The Burger Court

ABC-CLIO SUPREME COURT HANDBOOKS

ABC-CLIO SUPREME COURT HANDBOOKS

The Burger Court

Justices, Rulings, and Legacy

Tinsley E. Yarbrough

ABC-CLIO

Santa Barbara, California • Denver, Colorado • Oxford, England

Library of Congress Cataloging-in-Publication Data

Yarbrough, Tinsley E., 1941–
   The Burger court : justices, rulings, and legacy / Tinsley E.
Yarbrough.
     p. cm.
   Includes bibliography and index.
   ISBN 1-57607-179-0 (alk. paper)
   1. United States. Supreme Court—History. 2. Burger, Warren E.,
1907– . 3. Constitutional history—United States. I. Title.
   KF8742.Y365 2000
   347.73'26'09047—dc21
                       00-010871

06 05 04 03 02 01 00   10 9 8 7 6 5 4 3 2 1

ABC-CLIO, Inc.
130 Cremona Drive, P.O. Box 1911
Santa Barbara, California 93116-1911

This book is printed on acid-free paper ∞ .
Manufactured in the United States of America

To Cole
Our free spirit

Contents

Series Foreword

T here is an extensive literature on the U.S. Supreme Court, but it contains discussion familiar largely to the academic community and the legal profession. The ABC-CLIO Supreme Court series is designed to have value to the academic and legal communities also, but each volume is intended as well for the general reader who does not possess an extensive background on the Court or American constitutional law. The series is intended to effectively represent each of fourteen periods in the history of the Supreme Court with each of these fourteen eras defined by the chief justice beginning with John Jay in 1789. Each Court confronted constitutional and statutory questions that were of major importance to and influenced by the historical period. The Court's decisions were also influenced by the values of each of the individual justices sitting at the time. The issues, the historical period, the justices, and the Supreme Court's decisions in the most significant cases will be examined in the volumes of this series.

ABC-CLIO's Supreme Court series provides scholarly examinations of the Court as it functioned in different historical periods and with different justices. Each volume contains information necessary to understand each particular Court and an interpretative analysis by the author of each Court's record and legacy. In addition to representing the major decisions of each Court, institutional linkages are examined as well—the political connections among the Court, Congress, and the president. These relationships are important for several reasons. Although the Court retains some institutional autonomy, all the Court's justices are selected by a process that involves the other two branches. Many of the significant decisions of the Court involve the review of actions of Congress or the president. In addition, the Court frequently depends on the other two branches to secure compliance with its rulings.

The authors of the volumes in the ABC-CLIO series were selected with great care. Each author has worked extensively with the Court, the period, and the personalities about which he or she has written. ABC-CLIO wanted each of the volumes to examine several common themes, and each author agreed to work within certain guidelines. Each author was free, however, to develop the content of each volume, and many of the volumes advance new or distinctive conclusions about the Court under examination.

Each volume will contain four substantive chapters. The first chapter will introduce the Court and the historical period in which it served. The second chapter will examine each of the justices who sat on the particular Court. The third chapter will represent the most significant decisions rendered by the particular Court. Among other things, the impact of the historical period and the value orientations of the individual justices will be developed. A fourth and final chapter will address the impact of each particular Court on American constitutional law—its doctrinal legacy.

Each volume will contain several features designed to make the volume more valuable to those whose previous exposure to the Supreme Court and American constitutional law is limited. Each volume will have a reference section that will contain brief entries on some of the people, statutes, events, and concepts introduced in the four substantive chapters. Entries in this section are arranged alphabetically. Each volume will also contain a glossary of selected legal terms used in the text. Following each of the four chapters, a list of sources used in the chapter and suggestions for further reading will appear. Each volume will also have a comprehensive annotated bibliography. A listing of Internet sources is presented at the end of the bibliography. Finally, there will be a comprehensive subject index and a list of cases (with citation numbers) discussed in each volume. ABC-CLIO is delighted with the quality of scholarship represented in each volume and is proud to offer this series to the reading public.

Permit me to conclude with a personal note. This project has been an extraordinarily rewarding undertaking for me as series editor. Misgivings about serving in this capacity were plentiful at the outset of the project. After tending to some administrative business pertaining to the series, securing authors for each volume was the first major task. I developed a list of possible authors after reviewing previous work and obtaining valuable counsel from several recognized experts in American constitutional history. In virtually every instance, the first person on my list agreed to participate in the project. The high quality of the series was assured and enhanced as each author signed on. I could not have been more pleased. My interactions with each author have been most pleasant, and the excellence of their work will be immediately apparent to the reader. I sincerely thank each author.

Finally, a word about ABC-CLIO and its staff. ABC-CLIO was enthusiastic about the project from the beginning and has done everything necessary to make this series successful. I am very appreciative of the level of support I have received from ABC-CLIO. Alicia Merritt, senior acquisitions editor, deserves special recognition. She has held my hand throughout the project. She has facilitated making this project a reality in every conceivable way. She has encouraged me from the beginning, provided invaluable counsel, and given me latitude to operate as I wished while keeping me on track at the same time. This project would not have gotten off the ground without Alicia, and I cannot thank her enough.

—Peter Renstrom

Preface

Richard M. Nixon promised, given the chance, to create a constitutional counterrevolution in the Supreme Court, substantially reversing the liberal-activist direction in which the nation's highest tribunal had moved under the leadership of Chief Justice Earl Warren. Nixon would appoint, he vowed, "strict constructionist" justices devoted to the Constitution's text and its framers' intent rather than bent on imposing on the nation their own liberal social and moral theories, cloaked in the guise of judicial interpretation. The president filled four vacancies on the Supreme Court—choosing Warren Earl Burger to replace Chief Justice Warren; Burger's childhood friend Harry A. Blackmun to fill the vacancy left by the ignoble resignation of Justice Abe Fortas after Nixon's two attempts to appoint southerners to that seat met defeat in the Senate; respected Virginia lawyer Lewis F. Powell Jr. to replace Hugo L. Black of Alabama; and William H. Rehnquist to replace John Marshall Harlan, the principal Warren Court critic of Court trends following the 1962 retirement of Justice Felix Frankfurter. In 1975 President Gerald R. Ford replaced Justice William O. Douglas with John Paul Stevens. Sandra Day O'Connor, appointed by President Ronald Reagan in 1981 to fill the seat vacated by the retirement of Justice Potter Stewart, was the last justice appointed to the Court during Chief Justice Burger's tenure.

In some respects Nixon could take pride in his handiwork. In the criminal justice field in particular, the Burger Court embarked on a significant campaign of retrenchment. Majorities reduced the Fourth Amendment exclusionary rule, for example, to a mere judicially created device for deterring police misconduct rather than a constitutional command, then refused to extend it to grand jury proceedings and "good faith" police seizures of evidence based on invalid warrants, among other contexts. The *Miranda* warnings met the same fate, with the Burger Court permitting the use of tainted confessions to impeach a defendant's trial testimony and to secure other evidence against suspects, while also holding that *Miranda* did not apply to grand jury proceedings or situations in which police in the field initiate interrogation of a suspect to avert an imminent danger to public safety. Also dramatically expanded were the circumstances under which police were permitted to conduct searches without a warrant, as well as other areas of police and prosecutorial discretion.

Nor were Burger Court decisions curbing the reach of civil liberties and judicial authority in general confined purely to the criminal justice arena. In a number of rulings announced early in Chief Justice Burger's tenure, the Court imposed potentially significant restrictions on access to the federal courts. It substantially limited, for example, a Warren-era ruling that had expanded the authority of federal district courts to intervene in state court proceedings involving laws that interfered with federal constitutional rights. It gave a narrow construction to a Warren Court precedent allowing federal taxpayers, as taxpayers, to challenge federal laws claimed to violate federal rights. And it proved decidedly more reluctant than its predecessor to find in ostensibly private conduct the requisite "state action" to subject it to constitutional obligations.

In the First Amendment field, moreover, the Burger Court expanded the reach of governmental authority over the distribution or exhibition of obscenity and narrowly construed a Warren Court decision guaranteeing a right to possess obscenity in the privacy of the home. It was also generally reluctant to expand upon the scope of rights given no explicit mention in the Constitution's text. Toward the end of Chief Justice Burger's tenure, for example, a narrow majority refused to recognize a right of consenting adults to engage in homosexual sodomy, finding no such guarantee deeply rooted in the nation's history and traditions.

The Burger Court was by no means as consistently restraintist in its exercise of judicial review, however, as President Nixon would have preferred. It significantly restricted but did not overrule the Fourth Amendment exclusionary rule or *Miranda* decision. Indeed, it did not reverse outright a single major Warren Court precedent. It was the Burger Court rather than the Warren Court, moreover, that first guaranteed, in *Roe v. Wade* (1973), a woman's right to abortion—a guarantee mentioned nowhere in the Constitution—and repeatedly reaffirmed that controversial precedent over the balance of Chief Justice Burger's tenure. The Court under Burger also extended constitutional protection to commercial speech for the first time. And while reluctant to expand beyond race or color the sorts of classifications considered constitutionally "suspect" and subject to strict judicial protection, the Burger Court included most discrimination against aliens among the constitutional suspects and characterized discriminatory statutes based on gender and illegitimacy as "quasi suspects" subject to varying degrees of heightened judicial review. It upheld death sentences in murder cases but was also the first Court to impose significant constitutional limitations on capital punishment schemes and hold the death penalty for rape disproportionate to the gravity of the offense.

The Burger Court's record included notable decisions regarding governmental power as well. Although it later overruled its 1976 *Usery* decision subjecting congressional regulations of state and local governments to strict judicial scrutiny, thereby relegating the fate of such controls once again to the political arena, Justice Rehnquist's *Usery* opinion would provide a philosophical basis for the current reflowering of state authority in Rehnquist Court federalism pronouncements. The Burger Court also handed down major decisions regarding the scope of presidential privilege to withhold documents from the courts and Congress; the immunity of presidents, members of Congress, and their aides from damage suits for official misconduct; and the "legislative veto," under which the executive's exercise of powers authorized by statute was subject to congressional veto. The Burger Court's record was thus neither a mirror image of the Warren era nor the constitutional counterrevolution Warren Court critics anticipated. Instead, it produced a considerable body of law in areas the Warren Court and its predecessors never confronted, while also remolding earlier precedents in both expansive and restrictive directions.

This book examines the Burger Court and its chief justice in that light. Chapter One introduces the reader to the justices, exploring the process and politics of the Nixon, Ford, and Reagan appointments to the Burger Court; assessing Burger's performance as chief justice; discussing major aspects of the Court's inner workings; and summarizing the Court's record. Chapter Two profiles each of the justices who served on the Court during Burger's tenure, including their backgrounds and judicial records. Chapter Three examines major Burger Court decisions in a variety of fields. And Chapter Four evaluates the Court and its chief justice.

Although responsibility for what follows is my own, a number of institutions and individuals were of invaluable help to my research and timely completion of the manuscript.

Generous grants from the Earhart Foundation were of tremendous assistance. I also appreciate the fine cooperation of manuscript curators at the Washington and Lee School of Law, repository for the Lewis F. Powell Jr. papers, and the Library of Congress, repository for the papers of other Burger Court justices available to researchers. The staff of East Carolina University's Joyner Library was extremely helpful, as was Cynthia Manning Smith, who once again provided flawless clerical support. Mrs. Smith's expertise, dedication, and friendship are a constant source of encouragement. Series editor Peter Renstrom and Alicia Merritt of ABC-CLIO were wonderfully cooperative at every stage of my efforts. Finally, as always, I am deeply thankful for the patience and good humor of my wife, Mary Alice; our daughter, Sarah, and her husband, Todd Ratner; and our son, Cole, to whom this book is affectionately dedicated.

—Tinsley E. Yarbrough

The Burger Court

PART ONE

Justices, Rulings, and Legacy

1

The Burger Court and the Period

Warren Earl Burger served as chief justice of the Supreme Court seventeen years, from 1969 to 1986. His predecessor, Earl Warren, had presided over the Court during a period of both unprecedented judicial expansion in the scope of constitutional liberties and intense public debate over the proper role of the courts in a democratic society. Through their interpretation of the Fourteenth Amendment, Warren-era majorities extended the right to counsel, protections against unreasonable search and seizure and compulsory self-incrimination, the right of trial by jury, and most other guarantees of the Bill of Rights to state criminal cases, substantially eliminating the double standard under which those basic safeguards had long been applied only to the national government and its officials. Police investigations and interrogation techniques were subjected to strict constitutional standards. The First Amendment became a broad safeguard for erotic expression and political protest, its religion clauses important guarantees to religious liberty and the separation of church and state. As the linchpin of Warren Court expansions of the nature and scope of constitutional rights, the equal protection guarantee became not only a potent weapon against racial and related forms of discrimination and malapportioned governmental bodies, but a meaningful barrier to laws classifying people on the basis of wealth, interstate travel, and status of birth. And in *Griswold v. Connecticut* (1965), a Warren Court majority first recognized a right of privacy to be implicit in the Constitution's text.

Such rulings made the Warren Court and its justices the objects of intense controversy and convenient targets for vote-seeking politicians, especially Republican presidents and would-be presidents hoping to broaden their party's voter base in the South and the nation. During his 1968 presidential campaign, Richard M. Nixon vowed to appoint "strict constructionist" federal judges who would "interpret" rather than "create" constitutional guarantees and in particular would restore a "balance" in judicial decisions between the "crime and peace forces" of the nation. Ultimately, of course, President Nixon's own criminal conduct in the Watergate scandal would force his resignation from the presidency in August 1974. As president, however, Nixon had the opportunity not only to replace Earl Warren with Warren Burger but also to name Harry A. Blackmun, Lewis F. Powell Jr., and William H. Rehnquist to seats previously held by Justices Abe Fortas, Hugo L. Black, and John Marshall Harlan. President Nixon's Republican successor, Gerald Ford, replaced Justice William O. Douglas with John Paul Stevens. Although Democrat Jimmy Carter had no opportunity to fill vacancies on the Court, Ronald Reagan appointed Sandra Day O'Connor the first woman justice in 1981, replacing Justice Potter Stewart and leaving Justices William Brennan, Byron R. White, and Thurgood Marshall the only remaining Warren-era holdovers on the high bench through the balance of Chief Justice Burger's tenure.

The Appointments

Presidential nominations to federal judgeships require approval or confirmation by a simple majority vote in the U.S. Senate. With three exceptions, Supreme Court nominations during the Burger era had an easy run in Senate confirmation proceedings. Chief Justice Burger's nomination raised hardly a ripple in the Senate Judiciary Committee, the body responsible for initial scrutiny of presidential choices to the federal bench. Shortly before his appointment to the Supreme Court, the future chief justice, a judge on the U.S. Court of Appeals for the District of Columbia and frequent critic of Warren Court criminal justice rulings, had told an audience at a judicial conference that close Warren Court civil liberties decisions could be undone "by so simple a happening as the advent of one or two new Justices" (*New York Times*, October 5, 1969). President Nixon obviously considered Burger an excellent prospect to lead such an effort, and Judiciary Committee conservatives readily agreed, while liberal senators raised few or no questions or did not show up at all for the hour-and-forty-minute hearing on June 3, 1969. In presenting the nominee to the committee, Senator Harry F. Byrd of Virginia quoted with approval from one of Burger's court of appeals dissents in a decision expanding the interrogation rights of suspects, then expressed the hope that the new chief justice would "continue to take a sane and sensible view of the problems of law enforcement," while decrying "the decisions of some courts which make it difficult for the authorities to maintain law and order." South Carolina Republican senator and 1948 Dixiecrat presidential candidate Strom Thurmond, a leading member of the committee, concurred, certain that Burger believed "in interpreting the law but not legislating" (Senate Judiciary Committee, 1969, 15, 20). In a five-minute private session following the hearing, the committee voted unanimously to confirm the nomination. On June 9 the full Senate approved the president's choice by a 74–3 vote.

Nixon's efforts to fill another vacancy on the high bench, however, would provoke considerable controversy. In 1968, while Lyndon B. Johnson was president,

The Burger Court from 1969 to 1970: (left to right, front row) John M. Harlan, Hugo L. Black, Warren E. Burger, William O. Douglas, and William J. Brennan Jr.; (left to right, back row) Thurgood Marshall, Potter Stewart, and Byron R. White. (Harris & Ewing, Collection of the Supreme Court of the United States)

Chief Justice Warren had resigned his position, effective on selection of a successor. Johnson nominated to the Court's center seat Justice Abe Fortas, a prominent Washington lawyer and presidential confidant whom the president had selected as an associate justice in 1965. Conservative senators used the Fortas confirmation proceedings as a platform for harsh attacks on Warren Court criminal procedure decisions and charged that the nominee's continuing role as a presidential adviser violated separation of powers. As a lame-duck president who had chosen not to seek reelection in 1968, President Johnson could do little in Fortas's behalf. When senators learned that Fortas had accepted a $15,000 honorarium from friends and former clients to teach a summer university course, Republicans and conservative southern Democrats launched a filibuster, obliging the president to withdraw the nomination at Fortas's request. In 1969, a news magazine published revelations that the justice had also received a $20,000 fee as a consultant to a charitable foundation headed by former client Louis Wolfson, which Fortas had returned after the industrialist's imprisonment for illegal stock transactions. Under heavy fire from President Nixon and Attorney General John Mitchell, Fortas resigned from the bench on May 4, 1969, giving the president a second vacancy to fill on the high Court.

Selecting Fortas's replacement was to be no easy task. On August 18 President Nixon first named Clement F. Haynsworth Jr., a South Carolina native, senior partner in one of that state's wealthiest law firms, Eisenhower appointee to the U.S. Court of Appeals for the Fourth Circuit, and that court's senior jurist in years of service and thus chief judge since 1964. The nominee had developed a moderately conservative record in civil liberties cases, especially those involving racial issues. In 1968, for example, the Supreme Court reversed his opinion upholding "freedom of choice" desegregation plans that permitted parents to select their children's schools, even though such arrangements left school systems largely segregated. It was not surprising, perhaps, given the number of wealthy corporate clients his law firm represented, that Haynsworth had also developed a conservative record in labor-management cases. By 1969 seven labor cases in which he participated had been appealed to the Supreme Court. He had taken an antilabor position in each and was reversed every time, by a unanimous Supreme Court in six of the seven cases. The nominee's racial and labor votes made him ideally suited to the Nixon administration's "southern strategy" for luring dissident southern Democratic voters into the Republican fold, but they hardly endeared Haynsworth to labor and civil rights groups, from whom his nomination provoked an immediate outcry.

Opposition to Haynsworth focused, however, on the nominee's insensitivity to ethical standards, especially complaints he had participated in two cases involving subsidiaries of companies in which he owned stock and had bought stock in another company between the time of the decision in a case involving that company and the announcement of the decision. The Committee on Federal Judiciary of the American Bar Association (ABA) gave Haynsworth a positive rating, unanimously at first and later by a divided vote. The Senate Judiciary Committee recommended his confirmation 10–7. But the concerns persisted, and a growing number of senators, including several Republicans who had led the ethics-based fight against Fortas's confirmation as chief justice, announced their opposition to the president's choice. On November 21 the Senate voted 55–44 to defeat the nomination.

President Nixon immediately denounced the Senate's "brutal, vicious and . . . unfair" attacks on Judge Haynsworth and vowed to nominate another "strict constructionist" southerner to the Court. On Attorney General Mitchell's recommendation, the president next chose Judge G. Harrold Carswell of Florida, an undistinguished former federal district judge with only six months of experience on the U.S. Court of Appeals for the Fifth Circuit. Nixon and Mitchell seemed certain that the Senate would lack the stomach to reject a second southern nominee. But reporters soon discovered a white supremacist speech Carswell had made as a Georgia state legislative candidate in 1948. The nominee, citing his youth and inexperience, disavowed his speech and gave assurances that he harbored no vestiges of racial prejudice. News reporters learned, however, that while a U.S. attorney in

Florida, Carswell was involved in a scheme to transform a municipally owned Tallahassee golf course into a private, segregated club. An examination of his record revealed, moreover, that his judicial and legal credentials were grossly inferior to those expected of a Supreme Court nominee.

Nor were certain of Carswell's Senate defenders much help. As the president's floor manager for the confirmation process, Nebraska Republican Roman Hruska, in a classic if unintended display of low congressional humor, proclaimed, "Even if [Carswell] is mediocre there are a lot of mediocre judges and people and lawyers. They are entitled to a little representation, aren't they, and a little chance? We can't have all Brandeises, Cardozos, and Frankfurters, and stuff like that there" (*Congressional Record*, Vol. 116, 7487). On April 8, 1970, the Senate rejected Carswell 51–45. Two weeks later he resigned his federal appeals court seat to make an unsuccessful run for the U.S. Senate in Florida's Republican primary.

The day after Carswell's defeat in the Senate, President Nixon angrily announced that he would make no further attempt to place a justice from the South on the high bench. "I will not nominate another Southerner," asserted Nixon, in a statement directed mainly, no doubt, at dissident southern Democrats, "and let him be subjected to the kind of malicious character assassination accorded both Judges Haynsworth and Carswell" (Woodward and Armstrong 1979, 75). By April 11, White House sources were indicating to reporters that the current front-runner in a field of three potential nominees was Judge Harry A. Blackmun of the U.S. Court of Appeals for the Eighth Circuit, a Tennessee native who had spent most of his life in Minneapolis-St. Paul and was a lifelong friend of Chief Justice Burger. On April 14, White House press secretary Ronald Ziegler announced Judge Blackmun's nomination.

As a Phi Beta Kappa graduate of Harvard University, Harvard Law School graduate, member of one of Minneapolis's largest firms, and counsel to the famed Mayo Clinic in Rochester, Minnesota, prior to his appeals court appointment by President Eisenhower in 1959, Judge Blackmun had solid credentials. His judicial record stamped him as a moderate on most civil rights and civil liberties issues, although generally conservative in his response to the claims of criminal suspects—an obvious plus with the Nixon White House. Blackmun had regularly voted to uphold death sentences but found such judgments personally painful, as he would later on the Supreme Court. And while he had rejected the efforts of a black couple to invoke a Reconstruction-era statute against private-housing discrimination in a decision the Supreme Court overturned in *Jones v. Alfred H. Mayer Co.* (1968), he had taken a firm position on the obligations of southern officials to desegregate public schools.

Given Blackmun's background and moderate judicial record, it was not surprising that his nomination encountered virtually no opposition in the Senate Judiciary Committee. Indiana Democrat Birch Bayh, a leader in the opposition to Haynsworth and Carswell, questioned Blackmun regarding his participation in three cases involving companies in which he held stock, as well as another in which he acquired stock in a firm after the decision of a case involving that company. But Bayh and others clearly saw those situations as far different in magnitude from the ethical concerns that doomed Judge Haynsworth's appointment. Under questioning from Senator Edward Kennedy (D.-Mass.), the nominee, who had been best man at Warren Burger's 1933 wedding, noted that his association with the chief justice had begun "when our respective mothers packed us off to Sunday school at age 4 or 5." But he also emphasized that they had never been associated or opposed in a case and that he did not "fear" whatever strains in their relationship might develop over cases coming before the Court were he to be confirmed: "I would have no hesitation whatsoever, and he is the first person to be aware of this, in disagreeing with him, or, if I may speak for him, . . . in his disagreeing with me. I think we respect each other" (Senate Judiciary Committee 1970, 40).

When Senator James Eastland of Mississippi, the committee chair, asked Blackmun for his impression of a pending bill calling for mandatory senior judge (or semi-retired) status at age seventy, the nominee responded without hesitation that "[a]n arbitrary age limit can lead to some unfortunate consequences," then added that many judges—he cited Oliver Wendell Holmes—"had performed great service for the country after age 70" (Senate Judiciary Committee 1970, 53). The nominee fielded other questions as well. He conceded, for example, that he had indeed observed in one case that the death penalty "was particularly excruciating for one who is not convinced of the rightness of capital punishment as a deterrent in crime" but also insisted that its use was "ordinarily . . . a matter for the discretion of the legislature" (Senate Judiciary Committee 1970, 59–60). The committee's decision was never in doubt. On May 5, members voted 17–0 in favor of confirmation. A week later, the full Senate concurred without a negative vote.

The retirements of Justices Black and Harlan in the fall of 1971 gave President Nixon two additional appointments to the Court. Initially, Little Rock lawyer Herschel Friday and Mildred Lillie, a California appeals court judge, appeared the likely White House choices. But the ABA judiciary committee gave Judge Lillie a negative rating by an overwhelming vote and divided evenly on Friday. When the ratings were leaked to the press, Attorney General Mitchell wrote the association a letter indicating that the Nixon administration was returning to its earlier practice of obtaining ABA evaluations only after nominations were announced. That same night, October 21, President Nixon announced on television his selection of Lewis F. Powell Jr. and William Hubbs Rehnquist to fill the Black and Harlan seats on the Court.

Lewis Powell's selection was a stroke of political and juridical genius. A Virginia native, Washington and Lee Law School graduate with a Harvard LL.M., and partner in Hunton, Williams, one of Richmond's most prestigious firms, the nominee not only satisfied the president's professed desire to place a southerner on the bench but as a

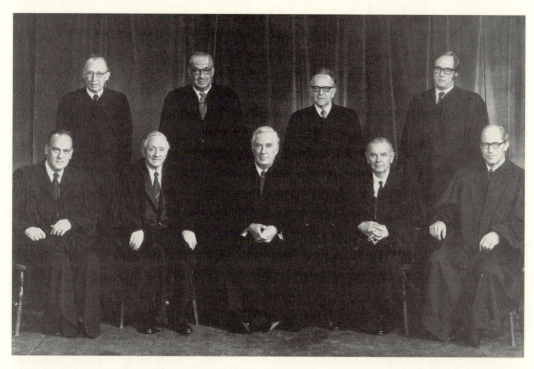

The Burger Court from 1972 to 1975: (left to right, front row) Potter Stewart, William O. Douglas, Warren E. Burger, William J. Brennan Jr., and Byron R. White; (left to right, back row) Lewis F. Powell Jr., Thurgood Marshall, Harry A. Blackmun, and William H. Rehnquist. (Harris & Ewing, Collection of the Supreme Court of the United States)

past president of the ABA (1964–1965), he was certain to garner the association's highest rating. Although clearly part of his state's conservative establishment, moreover, Powell enjoyed a reputation as a racial moderate who had opposed Virginia's policy of "massive resistance" against school desegregation and presided over the largely peaceful integration of Richmond's schools as chairman of the city's board of education from 1952 to 1961. As a member of a Richmond department store's board of directors, he had also been instrumental in the store's decision to desegregate its dining room without pressure from sit-in demonstrations. Yet Senate conservatives no doubt took comfort in Powell's assertion during the confirmation proceedings that the Warren Court "went further than I would have gone" in *Miranda v. Arizona* (1966) and other decisions imposing strict standards on police questioning of suspects (Senate Judiciary Committee 1971, 257). Following a cursory hearing, Judiciary Committee members unanimously endorsed his nomination; on December 6, the full Senate concurred 89–1.

Nixon's choice to replace Justice Harlan was to be decidedly more controversial. Excerpts from a transcript of a conversation the president had with members of his staff in the Oval Office on July 24, 1971, suggest that Nixon's knowledge of his future Supreme Court nominee, not to mention respect for his abilities, was limited. During a tirade against Justice Department staffers, Nixon had derided "that group of clowns we had around there. Renchburg and that group. What's his name?" "Renchquist," Nixon assistant John Ehrlichman replied. "Yeah," the president retorted, "Renchquist" (Abraham 1999, 268). But William H. Rehnquist possessed impeccable professional credentials. He had graduated first in his law class at Stanford, clerked for Supreme Court Justice Robert H. Jackson, practiced law for many years in Phoenix, and headed the Office of Legal Counsel in the Nixon Justice Department.

Rehnquist had also, however, opposed adoption of a Phoenix city ordinance forbidding racial discrimination in restaurants and other places of public accommodation. As a conservative Republican and follower of Arizona senator Barry Goldwater, he had played an active role in challenging the qualifications of would-be minority voters at the polls. In the Office of Legal Counsel, moreover, he had supported warrantless wiretapping of criminal suspects, military surveillance of political dissidents, abolition of the exclusionary rule forbidding use of illegally seized evidence in court, elimination of the *Miranda* warnings police were required to give before questioning suspects, "preventive detention" before trial of suspects deemed likely to commit violent crimes if released on bail, and "no knock" authority for police to enter dwellings without notice to occupants. The nominee's background and controversial issue positions provoked considerable public outcry, and the American Civil Liberties Union (ACLU), for the first time in its history, announced its opposition to a judicial nominee.

Before the Judiciary Committee, Rehnquist skillfully sought to soften his civil rights image, assuring senators, for example, that he no longer opposed public accommodations laws. But several committee Democrats grilled him closely on a variety of matters. Senator Philip Hart of Michigan referred to two magazine articles the nominee had written early in his career. In one Rehnquist attacked two decisions in which the Supreme Court, speaking through Justice Black, had voted to uphold the claims of Communists denied admission to the bar. In condemning rulings based on what Rehnquist had termed "charity and ideological sympathy," asserted Senator Hart, the nominee appeared to have been suggesting that those decisions were based on the justices' "sympathy for Communist ideology." The senator found equally disturbing a Rehnquist article on the supposed "liberal" biases of Warren Court clerks, the young recent law graduates who assisted justices with their work. The clerks, Rehnquist had written, displayed "extreme solicitude for the claims of Communists and other criminal defendants, expansion of the Federal power at the expense of state power, great sympathy for any Government regulation of business, in short, the political philosophy now espoused by the Court under Chief Justice Earl Warren" (Senate Judiciary Committee 1971, 28). Hart also questioned Rehnquist's testimony before a Senate subcommittee on constitutional rights that government surveillance of political gatherings would not chill or inhibit the exercise of First Amendment freedoms.

Although applauding the nominee's reputation as a "superb craftsman" with an "extremely gifted" legal mind, Senator Kennedy challenged Rehnquist's contentions in various settings as a member of the Nixon administration that congressional efforts to impose a time limit on U.S. involvement in the Vietnam War posed an unconstitutional interference with presidential war powers. Recalling the nominee's published statements that nonviolent as well as violent civil disobedience should be met with "force," Kennedy also questioned Rehnquist about the shooting of peaceful student antiwar protesters by National Guardsmen at Kent State University. When the nominee replied that the matter had been outside his area of responsibility at the Justice Department, the senator asked Rehnquist about his role in the administration's efforts to prevent newspaper publication of excerpts from a classified Department of Defense history of the Vietnam War popularly known as *The Pentagon Papers*. Avoiding a direct response, Rehnquist cited the attorney-client privilege he enjoyed as adviser to the attorney general but conceded he had advised Attorney General Mitchell that the government might succeed in the effort, later struck down by a 6–3 Supreme Court majority in *New York Times Co. v. United States* (1971).

A number of other committee Democrats questioned Rehnquist to similar effect, while Republican senators and a number of Democrats praised the president's good judgment. When it was over, the committee voted 12–4 to confirm, with Senators Hart, Kennedy, Bayh, and John Tunney (D.-Calif.) casting the negative votes.

Following the committee vote, a memorandum surfaced that Rehnquist had written as a clerk for Justice Jackson, while *Brown v. Board of Education* and other cases challenging segregation in public schools were pending before the Court. In the memorandum Rehnquist complained about liberal "colleagues" and recommended that the Court reaffirm *Plessy v. Ferguson*, the 1896 decision upholding state power to require "separate but equal" accommodations for the two races in public and private facilities. Opponents of confirmation urged Senator Eastland to reopen the hearing. In a letter to the Mississippi Democrat, however, Rehnquist claimed that the memorandum had been written at Justice Jackson's request, as a statement of the justice's views rather than Rehnquist's own position—a doubtful assertion, given the wording of portions of the memorandum, and one that the late justice's longtime secretary, among others, vehemently challenged.

Eastland refused to reopen committee consideration of the nomination. But Senate floor debate lasted a week, with Senator Bayh leading a filibuster against confirmation. Rehnquist's supporters were unable to muster the two-thirds vote then necessary to invoke cloture, cutting off further debate on the matter. As the Congress's Christmas recess neared, however, opponents yielded. On December 10, 1971, the Senate voted 68–26 to confirm, a comfortable margin but at that point second only to the vote on Chief Justice Hughes's confirmation in the number of negative votes cast against a successful nominee. On January 7, 1972, Rehnquist and Lewis Powell took the oath as associate justices.

Powell and Rehnquist were President Nixon's last nominations to the Supreme Court. But President Ford, who succeeded to the presidency on Nixon's resignation August 9, 1974, filled one vacancy during his brief White House tenure, 1974–1977. Ironically, the president's opportunity arose with the retirement of Justice William O. Douglas, against whom Ford, then a Republican Michigan congressman, had mounted an abortive impeachment effort in 1970. On October 29, 1973, Douglas, appointed to the Court by President Franklin D. Roosevelt in 1939, had become the longest-serving justice in Supreme Court history; by November 1975, he had served thirty-six and a half years on the high bench. But a severe stroke in January of that year had forced his absence from the bench through most of the first half of 1975, while he underwent physical therapy. The justice returned to the Court that fall, hopeful of continuing his work. But tormented with intense and constant pain, as well as his colleagues' decision to delay indefinitely rulings in which he would cast the deciding vote, Douglas finally yielded to the entreaties of his wife and friends, retiring from the bench on November 12, 1975.

Shortly after Douglas's announcement, President Ford met with Attorney General Edward Levi, the distinguished president and law dean of the University of Chicago, asking that Levi develop a list of potential nominees and that the attorney general not exclude women from the list. Reinstating the tradition President Nixon had discarded, Ford planned to have the names of potential nominees submitted to the ABA's judiciary committee. A number of persons close to the president, including his wife, Betty Ford, urged appointment of a woman. But the names of only two women—Housing and Urban Development secretary Carla Hills and U.S. District Judge Cornelia G. Kennedy—made the list of eleven possible nominees submitted to the ABA.

Also on the president's list was Judge John Paul Stevens of the U.S. Court of Appeals for the Seventh Circuit. Appointed by President Nixon to the circuit bench in 1970, Stevens was a member of a prominent Chicago family. A Phi Beta Kappa graduate of the University of Chicago with a Northwestern University law degree and former clerk to Supreme Court Justice Wiley Rutledge, Stevens had specialized in antitrust law at the Chicago firm he helped to found and had lectured on antitrust law at Northwestern and the University of Chicago. A nominal Republican with limited involvement in politics and no intense ideological leanings, the nominee had developed a moderately conservative record on the circuit bench. Noted for well-crafted, scholarly, eminently readable judicial opinions, he had ranked twelfth in a recent national survey of appeals court judges. The ABA judiciary committee accorded him its highest rating, and influential Illinois Republican senator Charles H. Percy was both a longtime friend and University of Chicago classmate. Most important, Attorney

General Levi, who had met Stevens when he lectured at the university, lobbied the president vigorously in Stevens's behalf. On November 28 Ford met with Levi and other presidential advisers, then spoke with Stevens briefly by telephone. That afternoon the president's press secretary announced Stevens's nomination.

Confirmation proceedings in the Judiciary Committee would span three days in December yet be largely uneventful. The week of President Nixon's 1974 resignation, Stevens had undergone heart bypass surgery. Senator Eastland began the questioning by asking the nominee about the status of his health. Noting that his mother was ninety-four and that his father had died a week before his eighty-eighth birthday, the fifty-five-year-old Stevens assured the committee his health was excellent. Had he any doubts whatever on that score, he added, "I would not be sitting here today" (Senate Judiciary Committee 1974, 10). Letters from the nominee's physicians attesting to his good health were also entered into the record.

As the hearing progressed, Stevens's well-known wit was equally evident. In his introduction of the nominee to the committee, Attorney General Levi characterized his opinions as a "joy to read." Senator Hart jokingly asked Stevens if all the litigants coming before him would agree with the attorney general's assessment. "He might be half right on that," the nominee shot back (Senate Judiciary Committee 1974, 13).

In 1969 Stevens had served as general counsel to a special Illinois commission established to investigate charges of judicial corruption. Based on evidence Stevens compiled, two Illinois Supreme Court justices had resigned from the bench. Among witnesses opposing his confirmation, however, was a Chicago man who claimed that Stevens had concealed evidence of misconduct by two state supreme court justices the witness claimed were "judicial lackeys" of Chicago mayor Richard J. Daley. But the witness, a failed bar applicant denied a law license by the Illinois high court, presented no evidence to support his charges, which Stevens's assistant counsel in the investigation branded "false, malicious and scurrilous" in an affidavit to the committee (Senate Judiciary Committee 1974, 194–195). Another witness argued that Stevens's nomination should be rejected so that a nonlawyer might be appointed to the bench, while a third complained that Stevens had ruled unfairly against him, costing the witness his livelihood.

The only credible opposition to Stevens's confirmation came from leaders of women's organizations, who contended that the nominee's judicial record reflected an insensitivity to discrimination based on gender. During his questioning of Stevens, Senator Kennedy raised such concerns. Stevens readily agreed that women had not yet achieved "full equality," but he was confident they were "marching definitely in that direction." He also assured the committee that he was "free of prejudice against either sex and [could] . . . rule impartially when members of one sex are engaged in litigation involving their rights to employment or other opportunities." During his tenure on the bench, his court had decided a total of five cases that arguably involved sex discrimination issues. In two he had dissented from the court's grant of relief to women litigants. In two others he supported relief for female litigants, and the ruling in the fifth case was a partial victory for a female plaintiff. "I think I come out about 50–50. But I do not think that is the correct way to analyze a judge's performance because it depends entirely on the mix of cases that one gets" (Senate Judiciary Committee 1974, 15).

The nominee's "simple standard" in gender discrimination cases, he said, was to determine whether the person involved would "have fared better . . . had he or she been of the opposite sex." Asked by Senator Kennedy to state his views regarding the Equal Rights Amendment (ERA), then before the state legislatures in an unsuccessful ratification effort, Stevens responded, "Well, I don't really know, Senator. I must confess that, other than the symbolic value of the amendment, I am not entirely clear how much it will accomplish beyond the equal protection clause of the 14th amendment itself" (Senate Judiciary Committee 1974, 15). When Kennedy inquired whether Stevens was more concerned about racial or sexual discrimination, the nominee first expressed a reluctance to answer, then observed, "I suppose, if I am asked to do so, I would be more concerned about the racial discrimination because I think [racial minorities] are a more disadvantaged group in the history of our country than the half of the population that is female" (Senate Judiciary Committee 1974, 16).

Such testimony was hardly a comfort to leaders of women's organizations opposed to the nomination. Margaret Drachsler of the National Organization for Women (NOW) first took aim at President Ford's failure to select a woman to fill the Douglas seat on the Court:

> After 200 years of living under laws written, interpreted, and enforced exclusively by men, we have a right to be judged by a court which is representative of all people, more than half of whom are women. The President owes us a duty to begin to eliminate the 200 years of discrimination against women. In our judicial system this would be partially accomplished by appointing a woman to the Supreme Court. (Senate Judiciary Committee 1974, 78–79)

But Drachsler reserved most of her scorn for Judge Stevens, rejecting his record in gender discrimination cases as inconsistent with Supreme Court precedent and federal law. "In many of his decisions," she asserted, "he has been at odds with his own circuit and other circuits. More importantly, he has rejected guidance from the Supreme Court decisions on these issues by which decisions he was bound as a circuit judge. His decisions have flown in the face of applicable law as duly passed by Congress, elected by the people, both men and women." When Senator Tunney asked whether her views might be "colored by the fact that Judge Stevens is not a woman," she insisted that NOW was not opposing the nominee solely because of his gender. "That is of secondary importance," she claimed. "We would not be down here opposing just anyone who was nominated to the court just because that person was a man. We are here specifically because of Judge Stevens's stands on these legal issues" (Senate Judiciary Committee 1974, 83–84). In a prepared statement to the committee, Nan Aron, president of the Women's Legal Defense Fund, assumed the same stance (Senate Judiciary Committee 1974, 227).

Not surprisingly, however, given Stevens's excellent professional credentials and moderate judicial record, his confirmation was never in doubt. On December 11 the committee recommended approval to the full Senate. Following brief floor discussion on December 17, the Senate confirmed the appointment 98–0. Rounding up senators and voting took four times longer than the debate preceding the vote.

Although Ford's successor, President Jimmy Carter, had no opportunities to fill seats on the Supreme Court during his one term in the White House, President Reagan got his only first-term chance to name a justice during his initial year in office. During his 1980 campaign, Reagan had vowed to name "the most qualified woman I can find" as one of his first appointments to the high bench. When Potter Stewart, a 1958 Eisenhower appointee, announced in June 1981 that he would retire on July 3, the new president made good on his promise. On June 23 Attorney General William French Smith provided Reagan with a list of approximately twenty-five possible nominees, nearly half of whom were women. By the end of the month, that list had been reduced to five, including Sandra Day O'Connor of the Arizona state court of appeals and Cornelia Kennedy of the U.S. Court of Appeals for the Sixth Circuit. On July 7 the president announced Judge O'Connor's nomination.

Daughter of a wealthy Arizona rancher, the first woman nominee to the Supreme Court was a Stanford undergraduate and law graduate who had practiced law in Phoenix and served as assistant Arizona attorney general, majority leader of the Republican-controlled state senate, and as a state trial judge before being named in 1980 by Governor Bruce Babbitt, a Democrat, to a seat on the state's intermediate appeals court. O'Connor's legislative record placed her clearly within the moderate to conservative Republican mainstream. In remarks made during a Williamsburg, Virginia, symposium on the state courts and federalism the previous January, moreover, she had argued that federal judges should generally defer to their state court counterparts in resolving federal constitutional issues raised in state cases. In the Arizona senate, however, she had also championed the repeal of provisions of state law discriminating against women and had voted in favor of the proposed ERA. Her mixed record helped her win endorsements from such ideologically diverse senators as Arizona's conservative Barry Goldwater and Democrat Ted Kennedy of Massachusetts, and NOW President Eleanor Smeal hailed the nomination of the first woman to the Court as a victory for the women's movement. While the ABA's judiciary committee withheld its highest rating, citing O'Connor's lack of extensive court experience, it found her clearly qualified in terms of her professional credentials, integrity, and judicial temperament.

The Burger Court from 1981 to 1986: (left to right, front row) Thurgood Marshall, William J. Brennan Jr., Warren E. Burger, Byron R. White, Harry A. Blackmun; (left to right, back row) John Paul Stevens, Lewis F. Powell Jr., William H. Rehnquist, and Sandra Day O'Connor. (National Geographic Society, Collection of the Supreme Court of the United States)

Members of one important segment of President Reagan's conservative constituency, however, vehemently opposed O'Connor's confirmation by the Senate. As an Arizona legislator, the nominee had cast four votes on abortion and related issues. In 1970 she voted in the state senate's judiciary committee to send to the floor a bill to repeal Arizona's extremely restrictive abortion statutes. Later she was a cosigner of a bill to make information about contraception more widely available to adults and minors. In 1974 she opposed a resolution urging Congress to adopt an antiabortion amendment to the U.S. Constitution, and that same year she voted against an amendment to a stadium construction bill for the University of Arizona limiting the availability of abortions.

O'Connor was hardly a proabortion activist. In fact, she had supported a state senate measure restricting the use of government funds to provide abortions for poor women, as well as a bill giving hospital employees the right to refuse to assist in performing abortions. But Reagan had taken a strong campaign stance against *Roe v. Wade*, the 1973 Burger Court decision recognizing a broad abortion right, and leaders of pro-life organizations were incensed that the president's first nominee to the nation's highest court had an ambivalent abortion record.

Two officials of the National Right to Life Committee, among other antiabortion activists, appeared before the Judiciary Committee in opposition to O'Connor's confirmation. Dr. Carolyn F. Gerster, the organization's vice-president for international affairs, reminded committee Republicans of the party's 1980 platform promise to "work for the appointment of judges at all levels of the judiciary who respect traditional family values and the sanctity of innocent human life." Dr. John C. Willke, the group's president, equated abortion with murder and compared the *Roe* decision with *Dred Scott v. Sandford*, the infamous 1857 Supreme Court decision denying citizenship rights to African Americans and declaring in effect, in Willke's words, "that an entire class of living humans were chattel." Willke agreed that few single issues were so fundamental that they should exert a controlling influence over the confirmation process. But abortion, in his judgment, clearly raised such an issue, just as G. Harrold Carswell's 1948 segregationist speech had "weighed heavily upon the minds of many Senators, and quite properly so," when his nomination was placed before the Senate twenty-two years later. "We believe that recognition of the right to life of the unborn child," asserted Willke, "is . . . just such a fundamental issue. Those who do not recognize this right, we suggest, should be disqualified from sitting on the Federal court" (Senate Judiciary Committee 1981, 282–283).

When it was his turn to question the witnesses, Ohio Democrat Howard Metzenbaum probed Willke and Gerster closely about their assertion that a nominee's position on abortion should exert a veto effect over the confirmation process. Observed Metzenbaum:

> I have concerns, whether it has to do with the right to life or any other single issue, as to what happens to the fabric of our democracy if we are to elect or defeat people, or nominees to the Supreme Court, based upon any one single issue. When [a recent lower court nominee] was before this Committee the issue was gun control. Now . . . the issue is right-to-life.

The senator cited several elements of Judge O'Connor's record with which he disagreed, as well as her memberships in racially discriminatory private clubs. Had he been president, he said, he "would not necessarily have appointed her." But Metzenbaum questioned whether he, "you or anyone else should judge any particular individual for elective office or appointive office based upon one issue" (Senate Judiciary Committee 1981, 287).

When Willke responded by drawing a distinction between a "single issue" and a "disqualifying issue" and comparing those supporting abortion with persons "in favor of [the] killing of 2-year-old girls," Metzenbaum asked,

> It does not bother you that the gun control people think that is the most important issue . . . that the single issue prayer-in-the-school people think that is the most

important issue . . . that there are so many groups who think that their issue is the only issue? Now you say that this has become the overriding, the paramount issue, but the fact is that a majority of people in this country have not indicated in the polls they agree with you, and seven Supreme Court Justices [the majority in the *Roe* case] have not indicated that they agree with you. Yet you feel that by reason of your position that that is the paramount issue, and that should disqualify this woman from being confirmed to the Supreme Court. . . . I . . . question the Americanism of any group in this country which says that one issue is enough of a basis to be for or against an appointee to the Supreme Court or an elected public official. (Senate Judiciary Committee 1981, 288–290)

North Carolina Republican John P. East came to the witnesses' defense. East, a protégé of Senator Jesse Helms (R.-N.C.) and an avowed pro-life advocate until his 1985 suicide, agreed with Willke and Gerster "that on occasion . . . there can be matters that become of such overriding importance that they could well up as, if not the litmus test, at least as a critical and decisive test in making that determination. . . . [I]t is not an unreasonable position" (Senate Judiciary Committee 1981, 291). East doubted, for example, that the Senate would confirm nominees with "a tainted record in their attitude on blacks or Jews or any other prominent group in the great American melting pot" merely because "they [were] rather strong on other things" or "[t]hey seem[ed] to make good sense on other things" (Senate Judiciary Committee 1981, 291).

Had Judge O'Connor taken a stronger antiabortion stance in her testimony before the committee, pro-life witnesses might have dropped their opposition to her confirmation. Dr. Gerster and the nominee had known each other since 1972, attended the same church, had the same friends; their children had been members of the same youth group. Had the nominee testified the way Dr. Gerster hoped, she had been prepared to forget her friend's ambivalent legislative record on the abortion issue, "tear up my testimony," and "enthusiastically support [the] nominee" (Senate Judiciary Committee 1981, 281).

Under questioning from committee chair Strom Thurmond (R.-S.C.), however, Judge O'Connor assumed the same sort of flexible abortion stance her legislative record reflected and her later Supreme Court opinions would adopt. Personally, she testified, she opposed abortion "as a matter of birth control or otherwise," considering it a legitimate object of legislative regulation, albeit one "subject to . . . constitutional restraints or limitations." She conceded that she had supported a 1970 bill to repeal Arizona's abortion law, but only, she insisted, because of the statute's extremely restrictive provisions, including a prohibition on abortions in rape cases. "[M]y own knowledge and awareness of the issues and concerns that many people have about the question of abortion has increased since those days. . . . I would not have voted, I think, . . . for a simple repealer thereafter." In explaining her 1973 cosponsorship of a bill to encourage the availability of contraceptive information, she asserted that perhaps the best way to reduce the incidence of abortion "was to enable people not to become pregnant unwittingly or without the intention of doing so." Her 1974 opposition to a measure urging Congress to adopt an antiabortion amendment stemmed from her concern, she said, that insufficient consideration had been given such action, while her vote against adding a restrictive abortion rider to a stadium construction bill had simply reflected her opposition to the addition of nongermane amendments to senate bills. The nominee emphasized, moreover, her support for a law that banned the funding of abortions for indigent women except where necessary to save the mother's life or in cases in which a pregnancy had resulted from rape or incest.

Whatever the effect of her testimony on abortion opponents, Judge O'Connor's statements regarding other issues relevant to the Supreme Court's work must have been comforting to conservative members of the Judiciary Committee. Anticipating later Supreme Court opinions in which she would champion state sovereignty against congressional statutes imposing obligations on the states (*Garcia v. San Antonio Metropolitan Transit Authority* [1985]), the nominee declared, for example, that she had "some concerns about seeing that State governments and local government are maintained in their abilities to deal with the problems affecting the people. The reason for that philosophically is because I think I would agree with those who think that the government closest to the people is best able to handle those problems" (Senate Judiciary Committee 1981, 122). When asked about school desegregation, she noted that she had voted in the Arizona senate for a memorial requesting federal action "to terminate the use of forced busing in desegregation cases." The 75-mile round-trip school bus ride she had endured daily as an eighth grader had left her with an abiding concern, she added, that the "transportation of students over long distances . . . can be a very disruptive part of any child's educational program" (Senate Judiciary Committee 1981, 119).

In the criminal justice field, moreover, she voiced support for the sort of "good faith" exception to the exclusionary rule under which she and other members of the Burger Court would allow the use in criminal trials of evidence that police illegally seized in a reasonable but mistaken belief their conduct was lawful (*United States v. Leon* [1984]). In mid-September the Judiciary Committee unanimously approved O'Connor's nomination. On September 21 the full Senate unanimously concurred after nominal floor debate marked mainly by such long pauses between remarks by the senators that one Democrat joked that tourists in the visitors' gallery might wish to join the discussion. In committee, however, Senator Jeremiah Denton (R.-Ala.), a onetime proponent of mandatory chastity belts for young women, had merely voted "Present" in mild protest against the nominee's refusal to attack the *Roe* decision. And North Carolina's Senator Helms announced to his colleagues that he was voting in O'Connor's favor only because of President Reagan's personal assurances that she shared the president's opposition to abortion. He had no reason to believe, added

Helms, that "Mrs. O'Connor would deliberately allow the President to be misled" (*New York Times*, September 22, 1981).

The Period

Warren Burger would serve as chief justice during four presidencies—Richard Nixon's, Gerald Ford's, Jimmy Carter's, and Ronald Reagan's—and during some of the most turbulent and divisive events in the nation's modern history, including the Vietnam War and its profoundly disturbing impact on the fabric of American society; the Watergate scandal and its aftermath; the seizure of the U.S. embassy in Tehran, Iran, and the ensuing nationally humiliating hostage crisis; and the development or continuation of intense political and legal debates over abortion, school desegregation, affirmative action, religious exercises in the public schools, women's rights, the permissible scope of political and artistic expression, the rights of suspects and defendants in criminal cases, and related national issues. The Burger Court became embroiled to one degree or another in most such controversies and was thus a key factor in the major political controversies of its era, a continuing object of political attack and praise, and a significant element in the campaign and administration agendas of Richard Nixon and Ronald Reagan.

During the early years of Chief Justice Burger's tenure, as in the Warren era, the Supreme Court repeatedly refused to review challenges to the Vietnam War in cases in which military draftees and other litigants contended that the war was unconstitutional in the absence of a formal declaration of war by Congress, while lower courts generally dismissed such suits by concluding that the plaintiffs could claim no direct and substantial personal injury to their legal rights and thus lacked "standing to sue," or that such cases raised "political questions" inappropriate for judicial intervention without grave risk of embarrassment to the nation abroad (e.g., *Sarnoff v. Shultz* [1972]). But when a 6–3 majority rebuffed the Nixon administration's efforts to prevent publication of *The Pentagon Papers*, two of the three dissenters were Nixon appointees—Chief Justice Burger, who refused to reach the free press issues raised in the case because of the haste with which the majority had disposed of the suit, and Justice Blackmun, who concluded that national security interests outweighed any harm to the newspapers' freedom of the press, while also noting that the First Amendment, albeit entitled to considerable deference, was merely one part of the Constitution (*New York Times Co. v. United States* [1971]). Nor was *New York Times* the only Burger Court ruling that grew out of the *Pentagon Papers* controversy. In an attempt to provide wider circulation for the papers, Senator Mike Gravel (D.-Alaska) read portions into the record at a Senate committee session, then arranged with a private firm for their publication. A federal grand jury investigating possible criminal violations arising from the papers' publication demanded that Gravel provide testimony as to how they came into his possession. And in *Gravel v. United States* (1972), the Burger Court held that Gravel's reading of the documents into the Senate record was protected from judicial inquiry under the constitutional provision safeguarding the "speech and debate" of members of Congress during the conduct of their official duties, but that the senator's private publication of the papers fell outside the scope of his legislative functions.

Consistent with President Nixon's 1968 campaign vows, his appointees to the Court helped to form majorities limiting litigant access to the courts (e.g., *Warth v. Seldin* [1975]) and curtailing the interrogation (e.g., *United States v. Mandujano* [1976]) and search and seizure rights (e.g., *United States v. Calandra* [1974]) of criminal suspects and defendants. On one highly controversial occasion, moreover, Justice Rehnquist sat in a case that involved a challenge to a Nixon administration policy he had helped to develop and had defended before Congress, providing the fifth vote to dismiss the suit and thus overturn a lower court decision invalidating the challenged scheme.

During his first year on the bench, Rehnquist participated in *Laird v. Tatum* (1972), in which a 5–4 majority dismissed for lack of standing a challenge to military surveillance of civilians about which the new justice had been questioned during his Senate confirmation proceedings. Following announcement of the Court's decision, the ACLU, which had furnished counsel for the *Laird* plaintiffs, filed a petition for rehearing and a motion that Justice Rehnquist recuse, or disqualify, himself from further participation in the case. As head of the Nixon Justice Department's office of legal counsel, ACLU lawyers contended, Rehnquist had appeared as an expert witness in Senate hearings on military surveillance practices. He also had intimate knowledge of the *Laird* case, had made public statements questioning the merits of the *Laird* plaintiffs' allegations, and before a congressional subcommittee had even rejected the assumption that they could allege that the surveillance scheme had imposed a sufficient chilling effect on their exercise of First Amendment rights adequate to give them standing to sue—the very ground on which the Court had later dismissed the suit.

Yet Rehnquist refused to withdraw from the case. Instead, in a highly unusual move, he issued a memorandum denying that his prior connection with the case constituted a conflict of interest. Justices Black and Frankfurter, he declared, had participated in cases involving laws they had helped to draft, and his failure to have participated in *Laird* would have resulted in a tie vote. To the justice's critics, however, that was precisely the point. The *New York Times* observed, for example, that the government had won the case only as a result of the justice's participation. Rehnquist's claim that he had a duty to participate to assure a decision in the case, the paper asserted, "seems only to underscore the impropriety of a former representative of Government to continue the Government's case on the Supreme Court—the court of last resort" (*New York Times*, October 11, 1972).

President Nixon and his administration were also the object, of course, of other Burger Court litigation. In 1975, the year after Nixon's resignation, the Court narrowly construed congressional statutes in overturning Nixon's efforts to prevent expenditure of federal funds appropriated by Congress. Presidents traditionally had asserted an impoundment power, that is, the authority to reduce or prevent the expenditure of congressional appropriations through instructions to Treasury Department officials. But Nixon impounded funds on a massive scale, not only making deep cuts in domestic programs but even terminating government programs through a total impoundment of the funds approved for their operations. In the Budget and Impounding Control Act of 1974, Congress eliminated the president's authority to even delay the expenditure of funds over congressional opposition and required the approval of Congress for a permanent impoundment of appropriations. The following year, moreover, the Court rejected impoundments undertaken by Nixon before the 1974 law's adoption. In *Train v. City of New York* (1975), the justices held that an appropriation statute specifying that certain funds "shall be allotted" did not allow the administration to withhold any portion of the appropriation, even though congressional authorization of the expenditures, stipulated elsewhere in the law, was for sums "not to exceed" the amounts appropriated.

Eight years after the president's resignation, the Court handed Nixon and his successors a major victory when it held in *Nixon v. Fitzgerald* (1982) that presidents are absolutely immune from damage suits for any conduct, however unconstitutional or illegal, falling within the broad range of their official duties. Dismissed in that case was the suit of a government whistle-blower fired by the administration after testifying before Congress about cost overruns and other mismanagement of government defense contracts.

The most significant Burger Court ruling that resulted from the political turmoil of the Nixon years, however, was *United States v. Nixon* (1974), the 8–0 ruling (with Justice Rehnquist not participating) that rejected the president's claim of executive privilege to withhold from the courts tapes and related evidence of his and his aides' involvement in the Watergate scandal. In the Watergate context, the Court concluded, the overriding judicial interest in securing evidence of criminal conduct outweighed the president's privilege claim.

The Ford White House largely avoided clashes with the courts. As part of his southern strategy to lure dissident white southerners into the Republican Party, President Nixon had assumed a strong stance against court-ordered busing and racial quotas to implement school desegregation, supporting "neighborhood schools," urging Congress to impose restrictions on judicial authority in the field, and planning to seek a constitutional amendment forbidding racial assignment of public school students until Watergate aborted his efforts. During his brief White House tenure, President Ford also opposed court-ordered busing but yielded to Attorney General Levi's recommendation that the administration not file a brief to that effect in a controversial Boston school desegregation case. In 1975 Ford sought congressional advice about the seizure of the American merchant vessel *Mayaguez* by Cambodian naval forces only after a sea and air rescue was under way, despite provisions of the 1973 War Powers Act obliging presidents generally to consult with congressional leaders before committing troops to combat in the absence of congressional authorization. But his action, widely supported in Congress and the nation, provoked no court challenge.

A number of important international situations dominated Carter administration litigation in the Burger Court. In 1979, the justices turned back, mainly on the ground that it was a political question, a challenge by Senator Barry Goldwater and other members of Congress to President Carter's termination of the U.S. defense treaty with Taiwan without consulting or securing prior approval of the Senate (*Goldwater v. Carter* [1979]). And in *Dames & Moore v. Regan* (1981), the Court upheld action taken by Carter, later affirmed by the Reagan administration, to end the Iranian hostage crisis. But the Court declined to review one of the more disturbing Carter administration reactions to the seizure of the U.S. embassy in Tehran. In November 1979 Carter's attorney general, Benjamin Civiletti, issued regulations under which Iranian nationals admitted to the United States as nonimmigrant college students were to report to immigration officials, providing evidence of their continuing full-time student status. Failure to comply would constitute grounds for deportation, as would conviction of any violent crime carrying a potential prison sentence of more than a year. In a class action brought by three Iranian students, a federal district judge invalidated the regulation on equal protection grounds and issued an injunction forbidding its further enforcement (*Narenji v. Civiletti* [D.D.C. 1979]). But the Court of Appeals for the District of Columbia reversed the ruling, citing the broad deference traditionally extended the executive in the field of foreign affairs (*Civiletti v. Narenji* [D.C.C.A. 1979]), and the Supreme Court refused to review the appeals court's ruling.

During Reagan's presidency the relationship between turbulent political and social developments in the nation and the Supreme Court became especially pronounced. To a greater degree than any of its post–World War II predecessors, the Reagan administration challenged important civil rights and civil liberties precedents of the era, including abortion rights and school desegregation, the Burger Court's acceptance of certain varieties of affirmative action programs for minorities in hiring and university admissions, decisions limiting religious programs in the public schools and government assistance to church-affiliated schools and colleges, restrictions on police interrogation and search and seizure tactics, and constitutional protection for erotic expression. Like Nixon, Reagan attempted to shape the direction of civil liberties law in part through presidential control over appointments to the federal bench. On Chief Justice Burger's retirement in 1986, for example, the president named Justice William Rehnquist, the most conservative-activist justice of the Burger era, to the Court's center seat, and Antonin Scalia, a jurist in some respects even more compatible with the Reagan constitutional agenda than the new chief justice, to replace Rehnquist as an associate justice. When the next vacancy arose, Reagan attempted to place Robert Bork, another nominee of the Rehnquist-Scalia mold, on the Court, turning to the more jurisprudentially moderate Anthony Kennedy only after the Bork nomination met defeat in the Senate and the nomination of Douglas Ginsburg, a Harvard law professor and recent Reagan appointee to the District of Columbia Court of Appeals, was hastily withdrawn in the midst of allegations of a financial conflict of interest and revelations of his marijuana use as a member of the Harvard law faculty.

The administration pursued its conservative judicial and civil liberties agenda in other ways as well. Not only did the Reagan White House push congressional legislation and constitutional amendment proposals to overturn or undermine Supreme Court precedents in such sensitive fields as abortion, school prayer, and criminal justice, but the administration also assumed a major role in litigation challenging prevailing precedent. William Bradford Reynolds, Reagan's controversial assistant attorney general for civil rights, was at the forefront of such efforts, and presidential counselor Edwin Meese III, who eventually replaced William French Smith as attorney general, regularly attacked the Supreme Court's failure to follow the "original intent" of the Constitution's framers and willingness to "create" rights under the guise of constitutional interpretation. Solicitor General Rex Lee, the chief representative of the United States and federal law before the Supreme Court, also aggressively pursued the administration's policy goals in the Court. In 1984, for example, Lee persuaded the justices to exempt from the exclusionary rule, forbidding use of the fruits of illegal searches in criminal trials, evidence seized in "good faith" by police acting under an invalid search warrant (*United States v. Leon* [1984]).

Ultimately, however, conflicts between Lee and other administration officials over the proper role of the solicitor general's office was apparently the cause of his 1985 resignation from the position. Lee's win-loss record in the Court had equaled or exceeded that of his recent predecessors. During the Court's 1984–1985 term, for instance, the Burger Court agreed to hear about 80 percent of the cases Lee's office filed, in contrast with about 3 percent of other petitions for review. And his office won 83 percent of the cases it filed or in which it had otherwise participated (usually by filing a "friend of the Court" brief supporting one of the parties in a case). The former Brigham Young University law dean's constitutional philosophy was also clearly consistent with the administration's stance on major civil liberties questions. A number of conservative political leaders had increasingly complained, though, that Lee was not pushing the Reagan judicial agenda with sufficient vigor.

For his part, Lee believed that an unduly aggressive posture against prevailing Supreme Court precedents with which the administration disagreed would undermine the unique relationship of trust and confidence the solicitor general's office enjoyed with the Court. Traditionally, the solicitor general had been considered the defender of federal law rather than a particular administration's policy agenda. In fact, when the solicitor concluded that the government had won a case in the lower courts through error, he was expected to file a confession of error with the Supreme Court, recommending that the lower court decision be reversed. Lee feared that vigorous pursuit of the administration's judicial goals on numerous fronts would jeopardize the Court's respect for his office and could undermine his position in individual cases. When announcing his resignation, Lee insisted that his departure, which had long been expected anyway, was in no way related to conflicts with William Bradford Reynolds or other administration officials, that he was leaving government and becoming a partner in the Washington office of a Chicago law firm only out of concerns for the educational needs of his seven children, three of whom would be in college that fall. In an interview, however, Lee stressed the importance of the rule of stare decisis, or precedent, to the American legal system: "Even though I might have some misgivings about certain precedents, where they are well established and it's obvious the Court isn't going to depart from them, it isn't smart to lecture the Justices about where they went wrong. . . . I'm the Solicitor General, not the Pamphleteer General" (Caplan 1987, 107).

Initially, Lee's successor, Charles Fried, a Harvard law professor said to be ambitious himself for a Reagan nomination to the high bench, rigorously pressed the administration's positions before the justices. But his stance apparently caused several members of the Court considerable consternation during the 1985–1986 term. That year, moreover, the rate of petitions from the solicitor general's office accepted by the Court fell to 57 percent from 80 percent the previous term. Sensitive to the situation, Fried stated publicly that his role as an aggressive administration advocate had not damaged the reputation of the office of solicitor general but also declared his intention to find a middle ground between what he called "being obdurate and being abject before the Court" (Caplan 1987, 263).

The Court

Although the Burger Court and its rulings were continuing objects of intense public debate as well as presidential, congressional, and state politics, its justices went about their work and day-to-day interactions in relative isolation from the close public scrutiny to which their legislative and executive counterparts were regularly subjected. As the Court's social and task leader responsible for assuring a collegial atmosphere among the justices as well as the timely completion of the Court's business, War-ren Burger was clearly no Earl Warren. With his impressive stature and flowing mane of silver hair, President Nixon's choice to lead the Court through what he hoped would be a profound constitutional counterrevolution certainly looked the part.

To a greater degree than any other chief justice since William Howard Taft (1921–1930), Chief Justice Burger labored tirelessly in behalf of reform in the quality of judicial administration and efficient caseload management. To one degree or another, he was involved in the establishment and enlargement of agencies dedicated to improving and streamlining federal and state court operations, the provision of administrative staff for federal and state judges, reduction in the size of civil juries and other reforms in that venerable institution, initiation of numerous innovations in federal court procedure, significant advances in opportunities for the continuing edu-cation of judges, and expansion of the Federal Judicial Center (first created in 1967) and its activities in behalf of judicial reform. And while Burger's opinions lacked the elegance of those of Oliver Wendell Holmes or Robert H. Jackson or the clarity and simplicity of Hugo Black's opinions, they were competent, workmanlike efforts.

From the first, however, justices and Court watchers alike compared Burger unfavorably with his predecessor. The social and political interpersonal skills Earl Warren had honed as governor of California and throughout his career in that state's politics had served him well on the Court. John Marshall Harlan, Felix Frankfurter, and a number of other colleagues with whom Warren frequently differed on issues confronting the justices no doubt considered the chief justice intellectually shallow and unduly result-oriented in his approach to constitutional interpretation. But War-ren's affable personality and acceptance of compromise and negotiation as inevitable elements of judicial decision making helped Warren greatly in promoting camaraderie and in guiding the Court to decisional results the chief supported, especially after Jus-tice Frankfurter's 1962 retirement from the bench. On the Burger Court, however, Jus-tices Brennan and Powell exerted far greater influence than the chief justice. Burger found the give-and-take of leadership on a court in which the chief justice was simply "first among equals" difficult, and his pugnacious temperament made it hard for him to suppress his personal preferences in the interest of at least an appearance of Court collegiality. Frequent press reports of the Court's dissatisfaction with his leadership undoubtedly originated on occasion with his colleagues, and the rate of concurring and dissenting opinions on his Court was the highest in the institution's history.

Part of the problem early in Burger's tenure was the chief justice's perhaps undue emphasis on Court ritual and the appearance of the building and grounds. Attempting to improve upon an already resplendent facility, which had quickly been dubbed the "Marble Palace" on completion of its construction in 1935, the chief justice embarked upon an extensive beautification campaign certain of his colleagues found both amus-ing and extreme. Several years into his tenure, Burger also apparently attempted to persuade his colleagues that their high-backed courtroom chairs should be of uniform size. But several justices ignored his suggestion, and such preoccupation with appearances made the chief the butt of pointed comments and jokes among his colleagues and Court staff. (One Warren Court holdover, for example, remarked to a visitor admiring the courtyard across a corridor from the justice's chambers—a partial result of Burger's handiwork—that his new chief was indeed "a good man . . . with flowers.")

The chief justice's approach to opinion assignments was another early source of concern. Since the days of Chief Justice John Marshall, the Court in most cases has issued an opinion of the Court explaining the rationale underlying the majority's decision. By custom, in cases in which the chief justice is in the majority, he has the prerogative of writing the Court's opinion or assigning the task to another majority justice; when he does not vote with the majority, the senior associate justice in the majority (in terms of years of service on the bench) makes the assignment. Not long into his tenure, Burger at times switched his vote in order to control the assignment of the Court's opinion in cases in which he initially had dissented—and thereby attempt to limit the ruling's impact as precedent.

During the Court's consideration of *Roe v. Wade* (1973), the chief justice resorted to a more complicated maneuver. Following oral argument in a case, the justices meet in a conference to discuss the case and reach a decision. When argument was initially held in the *Roe* case in the fall of 1971, Justices Powell and Rehnquist had not yet been confirmed by the Senate to replace Black and Harlan. In conference Chief Justice Burger suggested that *Roe* presented such sensitive issues that it should be scheduled for reargument before a full Court after the two latest nominees had taken their seats. On the merits of the constitutional issues raised in *Roe*, Burger thought that the restrictive Texas abortion law at issue in the case might be unconstitutionally vague, failing to inform people with sufficient clarity what abortions it prohibited and allowed. But he rejected the notion that the law violated the privacy rights of women. Justice White, who would ultimately be one of two *Roe* dissenters, also recommended reargument and was reluctant to include abortion rights among unenumerated constitutional safeguards. But Justices Douglas, Brennan, Stewart, and Marshall—a majority of the seven justices then participating in the case—disagreed, arguing that the right of privacy that the Court had recognized in earlier cases was sufficiently broad to include a right to abortion. And Justice Blackmun, at that point the Court's junior member, seemed inclined toward that position also. The chief justice thus appeared to be in the minority. He nonetheless assigned Justice Blackmun to write the Court's opinion. And when Douglas, the Court's senior associate justice, complained, Burger responded that the issues were so complex and the views of the various justices at conference so complicated that he had simply recorded no vote in the case. The ultimate outcome, he added, must thus depend on whether a majority of justices joined Blackmun's opinion.

When Justice Blackmun circulated a draft opinion resting a decision in the case on vagueness grounds rather than on the majority's recognition of an abortion right, Douglas and Brennan noted the discrepancy between Blackmun's draft and conference discussion of *Roe*. Blackmun then circulated a memorandum indicating that he now believed the case should be reargued before a full nine-member Court. By that point, Powell and Rehnquist had taken their seats. When they indicated they would vote for reargument even though they had not participated in the original proceedings, an angry Justice Douglas threatened to file a statement opposing the move but ultimately relented, simply noting instead his dissent from the reargument order (O'Brien 1996, 25–36).

Following reargument during the Court's 1972–1973 term, a 7–2 majority, speaking through Justice Blackmun, recognized a broad abortion right. Burger had eventually joined Blackmun's opinion but emphasized in a brief concurring opinion that the *Roe* Court "[p]lainly . . . rejects any claim that the Constitution requires abortion on demand" (*Roe v. Wade*, 208). That left only White and Rehnquist in dissent. Ultimately, therefore, a 7–2 majority of the full Court assumed the stance the truncated 4–3 majority had originally supported. Given the controversy *Roe* was to provoke, a decision by a 7–2 majority of the full Court was undoubtedly preferable to decision by four justices. The chief justice's questionable tactics, however, had delayed disposition of *Roe* by a term.

On one extremely significant occasion, moreover, Burger's reluctance to compromise resulted in the conversion of an opinion of the Court he had originally assigned himself into an opinion he signed but that was actually a collegial effort among the justices. When the Court voted in *United States v. Nixon* (1974) to reject the president's assertion of executive privilege in his abortive effort to withhold Watergate evidence from the courts, Burger circulated a draft opinion in the case. Convinced that their chief was assuming a position unduly deferential to presidential authority, his colleagues bombarded Burger with suggestions, along with threats to file separate opinions if substantial portions of his draft were not modified. The final version carried Burger's name but was the product of extensive negotiation, with various justices assuming major roles in writing different sections of the Court's opinion.

Chief Justice Burger, of course, was not the only cause of friction among the justices. When Justice Douglas declined to retire following his 1975 stroke, seven justices decided that he should be assigned no opinions and that the Court would hand down no ruling during the 1975–1976 term in cases decided by a 5–4 vote with Douglas in the majority. Justice White vigorously objected to his colleagues' decision. In the past when he had dissented from the Court's actions, White wrote the chief justice, he had "thought the decision being made, although wrong in my view, was within the powers assigned to the Court by the Constitution." But in White's judgment, the Court's treatment of their colleague "exceeds its powers and perverts the constitutional design." The Constitution, contended the justice, permitted the removal of justices through impeachment, "but it nowhere provides that a Justice's colleagues may deprive him of his office by refusing to permit him to function as a Justice." If there was doubt about Douglas's competence, White also could not understand why the justice's vote should be considered in any case, not merely those in which his was the deciding vote. He questioned whether even congressional authorization for removal of a justice for medical reasons would pass constitutional muster. "But Congress has taken no such action," he declared, "nor has it purported to vest power in the Court to unseat a Justice for any reason." The justice found equally objectionable his colleagues' failure to discuss the matter with Douglas or obtain from him his physicians' assessment of his health. White had no doubt that Douglas's illness was severe and that he should retire. "Although he has made noble efforts—very likely far more than others would have made—there remain serious problems that would best be resolved by his early retirement." That decision, however, was for Douglas to make. "The Constitution opted for the independence of each federal judge, including his freedom from removal by his colleagues" (Byron R. White to Warren E. Burger, October 20, 1975, Powell Papers, Box 129).

On November 12, 1975, Justice Douglas wrote President Ford that he was retiring, effective that day. The president who some years earlier had pressed for the justice's impeachment in the House of Representatives, acknowledged the letter "with profound personal sympathy" and "this nation's great gratitude" for Douglas's record years of service on the high bench (Gerald R. Ford to William O. Douglas, November 12, 1975, Powell Papers, Box 129). The justice's colleagues, too, expressed their gratitude. But Douglas would find complete separation from the Court he had served more than thirty-six years very difficult. As a justice, he had the assistance of one law clerk and two secretaries, declining the second clerk to which associate justices were then entitled. In a memorandum to the justices following his retirement, however, he requested the assignment of two clerks and two secretaries, in part to assist him in writing a history of the Court (Memorandum to the Conference, December 17, 1975, Powell Papers, Box 129). In a December 20 letter to the chief justice, he also indicated an interest in participating in cases brought to the Court but not yet decided at the time of his retirement. His colleagues agreed to allow Douglas two secretaries rather than the one ordinarily assigned retired justices and the clerk authorized those who assumed judicial duties in the lower federal courts. In a December 22 letter signed by all the justices on the Court at the time of his retirement, however, they gently but firmly pointed out that while retired justices could take assignments on lower courts, they could not be assigned any duties of a Supreme Court justice, even in cases submitted to the Court but not decided before their retirement (Letter from the justices to William O. Douglas, December 22, 1975, Powell Papers, Box 129).

Despite his precarious health, Justice Douglas did not die until January 1980, and his plans to write a history of the Court might not have been so far-fetched. Over the years the justice had authored more than thirty volumes on a variety of topics, and his fine autobiography appeared only a year before his stroke and retirement. Although unrealistic in his case, moreover, his suggestion that retired justices be permitted to participate in the Court's work was in fact one of several recommendations advanced during the Burger era for assisting the Court to cope with its mounting caseload.

During the Warren and Burger eras, the Court's docket had grown tremendously, from fewer than 2,000 cases in the 1960–1961 term to over 5,000 in 1980–1981, while the small number of cases given full review had remained relatively constant at about 150 annually. Most litigants attempt to bring their cases to the Court through a writ of certiorari, a discretionary procedure under which a writ authorizing review of a case is granted if four or more justices consider it sufficiently meritorious but is otherwise denied. The overwhelming majority of certiorari petitions are denied each term, but as the Court's overall docket grew, the justices were presumably obliged to devote more and more time to culling from the thousands of petitions filed every year the relatively few deemed worthy of review.

Concern that the justices' increasing screening duties were interfering with their attention to cases given full review prompted a variety of proposals for relieving the Court's apparent caseload management problems. Early in Chief Justice Burger's tenure, for example, a study group headed by Harvard law professor Paul Freund proposed creation of a National Court of Appeals, quickly dubbed a "Junior Supreme Court," to assume a substantial portion of the Supreme Court's screening function. Initially to be composed of seven judges reassigned temporarily from the U.S. courts of appeals, the intermediate appellate courts in the federal judiciary, the proposed court would review the Supreme Court's certiorari petitions, rejecting about 90 percent and forwarding the remainder to the high court for further screening and review. Justice Stevens later proposed a more extreme version of the study group's plan, and several other justices found such proposals appealing. But other members of the Court, most notably Justice Brennan, contended that the proposed scheme would violate the Constitution's requirement of "one" Supreme Court, attempted to separate two inherently interconnected functions of the Court (screening and deciding cases), and would undermine the justices' need to keep abreast of developing legal issues confronting the nation through review of all certiorari petitions. (For a summary of various recommendations, see "Law Clerks: The Transformation of the Judiciary," 1–110.)

Although the study group and Stevens proposals, among other suggestions to lighten the Court's caseload, were not adopted, the justices did modify the screening process internally in an effort to make their work more manageable. At Justice Powell's suggestion in 1972, a majority of the justices began participating in a "cert. pool." Traditionally, each justice's clerks have played a major role in screening certiorari petitions and preparing memoranda recommending to the justice they serve whether review should be granted or denied in each case before the Court. Under the pool arrangement, participating justices shared memos prepared by their pool of clerks, eliminating the obligation of the clerks in each chamber to review all petitions. The approach arguably gives tremendous influence to the clerk who prepares the pool memo in a given case, but most justices' chambers have participated in the pool since its inception. At this writing, the practice continues in the Rehnquist Court; only Justice Stevens does not participate.

The Record

The number of unanimous and nonunanimous opinions issued by the Court each term ranged from a low of ninety-four in the 1969 term, Burger's first year on the high bench, to a high of 167 in the 1981 term, with an average of 146 opinions issued per term.

As noted earlier, the Court's dissent rate reached historic high levels during Chief Justice Burger's tenure. The dissent rate for cases given full review during Earl Warren's last term was 66 percent. The dissent rate rose to 71 percent in Burger's first term and exceeded 81 percent in his second term. The rate for the 1971 term remained high at 78 percent and continued to be high in subsequent terms until a dip to 66 percent in the 1976 term. The lowest dissent rate for the Burger Court's first decade was 64 percent in the 1978 term. But while the rate rose to 75 percent the following term, the rates for the next five terms were below 70 percent, with record lows of 60 percent in the 1983 and 1984 terms. Although the dissent rate for the 1985 term, Burger's last, reflected an increase to 69 percent, the data reveal a very contentious Court during his first decade and a generally reduced level of dissent thereafter. (This discussion is based on Goldman 1999, 144–153.)

Table 1.1 indicates the dissent rates for individual Burger Court justices. When Justices Powell and Rehnquist replaced Black and Harlan during the 1971 term, the conservative shift in the Court's membership led to an increased rate of dissent among the most liberal justices—Douglas, Brennan, and Marshall. For the 1971–1974 terms, after all four Nixon appointees were on the bench, Douglas's dissent rate, as Table 1.1 shows, averaged nearly 44 percent over about 30 percent the previous two terms, while Brennan's average dissent rate increased from 21.6 to 29.8 percent in that period and Marshall's from 16.8 to 27.7 percent. Burger's dissent rate, by contrast, dropped from 20.2 to 14.1 percent. Following Douglas's replacement with Stevens, Brennan's and Marshall's dissent rates increased to 35.2 and 32.6 percent, respectively, while the moderately conservative Burger, Powell, Stewart, and White had rates of 15.7, 9.7, 15.9, and 15.2 percent. Not surprisingly, given his highly individualistic approach to issues confronting the Court, Justice Stevens had a dissent rate of 21.9 percent, while Rehnquist, the most conservative Burger Court justice, had a 22.8 percent dissent rate in the 1975–1977 terms. That pattern continued for the balance of the Court, with Brennan and Marshall registering the highest dissent rates, and the conservative Rehnquist and unpredictable Stevens the next highest rates, while the rates for the moderate conservatives ranged from 11.5 percent for Justice Powell to somewhat higher figures for the others during the 1981–1985 term. Justice Blackmun, whose voting record became increasingly liberal over the years of his tenure, had an 18.3 percent dissent rate during the same period. The overall average dissent rate for Burger Court justices was 20 percent, compared with 14 percent in the later Warren era (1962–1968 terms). Only four, or 36.4 percent, of the eleven justices of the later Warren Court had dissent rates exceeding 20 percent, moreover, while nine of the thirteen justices who served during part or all of the Burger era had dissent rates above 20 percent.

Judicial scholars have long grouped Supreme Court justices into blocs based on similar voting patterns in nonunanimous cases. Table 1.2 indicates liberal and conservative blocs identified for each of the seventeen terms Warren Burger served in the Court's center seat. Justices Brennan and Marshall were consistently part of the liberal bloc throughout the Burger era, as was Justice Douglas until his 1975 retirement. Burger, Rehnquist, and Blackmun, in that order, formed the conservative bloc's core until the 1977 term, with Burger and Blackmun voting together in about 90 percent of nonunanimous civil liberties cases.

After that, as Blackmun developed more moderately liberal voting patterns, he and the chief justice were less cohesive, and in Burger's last term the two agreed in only 40 percent of cases. During the 1981, 1982, and 1985 terms, in fact, Blackmun agreed more with Brennan and Marshall than with Chief Justice Burger. But those were the only terms when Blackmun was not allied with a conservative bloc. Rehnquist and Burger, in contrast, were consistently allied, agreeing 84 percent of the time in the 1980 term, 88 percent in 1983–1984, and 90 percent in the 1985 term. Justice O'Connor, after joining the Court in 1981, was also regularly part of the conservative bloc. During his first seven years on the Court, Justice Stevens fluctuated between conservative and liberal blocs, but from the 1981 term to the end of Burger's tenure, Stevens formed part of the liberal bloc. The term that Powell and Rehnquist joined the Court, Justice Stewart had also moved briefly into the liberal bloc, but after the 1971 term Stewart was a steadfast member of the conservative bloc. And Justice White helped form a conservative bloc every term of the Burger era.

As Table 1.3 indicates, the arrival of the Nixon appointees also occasioned a serious drop in the Court's support for civil liberties claims. During Burger's first two terms, the support rate averaged 55 percent, in contrast with rates of 89, 75, and 76 percent for Douglas, Brennan, and Marshall. The support rate for the 1971–1974 terms was 46 percent, only 37 percent for 1975–1977, 41 percent in the 1978–1980 terms, and 38 percent for 1981–1985. Unlike Chief Justice Warren, Burger had a consistently lower civil liberties support record than the Court's overall record, even as the proportion of cases decided in favor of civil liberties claims dropped significantly from the Warren Court level. During Warren's last term, some 75 percent of all cases decided with full opinion favored the civil liberties claim, in contrast with the substantially lower rates during the Burger era.

The Burger Court was also considerably less supportive of safeguards for economic underdogs or government regulation of business than its predecessor. In contrast with the Warren Court's 70 percent record of support for economic liberalism claims in the 1962–1968 terms, the Burger Court, as Table 1.4 indicates, had a 52 percent support level in 1969–1970, 42 percent in 1971–1974, 51 percent in 1975–1977, 46 percent in 1978–1980, and 60 percent in 1981–1985. Over that period Warren Court holdovers Brennan and Marshall became even more liberal on economic issues, while Douglas maintained a high level of support throughout his tenure and Justice White displayed a considerably more liberal bent in such cases than in civil liberties cases. Justice Rehnquist was least sympathetic to economic liberalism claims, followed near the end of Burger's tenure by O'Connor, Burger, and Powell. Justice Blackmun became more moderate to liberal on economic questions as well as civil liberties issues near the end of the Burger era.

Table 1.1 Dissent Rates (in percentages), Burger Court

Justice	1969–1970 Terms	1971–1974 Terms	1975–1977 Terms	1978–1980 Terms	1981–1985 Terms
Black	23.9	—	—	—	—
Blackmun	15.0	10.9	13.7	15.6	18.3
Brennan	21.6	29.8	35.2	32.5	32.4
Burger	20.2	14.1	15.7	14.7	12.7
Douglas	29.4	43.9	—	—	—
Harlan	16.9	—	—	—	—
Marshall	16.8	27.7	32.6	34.5	34.0
O'Connor	—	—	—	—	13.8
Powell	—	10.3	9.7	14.9	11.5
Rehnquist	—	18.7	22.8	24.8	19.9
Stevens	—	—	21.9	22.0	28.4
Stewart	15.4	16.1	15.9	20.7	—
White	14.1	10.9	15.2	13.3	12.4
The Court	76.9	77.7	72.1	69.4	64.3

Source: Goldman, *Constitutional Law: Cases and Essays*, 2nd ed. (1991), p. 146. Reprinted with permission.

Table 1.2 Voting Blocs on the Supreme Court in Nonunanimous
Civil Liberties Decisions, the Burger Court

Term	Bloc Membership	Average Agreement of Justices in Bloc (%)	Type of Bloc
1969	Douglas, Brennan, Marshall	79	Liberal
	White, Harlan	86	Conservative
	Stewart, Burger, Black	62	Conservative
1970	Douglas, Brennan, Marshall	83	Liberal
	Burger, Blackmun, Harlan, Stewart, White, Black	68	Conservative
1971	Douglas, Brennan, Marshall, Stewart	74	Liberal
	Burger, Blackmun, Rehnquist, Powell, White	81	Conservative
1972	Douglas, Brennan, Marshall	86	Liberal
	Burger, Blackmun, Rehnquist, Powell, White, Stewart	73	Conservative
1973	Douglas, Brennan, Marshall	85	Liberal
	Stewart, Powell, White	77	Conservative
	Burger, Blackmun, Rehnquist	83	Conservative
1974	Douglas, Brennan, Marshall	79	Liberal
	Burger, Blackmun, Rehnquist, Powell, White, Stewart	74	Conservative
1975	Marshall, Brennan	97	Liberal
	Burger, Blackmun, Rehnquist, Powell, White, Stewart, Stevens	72	Conservative
1976	Brennan, Marshall, Stevens	75	Liberal
	Burger, Rehnquist, White, Blackmun, Powell, Stewart	73	Conservative
1977	Brennan, Marshall	90	Liberal
	Powell, Blackmun	75	Conservative
	White, Burger, Stewart, Rehnquist, Stevens	61	Conservative
1978	Brennan, Marshall, Stevens	75	Liberal
	White, Blackmun	80	Conservative
	Burger, Stewart, Rehnquist, Powell	76	Conservative
1979	Brennan, Marshall, Stevens	82	Liberal
	Powell, Stewart	78	Conservative
	Burger, White, Blackmun, Rehnquist	64	Conservative
1980	Brennan, Marshall	89	Liberal
	Burger, White, Blackmun, Rehnquist, Powell, Stewart, Stevens	65	Conservative
1981	Brennan, Marshall	91	Liberal
	Stevens, Blackmun	67	Moderate
	Burger, Rehnquist, Powell, White, O'Connor	75	Conservative
1982	Brennan, Marshall, Stevens, Blackmun	70	Liberal
	Burger, Powell, White, Rehnquist, O'Connor	79	Conservative
1983	Brennan, Marshall, Stevens	72	Liberal
	Burger, Powell, White, Rehnquist, O'Connor, Blackmun	78	Conservative

1984	Brennan, Marshall, Stevens	77	Liberal
	Burger, White, Rehnquist, Powell, O'Connor, Blackmun	75	Conservative
1985	Brennan, Marshall, Stevens, Blackmun	70	Liberal
	Burger, Rehnquist, O'Connor, White, Powell	79	Conservative

Source: Goldman, *Constitutional Law: Cases and Essays*, 2nd ed. (1991), p. 148. Reprinted with permission.

Table 1.3 Pro–Civil Liberties Voting of the Justices on the Burger Court in All Decisions with Full Opinion (percentage of votes in favor)

Justice	1969–1970 Terms	1971–1974 Terms	1975–1977 Terms	1978–1980 Terms	1981–1985 Terms
Black	54	—	—	—	—
Blackmun	35	38	33	44	54
Brennan	75	83	77	81	80
Burger	36	31	23	25	23
Douglas	89	93	—	—	—
Harlan	47	—	—	—	—
Marshall	76	85	78	82	83
O'Connor	—	—	—	—	28
Powell	—	39	34	36	31
Rehnquist	—	22	13	13	17
Stevens	—	—	53	59	61
Stewart	46	59	42	41	—
White	50	44	37	43	33
The Court	55	46	37	41	38

Source: Goldman, *Constitutional Law: Cases and Essays*, 2nd ed. (1991), p. 149. Reprinted with permission.

Table 1.4 Pro–Economic Liberalism Voting of the Justices on the Burger Court in Nonunanimous Decisions with Full Opinion (percentage of votes in favor)

Justice	1969–1970 Terms	1971–1974 Terms	1975–1977 Terms	1978–1980 Terms	1981–1985 Terms
Black	58	—	—	—	—
Blackmun	27	38	50	61	76
Brennan	78	85	92	80	87
Burger	16	19	30	33	33
Douglas	78	78	—	—	—
Harlan	31	—	—	—	—
Marshall	61	73	86	85	91
O'Connor	—	—	—	—	31
Powell	—	29	41	37	33
Rehnquist	—	21	28	13	24
Stevens	—	—	53	40	52
Stewart	33	40	39	36	—
White	68	53	67	61	64
The Court	52	42	51	46	60

Source: Goldman, *Constitutional Law: Cases and Essays*, 2nd ed. (1991), p. 152. Reprinted with permission.

References

Abraham, Henry J. *Justices and Presidents: A Political History of Appointments to the Supreme Court.* 4th ed. Lanham, Md.: Rowman and Littlefield, 1999.

Caplan, Lincoln. *The Tenth Justice: The Solicitor General and the Rule of Law.* New York: Alfred A. Knopf, 1987.

Goldman, Sheldon. *Constitutional Law: Cases and Essays.* 2nd ed. New York: Harper & Row, 1991.

O'Brien, David M. *Storm Center: The Supreme Court in American Politics.* 4th ed. New York: Norton, 1996.

Powell, Lewis F., Jr. Papers. Washington and Lee University, Lexington, Va.

U.S. Congress. Senate. Committee on the Judiciary. *Hearing, Nomination of Judge Sandra Day O'Connor of Arizona to Serve as an Associate Justice of the Supreme Court of the United States.* 97th Cong., 1st sess., 1981.

———. *Hearing, Nomination of John Paul Stevens, of Illinois, to Be an Associate Justice of the Supreme Court of the United States.* 94th Cong., 1st sess., 1974.

———. *Hearing, Nominations of William H. Rehnquist, of Arizona, and Lewis F. Powell, Jr., of Virginia, to Be Associate Justices of the Supreme Court of the United States.* 92d Cong., 1st sess., 1971.

———. *Hearing, Nomination of Harry A. Blackmun, of Minnesota, to Be Associate Justice of the Supreme Court of the United States.* 91st Cong., 2d sess., 1970.

———. *Hearing, Nomination of Warren E. Burger, of Virginia, to Be Chief Justice of the United States.* 91st Cong., 1st sess., 1969.

Woodward, Bob, and Scott Armstrong. *The Brethren: Inside the Supreme Court.* New York: Simon & Schuster, 1979.

2

The Justices

T he membership of the Burger Court encompassed the modern Supreme Court's entire history. Hugo Lafayette Black, appointed by President Roosevelt in 1937, served through the Hughes, Stone, Vinson, and Warren eras, as well as for the first two terms of Chief Justice Burger's tenure, retiring from the bench and dying in September 1971. William Orville Douglas, a 1939 Roosevelt appointee, would serve an even longer tenure than Black—indeed, the longest in the Court's history to date—over thirty-six years, including the first six terms of the Burger Court. Like Justice Black, John Marshall Harlan, appointed by President Eisenhower in 1955 and the grandson of the first Justice Harlan, served only during Burger's first two terms, dying on December 29, 1971. But three other justices appointed to the Court during the Warren era—William Joseph Brennan Jr., a 1956 Eisenhower appointee; Byron Raymond White, chosen by President Kennedy in 1962; and Thurgood Marshall, appointed by Lyndon Johnson in 1967—served through the entire Burger era and into Chief Justice William H. Rehnquist's tenure, retiring in 1990, 1993, and 1991, respectively. And Justice Potter Stewart, a 1958 Eisenhower appointee, served on the Burger Court until 1981. Two of President Nixon's three associate justices, Harry Andrew Blackmun and Lewis Franklin Powell Jr., served into the Rehnquist era, Powell until 1987 and Blackmun until 1994, while Nixon's third appointee as associate justice became President Reagan's choice to replace Burger in 1986. John Paul Stevens, appointed to the Burger Court by President Ford in 1975, continues on the Rehnquist Court at this writing, as does Sandra Day O'Connor, appointed by Reagan in 1981. This chapter examines in order of appointment to the Court the backgrounds and records of the fourteen justices who served during at least a portion of Chief Justice Burger's tenure.

Roosevelt Court Justices

During Franklin D. Roosevelt's first term in the White House (1933–1936), a laissez-faire majority on the Supreme Court made a shambles of his New Deal plan for

Table 2.1 Burger Court Justices

Justice	Birth Year	App't Year	App't Pres.	App't Age	Burger Court	Replaced
Black	1886	1937	Roosevelt	51	83–85	Van Devanter
Blackmun	1908	1970	Nixon	61	61–77	Fortas
Brennan	1906	1956	Eisenhower	50	61–78	Minton
Burger	1907	1969	Nixon	61	62–79	Warren
Douglas	1898	1939	Roosevelt	40	71–77	Brandeis
Harlan	1899	1955	Eisenhower	55	70–72	Jackson
Marshall	1908	1967	Johnson	59	61–78	Clark
O'Connor	1930	1981	Reagan	51	51–56	Stewart
Powell	1907	1972	Nixon	65	65–79	Black
Rehnquist	1924	1972	Nixon	48	48–61	Harlan
Stevens	1920	1975	Ford	55	55–66	Douglas
Stewart	1915	1958	Eisenhower	43	54–71	Burton
White	1917	1962	Kennedy	44	52–69	Whittaker

pulling the nation out of severe economic depression. Invoking state reserved powers, a narrow construction of congressional and presidential regulatory authority, and a "substantive due process" interpretation of the Fifth and Fourteenth Amendment due process clauses used to invalidate laws the justices considered "unreasonable" interferences with property interests, the "Old" Court, as it was later to be known, declared unconstitutional much federal recovery legislation and state economic controls as well. President Roosevelt had no first-term opportunities to alter the Court's membership, and Congress rejected his Court-packing plan early in his second term, denying him the chance to add up to six additional justices to the high bench and change the direction of the Court's economic rulings.

In the spring of 1937, however, the Court began consistently to uphold both federal and state economic regulations. At least one justice (Owen Roberts) whose voting patterns shifted during that watershed period later argued defensively that the justices had not caved in to political pressure but that instead the post-1936 legislation the Court invariably upheld had simply been more carefully drafted to avoid constitutional defects than the laws struck down during Roosevelt's first term. But Washington wits joked that certain members of the nine-man body had decided that "a switch in time would save nine."

Hugo Black

Roosevelt's second and succeeding terms also offered him the chance to fill numerous vacancies on the high bench. Indeed, at his death in 1945, FDR had filled all but one of the seats on the Court. Roosevelt's first choice for the bench, in August 1937, was Senator Hugo Black of Alabama, one of the staunchest congressional proponents of the Court-packing bill and a vehement critic of the Old Court's laissez-faire economic decisions. Born in rural Clay County, Alabama, in 1886, the son of a store-keeper and farmer, Black's relatively humble roots, two-year law program at the University of Alabama, and brief tenure as a Birmingham police court judge offered little cause for optimism about the ultimate directions of his life and career. But Black's intelligence, drive, and iron will, inherited largely from his beloved mother, enabled him to overcome his modest background and initial prospects. By the early 1920s, he was a prominent Birmingham lawyer, in 1926 he was elected to the U.S. Senate, and in 1937 he became the first justice of the "Roosevelt Court."

Black's selection to the nation's highest court was as controversial as it was remarkable. Birmingham business leaders considered the populist Democrat, whose clients had included labor unions, a "Bolshevik," and as a local prosecutor he drafted a grand jury report accusing police officers in Bessemer, a blue-collar Birmingham suburb, of using third-degree tactics on suspects, especially persons of color. Yet as defense counsel in the notorious 1921 murder trial of a white man accused of killing a Roman Catholic priest who had married the defendant's young daughter to a middle-aged Puerto Rican, Black had appealed to the racial and religious bigotry of jurors in winning his client's acquittal. In 1923 he had also joined the Ku Klux Klan (KKK). At the beginning of his first Senate campaign in 1926, he resigned his Klan membership, and in later years he said that he had joined the group largely because many Alabama jurors, before whom he regularly argued cases, were also members. Even so, he won election with KKK support and remained politically indebted to the Invisible Empire until the early 1930s. As an ardent Senate New Dealer, though, he had alarmed even President Roosevelt with his attacks on economic privilege and support for a thirty-hour workweek. His heavy-handed Senate investigations of government ties to big business, moreover, led to charges he was bullying the business community.

Controversy also followed the Alabamian to the Supreme Court. Public revelations of his Klan membership shortly after his appointment to the bench aroused a national furor. Indeed, one group labeled October 4, 1937, his first day on the Court, as "Black Day." The liberal civil liberties record the new justice quickly forged largely allayed such concerns, but certain civil libertarians were never comfortable with the ex-Klansman's presence on the bench and found especially offensive his decision for the Court in *Korematsu v. United States* (1944), upholding World War II sanctions against Japanese Americans. Nor were such concerns ever entirely alleviated: In a 1967 newspaper interview published after his death, Black defended the blanket regulations military authorities had imposed, saying, "They all look alike to a person not a Jap" (*New York Times*, September 26, 1971).

An exceptionally tenacious, wily defender of positions he thought important, Justice Black often antagonized those justices with whom he most frequently differed, especially Robert H. Jackson and Felix Frankfurter, who considered their colleague insufficiently deferential to legislative and executive authority. But Black was

Hugo Lafayette Black (Harris & Ewing, Collection of the Supreme Court of the United States)

not merely one of the Court's most controversial justices; he was also one of its intellectual leaders, despite his modest academic credentials, about which Justice Frankfurter, a former Harvard law professor, was especially scornful. Black embraced a positivist conception of the judge's function that many considered outmoded and unworkable. Under his positivist jurisprudence, judges were to construe the meaning of constitutional provisions according to their literal meaning and the intent of their framers rather than be guided by their personal notions of what was reasonable, fair, just, or socially desirable. Where the Constitution's text or the historical record proved unavailing, he agreed that judges could assign a constitutional provision the meaning they thought to possess the greatest intrinsic merit. In his judgment, however, such penumbral situations rarely arose. Black preferred, moreover, relatively fixed constructions of constitutional provisions that limited the discretion of judges to decide cases according to their personal predilections.

During much of his judicial career, Justice Black's positivism led him largely in liberal-activist directions. Asserting that the Old Court majority had simply engrafted its laissez-faire economic theories onto the Constitution's text, for example, he was one of the leaders of the Roosevelt Court's dismantling of such precedents. According a literal, absolutist interpretation to the First Amendment's command that government make "no law" abridging freedom of speech and other liberties guaranteed there, he opposed all laws against obscenity (*Roth v. United States* [1957]) and libel (*New York Times v. Sullivan* [1964]). Convinced that the Fourteenth Amendment's framers had intended the broadly worded provisions of its first section to make fully binding on the states all the guarantees of the federal Bill of Rights, he favored the complete elimination of the double standard under which for much of his tenure most of the Bill of Rights had been applicable to national officials alone (*Adamson v. California* [1947]). And while a majority never adopted his "total incorporation" thesis, he had the satisfaction during his last decade on the bench of watching the Court apply most Bill of Rights safeguards to the states via a "selective incorporation" approach to the Fourteenth Amendment's meaning (*Duncan v. Louisiana* [1968]).

The positivist conception of the judge's function that Justice Black embraced also limited, however, the degree to which the judiciary could intrude on the other branches and levels of government. Since the Fourth Amendment prohibited only "unreasonable" searches and seizures of "persons, houses, papers, and effects," he recognized relatively broad power for police in that field and objected to the amendment's extension beyond the seizure of the tangible items mentioned in its text to eavesdropping. He doubted, too, that any warrant authorizing the bugging of possible future conversations could ever satisfy the amendment's requirement that search warrants "particularly describ[e]" the things to be seized (*Katz v. United States* [1967]). He refused to agree, moreover, that the First Amendment's guarantee to "freedom of speech" went beyond its literal language to include "symbolic speech"—

to conduct such as flag-burning, that is, intended to communicate ideas or feelings (*Street v. New York* [1969]). He also insisted that people could exercise First Amendment freedoms only where they had a right to be for such purposes. He spoke for a 5–4 majority, for example, in sustaining the trespass convictions of civil rights demonstrators who held a peaceful protest on the grounds of a local jail (*Adderley v. Florida* [1966]) and vigorously dissented when the justices upheld the right of students to wear black armbands on public school property as a symbol of protest against U.S. military policies (*Tinker v. Des Moines Indep. School Dist.* [1969]).

Black was especially concerned at the potentially open-ended meaning judges might assign the Constitution's equal protection and due process guarantees. For that reason, he preferred to limit equal protection largely to its historic racial context. He thus dissented when a majority struck down a poll tax requirement for state elections, contending that states possessed broad power to impose nonracial restrictions on the franchise (*Harper v. Virginia Board of Elections* [1966]). Just as he had vigorously opposed the use of substantive due process to strike down economic laws a majority considered unreasonable during the laissez-faire era, moreover, he also rejected the modern Court's resort to that doctrine in adding noneconomic personal rights to the Constitution's meaning. In *Griswold v. Connecticut* (1965), a 7–2 majority invoked substantive due process and related rhetoric to recognize an unenumerated right of marital privacy and overturn a broad state ban on the use of contraceptives. Black dissented, accusing majority justices of embracing a "natural law" jurisprudence that unconstitutionally made lawmakers of judges. He had no doubt the challenged law was unwise but insisted that the appropriate medium for keeping the Constitution "in tune with the times" or current conceptions of "justice" was the amendment process, not the transformation of judges into a "bevy of Platonic Guardians." Although the justices did not directly confront the abortion issue before his retirement from the bench, Black's conference remarks made it clear that he would also have filed a vigorous dissent in *Roe v. Wade* (1973), recognizing a broad due process right of women to abort unwanted pregnancies.

Just as the justice favored the complete rejection of substantive due process, Black also opposed use of the due process guarantee to recognize procedural rights not mentioned or implied in the Constitution's text. When the Court concluded in *In Re Winship* (1970), for example, that proof of a defendant's guilt beyond a reasonable doubt was a requirement of procedural fairness implicit in due process, he again dissented. In English law due process had originally required only that government follow the "law of the land," that is, preexisting laws and procedures, when interfering with a person's life, liberty, or property; it was not a guarantee to substantive "reasonableness" or procedural "fairness" to be defined by judges. The Court, argued Black, should stick to that relatively fixed, law-of-the-land conception of due process rather than construe it as an open-ended, continuing invitation to judges to engraft their own preferences—procedural or substantive—onto the Constitution's text and the intent of its framers.

William O. Douglas

President Roosevelt's fourth appointee to the Court would also enjoy a tenure—the longest in history to date—that extended into the Burger era. The second of three children, William O. Douglas was born in Maine, Minnesota, in 1898 but spent most of his youth in the west, where his father's calling as a Presbyterian home missionary took the family shortly after young William's birth. When his father died in 1904, Douglas's mother settled with her children near relatives in Yakima, Washington.

Although raised in grinding poverty and crippled by polio, Douglas resolutely overcame the adversities of his youth. He, his sister, and brother contributed to the family's finances with odd jobs and work in area orchards. After excelling in high school, where he was valedictorian, he attended Whitman College on a scholarship, graduating Phi Beta Kappa in 1920. Following undergraduate study, Douglas taught English and Latin at Yakima's high school for two years, but in 1922 he took a train east, herding a carload of sheep to pay his fare, and enrolled at New York's Columbia Law School. Graduating second in his law class, he was hopeful of becoming a clerk to Supreme Court justice Harlan Fiske Stone. When a clerkship eluded him, he joined a prominent Wall Street firm (now Cravath, Swaine & Moore), but after two unsatisfying years there left Wall Street to teach law, first at Columbia (1927–1929), then at Yale (1929–1934), where he specialized in corporate law. At Yale he became one of the youngest professors to hold an endowed chair and became thoroughly imbued with the legal realist movement then flourishing there and its conception of law as a device for promoting social change and of judges as social engineers.

Like several other prominent depression-era scholars, Douglas went to Washington to work in the Roosevelt administration, where he became a member of the Securities and Exchange Commission (SEC) in 1936 and the commission's chair the following year, while also developing close ties with Secretary of the Interior Harold Ickes and other members of FDR's inner circle. When Justice Louis D. Brandeis retired from the Court in early 1939, Douglas's intimate connections with the Roosevelt White House paid off. After filling his initial Supreme Court vacancies with two southerners (Black in 1937 and Kentuckian Stanley Reed in 1938) and an easterner (Felix Frankfurter in 1939, a month before Brandeis's retirement), the president had promised to appoint a westerner to the next seat to become available on the high bench.

Although Douglas had spent his youth on the West Coast, FDR considered him an easterner from Yale. Some questioned, moreover, his enthusiasm for the New Deal and commitment to vigorous regulation of the stock market. But an uncompromising Douglas speech attacking financial interests and filled with New Deal zeal helped to dispel

William O. Douglas (Harris & Ewing, Collection of the Supreme Court of the United States)

such concerns, and friends joined Douglas in building a broad base of support for his nomination. In late March the president submitted his name to the Senate, which approved his appointment in early April by a 62–4 vote. The four confirmation opponents, all Republicans, branded the nominee, ironically enough, a tool of Wall Street.

Among Justice Douglas's most lasting contributions to American law were his opinions for the Court in a variety of World War II cases involving government regulation of business. But he would be best remembered as perhaps the most consistent defender of civil liberties claims ever to occupy a seat on the high bench. Through most of their years together on the Court, Douglas and Roosevelt's first appointee, Hugo Black, were regularly allied in such cases. They initially joined the Court in upholding compulsory school flag programs in *Minersville School District v. Gobitis* (1940) but later announced that *Gobitis* had been wrongly decided (*Jones v. Opelika* [1942]), then helped to form a majority in *West Virginia Board of Education v. Barnette* (1943), declaring flag programs a violation of free speech and religious liberty.

Although apparently with considerably less enthusiasm than his colleague, Douglas also joined Black's *Korematsu* opinion. After World War II they regularly challenged government regulations of subversive speech. In *Terminiello v. Chicago* (1949), Douglas spoke for a majority that included Black in overturning the conviction of a Catholic priest arrested by police after his harangue to a packed auditorium audience attracted a hostile crowd, which denounced the speaker as a pro-Fascist anti-Semite. The trial judge, concluded Douglas, had construed the disorderly conduct statute under which Terminiello was convicted to reach speech that merely provoked anger and controversy rather than the clear and present danger of illegal action required by First Amendment precedents for the suppression of expression.

More often, however, the duo were in dissent from postwar rulings sustaining governmental authority against the First Amendment and related claims of Communists. Embracing an absolutist interpretation of the amendment, both vigorously dissented, for example, in *Dennis v. United States* (1951), in which a 6–2 majority upheld the convictions of eleven Communist Party leaders and a plurality invoked a version of the clear and present danger test extremely deferential to government. Black, joined by Douglas and Chief Justice Earl Warren, filed another vehement dissent in *Barenblatt v. United States* (1959), upholding the contempt-of-Congress conviction of a college instructor who refused to answer questions before a House Un-American Activities Committee inquiry regarding his political beliefs and membership in a Communist club at the University of Michigan. Douglas also concurred in the absolute protection Black extended obscenity and libel and joined his colleague in advocating complete application of the Bill of Rights in state cases, as well as his expansive interpretations of the right to counsel and guarantees against compulsory self-incrimination and double jeopardy.

Yet Douglas and Black adhered to fundamentally different conceptions of jurisprudence that led them to part company often during their last decade together on the Court. The two differed on a number of issues of national power and federalism. Since the Constitution's language granted Congress, not the federal courts, power over interstate commerce, the literalist Black opposed the line of decisions in which a majority assumed authority to rule on the reasonableness of state regulations of interstate trade, while the more pragmatic Douglas considered such decisions a viable way to limit state interferences with national commerce in commercial fields Congress had not fully occupied with national law (*Southern Pacific Co. v. Arizona* [1945]). Black was more willing than Douglas, moreover, to invoke federal principles in limiting national judicial authority over state court proceedings. During his last term, for example, Black spoke for the Court in *Younger v. Harris* (1971), reaffirming earlier decisions drastically restricting the power of federal district courts to issue injunctions stopping pending state criminal prosecutions, even under state laws that violated First Amendment rights. In a *Younger* dissent, Douglas, for his part, favored federal court intervention in such cases.

Their jurisprudential differences were most pronounced, though, in cases dealing with the scope of civil liberties. Although Black's positivism placed a ceiling as well as a floor on the content of constitutional rights, confining them largely to guarantees mentioned in the document's text or intended by its framers, Douglas's legal realism envisioned the Constitution as an ever-expanding civil liberties repository with presumably no limit to its ultimate scope. Thus, while Douglas joined Black's total incorporation thesis, he did not limit constitutional guarantees to those enumerated in the Bill of Rights and elsewhere in the Constitution. In *Griswold v. Connecticut* (1965), for example, Douglas spoke for the Court over Black's pointed dissent in holding that the specific guarantees of the Bill of Rights include within their scope unenumerated, "penumbral" rights, such as a guarantee to marital privacy. And while Black favored limiting the equal protection guarantee largely to racial discrimination, Douglas wrote or joined opinions subjecting other "suspect" forms of discrimination, including illegitimacy (*Levy v. Louisiana* [1968]), to strict judicial review and also construing equal protection to provide meaningful coverage to "fundamental rights" not mentioned in the Constitution's text, among them the rights to vote (*Harper v. Virginia Board of Elections* [1966]), interstate travel, and welfare benefits (*Shapiro v. Thompson* [1969]).

Not only did Douglas's jurisprudence place few, if any, substantive limits on the ultimate scope of civil liberties, but especially in later years his opinions, like certain of the more than thirty books he found time to write during his career, took on a casual (indeed, sloppy), intellectually shallow look. He appeared to delight, moreover, in embracing extreme legal positions, including the claim that trees should be accorded standing to sue in environmental cases (*Sierra Club v. Morton* [1972]). As his opinions became a frequent target of scholarly criticism, his liberal voting record infuriated conservative politicians. His unorthodox personal life fueled outrage as well. After divorcing his wife of nearly thirty years in the early 1950s, the justice had remarried three times, on the last occasion to a twenty-two-year-old, when he was sixty-six.

In 1970 the controversy surrounding the justice came to a head in the Congress. A week after the Senate rejected President Nixon's Supreme Court nomination of Clement Haynsworth that year, House Republican leader Gerald Ford introduced a resolution calling for Douglas's impeachment. Congressional Republicans were especially critical of the justice's connections with a foundation said to have received substantial income from Nevada gambling interests. But the Democratic-controlled House Judiciary Committee found no basis for the allegations, and various members of the national press editorialized that Congressman Ford's real concern was with the justice's judicial record. Douglas continued on the Court until 1975, when a severe stroke ultimately forced his reluctant retirement from the bench. Before his death in 1980, however, Congress honored the lifelong hiker and nature lover with the designation of parkland along a favorite Washington walking trail as the William O. Douglas National Park.

Warren Court Holdovers

Hugo Black and William O. Douglas were not the only justices tying the Burger Court to the past. A number of justices appointed during the Warren era continued to serve for all or a portion of Chief Justice Burger's tenure in the Court's center seat. President Eisenhower's 1953 appointment of Earl Warren, a California governor from the GOP's moderate-to-liberal wing with no previous judicial experience, was hardly greeted with unrestrained enthusiasm by the party's business conservative core; and the new chief justice's masterful engineering of a unanimous ruling the next year in *Brown v. Board of Education*, outlawing state-mandated racial segregation in the public schools, had dashed, if only briefly, Republican hopes of breaking the Democrats' nearly century-long hold on the white South. For his second selection to the high bench, therefore, Eisenhower chose a nominee with impeccable Republican establishment credentials, close ties to the business community, and at least a modicum of prior court experience.

John Marshall Harlan

Senior partner and chief litigator in one of Wall Street's most prestigious firms before being appointed by Eisenhower in 1954 to the U.S. Court of Appeals for the Second

Circuit, John Marshall Harlan was the grandson and namesake of the first Justice Harlan, the Kentucky slaveholder and opponent of abolition who became a great champion of civil rights on the Court. The younger Harlan was born in Chicago in 1899. His father, John Maynard Harlan, was a colorful lawyer, city alderman, and unsuccessful mayoral candidate who railed against the city's traction (streetcar) interests but ultimately made his peace with them, becoming their counsel on a lucrative retainer.

The financial security John Maynard's new clients provided, as well as the family's excellent social standing, placed the Harlans at the center of Chicago society. But young John Marshall spent little of his life there. Packed off at an early age to a Canadian boarding school, where he excelled in academics and sports, he spent his summers at Justice Harlan's Quebec summer home. Following a final year of preparatory education at the Lake Placid School in New York, he enrolled in the Princeton class of 1920. After compiling an outstanding record at Princeton, where he was president of the student newspaper, he attended Oxford on a Rhodes scholarship, finishing his three years of study there with a "first" in jurisprudence and placing seventh in a class of 120.

On his return from England, Harlan obtained a position with what is now Dewey, Ballantine, one of New York City's finest Wall Street firms, and also completed New York Law School's two-year program in a year, securing the skills necessary for an American law practice that his jurisprudential studies at Oxford had hardly provided him. The firm's chief litigator, Emory Buckner, quickly became the young associate's mentor and the most significant influence on his rapidly developing career. When Buckner became U.S. attorney for New York's southern district in 1925, Harlan became his chief assistant, vigorously enforcing the national prohibition law both detested. In the late 1920s, when Buckner became a special state attorney general prosecuting the Queens borough president on municipal graft charges, Harlan was again the elder attorney's top assistant. By that early point, too, he had become second only to Buckner as their firm's principal litigator, and when his mentor's health began to fail in the 1930s, Harlan increasingly assumed leadership of the firm's litigation team. In his first major case, he successfully defended heirs to the estate of the eccentric New York millionaire Ella Wendel from more than 2,000 claimants; by the end of the decade he had become the firm's chief advocate.

Following service in military intelligence during World War II, Harlan returned to his firm and an impressive array of corporate clients. By the early 1950s, he was considered one of the nation's foremost litigators in antitrust and related suits. In a lengthy Chicago trial, he successfully defended the Du Pont brothers and a number of their corporate interests from antitrust charges growing out of the defendants' grip on General Motors and the United Rubber Company. When the Supreme Court, speaking through Justice William Brennan, reversed the trial court in that case

John Marshall Harlan (Harris & Ewing, Collection of the Supreme Court of the United States)

shortly after Harlan assumed his seat on the high bench, he properly recused himself from participation but privately vented his outrage at the Court's action to Justice Felix Frankfurter, one of the dissenters in the case.

Even before the district court ruling in the Du Pont suit, however, Harlan's career had taken a new and permanent direction. Although never very active in partisan politics, he had played a role in several GOP campaigns. More important, his circle of friends included New York governor and Republican presidential candidate Thomas E. Dewey, for whom Harlan had served briefly as chief counsel to the state crime commission, as well as Dewey's close associate Herbert Brownell, who became the first attorney general in the Eisenhower administration. When a vacancy arose on the Court of Appeals for the Second Circuit, Brownell offered Harlan the position. The future justice—whose public service lineage included not only his grandfather but also an uncle who had been an interstate commerce commissioner and an aunt who had served as secretary to the wives of several Republican presidents—accepted, despite serious reservations on the part of several senior partners in his law firm.

Harlan's brief tenure on the Second Circuit was confined largely to tax cases and other mundane matters. In *United States v. Flynn* (1954), the one notable exception to that pattern, Harlan spoke for a three-judge panel in upholding the convictions of twelve Communists under the Smith Act, a federal statute forbidding advocacy of the illegal overthrow of government and membership in organizations with such goals. In *Flynn*, Harlan gave the clear and present danger test an interpretation so deferential to government that one commentator was reminded of the archaic English law of constructive treason, which permitted prosecutions for treason against the crown even without direct proof of illegal conduct.

Flynn, of course, hardly damaged Harlan's reputation with the Eisenhower administration. One of Attorney General Brownell's motivations for offering Harlan the appeals court post was to provide him with the prior judicial experience, however brief, the Eisenhower White House insisted Supreme Court nominees possess after Governor Warren's appointment as chief justice. When Robert H. Jackson, another New Yorker, died in October 1954, Harlan was Brownell's candidate to fill Jackson's seat. Segregationist southern Democrats and conservative Republicans delayed his confirmation by the Senate for nearly five months, using the proceedings for attacks on the Court's recent school desegregation ruling in the *Brown* case and on Harlan's nominal membership in the Atlantic Union Council, which critics considered a hotbed of "one worlders" and threat to American sovereignty. Harlan's confirmation was never in doubt, but the Senate vote to approve the appointment was 71–11, with fourteen other senators abstaining.

On the bench Harlan quickly joined the restraintist voting bloc headed by Justice Frankfurter, whom the new justice had met years before through his mentor Emory Buckner, one of Frankfurter's closest friends. Developing a jurisprudence that closely resembled Frankfurter's, Harlan contended that the political processes and principles of federalism and separation of powers were ultimately more effective safeguards of individual liberty than constitutional guarantees, although also embracing the corollary view that judicial construction of the latter should give due deference to the importance of the former in a free society.

Harlan's regard for the "passive virtues" of judicial self-restraint did not mean, of course, that he invariably rejected civil liberties claims. His opinion for the Court in *NAACP v. Alabama* (1958) was the first to include freedom of association within the First Amendment's scope; his dissent in *Poe v. Ullman* (1961) embraced a constitutional right of privacy four years before a majority reached that judgment in the *Griswold* case; and in his final term he spoke for the Court in *Cohen v. California* (1971), upholding the public display of an offensive epithet and rejecting governmental power to cleanse the public vocabulary of vulgar speech. Although extremely deferential, moreover, to government assertions of national security claims—as his *Flynn* opinion and last-term dissent from a majority's extension of constitutional protection to publication of *The Pentagon Papers* in *New York Times Co. v. United States* (1971) made clear—Harlan's narrow constructions of the Smith Act in *Yates v. United States* (1957) and *Scales v. United States* (1961) made successful prosecution of subversive advocacy and membership exceedingly difficult.

In the main, however, Justice Harlan's voting patterns reflected his deference to governmental power, especially state authority. In *Barenblatt v. United States* (1959) and related cases, for example, he rejected Justice Black's First Amendment absolutism, following instead a balancing approach that accorded government wide latitude. In the criminal procedure field, moreover, he rejected the *Miranda* restrictions on police interrogation of suspects and extension of the Fourth Amendment exclusionary rule to state cases in *Mapp v. Ohio* (1961).

A number of key elements guided Harlan's approach to issues confronting the Court. Not surprising given his Oxford experience, he was a common-law jurist who placed a premium on the need to decide cases according to the precedents, or legal principles established in earlier cases. When able to distinguish a precedent with which he did not agree, he took advantage of the situation. When, for example, a majority inappropriately, in his judgment, construed the equal protection clause and other constitutional provisions to require reapportionment of the districts from which legislators and other government officials were elected, he opposed not only the earlier rulings in that field (e.g., *Reynolds v. Sims* [1964]) but each later extension of the one person, one vote principle applied in such cases as well—extensions applicable to different governmental units and thus distinguishable, to his mind, from previous decisions (*Avery v. Midland County* [1968]). The Warren Court's failure to muster a majority definition of obscenity after 1957 meant no binding precedent in that intractable field, thus freeing Harlan to continue espousing his position that federal obscenity controls should be narrowly confined while states were given broad authority over public health, safety, and morals. Where no such options were available, however, Harlan scrupulously honored even those precedents with which he most strenuously disagreed.

Consistent with the common-law tradition, Harlan also readily accepted the creative role judges play when construing constitutional provisions. But unlike his jurisprudential antagonist and close personal friend Hugo Black, he believed that adherence to the doctrine of self-restraint, rather than attempts to confine judges within the constraints of what were, to him, generally elusive quests for literal meaning or the intent of a constitutional provision's framers, was the proper way to curtail judicial power. Along similar lines, he favored narrow constitutional interpretations closely tied to the facts of individual cases rather than sweeping rulings with potentially broad future impact as binding precedent. Harlan's opposition to the Warren Court's expansive construction of the equal protection guarantee in reapportionment and other cases (*Shapiro v. Thompson* [1969]) reflected this concern, as did his disapproval of the incorporation of most Bill of Rights guarantees into the Fourteenth Amendment's restrictions on state power (*Duncan v. Louisiana* [1968]). And while Harlan, like Justice Frankfurter, embraced a flexible, evolving, "fundamental fairness" conception of due process that could be invoked, as Justice Black argued, to expand indefinitely the scope of constitutional rights, in Harlan's hands that vague guarantee was typically accorded a narrow meaning strictly confined to the circumstances of the particular case. In *Boddie v. Connecticut* (1971), decided in his last term, for example, he spoke for a majority invoking due process to overturn filing-fee requirements for indigents seeking to initiate divorce proceedings but made clear that his position was based on the state's absolute monopoly over the granting of divorces and was unlikely to be extended to other fields.

Finally, Harlan, like law professor Herbert Wechsler, contended that judicial decisions must be truly principled, based on reasoning that transcended the immediate results of individual cases—that reflected, in short, "neutral" legal principles rather than judicial conceptions of "justice" or social utility. Although supporting desegregation rulings, for example, he was concerned that the Court avoid the appearance of favoritism toward particular groups or causes.

Substantial loss of his eyesight made Harlan's work on the Court increasingly difficult during his last years, and debilitating cancer obliged him to retire from the bench in the fall of 1971. He died in late December of that year. Justice Harlan is often perceived, unfortunately, as merely another vote for Felix Frankfurter's jurisprudence. But particularly since Frankfurter left the bench in 1962, at the beginning of the Warren Court's most liberal-activist period, Harlan, not Frankfurter, arguably was the most significant critic of Warren Court trends.

William J. Brennan Jr.

In some respects Dwight Eisenhower's selection of William J. Brennan Jr. as his third Supreme Court nominee was as unlikely as his choice of John Harlan had seemed an eminently logical decision for a Republican president. Indeed, Ike would later complain that his appointments of Brennan and Warren were the worst mistakes of his presidency, while critics saw them as among the few bright spots of an otherwise lackluster administration unduly insensitive to mounting racial and related problems confronting the postwar nation. Born in 1906 in Newark, New Jersey, Brennan was the second of eight children of Irish Catholic immigrant parents. His father had migrated to the United States in 1890, earning a livelihood initially by shoveling coal in a brewery. Later the elder Brennan was active in the labor movement, becoming a leader in the American Federation of Labor, then moved into local government, where he served as Newark's commissioner of public safety from 1917 to 1930. Having to struggle to overcome his own impoverished roots instilled in William Sr. a strong sense of social responsibility and drive to succeed that he passed on to his children.

Although the family's financial status improved steadily over time, young Brennan and his siblings witnessed firsthand social injustices and social unrest in Newark. Like most youths of his era, he earned pocket money working in a gasoline station and making change for Newark trolley-car passengers. But he and his father had ambitious plans for Brennan's pursuit of a career in the law. Following graduation from high school in 1924, he attended the prestigious Wharton School of Finance and Commerce at the University of Pennsylvania, graduating with honors in 1928. He then entered Harvard Law School on a scholarship. His teachers included his future Supreme Court colleague Felix Frankfurter, and he graduated in 1931, ranking among the top ten students in his class.

Admitted to the New Jersey bar in 1932, Brennan joined the Newark firm that, when he was made partner, became Pitney, Hardin, Ward, and Brennan. As a trial advocate specializing in labor law, he played a major role in resolving a number of difficult labor-management disputes. During World War II, he served in the army, primarily in positions connected with procurement and the administration of civilian personnel. Entering as a major, he rose to the rank of colonel and received a Legion of Merit for his work in procurement. In 1945 Brennan returned to his firm, serving as counsel to a number of larger manufacturers in their labor disputes and advocating the use of compulsory arbitration for the resolution of disputes involving utility companies. He also became a leader in a successful campaign for adoption of a new state constitution that streamlined New Jersey's court system, helping to make it one of the most outstanding in the nation.

Largely as a result of his involvement in state court reform, Brennan became a state judge in 1949, progressing in a mere three years through every level of the New

William J. Brennan Jr. (Ken Heinen, Collection of the Supreme Court of the United States)

Jersey judiciary. Republican governor Alfred E. Driscoll first appointed Brennan, a Democrat, to a superior court trial seat, then the next year assigned him to the superior court's appellate division. His efforts to relieve the appellate division's congested court calendar quickly attracted the attention of Arthur T. Vanderbilt, the distinguished chief justice of New Jersey's supreme court. On Vanderbilt's recommendation, Governor Driscoll in 1952 appointed Brennan to the state supreme court.

Brennan's tenure on New Jersey's supreme court prepared him well for service on the nation's highest tribunal. A collegial body that, like its national counterpart, functioned without panels and largely determined the cases it chose to hear, the New Jersey high court, under Vanderbilt's leadership, was decidedly activist, regularly using its decisions for broad pronouncements on public policy. Foreshadowing by several years the U.S. Supreme Court's reapportionment rulings, for example, it ordered reallocation of New Jersey's congressional districts on a population basis. During his tenure there, Brennan also confronted other issues he was later to encounter on the Supreme Court, supporting, among other things, a broad reading of the privilege against compulsory self-incrimination and church-state separation in a dispute involving the Gideon Society's distribution of Bibles in public schools. In contrast with the position he was later to assume in subversive advocacy and membership cases, he joined a unanimous decision upholding the constitutionality of New Jersey's Communist control statute. In speeches around the state, however, he compared the smear campaigns of the McCarthy era with the Salem witch trials. As chairman of a committee on judicial reform, Brennan also was a crusader for speedier court proceedings and pretrial settlement of legal disputes.

Brennan's term on the state supreme court was not scheduled to end until 1959. But when Justice Sherman Minton resigned from the Supreme Court in October 1956, President Eisenhower offered the New Jersey native a recess appointment, to be formalized when Congress reconvened the following January. As a Democrat and social progressive with strong ties to organized labor, Brennan may have given Ike some pause. But at age fifty, with considerable prior judicial experience on one of the nation's finest state supreme courts and solid academic and professional credentials, he appeared an excellent prospect in many respects. New Jersey's chief justice Vanderbilt, a Republican, had long advanced his nomination, and the support of the president's appointments secretary, a Brennan friend from boyhood, was hardly a hindrance either. Apparently, too, Eisenhower or his aides mistakenly relied on a conservative speech Brennan had not written but merely delivered for an ailing Arthur Vanderbilt. And appointment of the first Roman Catholic to a Supreme Court seat since Justice Frank Murphy's death in 1949 would also do no harm in a presidential election year, while the GOP president's elevation of a Democrat to the Court would further buttress Eisenhower's bipartisan image to a largely Democratic national electorate. After a twenty-minute chat with the president, Brennan accepted an offer to assume Justice Minton's seat. Senate confirmation was delayed until March, in part as a result of North Dakota Republican senator William Langer's childish continuing campaign—begun with Earl Warren's 1953 appointment—against approval of any nominee until one was selected from his home state. But when a Senate vote was finally taken, only Senator Joseph McCarthy (R.-Wis.), who apparently had neither forgotten nor forgiven Brennan's earlier attacks on the senator's red-baiting politics, cast a negative vote.

Particularly after 1962, when Justice Arthur J. Goldberg's appointment to the high bench to replace Felix Frankfurter gave the Court's liberal-activist bloc a voting edge, Justice Brennan became the most significant justice on the Warren Court, even exceeding its popular chief justice in influence among the Court's members. A master at coalition-building with a winning personality, Brennan largely charted the Court's course during the balance of the Warren era. He and the chief justice were particularly close, holding regular strategy sessions before the justices' weekly conferences for the discussion and decision of pending cases, and Warren often gave Brennan choice opinion assignments, including *Baker v. Carr* (1962), launching the reapportionment revolution, which Warren considered the most important ruling of his tenure. But Brennan was even more likely than Warren to be on the winning side in the Court's deliberations. The justice for whom "five"—the number of votes needed for a majority—was the most significant word in the Court's lexicon had the lowest dissent rate of any member of the Warren Court. In 1968–1969, Warren's last term, for example, Brennan dissented only in slightly over 1 percent of the cases decided.

Brennan stood, in short, squarely at the Warren Court's center, resolutely liberal yet more flexible in his jurisprudence than other justices with similar records and thus more likely to build majority support for his positions. In *New York Times v. Sullivan* (1964), one of his most significant opinions, he declined to join Justices Black, Douglas, and Goldberg in according the press absolute immunity from libel suits for criticism of the conduct of public officials. Instead, Brennan erected a more flexible "actual malice" standard recognizing broad press freedom but permitting libel actions against knowing or reckless falsehoods as opposed to innocent errors. Despite the Fifth Amendment's prohibition against compelling a suspect "in any criminal case to be a witness against himself," Brennan, over the dissents of Warren, Black, and Douglas, held in *Schmerber v. California* (1966) that the self-incrimination guarantee applied only to the compulsion of "testimonial evidence," not such "physical evidence" as blood and hair samples. And in the subversive advocacy field, he led the later Warren Court in overturning essentially on procedural grounds regulations aimed at "subversive" beliefs and associations. In *Keyishian v. Board of Regents* (1967), for example, he spoke for a 5–4 majority in striking down New York laws and administrative rules designed to prevent employment of "subversive" teachers and professors in state institutions and dismiss those found guilty of "treasonous or seditious" conduct.

The scheme's prohibitions on the advocacy of the violent overthrow of government and membership in such organizations were so unduly vague, concluded Brennan, that they could be applied against expression and associations protected by the First Amendment as well as that subject to government control.

Unlike Justice Douglas, Brennan was also a leader in the development of constitutional doctrine on the Warren Court. In *Keyishian* and other cases, he was the principal architect of the vagueness and overbreadth doctrines. Under those standards, laws affecting First Amendment freedoms were to be narrowly and clearly written to avoid the risk of interference with protected expression and associations. Laws so vague or broad in their reach that they imposed an inhibiting or "chilling effect" on the exercise of protected rights were declared unconstitutional on their face and could not be enforced, even against persons whose conduct was subject to prosecution under a clearly and narrowly drafted law.

Brennan was responsible as well for the principal obscenity opinions of the Warren era. When the Court for the first time adopted a modern, relatively liberal definition of obscenity in *Roth v. United States* (1957), he was the Court's spokesman. And while a majority position on that intractable issue could not again be mustered for the balance of the Warren era, he authored plurality opinions in *Memoirs v. Massachusetts* (1966) and other cases that accorded even broader protection for erotic expression than that recognized in *Roth*, limiting obscenity to material "utterly" lacking in any social value whatsoever.

Brennan also played a significant doctrinal role in Warren Court equal protection developments. When the justices began to insist in the late 1960s that any school desegregation plan actually result in changes in the racial composition of public schools, Brennan also spoke for the Court. In *Green v. New Kent County* (1968), for example, he rejected the contention that a "freedom of choice" pupil placement plan satisfied the *Brown* mandate even though it had resulted in little desegregation. In the reapportionment field, moreover, he not only authored *Baker v. Carr* (1962) but also wrote the Court's opinion in *Kirkpatrick v. Preisler* (1969), striking down a 3.1 percent population deviation in a state's congressional districting plan and declaring that no deviation from absolute population equality in congressional districts could be considered *de minimis* and thus beyond the scope of judicial scrutiny.

As author the same year of the Court's opinion in *Shapiro v. Thompson*, striking down a one-year residency requirement for the receipt of welfare benefits, he also made a major contribution to the fundamental rights branch of modern equal protection philosophy. Under that element of equal protection doctrine, laws that burdened the enjoyment of fundamental rights or interests, including those not mentioned in the Constitution's text, would be declared a violation of equal protection unless shown to be necessary to serve a compelling governmental interest. The challenged residency requirement, declared Brennan for the *Shapiro* majority, interfered with the fundamental right of interstate travel. In a passage particularly disturbing to Justice Harlan, among other dissenters in the case, Brennan further implied that the Constitution recognized a fundamental right to welfare benefits when he suggested that laws burdening access to the necessities of life should also be subjected to strict judicial scrutiny.

Even when Brennan did not author the principal opinion in a Warren Court case, he often played a key role in developing its underlying rationale. Correspondence between Brennan and Douglas reveals Brennan's significant influence on his colleague's opinion for the Court in the *Griswold* case, recognizing a constitutional right of privacy and invalidating Connecticut's broad ban on the use of contraceptives. Probably in a futile effort to secure Justice Black's vote, Douglas initially circulated a draft opinion resting the ruling on First Amendment free association grounds. The physician appellants in *Griswold* were prosecuted for aiding and abetting patients in the use of contraceptives, and Douglas reasoned that the challenged law thus interfered with the doctor-patient relationship. But Brennan convinced his colleague that "a more fruitful approach," with greater potential for extension to other issue areas, would be based on a right of marital privacy lying within the shadow of various explicit Bill of Rights safeguards.

The arrival of Chief Justice Burger and the other Nixon appointees significantly diminished Brennan's influence on the Court. When in the majority, he was more rarely assigned to write the Court's opinion in major cases. Chief Justice Burger assigned Justice Harry Blackmun rather than Brennan, for example, to write the Court's opinion in *Roe v. Wade* (1973). Far more often than in the Warren era, moreover, he was in dissent. When a 5–4 majority, in *Miller v. California* and *Paris Adult Theatre v. Slaton* (1973), embraced a definition of obscenity more deferential to government than Brennan's plurality standards had been, the justice dissented. Clear obscenity standards sufficiently sensitive to First Amendment requirements, he now argued, simply could not be drafted; governmental authority in the obscenity field should thus be limited to protecting minors and unconsenting adults from exposure to erotica.

Brennan was regularly on the losing side of other Burger Court debates as well. Only he and Justice Marshall argued for the complete abolition of the death penalty (*Gregg v. Georgia* [1976]). They watched in horror as Burger Court majorities not only substantially curtailed application of the Fourth Amendment exclusionary rule and the *Miranda* warnings required of police before in-custody questioning of suspects in criminal cases but also restricted Brennan's newly sculpted fundamental rights branch of equal protection doctrine to rights stated or implied in the Constitution, refusing to include among such rights a guarantee to welfare benefits (*Dandridge v. Williams* [1970]) and an equally funded public school education (*San Antonio Independent School District v. Rodriguez* [1973]).

Brennan also objected to the Burger Court's reluctance to add to the types of discrimination considered inherently "suspect" and thus subject to strict judicial review. When the Court, for example, backed away from Warren Court rulings subjecting to close scrutiny laws disfavoring people on the basis of their status of birth, he bitterly protested. He filed a vigorous dissent, for example, when a majority sustained a Louisiana law that prevented illegitimate children from sharing in the estate of a father who had died without a will (*Labine v. Vincent* [1971]).

The justice played a major role, however, in the Burger Court's decision to subject gender classifications to heightened scrutiny. In *Frontiero v. Richardson* (1973), he spoke for a plurality in equating gender classifications with discrimination based on race or color. The former, like the latter, argued Brennan, were based on an immutable accident of birth irrelevant to legitimate governmental interests. Women, like African Americans, had long been the victims of purposeful discrimination, and endorsement by Congress and most states of the proposed Equal Rights Amendment, then pending in the state legislatures, reflected a national judgment that sex discrimination was inherently invidious and should be subjected to close judicial scrutiny. Although Brennan could not command a majority for that proposition, he later spoke for the Court in *Craig v. Boren* (1976), declaring laws based on gender a quasi-suspect form of discrimination and requiring that they be substantially related to the achievement of important government objectives.

Brennan also scored a number of successes in Burger Court affirmative action cases. Although unable to marshal a majority to sustain the medical school racial admissions quota at issue in *Regents of the University of California v. Bakke* (1978), he and like-minded colleagues joined Justice Lewis Powell, the pivotal vote in *Bakke*, in declaring that a state university could appropriately consider race, along with other nonacademic admission criteria, in promoting its compelling interest in securing a diverse student body. The following year, moreover, Brennan spoke for a 5–2 Court in *United Steelworkers v. Weber* (1979), upholding a provision of a collective-bargaining agreement under which half of all craft training jobs at an aluminum plant were to go to blacks until the proportion of African Americans in those positions approximated their percentage of the local labor market. Provisions of Title VII of the 1964 Civil Rights Act, forbidding racial discrimination in employment, were not intended by Congress, concluded Brennan over the vigorous dissents of Chief Justice Burger and Justice Rehnquist, to prohibit the adoption of such voluntary programs by a private company.

Although often in dissent, Brennan did achieve occasional victories in the Rehnquist Court until his retirement in 1990. In *Metro Broadcasting v. Federal Communications Commission*, decided in his last year on the bench, he spoke for a 5–4 majority that endorsed greater judicial deference toward affirmative action programs adopted by Congress than those enacted by state and local governments. In a variety of public settings, he also answered critics who charged him and like-minded colleagues with imposing their own ethical and social preferences on the nation in the guise of constitutional interpretation, contrary to democratic principles and the prerogatives of elected officials. In a series of highly publicized exchanges with Reagan attorney general Edwin Meese, although neither ever mentioned the other by name, Brennan declared that the Constitution was an evolving document that judges were obliged to adapt to contemporary societal needs and dismissed arguments for constitutional interpretations based on language and the intent of the framers as illusory and thus arrogance cloaked in humility.

Potter Stewart

President Eisenhower's final appointee, as well as his last to serve into the Burger era, was Potter Stewart, who was on the Court from 1958 until 1981, the first year of Ronald Reagan's presidency. Stewart (who died in 1985) stepped aside to give the Republican president an opportunity to make his first appointment to the high bench. Like his colleagues Frankfurter and Harlan, Stewart would demonstrate during his twenty-three years on the Court a high regard for precedent, majoritarian institutions, and the role of the states in the federal system, as well as doubt whether most constitutional rights possessed a clear, readily definable scope. But Stewart would not defer to government as often as Frankfurter and Harlan. Instead, he developed a decidedly mixed voting record, becoming a classic swing justice.

Stewart was born in 1915 into a wealthy and prominent Ohio Republican family. His paternal grandfather was a distinguished Union soldier in the Civil War. His father, James Garfield Stewart, was a member of the Cincinnati city council from 1933 to 1947, the city's mayor from 1938 to 1947, and a justice of the Ohio Supreme Court from 1947 until his death in 1959, as well as an unsuccessful 1944 Ohio gubernatorial candidate. The marriage of Potter's parents ended in divorce, but he, his sister, and brother apparently had a pleasant childhood. After study at Cincinnati's University School and Hotchkiss in Connecticut, he graduated Phi Beta Kappa from Yale in 1937. Following a year at Cambridge on a Henry fellowship, he attended Yale's law school, where he made law review, won the moot court competition, and graduated with honors in 1941.

After a year with a Wall Street firm, Stewart entered the navy and spent most of World War II on oil tankers in the Atlantic and Mediterranean—"floating around on a sea of 100-octane gas," he later said, "bored to death 99 percent of the time and scared to death 1 percent" (*New York Times*, October 8, 1958). Whatever the ultimate impact of his wartime experience on his later career, his navy service put the patrician future justice in close contact with enlisted men from backgrounds quite different from his own. He also served as defense counsel in a number of summary court-martial proceedings.

After the war Stewart returned briefly to the New York firm, but following participation there in a campaign against the reelection of a member of the U.S. House

Potter Stewart (Harris & Ewing, Collection of the Supreme Court of the United States)

of Representatives with reputed mob ties, he went back to Cincinnati, becoming a lit-igator in a large firm whose prominent clients included Procter and Gamble and that numbered among its senior partners President Truman's secretary of commerce. Stewart was made a partner in the firm in 1951 but, like his father, also became active in Cincinnati politics, winning election to the city council in 1949 and 1951 and serv-ing one term as vice-mayor. He also vigorously campaigned in behalf of the presiden-tial aspirations of conservative Ohio senator Robert A. Taft, with whom the Stewart family had long been closely associated. In 1952, however, he shifted his allegiance fortuitously to the more politically moderate Dwight Eisenhower, while maintaining close ties to Ohio's conservative GOP establishment, including the state's junior sen-ator, John Bricker. When a vacancy arose on the U.S. Court of Appeals for the Sixth Circuit in 1954, Bricker brought Stewart to President Eisenhower's attention. Impressed with his naval service, excellent academic and professional credentials, and ties to the Republican Party, the president chose the thirty-nine-year-old Ohioan to fill the circuit vacancy.

On the court of appeals, Stewart began to acquire the reputation for succinct, lucid, closely reasoned opinions he was to enjoy on the Supreme Court. But his cir-cuit tenure would also be brief. On October 6, 1958, Stewart's fellow Ohioan Justice Harold H. Burton announced his retirement. The following day Stewart was named to a recess appointment on the high bench. He possessed fine qualifications. His was Eisenhower's third recess appointment, however, and a number of senators were increasingly irritated at the administration's resort to the recess arrangement as a way of placing a justice on the bench, even if in theory only temporarily, prior to the Senate confirmation process required by the Constitution.

The submission of Stewart's nomination to the Senate in January gave conser-vative Republicans and southern Democrats a further opportunity to rail against the Supreme Court's civil rights and "pro-Communist" decisions, as well as any strains of liberalism in Stewart's thinking and appeals court record. But the nominee stood his ground, telling segregationist South Carolina senator Olin Johnston at one point that he should not vote for confirmation based on any assumption Stewart would vote to overturn the *Brown* ruling. To the question whether the Constitution had the same meaning as when it was first adopted, the nominee also replied that, in his judgment, the framers used language capable of being adapted to a changing society.

When the Judiciary Committee voted 12–3 to approve Stewart's nomination, opponents continued their attacks on the Senate floor. But there, as in committee, they reserved their complaints largely for the Court rather than the nominee. On May 5, 1959, the Senate voted 70–17 to confirm, with southerners casting every negative vote.

During the first years of his tenure, Stewart regularly joined the passivist bloc committed to judicial self-restraint that Justice Frankfurter headed, frequently giving it the fifth vote needed to reject a civil liberties claim. After Justice Goldberg replaced

Frankfurter in 1962, the liberal-activist bloc assumed a fairly solid majority, and Stewart's influence in civil liberties cases diminished substantially for the balance of Chief Justice Warren's tenure. Following President Nixon's selection of Chief Justice Burger to replace Warren in 1969 and subsequent appointments of Blackmun, Powell, and Rehnquist, Stewart's position, like that of Justice Byron R. White, a Kennedy appointee, assumed renewed significance, with theirs the pivotal and restraintist vote(s) in many cases. Throughout his career, however, Stewart was to be a true moderate, assuming a restraintist stance in many cases but also keenly sympathetic to free press, obscenity, and religious liberty claims, as well as those based on civil rights statutes.

Given his early life, political career, and court of appeals record, Stewart's moderate Supreme Court record was hardly surprising. Although a lifelong Republican, he had been a vigorous supporter of Franklin Roosevelt and the New Deal at Yale. Yet during a bitter city council race in 1953, he joined those demanding the resignation of a Cincinnati planning commissioner (and political opponent) who was once associated with a Marxist study group, as well as two other commissioners who had merely "known" of their colleague's Communist ties. "[T]he Republican Party," declared Stewart at the time, "is made up of men and women who are loyal Americans" (Lamb and Halpern 1991, 380). In a concurrence for *Wellman v. United States* (1957), a Sixth Circuit Smith Act case, however, he agreed that defendants whose convictions had been vacated by the Supreme Court should be retried rather than set free, yet he found unrewarding "the efforts to discern the germ of illegal advocacy in [the] handful of equivocal statements culled from the present record" in the case (p. 608).

Nor was Stewart's moderate approach to civil liberties issues on the circuit bench confined to subversive advocacy and membership cases. When a district court approved a school board's plan to delay desegregation several years pending construction of new buildings, he and another judge formed a majority on a three-judge panel reversing the lower court. Unlike his colleague, however, Stewart favored denying relief until the beginning of the next school year (*Clemons v. Board of Education* [1956]). And of more than twenty judges reviewing the case of a young black who pled guilty hours after his arrest and was sentenced to life imprisonment for the rape of a white woman, only Stewart found a constitutional violation. "[S]wift justice," he pointedly observed, "demands more than just swiftness" (*Henderson v. Bannan* [1958], 390).

On the Supreme Court, Stewart's voting record was equally mixed. He spoke for the Warren Court, for example, in significantly curtailing the power of police to conduct warrantless searches incident to arrest (*Chimel v. California* [1969]) and subjecting electronic surveillance to the Fourth Amendment's warrant requirements (*Katz v. United States* [1967]) yet dissented in *Miranda* and joined a Burger Court majority in authorizing warrantless consent searches even where police did not inform suspects of their right to refuse consent (*Schneckloth v. Bustamonte* [1973]). He spoke for Warren (*Jones v. Alfred H. Mayer Co.* [1968]) and Burger (*Runyon v. McCrary* [1976]) Court majorities broadly construing a Reconstruction-era congressional statute to reach private discrimination in housing and contracts, while also declaring that Congress, under its authority to enforce the Thirteenth Amendment, could outlaw as vestiges of slavery all forms of racial discrimination. But he rejected a congressional voting rights regulation forbidding states to impose voter requirements (such as a fairly administered literacy test) the Court had previously upheld as constitutional, joining Justice Harlan in a dissent contending that the courts, not Congress, had the final power to construe the Constitution's meaning (*Katzenbach v. Morgan* [1966]).

Stewart's status as a swing voter on the Burger Court was clearly evident in death penalty cases. Confronted in *Furman v. Georgia* (1972) with a capital punishment provision that in no way limited the discretion of judges and jurors, Stewart provided the fifth vote to invalidate the statute at issue there, terming infliction of a death sentence under such a law comparable to being struck by lightning. But when states revised their death penalty statutes to limit the discretion of jurors and courts, and thus the likelihood of arbitrary and capricious imposition of capital sentences, Stewart helped to form a majority upholding such laws (e.g., *Gregg v. Georgia* [1976]). In fact, he was on the majority side in all thirty-six death penalty cases decided between 1971 and his 1981 retirement from the bench.

Although Stewart's moderate voting record on the circuit and supreme benches is thus easily documented, his approach to constitutional interpretation is more difficult to explain and understand. In various public addresses over his career, he often emphasized that judges should not decide cases according to their own notions of what is "good, wise or politic," adding, "*That* function is the function of the people's elected representatives, to be carried out by the executive branch of government." The Constitution's text and judicial precedents were, in his judgment, the judge's "primary [interpretive] tools" (Lamb and Halpern 1991, 381). His explications of the proper approach to constitutional interpretation bore a striking resemblance, in fact, to Justice Black's opinions and off-the-bench writings extolling a jurisprudence based on faithful adherence to text and the framers' intentions. When Black assumed that stance in the *Griswold* case, charging the majority with creating a right of privacy, Stewart joined his colleague's dissent and filed one of his own, proceeding along similar lines.

Given his position in *Griswold*, Stewart might have been expected to dissent in *Roe v. Wade* (1973), when the Court invoked substantive due process in extending the privacy right to a women's decision to abort a pregnancy. But the justice joined the *Roe* majority, explaining that he now considered *Griswold* "one in a long line of" cases recognizing unenumerated substantive rights via the due process guarantee and agreed that due process covered other freedoms than those explicitly stated in the Bill of Rights. Two fundamental elements in Stewart's jurisprudence help to reconcile, however, the apparent inconsistencies in his *Griswold* and *Roe* votes. First, his *Roe* stance can be viewed simply as reflecting his high regard for precedent, including that established in *Griswold*. Second, unlike Justice Black, who generally found clear commands in the Constitution's text and the history surrounding adoption of its provisions, Stewart rarely discovered such constitutional clarity. Instead, he believed the Constitution's framers intentionally couched many of its passages in general, relatively open-ended language. But for Stewart, in contrast to certain of his brethren, the document's general language was a call for judicial restraint, not an invitation for activist exercise of judicial review. Until the precedent established in *Griswold*, therefore, Stewart declined to invoke general constitutional language to recognize a right of privacy. Once bound by that precedent, however, he accepted it, agreeing with the *Roe* majority that the Constitution protected a variety of unenumerated privacy rights.

Another element crucial to an understanding of Stewart's judicial philosophy was his commitment to federalism and the position of the states in the federal scheme. He joined, for example, the 5–4 majority in *National League of Cities v. Usery* (1976), striking down an otherwise valid exercise of congressional power over interstate commerce on the ground it interfered with "integral" state functions.

Although the elements of Stewart's jurisprudence typically produced mixed voting patterns, he assumed a decidedly liberal stance in certain civil liberties areas, especially in cases involving freedom of the press and related issues. Initially uncertain in college whether to pursue a career in law or journalism, Stewart had headed Yale's student newspaper and also worked briefly as a reporter for the Cincinnati *Times-Star*. On the Court he was a vigorous if unsuccessful proponent of a testimonial (*Branzburg v. Hayes* [1972]) and search (*Zurcher v. Stanford Daily* [1978]) privilege for the media, arguing as well that reporters might enjoy greater access to jails and related government facilities than the general public (*Houchins v. KQED* [1978]). Ultimately, moreover, he joined Justice Brennan and other Burger Court dissenters who favored limiting governmental authority in the obscenity field to the protection of minors and unconsenting adults. Even in the free press area, however, Stewart did not inevitably embrace First Amendment claims. Thus, he authored a number of Court opinions rejecting press claims of a right of access to jails and other facilities not open to the public (*Pell v. Procunier* [1974]).

Byron R. White

Although three of President Eisenhower's Warren Court appointees (Harlan, Brennan, and Stewart) continued into the Burger era, only one of President Kennedy's two

Byron R. White (Joseph Bailey, National Geographic Society, Collection of the Supreme Court of the United States)

Supreme Court choices would have that distinction—Byron R. White, whose tenure extended from 1962 until his retirement in 1993. Born in Fort Collins, Colorado, in 1915, White spent his youth in Wellington, a small Colorado lumber and sugar beet farming community near the Wyoming border, where his father, a lumber dealer and staunch Republican, served one term as town mayor. In his youth Byron worked as a railroad section hand, and he and his brother brought in a sugar beet crop. He also excelled at sports and academics in high school, graduating first in his tiny senior class and gaining his first taste of gridiron fame as well. At the University of Colorado, White repeated that performance. While holding part-time jobs as a waiter in fraternity and sorority houses, he compiled a superb academic record, graduating Phi Beta Kappa and first in a class of 267. His football prowess was perhaps even more outstanding. Earning the nickname "Whizzer" for his skill at eluding his opponents, he became an All-American running back, leading his Colorado team to an undefeated season and slot in the Cotton Bowl his senior year. The collegiate champion for scoring, rushing, and total offense in the 1937 season, he also excelled at baseball and basketball.

White's outstanding undergraduate record earned him a Rhodes scholarship at Oxford, where he intended to study law. But when the Pittsburgh Steelers (then the Pittsburgh Pirates) offered him a lucrative football contract, he postponed enrollment at Oxford, telling family and friends that a year's income with the Pittsburgh team would pay his way through law school. After a season with Pittsburgh, where he led the league in ground-gaining runs, White entered Oxford in January 1939. When World War II erupted in Europe the following fall, he returned to the United States, where he entered Yale Law School and also signed with the Detroit Lions for two additional seasons of professional football. In July 1941, while studying law, he tried to join the marines but was rejected because of color blindness. Accepted into the navy the following year, he served as an officer with naval intelligence in the Solomon Islands. In 1946, after winning two Bronze Stars and a presidential citation, he resumed law study at Yale, graduating with honors that fall. A year as a clerk to Chief Justice Fred M. Vinson—making White the first clerk later to serve as a justice—followed, after which he went back to Colorado, where in 1947 he became an associate with a prominent Denver firm engaged in civil practice.

White remained in private practice until 1961, when John F. Kennedy's election to the White House brought the future justice back to Washington. Until 1960 White's involvement in politics had been limited to minor local positions in the Democratic Party. On several occasions over the years, however, he had been brought in contact with Kennedy, whom he first met in England when he was at Oxford and the future president's father was U.S. ambassador to the Court of St. James. Kennedy and White became friends when the two served in the Pacific during the war. In fact, White prepared the intelligence report on the sinking of Kennedy's PT 109, which, according to the justice's biographer, may have glossed over the future president's irresponsibility in the incident. White's Supreme Court clerkship also coincided with Kennedy's first term in Congress. When Kennedy made his 1960 run for the Democratic presidential nomination, White became head of his Colorado campaign committee and was later credited with delivering twenty-seven of the state's forty-two national convention delegate votes for Kennedy's nomination. During the general election campaign, White headed the national Citizens for Kennedy organization, dedicated to attracting Republicans and Independents to the candidate's fold.

Following the election, White became deputy attorney general in the Kennedy Justice Department, where he worked closely with the president's brother Robert, the attorney general. As deputy attorney general, he assumed major responsibility for federal judicial appointments. He also played a key role in a number of major civil rights crises, including the vicious assaults on freedom riders in Alabama. But White's tenure in the executive branch would last only a little over a year. When a mental health crisis led to the resignation of Justice Charles Whittaker in 1962, the president, with Attorney General Kennedy's strong backing, nominated White to Whittaker's seat. Members of the press expressed concern about the nominee's lack of judicial experience. But the American Bar Association gave White its highest rating, and the Senate Judiciary Committee unanimously recommended confirmation. On April 11 the Senate approved the nomination by a voice vote; several days later White became the youngest justice on the Warren Court.

White's judicial and constitutional philosophy would be even more difficult to discern than Justice Stewart's. In general, his record reflected respect for majoritarian institutions, a reluctance to read unenumerated rights into the Constitution's meaning, and a preference for narrow rulings closely tied to the circumstances of particular cases. It is a much easier task, however, to examine White's approach in specific issue areas than to discover and delineate an overarching jurisprudence.

In the field of separation of powers, White was the Burger Court justice most likely to champion judicial and legislative authority over executive prerogative. Thus, he spoke for the Court in reaffirming the absolute immunity of judges from damage suits even in cases involving egregious and knowing judicial violations of individual rights (*Stump v. Sparkman* [1978]), and he authored the Court's opinion in *Gravel v. United States* (1972), extending to legislative aides the broad immunity from inquiry accorded members of Congress by the Constitution's speech and debate clause. But he dissented from the Court's ruling in *Nixon v. Fitzgerald* (1982) recognizing the absolute immunity of presidents from damage suits based on their official conduct. Totally immunizing presidents from such suits, even when they knowingly violated individual rights, placed presidents, declared White, above the law. Earlier, moreover, he had spoken for a majority in granting cabinet officers only a limited, qualified immunity from suit (*Butz v. Economou* [1978]). And in *Wood v. Strickland* (1975), he extended that standard to suits against school officials and most other administrators, holding them liable if they knowingly violated a person's rights or reasonably should have known their conduct was illegal. In one of the most closely reasoned and penetrating dissents of his career, he also objected to the Court's broad rejection of the legislative veto, under which proposed presidential actions were first subjected to review and possible rejection by Congress. Scorning as naive the textbook reading of separation of powers reflected in the Court's opinion in *INS v. Chadha* (1983), White saw the legislative veto as a useful device for assuring that executives remained subject to Congress's will when exercising the broad discretion given them in congressional statutes.

During the depression White had become a Democrat with strong admiration for President Roosevelt's New Deal policies. It was not surprising, therefore, that on the Court the justice typically assumed a strongly nationalist position in cases involving conflicts between federal and state power. In *National League of Cities v. Usery* (1976), for example, he joined Justice Brennan's dissent when a majority struck down a congressional statute subjecting state and local governments to federal wage and hour standards. When the Court reversed *Usery* in the 1985 *Garcia* case, White joined Justice Blackmun's majority opinion reaffirming the traditional position that the political process, not the courts, was the proper remedy for excessive congressional interference with state and local authority.

In civil liberties cases, White developed a moderately conservative record while assuming a liberal position in most equal protection cases and certain other issue areas. An early critic of the 1971 *Lemon* test, which limited governmental ties with religion, White consistently supported government assistance to religious schools and colleges. In *Committee for Public Education and Religious Liberty v. Regan* (1980), for example, he spoke for the Court in sustaining a New York law reimbursing parochial schools for administering state-prepared examinations. He also was relatively rarely a supporter of free speech claims and especially the First Amendment arguments of the press, for which he appeared to harbor a distaste going back to his youth and what he considered unfair and inaccurate reporting of his football exploits. In *Branzburg v. Hayes* (1972), he spoke for the Court in rejecting a testimonial privilege for newspersons, characterizing as highly speculative their contention that their appearances in grand jury and judicial proceedings would jeopardize press relationships with confidential informants and thus limit the free flow of information. For White, it was more important to do something about crime than write about it. The justice also authored majority opinions upholding restrictions on the political activities of civil servants and requiring that regulations of expression suffer from "substantial" overbreadth before being struck down on their face as First Amendment violations (*U.S. Civil Service Commission v. National Association of Letter Carriers* [1973]; *Broadrick v. Oklahoma* [1973]). White joined, too, *Miller v. California* (1973) and other rulings expanding governmental power over obscenity and wrote the Court's opinion in *New York v. Ferber* (1982), approving broad state authority over the use of minors in depictions of sexual activity.

White's stance in criminal cases was similarly that of a moderate conservative. He joined the 5–4 majority in *Furman v. Georgia* (1972), declaring the death penalty statute at issue there inherently arbitrary, but he made clear in a concurring opinion that its infrequent imposition was largely responsible for his *Furman* vote. In *Gregg v. Georgia* (1976), he joined the Court in upholding a death penalty law that included provisions designed to limit the discretion of juries and judges. Unlike the majority, he also had no constitutional objections to mandatory imposition of the death penalty in murder cases (*Roberts v. Louisiana* [1976]), although he later spoke for the Court in striking down the death penalty for rape as disproportionate to the gravity of the offense (*Coker v. Georgia* [1977]). A bitter dissenter from the Warren Court's *Miranda* ruling, he generally joined Burger Court decisions limiting that controversial decision's scope. He was also the principal architect of the "good faith" exception to the Fourth Amendment exclusionary rule, upholding for the Court in *United States v. Leon* (1984) the use in court of evidence seized by police relying on an invalid search warrant. While speaking for Warren and Burger Court majorities, moreover, in *Duncan v. Louisiana* (1968), extending the jury trial to state criminal trials, and *Taylor v. Louisiana* (1975), expanding judicial oversight of discrimination in jury selection, White also spoke for the Court in *Williams v. Florida* (1970) and *Apodaca v. Oregon* (1972), sustaining juries of six rather than twelve members and nonunanimous state jury verdicts.

In a variety of equal protection cases, White generally assumed a staunch but not entirely predictable antidiscrimination stance. He dissented in *Palmer v. Thompson* (1971) when a majority upheld the decision of Jackson, Mississippi, to close its swimming pools rather than desegregate them, as well as *Milliken v. Bradley* (1974), which struck down a trial judge's order that students be bused between the predominantly black Detroit school district and predominantly white suburban districts. But while he would have upheld the affirmative action quota at issue in the *Bakke* case and joined the majority in the *Weber* case, upholding a racial employment quota in a private company, he later became a rather consistent opponent of affirmative action programs (e.g., *Firefighters v. Stotts* [1984]). Although he joined most of the early reapportionment decisions and dissented when the Burger Court, in *Mobile v. Bolden* (1980), sustained at-large city commission elections under a scheme that had never resulted in the election of an African American commissioner, he found certain of the Court's election rulings unreasonable restrictions of state discretion (*Kirkpatrick v. Preisler* [1969]). A staunch opponent of gender discrimination, he dissented when a majority upheld male-only military draft registration in *Rostker v. Goldberg* (1981). But in *Grove City College v. Bell* (1984), he spoke for the Court in construing a congressional statute to require a cutoff of federal funds only in those programs of an educational institution that actually engaged in gender discrimination, not the entire facility. (Congress later overturned the Court's interpretation of the law.)

White also produced a mixed record in cases involving recognition of constitutional rights not mentioned in the Constitution's text. He joined the *Griswold* majority, declaring in a concurrence that the Connecticut contraceptive ban at issue was an arbitrary interference with individual liberty that violated substantive due process. But he was one of two dissenters in *Roe v. Wade* (1973), and speaking for the majority in *Bowers v. Hardwick* (1986), he rejected claims to constitutional protection for homosexual sodomy. Emphasizing that the Court's legitimacy was at greatest risk when it extended constitutional protection to unenumerated rights, White insisted for the majority that such guarantees must be limited to rights deeply rooted in the nation's history and tradition.

Thurgood Marshall

Justice White probably developed a more conservative Supreme Court record than President Kennedy and his brother Robert had anticipated. Lyndon B. Johnson, by contrast, could not possibly have entertained any doubts about the sort of judicial and constitutional philosophy Thurgood Marshall would embrace on the Court. The first African American appointee to the high bench and the only Johnson nominee to continue into the Burger era, Marshall's pivotal role in the modern civil rights movement for thirty years prior to his appointment made the direction of his Supreme Court career virtually a foregone conclusion.

Marshall's great-grandfather was captured in Africa and brought as a slave to Maryland's eastern shore. The future justice was born in Baltimore in 1908. His father was a Pullman car waiter and later a steward at an all-white Chesapeake Bay yacht club; his mother was an elementary school teacher. The family resided in an elite, formerly all-white Baltimore neighborhood, where they enjoyed the status accorded light-skinned blacks of that period in the black community. Initially named Thoroughgood after his paternal grandfather, by second grade Thurgood had adopted the simpler spelling of his first name.

Thurgood was a precocious but unruly elementary school student, frequently dispatched to the school basement to memorize passages of the Constitution as punishment for infractions of school regulations. That experience gave him his first awareness of the stark contrast between the Constitution's promise of equality and the harsh reality of segregation and racial injustice in Baltimore. A popular student at Frederick Douglass High School, the city's only secondary school for blacks, he organized the debate team, won most of its competitions, and graduated with honors. Following high school, Marshall enrolled at Lincoln University near Philadelphia, the nation's oldest educational institution for blacks. His mother pawned her wedding

Thurgood Marshall (Joseph Lavenburg, National Geographic Society, Collection of the Supreme Court of the United States)

and engagement rings to help with his college expenses, while Marshall worked part time as a busboy, waiter, baker, and grocery clerk. Consistent with his mother's wishes, he originally intended to study dentistry. But when he excelled at debate in college, as he had in high school, he changed his major to prelaw. Although a care-free, not very dedicated student by his own account, he graduated from Lincoln with honors in 1929.

When the all-white University of Maryland denied Marshall admission on the basis of his race, he enrolled at Howard University in Washington, D.C. Howard's law faculty then included a number of gifted black professors, including William Hastie and Charles Hamilton Houston, who became vice-dean of the law school in 1929 and profoundly influenced Marshall and other Howard students during his fifteen-year tenure there. Viewing law as a social tool, Houston stressed a "rights-oriented," "result-oriented" approach to legal issues, converting the law school into a laboratory for the development of legal strategies against racial discrimination. In 1933 Marshall graduated from Howard not only with academic honors at the top of his class but with a firm commitment to use the law as an instrument of social change.

Following admission to the Maryland bar, Marshall opened a private practice in Baltimore but very soon also became associated with the local branch of the National Association for the Advancement of Colored People (NAACP). After a year as a vol-unteer, he became counsel for the local branch and in 1935 collaborated with Charles Houston in winning his first major civil rights victory—a ruling from the Maryland court of appeals ordering the state university's law school to admit a black student. In 1936 Marshall began a two-year stint with Houston as assistant counsel to the NAACP's New York branch. When his mentor resigned as a result of illness in 1938, Marshall became special counsel in charge of litigation. The following year he helped to found the NAACP's Legal Defense and Educational Fund (LDF) to launch a legal assault on racial segregation. From 1950 to 1961, he served as the LDF's chief coun-sel and director, becoming the principal architect of the NAACP's campaign to deseg-regate the public schools through litigation.

"Shuffling through Dixie," as Marshall later termed it, the future justice spent much of his time traveling about the South, creating a network of lawyers to recruit plaintiffs for local challenges to segregated schools. He also coordinated the associ-ation's appeals to higher courts and argued cases before the Supreme Court. Win-ning twenty-nine of thirty-two cases he argued before the high bench, he achieved his most important victory in *Brown v. Board of Education* (1954), when a unani-mous Warren Court embraced his proposition that segregated schooling generated feelings of inferiority in minority children that adversely affected their ability to learn and thus provided them an "inherently unequal" education. He also brought challenges to discrimination in voting, housing, public accommodations, and other facilities. When black soldiers were disciplined in Korea and Japan, he traveled there in 1951, eventually securing reduced sentences for twenty-two of forty soldiers who claimed they had received unfair trials.

As his biographer Mark Tushnet has aptly observed, Marshall made his most significant contributions to constitutional development while counsel for the NAACP. The return of the White House to Democratic control in 1961 following the Eisenhower years provided him with additional opportunities for public service. In 1961 President Kennedy nominated Marshall to a seat on the Court of Appeals for the Second Circuit. Although segregationist senators stalled his confirmation for nearly a year, the Senate approved his appointment in September 1962 by a 54–16 vote. During his Second Circuit tenure, Marshall authored nearly 100 majority opinions, none of which was reversed in the Supreme Court. Among his rulings were decisions invalidating loyalty requirements for New York teachers and expanding the search and seizure rights of suspects in criminal cases. In holding the states subject to the Constitution's ban on double jeopardy, moreover, he foreshadowed by several years the Supreme Court's ruling to the same effect in *Benton v. Maryland* (1969), which he also authored.

In August 1965 Marshall became U.S. solicitor general less than a month after President Johnson submitted his name to the Senate. Third in rank in the Justice Department, the solicitor general is the principal representative of the United States and federal law before the Supreme Court. During his brief tenure as the first black to hold that position, Marshall argued nineteen cases before the Court, winning fourteen. His victories included *United States v. Guest* (1966) and *United States v. Price* (1966), in which the Court gave broad constructions to Reconstruction-era federal civil rights statutes. The *Guest* Court sustained federal authority to prosecute Ku Klux Klansmen who murdered a black interstate traveler on a Georgia highway; *Price* upheld the federal prosecution of a sheriff, sheriff's deputy, and Klansmen charged with a conspiracy to violate the federal rights of three civil rights workers murdered in Neshoba County, Mississippi. Ironically, in one of the few cases he lost, Marshall argued for the government against the Court's recognition of the right to court-appointed counsel during questioning that a 5–4 majority required in *Miranda v. Arizona* (1966) and that he later strongly defended as a justice.

Since President Johnson had vowed to appoint the first woman or black to the Supreme Court, Marshall's selection as solicitor general was widely viewed as a mere preliminary to his elevation to the high bench. When Justice Tom Clark of Texas, the grandson of a Confederate soldier, retired from the Court in 1967 to enable the president to appoint his son Ramsey to the post of attorney general, Johnson chose Marshall, the grandson of a Union solider and great-grandson of a slave, to fill Clark's seat. The nomination went to the Senate in June 1967; on August 30, Marshall won confirmation by a vote of 69–11. At least one columnist scored the president's creation of what was bound to become a "Negro seat" on the Court and doubted Marshall would bring much intellectual distinction to the body. As a symbol of the administration's commitment to civil rights, however, the president could have made no more appropriate choice for the seat he was to hold until his retirement in 1991.

For the balance of Chief Justice Warren's tenure, the new justice was a consistent member of the liberal majority, authoring a number of important rulings, including not only the decision extending the double jeopardy guarantee to the states but also *Stanley v. Georgia* (1969), recognizing a right to possess obscenity in the privacy of the home. Following the appointments of Chief Justice Burger and the other Nixon justices, Marshall occasionally spoke for the Court in major cases. In *Police Department v. Mosley* (1972), for example, he struck down an ordinance forbidding picketing near schools that exempted labor picketing from its coverage. In *Memorial Hospital v. Maricopa County* (1974), he extended the Warren Court precedent established in *Shapiro v. Thompson* (1969) by overturning a residency requirement for receipt of nonemergency medical care on the ground it might inhibit the right of indigents to interstate travel. And in *Linmark Associates v. Township of Willingboro* (1977), he rebuffed a township that attempted to stem "white flight" from an integrated neighborhood by adopting an ordinance prohibiting the posting of "For Sale" signs on front lawns. Such a ban on information that was neither false nor misleading, declared Marshall, breached the First Amendment. He even authored Burger Court opinions rejecting civil liberties claims. In *Gillette v. United States* (1971), for example, Marshall sustained governmental authority to deny military draft exemptions to draftees who objected only to their participation in "unjust" wars.

On the Burger Court, however, Marshall, like Justice Brennan, found himself increasingly in dissent. He largely relied on Brennan for the development of doctrinal attacks on conservative Burger Court decisional trends, albeit with notable exceptions. When the Court dramatically curtailed the suspect categories and fundamental rights branches of modern equal protection philosophy, limiting fundamental rights to those stated or implied in the Constitution and declining to expand the suspect categories concept beyond race to poverty and other bases of classification, Justice Marshall proposed adoption of an alternative approach to such cases. He favored abandoning the "two-tiered" formula under which certain forms of discrimination never survived scrutiny while others were subjected to virtually no judicial review whatever, even if they interfered with important individual interests. In its place he proposed adoption of a more flexible, "sliding scale" approach under which the degree of judicial scrutiny imposed on a particular form of discrimination would depend on the nature of the group affected, the extent to which it had previously been the target of purposeful discrimination by government, and the importance of the interests the challenged law affected. When the Court, in *San Antonio Independent School District v. Rodriguez* (1973), applied the lenient, rational-basis equal protection standard in upholding a state scheme for financing public schools largely through local property taxes, despite wide district disparities in per student spending, Marshall objected. Emphasizing that education was very closely related to the enjoyment of First Amendment and voting rights, he contended that the challenged regulation should have been subjected to more probing scrutiny than the majority applied.

The Court never adopted Marshall's approach, which he set out primarily in his dissents for *Dandridge v. Williams* (1970) and *Rodriguez*. But a majority did begin to take a more flexible approach to equal protection issues, as reflected, for example, in its treatment of gender-based laws as "quasi suspect."

Marshall made forceful contributions to other Burger Court constitutional debates as well. Although he and Brennan were the Court's only proponents of the death penalty's complete abolition, Marshall was probably the more effective of the two in attacking the use of public opinion surveys as a justification for capital punishment. Were the public truly informed about the death penalty and the circumstances of its infliction, he contended, they would reject it as inherently arbitrary, immoral, and shocking to the conscience (*Gregg v. Georgia* [1976]). He took pleasure in pointing out that an inmate's execution was a more expensive proposition for the state than life imprisonment. Marshall was also a vigorous supporter of affirmative action as an appropriate means of correcting the effects of past systematic discrimination against minorities. And while he rarely wrote major opinions in cases dealing directly with racial discrimination, his very presence on the Court had an undoubted impact on the sensitivity of certain of his colleagues to racial claims.

The Nixon Appointees

President Johnson not only appointed the first African American to the Supreme Court, but he also sought to elevate Abe Fortas, whom he had chosen as an associate justice in 1965, to the Court's center seat, to replace Earl Warren with another liberal-activist chief justice. Warren was certainly obliging, announcing in 1968 that he would leave the high bench on which he had served since 1953 once the president's nomination of a new chief justice had been confirmed by the Senate. By that point, however, Johnson was a lame-duck president as a result of his decision not to seek reelection, and the Fortas nomination collapsed in the face of mounting ethical questions about the nominee's fitness for the position. Selection of a new chief justice fell, therefore, to Richard M. Nixon, President Johnson's White House successor. Anxious to make good on his 1968 campaign promise to appoint "strict constructionist" justices who would reverse the liberal trends of the Warren era, Nixon chose federal appeals court judge Warren E. Burger to lead what he hoped would be a constitutional counterrevolution on the Court.

Abe Fortas (Harris & Ewing, Collection of the Supreme Court of the United States)

Warren Burger

Nixon's chief justice was born in St. Paul, Minnesota, in 1907. The fourth of seven children, Warren Burger was raised in a Swiss-German Protestant family of modest circumstances not unlike those in which the president was reared. Burger's father was a railroad cargo inspector and traveling salesman; his mother, it has been said, ran an "old-fashioned German house" based on respect for traditional values and "common sense." As a boy, Warren devoured the rags-to-riches exploits of Horatio Alger and began delivering newspapers at age nine to help with the family's finances. In high school he not only played cornet and bugle but also participated in five sports, served as student council president, headed the student court, and edited the school newspaper, while working in the summer on a farm and holding jobs as a track coach, lifeguard, truck driver, and camp counselor.

Although Burger's high school record was not outstanding, he won a scholarship to Princeton based on his extensive extracurricular activities. When the Princeton offer proved financially inadequate to meet his needs, he declined that opportunity, enrolling instead in extension courses at the University of Minnesota. After two years at the university, he attended night classes at the St. Paul College of Law (now the William Mitchell College of Law) while earning a living as a life insurance salesman. In 1931 he graduated with honors and that same year won admission to the Minnesota bar.

As a young associate in a St. Paul firm, Burger's income was less than that he had received selling life insurance. But he became a partner in 1935 and gained a reputation as a capable attorney in a practice devoted primarily to corporate, real estate, and probate law. From 1931 to 1953, he also taught contract law at his alma mater, and in 1935 he served as president of the local junior chamber of commerce. Although rejected for military service as a result of a spinal condition, he also served from 1942 to 1947 as a member of his state's emergency war labor board. After World War II, moreover, he held two positions connected with civil rights, serving as a member of the governor's interracial commission from 1948 to 1953 and as the first president of St. Paul's Council on Human Relations, where he was responsible for efforts to improve the relationship between city police and racial minorities.

The future chief justice played an active role, too, in partisan politics. A lifelong Republican, he helped to found Minnesota's first Young Republican organization in 1934 and figured prominently in Harold Stassen's successful 1938 gubernatorial campaign. In 1948 he served as floor manager of Stassen's abortive effort to secure the party's presidential nomination at the Republican National Convention in Philadelphia. He again managed Stassen's campaign at the 1952 GOP convention. But when General Eisenhower and conservative Ohio senator Robert A. Taft emerged as the leading contenders, Burger fortuitously threw his support to Eisenhower, helping to secure his nomination on the first ballot.

Warren Earl Burger (Robert S. Oakes, National Geographic Society, Collection of the Supreme Court of the United States)

Burger's support for the Eisenhower effort was soon rewarded. In 1953 the president appointed him to head what is now the Justice Department's civil division, with responsibility for all government civil litigation except antitrust and land cases. In his new capacity, he handled a number of cases involving the shipping industry and also oversaw proceedings leading to a federal court injunction issued under the controversial Taft-Hartley Act to end a longshoremen's strike on the East Coast. But Burger's most controversial action as an assistant attorney general in the Eisenhower Justice Department grew out of his role in a case involving John P. Peters, a Yale professor dismissed from his position as a consultant to the U.S. Public Health Service in 1953 on loyalty-security grounds. When Peters appealed to the Supreme Court, Solicitor General Simon E. Sobeloff, convinced that Peters's constitutional rights had been violated, refused to handle the case. Burger agreed to take Sobeloff's place, arguing that under the doctrine of separation of powers, the judiciary had no authority over the hiring or discharge of government employees. In *Peters v. Hobby* (1955), however, the Court ruled in Peters's favor, albeit on narrow procedural grounds.

In 1955 Burger accepted the administration's offer of a seat on the U.S. Court of Appeals for the District of Columbia, perhaps the most important of the federal appeals courts because of its large docket of cases involving federal administrative agencies and departments in the nation's capital. Largely as a result of charges raised by former Justice Department employees he had dismissed for incompetence, Burger's confirmation by the Senate was delayed for several months. In April 1956, however, he took his place on the circuit bench.

During his thirteen years on the D.C. appeals court, Burger developed a largely conservative record, especially in cases involving the rights of suspects and defendants in criminal cases. In his circuit opinions, he attacked the Warren Court's *Miranda* decision, as well as its earlier controversial ruling in *Mallory v. United States* (1957), holding that confessions secured from suspects following arrest are inadmissible in federal court if there was an unreasonable delay between arrest and the defendant's arraignment before a judge. He was also a critic of the expanded insanity defense the D.C. circuit had adopted in *Durham v. United States* (1954). Under the *Durham* rule, which other courts declined to adopt and several federal circuits specifically rejected, defendants could not be held criminally responsible for conduct that resulted from a mental disease or defect. Burger contended that the rule ignored the moral basis of criminal law. In public statements, however, he called for a complete overhaul of the penal system with a greater emphasis on the rehabilitation of inmates. He also spoke for the circuit in an important 1966 case requiring the Federal Communications Commission (FCC) to hear the complaints of civil rights and church groups regarding the allegedly biased programming practices of a Jackson, Mississippi, television station.

Despite his lengthy circuit tenure, Burger, like most jurists, remained virtually unknown to the public. Even though he was mentioned as a possible successor to

Chief Justice Warren, his selection came as something of a surprise to most Court watchers. But his nomination was well received, especially by conservatives but even among certain liberal journalists and lawyers who considered him a more moderate judge than President Nixon might have selected. And for a law-and-order president bent on curtailing expansive Warren Court precedents expanding the rights of criminal suspects and defendants, Burger's conservative circuit court criminal procedure record made him an ideal Nixon choice for the Court's center seat. Senate reception to the nomination, as noted in the previous chapter, was very positive. After a brief and essentially perfunctory hearing, the Judiciary Committee unanimously recommended his confirmation; the full Senate concurred by a 74–3 vote, and Burger took the oath from Chief Justice Warren on June 24, 1969.

The difficulties Chief Justice Burger encountered as the Court's leader were examined in Chapter One. As a judicial craftsman, though, he proved an entirely competent, if hardly extraordinary, jurist. His most significant opinions involved disputes over separation of powers among the branches of the national government. The initial draft of his self-assigned opinion for a unanimous Court in *United States v. Nixon* (1974), it will be recalled, was entirely too deferential to presidential prerogatives for his brethren. But the final version, while more a collegial effort than the chief justice's own handiwork, did recognize a presidential confidentiality privilege mentioned nowhere in the Constitution's text, declared it presumptively valid, and placed a heavy burden on those seeking to override its assertion in a particular case. In *INS v. Chadha* (1983), arguably the most important opinion of his career, Burger invoked a formalistic, textbook version of separation of powers and literal reading of pertinent constitutional provisions to strike down the legislative veto. The Constitution required that laws be passed by both houses of Congress and presented to the president for his review, declared the chief justice, and a congressional veto of proposed presidential action simply could not be squared with that constitutional arrangement. Burger's opinion for the Court in *Bowsher v. Synar* (1986), decided in his last term, similarly declared the Gramm-Rudman-Hollings budget-deficit-cutting law invalid for conferring executive functions on the comptroller general, a legislative officer removable by Congress. An official subject to congressional control, the chief justice reasoned, could not exercise executive powers.

Along similar lines, the chief justice also generally favored a narrow construction of the Constitution's speech and debate clause, protecting members of Congress from executive and judicial intrusions on their legislative work. Speaking for the Court in *Hutchinson v. Proxmire* (1979), for example, he held that the clause did not immunize a U.S. senator from a libel suit based on statements made in a congressional press release or newsletter, neither of which was essential to the legislative process. As long as congressional activity fell within the sphere of the legislative function, however, Burger extended the clause a relatively broad reading. When Mississippi senator James Eastland's Internal Security Subcommittee subpoenaed the records of an antiwar group, the group sought an injunction, claiming that enforcement of the subpoena would impose a chilling effect on their free expression rights. Without reaching the First Amendment issue, the Court, per Burger, held that subcommittee members and their aides were completely immune from suit because their investigation was within the scope of legitimate legislative activities (*Eastland v. Servicemen's Fund* [1975]).

Burger also sought to limit judicial encroachment on the other branches and levels of government. The Warren Court expanded the circumstances in which a plaintiff's status as a federal taxpayer conferred standing to challenge the validity of a congressional spending program. But in *United States v. Richardson* (1974) and *Schlesinger v. Reservists Committee to Stop the War* (1974), dismissing challenges to secret funding of the Central Intelligence Agency (CIA) and positions in the military reserves for members of Congress, Burger narrowly confined the Warren Court precedent to its facts. Burger also wrote the Court's opinion in *Laird v. Tatum* (1972), dismissing as unduly speculative the claim of antiwar protesters that army surveillance of their activities inflicted a chilling effect on their exercise of protected First Amendment rights.

Burger was highly critical of what he considered the irresponsibility of the press, extremely sensitive to media criticism of his work, and zealous in his efforts to protect the secrecy of the Court's inner workings from press display. He also joined decisions rejecting testimonial and related special First Amendment privileges for the press and authored *Miller v. California* (1973) and other decisions expanding government control over erotic expression. During his tenure, however, he wrote a number of important decisions upholding free press claims. In *Nebraska Press Association v. Stuart* (1976), he largely rejected the authority of judges to issue gag orders against the press as a means for insulating criminal proceedings from prejudicial publicity. *Miami Herald Publishing Co. v. Tornillo* (1974) invalidated as an undue interference with press editorial discretion a Florida statute requiring newspapers that attacked a political candidate to provide free reply space. And in *Richmond Newspapers, Inc. v. Virginia* (1980), Burger authored the Court's opinion requiring open trials as a means of promoting public confidence in the judicial process.

The chief justice developed an equally mixed record in other constitutional areas. He spoke for the Court, for example, in *Wisconsin v. Yoder* (1972), rejecting compulsory high school education for the Amish as a violation of their religious beliefs. In *Lemon v. Kurtzman* (1971) he announced a controversial three-part religious establishment test requiring substantial separation of church and state. Yet he also authored *Marsh v. Chambers* (1983), which emphasized long practice to uphold a state's provision of paid legislative chaplains against a First Amendment challenge.

The Court's first school desegregation ruling after Burger became chief justice was a per curiam opinion in *Alexander v. Holmes County Board of Education* (1969), a Mississippi case ordering the termination of dual school systems "at once." He also authored the Court's ruling in *Swann v. Charlotte-Mecklenburg Board of Education* (1971), upholding broad remedial power for federal judges to convert school systems with a history of de jure, or state-enforced, segregation into unitary systems.

Much later he spoke for the Court in *Fullilove v. Klutznick* (1980), according Congress greater deference than the states in affirmative action cases. But his original draft opinion in the *Swann* case was considerably less deferential to the power of lower courts in desegregation cases, and he also spoke for the majority in *Milliken v. Bradley* (1974), exalting local control over public schools in rejecting cross-district desegregation decrees. In *Griggs v. Duke Power Co.* (1971), he upheld application of Title VII of the 1964 Civil Rights Act to forbid employment tests unrelated to job skills, concluding, too, that a job test's racially disparate effect, rather than proof of discriminatory intent, was sufficient to establish a Title VII violation. But in *Bakke*, *Weber*, and most other cases, he opposed affirmative action programs. Nor did he generally favor expansive equal protection doctrines in nonracial litigation. Burger spoke for the Court in *Reed v. Reed* (1971), the first decision striking down a law that discriminated on the basis of gender. But he refused to join the argument that gender classifications, like those based on race, were inherently suspect and subject to strict judicial scrutiny.

In the main Chief Justice Burger developed a conservative record during his seventeen years on the supreme bench, especially in criminal justice cases. He was the Court's most vociferous critic of the Fourth Amendment exclusionary rule and the *Miranda* doctrine. Indeed, next to William Rehnquist, the Burger Court's chief justice compiled its most conservative voting record.

Harry A. Blackmun

Although Chief Justice Burger's conservative record must have given the president who appointed him considerable satisfaction, Nixon undoubtedly accorded Burger's boyhood friend, Harry A. Blackmun, the president's second selection to the high bench, mixed reviews at best. Born in 1908 in Nashville, Illinois, where his mother's family owned a flour mill, Blackmun grew up in Minneapolis and St. Paul, Minnesota. His father tried his hand at a succession of business careers, including fruit wholesaler, grocery and hardware store proprietor, bank official, and insurance salesman. Imbued with a strong work ethic and raised in a devoutly Methodist family, Blackmun was a quiet, serious, hardworking youth and diligent scholar considered by some a teacher's pet, yet he also had a playful, mischievous side to his personality. He and Warren Burger first met in Sunday school at age four or five, attended the same elementary

Harry A. Blackmun (Joseph D. Lavenburg, National Geographic Society, Collection of the Supreme Court of the United States)

school, delivered newspapers and played tennis together, and would remain close friends for life. When Burger married, Blackmun was his friend's best man.

After high school, however, their paths separated. While Burger remained in Minnesota for college and law school, Blackmun went away to Harvard on a partial scholarship, working as a janitor and tutor to supplement his income. An outstanding student, he majored in mathematics, was inducted into Phi Beta Kappa, and graduated with highest honors in 1929. Although initially interested in pursuing a medical career, he instead enrolled in Harvard's law school, where his professors included Felix Frankfurter. Following graduation in 1932, he won admission to the Minnesota bar and clerked for a year with Judge John B. Sanford of the U.S. Court of Appeals for the Eighth Circuit, on which Blackmun would later serve. In 1934 he joined a Minneapolis firm, eventually becoming a partner and specializing in tax law and estate planning. In 1935–1941 and in 1945–1947, he was also a part-time instructor at the St. Paul and University of Minnesota law schools. But in 1950 he, his wife, and daughters moved to Rochester, Minnesota, where he became resident counsel at the famed Mayo Clinic.

Blackmun was never as active in politics as Burger. In 1945 and 1948, however, he supported Democrat Hubert H. Humphrey in his successful campaigns for the mayorship of Minneapolis and a U.S. Senate seat. In 1959 President Eisenhower nominated him for a seat on the Eighth Circuit court of appeals with the support of Humphrey and his friend, Warren Burger, who was then on the D.C. court of appeals and before that had headed the Justice Department's civil division in the Eisenhower administration.

The voting record Blackmun compiled on the court of appeals was moderately liberal on racial civil rights issues, moderately conservative in most other civil liberties litigation, and distinctly progovernment in cases involving the claims of criminal suspects and defendants. The Supreme Court reversed his 1967 refusal to construe a Reconstruction-era civil rights statute as authority for suits against private (as opposed to state-enforced) racial discrimination in housing. But he also spoke for the circuit in overturning a desegregation plan that had actually perpetuated segregated schools and in ordering an Arkansas school district to rehire black teachers following the closing of an all-black school. In 1961 he authored an opinion reversing the conviction of a black defendant under a jury system that systematically discriminated against would-be jurors who were black. He also subjected the Minnesota legislature to the Supreme Court's reapportionment rulings and ordered the Communist Party placed on the state's ballot.

But Blackmun rarely supported criminal justice claims. He agreed, for example, that a defendant could be tried in separate proceedings for the robbery of two players in a poker game—a ruling the Supreme Court reversed on double jeopardy grounds in *Ashe v. Swenson* (1970). He also voted to affirm death sentences despite grave personal doubts that capital punishment was morally right or served as an effective deterrent to crime. In a ruling later reversed by the Supreme Court in *Pope v. United States* (1968), for example, he upheld a provision of the federal bank robbery statute under which a death sentence could be imposed only on a jury's recommendation, even though such a scheme deterred defendants from exercising their right to jury trial. His opinions in conscientious objector and related cases often reflected his dismay at the growing permissiveness and disrespect for traditional institutions in American society.

When the Senate refused to confirm President Nixon's nominations of Clement Haynsworth and G. Harrold Carswell to replace Justice Abe Fortas, who had resigned under fire in May 1969, the president nominated Blackmun to the Fortas seat. The "third man," as Blackmun later regularly referred to himself, won easy approval in the Senate and took his seat on the high bench June 9, 1970, over a year after Fortas's resignation. Given their close friendship and Burger's apparent role in Blackmun's nomination, Court watchers quickly dubbed the pair the "Minnesota Twins." For a time, the label appeared apt. During 1970–1971, Blackmun's first full term, the two voted alike in 95.8 percent of nonunanimous cases, including all but one of the Court's criminal procedure rulings. Even in the early years, however, Blackmun was more supportive of civil liberties claims than Burger or Rehnquist. Beginning with the 1975 term, the Burger-Blackmun rate of agreement declined steadily, and by the early 1980s Blackmun was more likely to be aligned with Justices Brennan and Marshall than with the chief justice and other Court conservatives. For the balance of Burger's tenure, he was the most liberal of the Nixon appointees to the Court; in Burger's final term Blackmun supported two-thirds of all civil liberties claims, behind only Marshall and Brennan.

Theories abound about the changing directions of Blackmun's voting record on the Court. His opinion for the Court in *Roe v. Wade* became the most controversial decision of the Burger era and one of the most hotly disputed in the Court's entire history. Some suggest that Blackmun's commitment to *Roe* and disappointment at conservative attacks on his opinion may have prompted greater sensitivity on his part to civil liberties claims generally. Others cite his well-known irritation at the "Minnesota Twins" label and particularly the degrading assumption that "Hip Pocket Harry" was a virtually certain vote for whatever position the chief justice embraced. That anger—and Burger's apparent insensitivity to his friend's feelings—may have motivated Blackmun, according to this thesis, consciously to attempt to distinguish his position from that of the chief justice on a variety of issues. Still others have contended that the ultimate outlines of Blackmun's jurisprudence were foreshadowed by the moderate record he developed on the circuit bench. In truth, of course, a variety of factors no doubt influenced the shifting directions of Blackmun's Supreme Court record. Throughout his career, however, he displayed considerable disdain for dogmatic, inflexible positions and, with notable exceptions, a soul-searching lack of certitude uncommon among jurists. That such a justice's voting patterns might change markedly over a lengthy tenure is hardly surprising, even if complicated to explain.

Justice Blackmun authored the Court's principal opinions in only a few issue areas of significance. Particularly in the early years, he often wrote or joined opinions favoring a narrow construction of First Amendment rights. In dissenting from the majority's support of free press claims in the *Pentagon Papers* cases, he favored a balancing of competing press and governmental interests and considerable deference to the latter, emphasizing that the First Amendment was merely "one part" of the Constitution. Extremely supportive of governmental authority over crude and offensive language, he frequently dismissed the public use of such expletives as immature antics unworthy of constitutional protection (e.g., *Cohen v. California* [1971]; *Gooding v. Wilson* [1972]) and joined the Court in *Miller v. California* (1973) and other rulings expanding governmental authority over erotic expression. But he also wrote *Virginia Board of Pharmacy v. Virginia Consumer Council* (1976) and other Burger Court decisions lifting the commercial speech exception to protected expression and holding, consistent with his distaste for constitutional absolutes, that advertisements could be regulated only to further substantial governmental interests.

Although generally opposed to expansion of equal protection philosophy, Blackmun in his first term also authored the Court's opinion in *Graham v. Richardson* (1971), adding alienage to the list of "suspect" classifications subjected to strict judicial scrutiny and striking down discrimination against aliens in the granting of welfare benefits. Later he spoke for majorities in declaring invalid attempts to exclude aliens from civil service jobs and college scholarships. And while he agreed that state police posts could be confined to U.S. citizens alone, he dissented when the Court upheld citizenship requirements for public school teachers and deputy probation officers.

But Blackmun's most significant and controversial opinion as the Court's spokesman was *Roe v. Wade* (1973), in which he drew on his years as counsel to the Mayo Clinic in recognizing a right of abortion, dividing pregnancies into three trimesters, and subjecting abortion controls in each trimester to strict judicial review. In subsequent cases he wrote or concurred in opinions reaffirming *Roe* and declaring unconstitutional a variety of abortion controls (e.g., *Planned Parenthood v. Danforth* [1976]). And when a majority upheld restrictions on funded abortions for indigent women, he wrote and joined Justices Brennan and Marshall in vigorous dissents (*Maher v. Roe* [1977]; *Harris v. McRae* [1980]), condemning, among other things, what he considered the majority's gross insensitivity to the plight of impoverished women. When the Rehnquist Court later rejected the strict trimester approach Blackmun had embraced in his *Roe* opinion, forbidding instead only "undue" burdens on a woman's decision to abort a pregnancy, Blackmun expressed relief that *Roe* had not been discarded entirely but also vigorously defended *Roe*'s trimester formula.

Blackmun's *Roe* opinion, the intense national debate it provoked, the justice's sensitivity to attacks on *Roe*, and his growing awareness of the impact of abortion controls apparently heightened his sensitivity to the plight of the weak and powerless. In *Wyman v. James* (1971), his very first opinion of the Court, the justice turned back Fourth Amendment challenges raised against the "home visits" to which welfare recipients were obliged to submit in order to continue receiving benefits. His majority opinion in *United States v. Kras* (1973) minimized the burdens a bankruptcy filing fee posed for the poor. But in holding alienage a suspect basis of classification in 1971, Blackmun had stressed the powerlessness of aliens as a group. After *Roe*, moreover, and particularly by the early 1980s, his concern for the disadvantaged had become pronounced. In Burger's last term, for example, he vehemently dissented when a majority in *Bowers v. Hardwick* (1986) upheld state authority to penalize homosexual sodomy. And in the *Bakke* case, he saw affirmative action programs as an appropriate temporary means for hastening the day when society would be truly integrated and racial discrimination truly a relic of the past.

Blackmun would be most consistently deferential to government in criminal procedure cases. He joined decisions diluting the exclusionary rule and *Miranda* doctrine, spoke for the Court in refusing to extend the jury trial to juvenile proceedings (*McKeiver v. Pennsylvania* [1971]), and recognized a variety of exceptions to the Fourth Amendment's warrant requirement (e.g., *South Dakota v. Opperman* [1976], upholding warrantless inventory searches of impounded automobiles). But even in the criminal justice field, there were limits to the justice's deference to government over the individual. He dissented in *Faretta v. California* (1975), when the Court upheld the right of defendants to refuse counsel and defend themselves, but his stance obviously reflected concern for the accused's best interests. Recalling the "old proverb that 'one who is his own lawyer has a fool for a client,'" he accused the *Faretta* majority of "bestow[ing] a *constitutional* right on one to make a fool of oneself" (p. 852).

While he dissented when a majority struck down a state death penalty statute in *Furman v. Georgia* (1972), he made clear in a dissenting opinion his deep personal abhorrence of capital punishment and that he simply considered its status largely a matter for legislative judgment rather than judicial review. In later years Blackmun gave death penalty challenges a mixed reception, joining the *Coker v. Georgia* (1977) majority, for example, in declaring capital punishment for rape disproportionate to the gravity of the offense. In his final term on the bench, the justice ultimately rejected capital punishment as inherently unconstitutional on the ground that no death penalty statute could be devised that would eliminate the arbitrariness inherent in its imposition. In another criminal justice field, moreover, he concluded that five-member juries were not of sufficient size to fulfill the jury's historic purposes (*Ballew v. Georgia* [1978]). And in *Scott v. Illinois* (1979), he argued that indigent defendants should be provided court-appointed counsel in any case in which the accused faced a possible punishment of more than six months' imprisonment, not merely where convictions actually resulted in imprisonment, as the Court had held.

There were also limits to Blackmun's deference to state authority in conflicts over national and state power in the federal system. He joined *Younger v. Harris* (1971) and other decisions largely rejecting federal district court intervention in pending state criminal and civil proceedings, but he also held for the Court that such suits were not forbidden when a state prosecution had only been threatened, not initiated (*Ellis v. Dyson* [1975]). Although he provided the pivotal vote, moreover, in *National League of Cities v. Usery* (1976), invalidating for the first time since 1936 a congressional regulatory statute on grounds of undue interference with state authority, he later spoke for the Court in *Garcia v. San Antonio Metropolitan Transit Authority* (1985), reversing *Usery* and relegating such disputes largely to the political arena. Nor was the shift in his position entirely unpredictable. As in many other issue areas, he had couched his initial support of *Usery* in equivocal terms. In federalism cases as in other fields, Justice Blackmun pursued a largely pragmatic, case-to-case jurisprudence not really amenable to broad generalization.

Lewis F. Powell Jr.

Lewis F. Powell Jr., President Nixon's third successful nomination to the Court, filed one of the most vigorous dissents of his career in the *Garcia* case. As the most influential justice of the Burger era, however, Powell was rarely a dissenter. His 1971 nomination to replace Justice Hugo Black was almost universally praised as one of the finest selections ever to the high bench.

Powell's family had settled in Virginia in colonial times; the first Powell to arrive, in fact, was one of the original Jamestown settlers. Lewis was born in 1907 at Suffolk, in southeastern Virginia, but spent most of his life in Richmond. Following graduation from the prestigious McGuire's University School in 1925, he enrolled at Washington and Lee, where he managed the football team, served as managing editor of the student newspaper, and was elected student body president, all the while compiling an outstanding academic record. Graduating Phi Beta Kappa in 1929, he remained at the law school. On completion of an LL.B. in 1931, he won admission to the Virginia bar but delayed law practice for a year in order to obtain a master's degree in law at Harvard, where his professors included Felix Frankfurter and Roscoe Pound, the distinguished legal scholar and Harvard law dean.

On returning to Virginia, Powell practiced law for two years in a Richmond firm, then began a long association with one of the city's oldest concerns. Made a partner in 1938 in what is now Hunton and Williams, he combined trial practice with representation of a variety of large commercial interests, becoming a director in eleven

Lewis F. Powell Jr. (Joseph Bailey, National Geographic Society, Collection of the Supreme Court of the United States)

major companies, including Phillip Morris, and a pillar of Richmond's civil and social life. From 1938 to 1941 he also taught evening classes at a Richmond business school.

During World War II, Powell joined the army air corps, rising to the rank of full colonel before his separation from the military in 1946. Serving as a combat and intelligence officer in the European and North African theaters, he earned several military honors, including the Legion of Merit and Bronze Star.

After the war Powell resumed his active law practice but also became increasingly involved in a variety of public service positions. In 1947 he chaired the commission that drafted a charter for Richmond's conversion to the city manager form of government. The next year he began a four-year appointment as a selective service hearing officer for Virginia's eastern district and an eight-year term with a governor's advisory council on the state's economy. In 1948 he was president of the local bar association and in 1950 president of the city's chamber of commerce.

Powell performed his most significant public service of that period, however, as chairman of the Richmond school board from 1952 to 1961. Although much of Virginia was pursuing a policy of massive resistance to racial integration of the public schools and schools were even closed in certain parts of the state in an effort to avoid desegregation, Powell followed a different approach. Under his leadership, black students were admitted without serious incident to Richmond's schools in 1959. Powell was hardly an aggressive leader in the struggle for racial equality. In 1963 the U.S. Court of Appeals for the Fourth Circuit concluded that certain of the school board's decisions during his tenure in fact helped to perpetuate segregation. He was also a member of two all-white private clubs, and at the time of his Supreme Court nomination his firm (which then included 100 lawyers) had never hired a black attorney. But Powell's moderate approach stood in marked contrast to the intransigence of most southern officials. As a director of Miller and Rhodes, the large Richmond department store his firm counted among its clients, he also played a role in the store's decision to desegregate its dining room before it could become a target of sit-in demonstrations.

Over the years Powell rose to national prominence in the activities of the legal profession. He was first elected to a national office in the American Bar Association in 1940, when he became chairman of the Junior Bar Conference. In later years he held other ABA positions and in 1964–1965 was its national president. He was also president of the American Bar Foundation, the association's research arm, in 1969–1971, as well as president of the American College of Trial Lawyers from 1968 to 1970. As an officer in the National Legal Aid and Defender Society and in other capacities, he worked tirelessly, too, in behalf of government-financed legal services for the poor.

Powell's superb professional credentials alone made him a formidable choice for a seat on the Supreme Court. But President Nixon was no doubt further impressed with his stated positions on a number of sensitive constitutional and policy issues. Observing that law-abiding citizens had nothing to fear, he had denounced critics of government wiretapping. In civil rights and antiwar contexts, he expressed fear that civil disobedience of whatever sort could degenerate into lawlessness and revolution. He suggested, moreover, that the Warren Court may have been unduly concerned with the rights of defendants and that it was perhaps time to focus greater attention on the rights of society generally.

Whatever the president's motivation, his nomination of Powell on October 21, 1971, to fill the vacancy created by fellow southerner Hugo Black's retirement and death was warmly received. Under other circumstances, the ABA might have been concerned about the nominee's advanced age (sixty-four at the time of Powell's nomination). But the association could hardly oppose one of its former national presidents, and its judiciary committee termed Powell "the best person available." The Virginia chapter of the NAACP also endorsed the nomination, and on December 6 the Senate made Powell the first justice from Virginia since Reconstruction, approving the president's choice by a vote of 89–1.

As a southern moderate, Lewis Powell had followed a cautious course through his native state's civil rights crises of the 1950s and 1960s, wedded firmly to the South's traditions yet obviously aware of the serious and enduring damage segregationist extremism could cause his state and region. On the Supreme Court, the justice generally assumed the same sort of middle-of-the-road stance—a posture that, combined with his considerable leadership skills and persuasive powers, made him the Burger Court's most significant justice.

At times Powell's pragmatic jurisprudence resulted in his position's becoming truly pivotal in important issues facing the Court. In *Regents of the University of California v. Bakke* (1978), the Court's first affirmative action ruling, four justices concluded that the minority admissions program at issue there violated a federal law forbidding racial discrimination by federally funded institutions. Four others argued that the challenged quota scheme helped remedy the effects of past discrimination against minorities, hastened the creation of a truly integrated and thus discrimination-free society, and promoted other legitimate and substantial governmental interests. Powell, in contrast, declared the quota invalid but also agreed that a university could include race and other nonmerit considerations in its admission formula to further its compelling interest in securing a diverse student body and thereby enhancing its students' educational experience; race simply could not be the *sole* factor in determining an applicant's admission eligibility. Earlier, when the Court confronted the jury unanimity issue in *Apodaca v. Oregon* (1972), Powell also cast the pivotal vote. Faithful to precedent, he agreed that federal juries must continue to render unanimous verdicts. But unwilling to embrace the proposition that the Fourteenth Amendment's due process clause imposed precisely the same procedural standards on states that the Court's constructions of the Bill of Rights required for federal proceedings, he also concluded that nonunanimous state jury verdicts satisfied Fourteenth Amendment due process requirements.

Although the ultimate impact of his stance was less clear, the justice played a similar role in *Branzburg v. Hayes* (1972), rejecting free press claims to a First Amendment privilege from grand jury testimony. Dismissing as highly speculative media contentions that grand jury appearances would inhibit their confidential sources and diminish the free flow of news, Justice White concluded for a *Branzburg* "majority" that reporters had the same obligations as other persons to assist grand juries in their inquiries; only when a subpoena was part of a bad-faith effort to harass a journalist should a court intervene in the media's behalf. In dissent, four justices contended that reporters were either absolutely immune under the First Amendment from grand jury subpoenas or privileged from testifying unless they possessed information available from no other source and of critical importance to the grand jury's investigation. In a concurrence, however, Justice Powell, the fifth member of the majority, concluded that a judge should weigh the competing press and prosecutorial interests to determine whether a media subpoena should prevail in a given case. The justice's stance led some to conclude, therefore, that the *Branzburg* vote was 4-1/2–4-1/2 rather than 5–4.

Powell developed a mixed record in other areas as well. One of the leaders in the Burger Court's efforts to curtail litigant access to the federal judiciary, he was particularly critical of the Warren Court's decision in *Flast v. Cohen* (1968), which held that a litigant's status as a federal taxpayer conferred standing to challenge the validity of federal programs (such as government assistance to religious schools) that the litigant claimed violated constitutional limitations on Congress's taxing and spending powers. When the Court, in *United States v. Richardson* (1974), dismissed a taxpayer suit against secret congressional funding of the CIA on the ground that the policy at issue was not an exercise of congressional financial authority, Powell filed a concurring opinion urging that *Flast* be limited strictly to its facts and emphasizing the dangers of making courts forums for the airing of generalized grievances more appropriate for legislative resolution.

Although he joined *Roe v. Wade*, Powell was generally indisposed to expand the scope of unenumerated rights accorded constitutional protection. He spoke for the majority, for example, in the *Rodriguez* case, limiting the rights given strict protection from discrimination under the equal protection guarantee to those stated or implied in the Constitution, and declining to include a right to an equal education among such guarantees. In the same case and elsewhere, he also displayed a reluctance to enlarge the scope of "suspect" classes given special judicial protection beyond race, color, and related factors. Thus, in *Rodriguez* he gave a narrow construction to precedents suggesting that poverty was a constitutional suspect.

The justice was equally skeptical of the Fourth Amendment exclusionary rule and *Miranda* doctrine that he, like the Burger Court majority, considered judicially created devices rather than constitutional requirements. Speaking for the majority in *Stone v. Powell* (1976), for example, he excluded from federal habeas corpus proceedings search and seizure claims defendants had already been given a full and fair opportunity to raise in the state courts. Strongly supportive of state authority in general, he also joined the 5–4 majority in the *Usery* case, which limited congressional authority over state and local governments under the interstate commerce clause. When a 5–4 majority in the *Garcia* case later overturned *Usery*, Powell, as noted earlier, vigorously dissented, scoring the Court's disregard for recent precedent and what he considered to be fundamental principles of federalism. And in his last term on the Court, the year following Chief Justice Burger's retirement, Powell was the Court's spokesman in *McCleskey v. Kemp* (1987), rejecting claims that gross racial disparities in a state's imposition of the death penalty established its violation of constitutional guarantees.

But Justice Powell's stance in such cases was hardly a firm predictor of his vote in similar suits. Assuming a strong separationist stance in religious establishment cases, he was on the winning side in some thirty suits and expressed concern that government assistance to religious schools created risks of political strife along sectarian lines. Whatever his general views regarding the constitutional status of public education, he provided the decisive fifth vote for the Court's ruling in *Plyler v. Doe* (1982), striking down the state's denial of a free public education to illegal alien children in Texas. And while he joined the Court in *Bowers v. Hardwick* (1986), upholding a state sodomy law against privacy claims, he found *Bowers*, as will be seen in more detail in the next chapter, an extremely frustrating case, later telling a law school audience his vote there was probably a mistake. Despite his general support of legislative judgments in the death penalty field, moreover, he spoke for the Court in *Booth v. Maryland* (1987), a decision the Rehnquist Court would later overrule, rejecting the prosecutor's use of victim-impact statements in the sentencing phase of a capital case. When the Court upheld a mandatory life sentence for recidivists in *Rummel v. Estelle* (1980), he dissented, contending that such a sentence was grossly disproportionate to the minor property crimes at issue in the case. In *Solem v. Helm* (1983), he spoke for the Court in distinguishing *Rummel* and striking down a mandatory life sentence without possibility of parole for a defendant convicted of a seventh nonviolent felony.

William H. Rehnquist

Whatever disappointment the moderately conservative Powell caused President Nixon must have been more than offset by his fourth appointee's record as the most

William H. Rehnquist (Dane Penland, Smithsonian Institution, Collection of the Supreme Court of the United States)

conservative Burger Court justice. Reared in a suburb of Milwaukee, Wisconsin, where he was born in 1924, William H. Rehnquist attended Kenyon College in Ohio for a year after high school, then served three years in the army air corps. Following military service, he entered Stanford, graduating Phi Beta Kappa with a political science major and next completing an M.A. there and a second master's degree at Harvard. Returning to Stanford for law school, he graduated first in his class and was editor of the law review. Rehnquist clerked for Supreme Court justice Robert H. Jackson from February 1952 until June 1953, then practiced law with a Phoenix firm from 1953 to 1956, when he formed a partnership with another young lawyer. That arrangement was dissolved the next year, and Rehnquist became an unlisted partner briefly in another firm. In 1958 he served as a special state prosecutor investigating fraud in the Arizona highway department. Two years later he formed a third partnership with a former lawyer for the Internal Revenue Service (IRS), with whom he remained until becoming an assistant attorney general in the Nixon administration.

Soon after arriving in Phoenix, Rehnquist had begun to establish a reputation as one of the state's most conservative Republicans. Before a GOP organization, he characterized Earl Warren, Hugo Black, and William O. Douglas as the Supreme Court's left-wing philosophers. In a 1957 magazine article, he attributed part of the liberal trends in the Warren Court to the leftist sympathies of the law clerks, accusing them of unconsciously slanting the materials they prepared for the justices' review of pending cases. He also became a close associate of prominent conservative Arizona Republicans, including Barry Goldwater and Richard G. Kleindienst, who served as state party chairman as well as national field director for the Goldwater and Nixon presidential campaigns in 1964 and 1968.

When Kleindienst became Nixon's deputy attorney general in 1969, Rehnquist was named assistant attorney general in charge of the Justice Department's Office of Legal Counsel, construing the Constitution and laws for the president and attorney general and providing legal advice to all executive agencies. In that capacity the future justice became a vigorous defender of a variety of controversial administration initiatives, from military surveillance of antiwar protesters, presidential war making in Southeast Asia, and mass police arrests of peaceful Washington demonstrators, to Nixon's tough anticrime package, including "no knock" police entries, pretrial detention without bail for potentially violent suspects, and warrantless electronic surveillance of suspects. He frequently declared in public settings his firm belief that Warren Court decisions had exhibited undue solicitude for defendants' rights and minimized important social interests in law and order.

When President Nixon chose Lewis Powell and Rehnquist in 1971 to replace Justices Black and Harlan, admirers and critics alike praised their impeccable intellectual, academic, and professional credentials. Unlike Powell, however, Rehnquist was the target of harsh criticism in the Senate confirmation process, as well as in the press and among leaders of liberal political organizations. Arizona residents signed affidavits accusing the nominee of attempting to intefere with the voting rights of minority voters at the polls. Other critics scored his conservative record in the Nixon Justice Department. And after the Judiciary Committee recommended his confirmation by a 12–4 vote, the memorandum he had written in opposition to school desegregation while clerking for Justice Jackson surfaced, provoking a futile effort by opponents to reopen the committee hearings. On December 10, 1971, the full Senate approved Rehnquist's appointment, but by a vote of 68–26, in marked contrast to the 89–1 vote for Justice Powell.

To a greater degree than other members of the Burger Court following Justice Black's retirement, Justice Rehnquist purported to embrace a legal positivist jurisprudence. Like Black, Rehnquist contended that judges should base their interpretations of the Constitution's meaning on its language and the intent of its framers rather than on their conceptions of justice, fairness, or social utility. Such an approach to constitutional interpretation, he argued, was the only one consistent with democratic majoritarian principles. Although Rehnquist agreed that the Constitution was "living" law, adaptable to changing circumstances, he maintained that Congress, through the exercise of its broad legislative powers, was the principal instrument for keeping constitutional provisions in tune with the times. In contrast to Justice Black, Rehnquist was willing to concede that the Constitution included unenumerated as well as express guarantees within its scope, but he accorded such rights no meaningful judicial protection, holding instead that government restrictions on their exercise should be sustained if at all related to some legitimate governmental purpose. For Rehnquist, a law rarely if ever would lack such a rational basis.

It could be argued that Rehnquist was faithful to his positivist jurisprudence in certain issue areas. He dissented in *Roe v. Wade*, for example, because he doubted the Fourteenth Amendment's framers had intended to include a right of abortion within the scope of due process and contended that even if abortion were in some sense a part of the liberty the amendment guaranteed against state infringement, it, like other Fourteenth Amendment freedoms, was subject to broad governmental control. In *Paul v. Davis* (1976), he spoke for a majority in rejecting meaningful constitutional protection for reputational privacy. And while assuming in *Kelley v. Johnson* (1976) that the liberty guaranteed in the due process clause encompassed some sort of right of personal appearance, he concluded for the *Kelley* majority that the personal appearance of police was subject to extensive regulation and upheld a police hair code as rationally related to the state's interests in promoting esprit de corps and assuring that officers were readily recognizable to the public.

Rehnquist joined the *Bowers* majority in refusing to include a right of homosexual sodomy within the meaning of due process. He was also reluctant to use equal protection as a safeguard for unenumerated rights or a meaningful weapon against gender and other nonracial classifications, preferring instead application of the lenient, rational basis standard of judicial review in such cases (e.g., *Craig v. Boren* [1976]). When a majority struck down a military dependency allowance provision favoring men over women, for example, Rehnquist filed a lone dissent, finding the challenged regulation rationally related to the government's legitimate interest in administrative convenience. Even in racial cases, moreover, he drew a clear-cut distinction between de facto and de jure segregation, insisting that only the latter—segregation rooted in law or other official practices—was subject to judicial remedy. Thus, in *Keyes v. School District* (1973), he filed a lone dissent against the Court's decision to uphold a district-wide desegregation plan where intentional discrimination had been found in only one part of the school district in question. He was also perhaps the Burger Court's most aggressive opponent of affirmative action, contending with Chief Justice Burger in the *Weber* case, for example, that federal law did not permit private companies even voluntarily to establish racial employment quotas.

Where a positivist approach to constitutional interpretation conflicted with fundamental elements in Rehnquist's political conservatism, however, the latter generally prevailed. His strong commitment to protecting the position of the states in the federal system at times overshadowed his positivist jurisprudence. Since the Constitution, as Justice Black long contended, confers the power over interstate commerce on Congress rather than the federal courts, Rehnquist's reluctance to join decisions invalidating state regulations of interstate commerce in the absence of conflicting congressional legislation (*City of Philadelphia v. New Jersey* [1978]) seemed compatible with his professed loyalty to constitutional text. But in speaking for the 5–4 *Usery* majority, invalidating an otherwise valid exercise of congressional power to regulate commerce on the ground that the statute at issue unconstitutionally interfered with state authority, he barely referred to the Constitution's text, relying instead on principles of state sovereignty mentioned nowhere in that document.

On similar nontextual grounds, he readily joined the many Burger Court rulings restricting federal court intervention in pending state court proceedings (e.g., *Hicks v. Miranda* [1975]). And when a lower federal court ordered Philadelphia to establish more effective procedures for sanctioning police violations of individual rights, he spoke for the Court in narrowly construing judicial authority over local administrative discretion (*Rizzo v. Goode* [1975]). In addition, he was a consistent proponent of the use of largely prudential and judicially created standing, political question, and related doctrines limiting litigant access to the federal courts and the sorts of questions they could resolve. Despite the absence of a textual basis for his position, he also supported absolute immunity from lawsuits based on official conduct not only for the president but for cabinet officers and presidential aides as well (*Butz v. Economou* [1978]; *Harlow v. Fitzgerald* [1982]). It is debatable, moreover, whether his adherence to a strict doctrine of separation of powers—as evidenced by his vote with the Court in *Buckley v. Valeo* (1976), invalidating a provision for congressional involvement in the selection of members of the Federal Election Commission, an executive body, and in *Bowsher v. Synar* (1986), striking down an executive role in national budget-balancing efforts for the comptroller general, a legislative office—had a firm basis in constitutional text.

Rehnquist's conservative political ideology as well as his positivist jurisprudence appeared to influence his reaction to many other issues before the Burger Court. A vigorous opponent of the exclusionary rule and *Miranda* doctrine, he consistently supported exceptions to their application as well as expansion of the circumstances under which warrantless searches were permissible. Speaking for the Court in *New York v. Quarles* (1984), for example, he announced yet another exception to the *Miranda* requirements, holding that police may question a suspect without administering the usual warnings where necessary to prevent an imminent threat to public safety. In *United States v. Robinson* (1973), moreover, he spoke for the Court in sustaining police authority to conduct a warrantless search incident to arrest, even in cases involving traffic or other petty offenses that provided no basis for suspicion the person arrested was armed or concealing drugs or other criminal evidence.

Rehnquist assumed an equally conservative stance in First Amendment cases. Convinced that the Court was reading into the amendment's religious establishment provision a requirement of undue separation of church and state its framers would have neither recognized nor tolerated, he argued that the clause was intended only to prevent government preference for particular religions (e.g., *Wallace v. Jaffree* [1985]). He also opposed the Court's extension of constitutional protection to commercial speech and was particularly scornful of the majority's decision striking down restrictions on the advertisement of contraceptives; the framers, he declared, would never have considered such expression entitled to constitutional protection (*Carey v. Population Services International* [1977]). In various contexts he favored a broad construction of the view that only governmental, or state, action was subject to constitutional oversight. He refused, for example, to equate the activity of a private club (*Moose Lodge v. Irvis* [1972]) and utility company (*Jackson v. Metropolitan Edison Co.* [1974]) with state action, even though both were subject to considerable state regulation.

The Ford Appointment

President Nixon's ignoble 1974 departure from the White House denied him the chance to place another William Rehnquist on the Court, and President Ford's only selection to the high bench was neither particularly conservative nor doctrinaire.

John Paul Stevens

The Chicago family into which John Paul Stevens was born in 1920 as the youngest of four sons was wealthy and prominent. Among his father's holdings were the city's LaSalle and Stevens Hotels, and although the family lost much of its wealth (including the Stevens Hotel) during the depression, they retained a comfortable lifestyle in their large home on the University of Chicago campus and a summer house in Michigan. A precocious youth who, according to one of his brothers, at age six could play bridge better than most adults, John Paul attended the university's high school, then the university itself, graduating Phi Beta Kappa in 1941. The next year he joined the navy. Serving from 1942 to 1945, he was stationed in Washington, where he was an intelligence officer on the staff of Admiral Chester W. Nimitz, working with a group assigned to break Japanese codes.

After the war Stevens enrolled in law school at Northwestern University in Chicago, becoming coeditor of the law review and graduating first in his class. Following a year as clerk to Supreme Court Justice Wiley Rutledge in 1947–1948, he joined a Chicago firm, where he developed an expertise in antitrust law. In 1951 and 1952, he returned briefly to Washington for service as associate counsel on a House judiciary subcommittee investigating monopolies. In 1952 he became a partner in a Chicago firm he helped to found. He also lectured on antitrust law at Northwestern in 1953 and at the University of Chicago in 1954–1955.

In 1969, as noted in the previous chapter, Stevens returned to public service as general counsel to an Illinois commission investigating judicial corruption. The next year, with the sponsorship of Illinois senator Charles Percy, President Nixon appointed him to a seat on the Court of Appeals for the Seventh Circuit, on which he served for five years, developing a solid judicial reputation.

Stevens's first judicial opinion on the circuit bench was a dissent from a decision of the full court of appeals affirming the Wisconsin legislature's summary contempt conviction of Father John E. Groppi, a leader in the antiwar movement, for disruption of a legislative session. Stevens contended that Father Groppi should have been given notice of the charges and an opportunity to respond. In *Groppi v. Leslie* (1972), the Supreme Court overruled the circuit majority, vindicating Stevens's stance in the case. Except in responding to search and seizure claims, however, he typically supported the police in criminal procedure cases, and his circuit record in general was difficult to categorize, his votes and opinions closely tied to the facts of particular cases.

When Justice Douglas's declining health forced his retirement in 1975, Stevens was in an optimum position to become Douglas's successor. Not only had he developed the sort of moderate circuit court record that was likely to appeal to a president pursuing a politics of harmony in the wake of the divisiveness of the Nixon adminis-

John Paul Stevens (Joseph Bailey, National Geographic Society, Collection of the Supreme Court of the United States)

tration, but he was also the longtime friend of Edward H. Levi, President Ford's attorney general and dean of the University of Chicago Law School during Stevens's years as a lecturer there. After the ABA assigned Stevens its highest rating, the Senate Judiciary Committee voted unanimously to approve his nomination. On December 17, 1975, the full Senate followed suit, voting 98–0 to confirm.

Although he ultimately would become one of the most liberal justices on the Rehnquist Court, Justice Stevens was something of a judicial maverick (or "Lone Ranger," as he was often called) from the beginning of his tenure on the high bench. In his first full term alone, he wrote far more concurring and dissenting opinions than any other justice, filing seventeen concurrences and twenty-seven dissents; he joined dissents without also writing a separate opinion on only two occasions. Apparently uninterested in building voting or philosophical alliances, Stevens often embraced a different rationale for his votes than that of the justices he joined. As one of the Court's more gifted writers, moreover, he frequently attacked his colleagues' positions in pointed and caustic terms. Nor did Stevens hesitate to back changes in procedure he thought might improve the quality and efficiency of the Court's work. Not only did he favor elimination of the rule of four, under which a minority of the nine justices could have a case brought up for review on a writ of certiorari, but he also was one of the few justices who favored creation of an intermediate tribunal to assist the Court in screening cases for possible review.

With a support rate of nearly 60 percent, Stevens could be characterized as a reasonably strong defender of civil liberties claims on the Burger Court, albeit with notable exceptions. Although he wrote few of the Court's opinions in religious establishment and free exercise cases, he was one of the stronger advocates for strict separation of church and state. In *Wallace v. Jaffree* (1985), for example, he spoke for the majority in striking down an Alabama law that set aside a moment of silence for prayer and meditation in the public schools, dismissing the argument of Justice Rehnquist, among others, that the establishment clause was intended only to prohibit government preference for particular sects.

In free speech and press cases, Stevens ranked different forms of expression, assigning a relatively low priority especially to sexually oriented material. Motivated in part by such thinking, he spoke for the Court in *Young v. American Mini Theatres* (1976), upholding special zoning restrictions on adult businesses; *FCC v. Pacifica Foundation* (1978), sustaining federal authority over offensive daytime radio broadcasts easily accessible to children; and *New York v. Ferber* (1982), affirming broad state power over erotic material depicting children. Emphasizing the First Amendment's core function in safeguarding political speech, he observed in *Young* that "[f]ew of us would march our sons and daughters off to war to preserve the citizen's right to see 'Specified Sexual Activities' in the theater of our choice" (p. 70). But Stevens questioned the wisdom of the emphasis on criminal prosecutions as a weapon against obscenity and urged a fundamental reexamination of the obscenity formula established in *Miller v. California* (1973). He appeared particularly concerned with the obligation of courts under *Miller* to determine the offensiveness of erotica, whether under a "national" or "local" standard (*Smith v. United States* [1977]).

Although he joined decisions that included commercial speech within the realm of protected expression, he also thought it important that the commercial speech concept not be assigned an unduly broad scope, since it enjoyed less protection than most other forms of expression (*Central Hudson Gas v. Public Service Commission* [1980]). To a greater degree than the majority, moreover, Stevens was willing to recognize a media right of access to public facilities traditionally closed to the public. He concurred in the Court's decision in *Richmond Newspapers, Inc. v. Virginia* (1980), upholding the right of the public (and press) to attend criminal trials, absent important interests justifying a closed proceeding. And earlier, when the Court rejected media claims of a right to visit portions of prisons not open to the public and interview inmates, he dissented, urging reasonable press access as a means of promoting public confidence in the penal system (e.g., *Houchins v. KQED* [1978]).

With his distaste for doctrinaire approaches to constitutional issues, Stevens favored a general balancing of competing interests in equal protection cases rather than application of varying standards of review for different types of discrimination. He filed a concurrence, for example, in *Craig v. Boren* (1976), when the Court applied an intermediate standard of judicial review to gender classifications and struck down a state law permitting young women to purchase beer at an earlier age than young men. "There is only one Equal Protection Clause," declared Stevens. "It does not direct the courts to apply one standard of review in some cases and a different standard in other cases" (pp. 211–212). The question for Stevens in the case was whether the state's defense of the challenged law as a traffic safety regulation was sufficient to justify the discrimination at issue. Finding it difficult to believe the law had actually reduced drunken driving or was based on anything more than a stereotypical attitude about the relative maturity of young men and women, the justice concluded that the statute violated equal protection.

He pursued a similar course in racial discrimination cases. Although contending in the *Bakke* case that Title VII of the 1964 Civil Rights Act imposed a flat ban on all race-conscious policies in federally funded programs, he refused to agree that all affirmative action programs were inherently unconstitutional. He filed a vigorous dissent in *Fullilove v. Klutznick* (1980), when a majority upheld a congressional statute setting aside 10 percent of federal public works contracts for minority businesses. But unlike Stewart and Rehnquist, who also dissented, Stevens stressed the lack of legislative findings of discrimination in such transactions and also questioned whether nonblack minority groups had suffered a history of discrimination sufficient to warrant the special treatment the law provided.

Stevens followed a similar flexible approach in substantive due process cases but was almost as likely to find a constitutional violation in such suits as Justices Brennan and Marshall. Although not on the Court when *Roe v. Wade* was decided, he accepted *Roe* and joined decisions invalidating certain abortion restrictions but not others. He saw no constitutional problem, for example, with a parental consent requirement for minors (*Planned Parenthood v. Danforth* [1976]). And in *H. L. v. Matheson* (1981), he concurred when the Court upheld a law requiring parental notification (but not consent) before a minor could obtain an abortion. He also joined *Maher v. Roe* (1977), sustaining a state law allowing the use of Medicaid funds for therapeutic, or medically necessary, abortions, but not for elective abortions. But when a majority in *Harris v. McRae* (1980) upheld a version of the federal Hyde amendment, which forbids government funding even of most therapeutic abortions for indigent women, Stevens dissented, finding the state's interest in fetal life insufficient to justify the denial of abortion funding when other necessary medical procedures were covered. In a dissent from the Court's *Bowers* decision, upholding a state sodomy ban as applied to homosexual conduct, he emphasized, moreover, that the Georgia statute at issue in the case did not distinguish between homosexual and heterosexual conduct. State intrusion on the privacy of either, he declared, was constitutionally forbidden.

In criminal justice cases, Stevens was much more likely than Justices Brennan and Marshall to support the government, but he supported criminal procedure claims in most cases, especially during Chief Justice Burger's last four terms. Although Stevens spoke for the Court in *United States v. Ross* (1982), broadening the permissible scope of warrantless searches to an unprecedented degree, he generally favored an expansive interpretation of search and seizure rights. He authored the Court's opinion, for example, in *Payton v. New York* (1980), which required a warrant for routine arrests of suspects in their homes, and he opposed the good-faith exception to the search warrant requirement recognized in *United States v. Leon* (1984). An opponent also of decisions creating exceptions to the *Miranda* doctrine, he was particularly scornful of the Court's conclusion in *Rhode Island v. Innis* (1980) that a police exchange with a suspect had not constituted "interrogation" subject to the *Miranda* requirements. Under the majority's approach, complained Stevens, police interrogation appeared limited to situations in which statements to a suspect were "punctuated with a question mark" (p. 312).

The First Woman Justice

Justice Stevens was Gerald Ford's only appointee to the Supreme Court, and President Carter had no opportunities to fill vacancies on the high bench. Justice Potter

Stewart's retirement in 1981, however, gave President Reagan his first and only chance to fill a seat on the Burger Court, although he later would not only elevate William Rehnquist to the tribunal's center seat but also appoint Antonin Scalia and Anthony Kennedy to the Rehnquist Court.

Sandra Day O'Connor

Reagan's selection of Sandra Day O'Connor as his first appointee enabled the new president to fulfill his campaign promise to choose the first woman justice and at the same time add a generally conservative voice to the Court, as well as a justice deeply committed to promoting the position of the states in the federal system. The oldest of three children, O'Connor was born in El Paso, Texas, in 1930 but spent most of her early life in southeastern Arizona on her father's 155,000-acre Lazy B Ranch, which her grandfather, a Vermont native, had founded thirty years before Arizona became a state. Growing up in that rugged setting, Sandra quickly learned to ride horseback, round up cattle, and drive a truck and tractor, repairing windmills and fences and performing other chores as her contribution to ranch operations.

Anxious for their daughter to secure a better education than available in the area's rural schools, Sandra's parents sent her at age five to live with her maternal grandmother in El Paso, where she attended the Radford School for girls. Homesick for the Lazy B, she returned to the ranch at age thirteen to attend school at Lordsburg, New Mexico. Because the school was 20 miles away, she was obliged to leave home before dawn and return after dark; that experience left her with an abiding concern about the adverse effects of lengthy school bus rides on a child's education. The next year she returned to El Paso for another year at Radford, then finished high school in Austin.

Following high school, O'Connor entered Stanford University, majoring in economics and graduating with honors in 1950. Two years later she received a law degree at Stanford; she was third in the class behind her future Supreme Court colleague William Rehnquist, the class valedictorian. After graduation she interviewed with firms in the Los Angeles and San Francisco area, but with no luck. Although an honor graduate and member of the law review board at one of the nation's more prestigious law schools, she received only one offer: The Los Angeles firm in which future Reagan attorney general William French Smith was a senior partner was willing to hire her as a legal secretary. She ultimately took a job as deputy county attorney in San Mateo, California, while her husband, John O'Connor, the son of a San Francisco physician she had met at Stanford, finished his law degree. When John joined the army judge advocate general's corps, serving three years in Frankfurt, Germany, O'Connor found a position there as a civilian lawyer with the Quartermaster Corps.

After military service the couple settled in Phoenix. John O'Connor would become a senior partner in a major local firm. Sandra established a solo practice in a

Sandra Day O'Connor (Dane Penland, Smithsonian Institution, Collection of the Supreme Court of the United States)

Phoenix suburb but devoted most of her time in the early years to raising their three sons and to civic affairs, including service on the county board of zoning adjustments, as a member of a governor's committee on marriage and the family, and as a volunteer in a school for blacks and Hispanics. She also held offices in the local GOP. Later, as noted in the previous chapter, she became a member of and Republican leader in the Arizona Senate, where she had a generally conservative but mixed voting record, even on abortion issues.

In 1974 O'Connor moved to the judicial branch of state government, winning a hard-fought election to a seat on the Maricopa County superior court. On the trial bench, she developed a reasonably tough reputation in criminal cases and imposed at least one death sentence but also demonstrated concern over prison conditions. After she resisted pressure to run against Democrat Bruce Babbitt in Arizona's 1978 gubernatorial election, Babbitt made her his first appointee to the Arizona court of appeals. In 1980 the state bar association ranked her only eighth among ten appellate judges. But 90 percent of the bar recommended her retention on the appeals court seat.

O'Connor's appellate record provided little inkling of her possible reaction to many of the controversial issues confronting the Burger Court. But her off-the-bench statements, as well as her legislative record, offered the Reagan administration cause for optimism that she favored further restrictions on national judicial power and deference to the states in federal-state conflicts. However great an obstacle her gender had posed for her early career development, moreover, it was obviously no problem for a president bent on appointing the first woman justice. Despite the opposition of antiabortion leaders concerned about her ambivalent state senate record on abortion legislation, all but one member of the Judiciary Committee voted to approve her nomination to replace Justice Stewart. On September 22, 1981, ninety-one members of the full Senate concurred with the committee's recommendation.

During her five terms on the Burger Court, Justice O'Connor clearly demonstrated the high priority she accorded state sovereignty in conflicts over national and local authority. Although she had not yet joined the Court when the *Usery* case was decided, she vigorously dissented when the 5–4 *Garcia* majority overruled *Usery* and sustained congressional power to impose regulations on state and local governments, leaving the correction of alleged congressional excesses once again largely to the political process. Joined by Justices Powell and Rehnquist, O'Connor exclaimed in dissent that

> [t]he true "essence" of federalism is that the States *as States* have legitimate interests which the National Government is bound to respect even though its laws are supreme. . . . If federalism so conceived . . . is to remain meaningful, this Court cannot abdicate its constitutional responsibility to oversee the Federal Government's compliance with its duty to respect the legitimate interests of the States. (p. 581)

Earlier O'Connor, joined by Burger and Rehnquist, had also dissented when a majority in *Federal Energy Regulatory Commission v. Mississippi* (1982) upheld provisions of a federal statute designed to reduce the nation's dependence on foreign oil in part by directing state utility commissions to "consider" adoption of federal rate and regulatory standards. Such "conscription" of state agencies to carry out federal policies, she declared, unduly interfered with state sovereignty.

O'Connor's opinion for the Court in *Michigan v. Long* (1983), however, seemed to reflect more opposition to expansions in the scope of individual rights than high regard for state courts in the federal system. Under an aspect of the abstention doctrine, the Supreme Court normally will refuse to decide federal legal issues raised in an appeal of a state court decision if the lower court ruling rested on an adequate and independent state law rather than a federal claim. The ultimate outcome of such a case would depend, after all, on the state law issue, however the Supreme Court might rule on federal questions raised in the case. In *Long* the Michigan Supreme Court had overturned an automobile search on both Fourth Amendment grounds and a comparable search and seizure guarantee in the state's constitution. Speaking for the majority, Justice O'Connor announced that the Court would now presume that such decisions rested primarily on federal rather than state grounds, absent a "plain statement" in the lower court's opinion that the decision was mainly based on state law. Following that approach, she then concluded that the state court decision was based on federal rather than state law and reversed the lower court's finding of an unconstitutional search and seizure. Given O'Connor's strong commitment to state authority, it was somewhat ironic that she would join, indeed author, an opinion expanding Supreme Court review of federal issues raised in state cases, as *Long* appeared to do. *Long* is perhaps more accurately viewed, however, as simply another Burger Court decision reflecting hostility to further expansion of individual rights, for it permits the Supreme Court to reject a federal constitutional claim that a state court has upheld under a state constitutional counterpart, unless the state court has made clear its decision rested on state law.

Although rarely assigned to write important majority opinions during Chief Justice Burger's tenure, O'Connor contributed considerably to doctrinal debates in a number of significant and controversial areas. Like several of her colleagues, she was very uncomfortable with the three-part religious establishment test announced in *Lemon v. Kurtzman* (1971), invalidating church-state relationships unless they had a secular purpose and a primary effect that neither advanced nor harmed religion, while also avoiding an excessive governmental entanglement with religion. O'Connor provided the crucial fifth vote in *Lynch v. Donnelly* (1984), which upheld a city's right to set up a nativity scene in its downtown shopping district as part of a seasonal display that included secular symbols of Christmas. In a separate concurrence, she rejected the *Lemon* analysis of establishment issues, proposing instead that government ties with religion be held to violate the establishment clause only if they intended or were perceived to endorse religion. O'Connor's approach prompted her to uphold certain forms of government contact with religion and reject others. She dissented, for example, in *Aguilar v. Felton* (1985), when the Court invalidated assignment of public school teachers to religious schools. (In *Agostini v. Felton* [1997] a Rehnquist Court majority embraced her position, overturning *Aguilar.*)

O'Connor also opposed the trimester formula for evaluating abortion controls that Justice Blackmun had announced for the Court in the *Roe* case. Instead, she preferred a more general standard under which the courts could forbid only those abortion regulations that imposed an "undue burden" on a woman's decision to obtain an abortion at any stage of a pregnancy. Dissenting in *Akron v. Akron Center for Reproductive Health* (1983), she complained that the *Roe* trimester construct was an unworkable legal standard, given continuing advances in medical technology. Under *Roe* no compelling interest justified any regulation of abortions during the first trimester (or approximately three months) of a pregnancy. Health risks to the mother justified reasonable regulation of abortion procedures during the second trimester, and during the third trimester, the period from which a fetus becomes viable (or capable of surviving independent of the womb) to term, the state's compelling interest in fetal life justified a ban on nontherapeutic abortions. But improvements in medical technology, declared O'Connor, were constantly modifying the timeline on which the trimester approach largely depended, reducing the previability stage of a pregnancy while also substantially eliminating the health risks abortions posed for the mother at every stage of a pregnancy. The more flexible undue-burden standard O'Connor advocated would, she believed, avoid such problems. When the Rehnquist Court reaffirmed the "essence" of *Roe* in *Planned Parenthood v. Casey* (1992), a plurality of justices adopted O'Connor's approach.

In criminal justice cases, O'Connor pursued a generally conservative course. She usually joined decisions creating exceptions to the Fourth Amendment exclusionary rule and *Miranda* doctrine and rejected most death penalty challenges. She objected, however, to the "public safety" exception to *Miranda* announced in *New York v. Quarles* (1984). In the First Amendment field, she wrote a number of rulings narrowing the concept of the "public forum," thereby restricting the scope of protected expression (e.g., *Cornelius v. NAACP Legal Defense and Educational Fund* [1985]). She also joined decisions restricting erotic expression and, in *Hudnut v. American Booksellers Association* (1986), supported full Court review of an Indianapolis ordinance that allowed women to seek damages from pornography distributors when they were the victims of sex crimes, while the majority summarily affirmed a lower court decision striking down the controversial law.

O'Connor's opinion for the Court in *Mississippi University for Women v. Hogan* (1982) was her most significant pronouncement in Burger Court equal protection cases. Applying the intermediate standard of scrutiny first adopted for gender discrimination in *Craig v. Boren* (1976), she found no substantial interest that justified the university's policy of keeping men out of its nursing school. In fact, emphasizing that the challenged policy simply reinforced the stereotype of nursing as an exclusively female profession, she expressed doubt that it could even satisfy the lenient, rational basis standard of review. O'Connor refused, however, to join other justices in declaring gender, like race, a suspect classification subject to strictest judicial scrutiny. She developed an equally moderate and flexible stance in racial cases, including affirmative action litigation. Like Justices Blackmun, Powell, and Stevens, therefore, she only partially fulfilled the expectations of the Nixon-Reagan constitutional agenda—albeit to a greater degree than her three colleagues in many issue areas.

References

Eisler, K. I. *A Justice for All: William J. Brennan, Jr.* New York: Simon & Schuster, 1994.

Lamb, Charles M., and Stephen C. Halpern, eds. *The Burger Court: Political and Judicial Profiles*. Chicago: University of Illinois Press, 1991.

3

Major Decisions

W hen Richard Nixon was able to replace four Supreme Court justices before the end of his first term in office, it was widely expected that many of the Warren Court's rulings would be short-lived. Such expectations were largely unfulfilled: The Burger Court's decisions generally kept faith with those of the Warren era. Highlighting the Burger Court's continuity with the past, however, obscures its important contributions to the development of American constitutional law—contributions both narrowing and expanding the scope of civil liberties, clarifying relationships among the branches of the national government, and setting the stage for later debates over the nature of federal-state relations that were to play such a prominent role in Rehnquist Court decision-making. This chapter examines major decisional trends on the Burger Court.

The Scope of Judicial Power

Warren-era precedents considerably expanded litigant access to the federal courts and the sorts of issues they were permitted to resolve. Most civil liberties guarantees, for example, forbid only governmental, or state, action, not private interferences with the freedoms they protect. But the Warren Court regularly extended such constitutional safeguards to private activities found to be significantly connected with government or to possess a "public" character. The rules limiting litigants' standing to sue in federal courts were also relaxed. In *Frothingham v. Mellon* (1923), the Supreme Court had held that the tax burden a national taxpayer shares with millions of other citizens posed insufficiently direct and substantial personal injury to constitute standing to challenge a federal spending program claimed to interfere with state authority under the Tenth Amendment. But in *Flast v. Cohen* (1968), the Warren Court, speaking through the chief justice, granted federal-taxpayer standing to litigants who attacked an exercise of Congress's taxing and spending authority claimed to violate a specific constitutional limitation on such power—in *Flast* a program of federal aid to religious schools said to violate the First

Amendment's ban on laws respecting an establishment of religion. Over the vigorous dissents of Justices Felix Frankfurter and John Marshall Harlan, moreover, the Warren Court rejected contentions that legislative malapportionment raised nonjusticiable, political issues (*Baker v. Carr* [1962]), substantially curtailing the "political question" doctrine previously used to keep a variety of sensitive issues out of the federal courts.

Yet particularly during the early years of Chief Justice Burger's tenure, the Burger Court restricted litigant and issue access to the federal judiciary. Over the dissents of Warren Court holdovers William J. Brennan and Byron R. White, joined by Nixon appointee Harry Blackmun, the Court dismissed a challenge by Arizona senator Barry Goldwater and other members of Congress to President Jimmy Carter's termination of the mutual defense treaty with Taiwan without Senate approval or consultation. A plurality of four justices, speaking through Justice William H. Rehnquist, rested their decision on political question grounds, while Justice Lewis F. Powell, noting that Congress had not yet confronted the president regarding his abrogation of the treaty, concluded that the dispute was not yet sufficiently developed, or "ripe," for judicial decision (*Goldwater v. Carter* [1979]).

The treaty case hardly signaled a reflowering of the political question doctrine, especially since it dealt with sensitive foreign affairs issues traditionally considered inappropriate for judicial review. In other areas, however, the Burger Court imposed potentially significant limitations on the sorts of litigants and issues the justices were willing to confront. Narrowly construing the conditions under which ostensibly private activities become state action for constitutional purposes, the Court, in *Moose Lodge v. Irvis* (1972), declined to subject to equal protection requirements a private club's refusal to serve the African American guest of a club member at its bar. The mere fact that the club was licensed to sell liquor and otherwise subject to state liquor regulations, Justice Rehnquist concluded for a 6–3 majority, did not amount to official support of the racial discrimination at issue in the case. Justice Douglas, joined by Justice Marshall, contended in dissent, however, that a state-imposed liquor license quota, filled for years in Harrisonburg, Pennsylvania, where the case arose, had the effect of restricting African American access to liquor in an area where liquor was available only in private clubs during much of each week. In a separate dissent, Justice Brennan, also joined by Justice Marshall, found the significant connection between Pennsylvania's liquor regulations and the club's discriminatory policies sufficient to justify a finding of state action in the case.

Douglas, Brennan, and Marshall were again in dissent when in 1974 the Court, speaking through Justice Rehnquist, rejected the claim of a Pennsylvania resident that a utility company violated her due process rights when it terminated her service without adequate notice or a hearing. Although the company enjoyed a state-created partial monopoly, was subject to extensive regulation, and provided services often handled by government directly, Rehnquist concluded that it was a private entity immune from due process requirements (*Jackson v. Metropolitan Edison Co.* [1974]).

The Burger Court also narrowly construed, then overturned, one of the Warren era's most controversial state-action decisions in the free expression field. In *Marsh v. Alabama* (1946), the Court, speaking through Justice Hugo Black, had held that a privately owned company town possessed all the attributes of any other municipality, save public ownership, and thus was subject to First Amendment requirements. The Warren Court's ruling in *Amalgamated Food Employees v. Logan Valley Plaza* (1968) extended *Marsh* to shopping center property over the vigorous dissent of Justice Black. A First Amendment absolutist, Black thought people had an unconditional right to engage in expression, but only where they had a right to be for such purposes. The company town involved in *Marsh* possessed all the attributes of a town and thus, in the justice's opinion, was subject to First Amendment requirements. But Black considered the shopping center a strange-looking town indeed. Requiring one to open its facilities to those wishing to engage in expression on its premises thus amounted, he contended, to state infringement on private property without due process of law.

Black's position ultimately prevailed. The Burger Court's decision in *Lloyd Corporation v. Tanner* (1972) confined *Logan Valley* largely to its facts, holding that shopping center property had First Amendment obligations only when (1) the expression at issue related to the facility's operations and (2) no alternative means of access to shopping center customers were available to would-be speakers and picketers. Justice Powell's opinion for the Court emphasized, moreover, the private property rights Justice Black had extolled in his *Logan Valley* dissent. It was hardly surprising, therefore, when the Court a few years later announced that *Lloyd Corporation* had in effect overruled *Logan Valley* (*Hudgens v. NLRB* [1976]).

The mootness and standing doctrines were other major tools the Burger Court invoked to limit litigant access to federal judges. Article III, the Constitution's judicial article, limits federal courts to deciding "cases or controversies." Drawing on this provision and on prudential considerations cautioning against undue judicial encroachment on the other branches and levels of government, the Supreme Court historically has held that federal courts cannot hear cases that have already been resolved, or rendered "moot," by circumstances or those in which litigants lack "standing to sue"—that is, cases in which parties fail to allege a direct and substantial injury to personal legal rights and interests or are unable to convince a court that it can provide meaningful relief for the harm the defendant is claimed to have caused. In *DeFunis v. Odegaard* (1974), the Court invoked the mootness doctrine to postpone its first ruling on the intractable affirmative action issue. Mario DeFunis filed suit when he was denied admission to the University of Washington's law school even though his academic credentials exceeded those of a number of minority applicants admitted under the school's preferential admissions program. While the case was in the courts, however, DeFunis attended law school under a lower court order and was about to graduate when his case reached the Supreme Court. A 5–4 majority dismissed his claims as moot, while dissenters emphasized that DeFunis had not yet graduated and could be dismissed were the Court not to decide his case, especially since the state had prevailed in the Washington supreme court.

The Burger Court was particularly expansive in its construction of the standing limitation on access to the judiciary. A number of its rulings were generous to plaintiffs. Two 1970 decisions, *Data Processing v. Camp* and *Barlow v. Collins*, gave a broad construction, for example, to the standing provisions of the federal Administrative Procedure Act (APA), under which litigants challenge the lawfulness of federal agency actions. Especially in cases arising under such statutes, the Court had also emphasized that a claim to standing may be based on aesthetic, environmental, and related interests, as well as economic injury. In *Sierra Club v. Morton* (1972), the Court did dismiss a challenge to a proposed ski resort in a national forest on the ground that the environmental group had alleged injury only to the environment, not to the personal interests of the organization and its members. But that hurdle proved relatively minor the next year when, in *United States v. SCRAP* (1973), several law students challenging a federal policy claimed to inhibit commercial use of recycled products were granted standing based on their claim that the disputed regulation (authorizing a surcharge on freight shipments) interfered with their enjoyment of nature.

Usually, though, the Court gave the standing doctrine an exceptionally restrictive reading. In 1973 the justices denied standing to the mother of an illegitimate child contesting the constitutionality of a Texas child support statute that consistently had been construed to apply only to the parents of legitimate children (*Linda R.S. v. Richard D.* [1973]). Justice Marshall, the author, surprisingly, of the Court's opinion, agreed that the appellant had suffered an injury as a result of the failure of her child's father to provide support payments. But he contended that the fixed penalty state law provided in such cases (as opposed to an indefinite jail sentence for civil contempt to induce compliance) would not necessarily assure that the father would meet his support obligations. Although in the Court's judgment the justices' intervention might thus have proved fruitless, Justice White expressed surprise in dissent at the majority's assumption that the threat of criminal punishment would have a doubtful impact on a person's conduct. "I had always thought," declared White, that "our civilization had assumed that the threat of penal sanctions had something more than a 'speculative' effect on a person's conduct" (p. 621).

In *Warth v. Seldin* (1975), one of the Court's most significant pronouncements on the reach of the personal injury standard, a majority denied standing to various litigants who claimed that the restrictive zoning ordinance of Penfield, a Rochester, New York, suburb, effectively prevented construction of housing for persons of low and moderate income. Low-income plaintiffs of Rochester, Justice Powell observed for the majority, had failed to establish, for example, a causal relationship between the town's zoning requirements and their claimed injury, and members of a nonprofit corporation interested in housing problems had not recently applied for a zoning variance permitting them to construct housing for persons with moderate incomes. But in an elaborate dissent joined by Justices White and Marshall, Justice Brennan scored the majority for failing to recognize the "interwoven interests" of several sets of plaintiffs in the case—interests that, taken together, warranted a grant of standing. The absence of recent attempts to secure a zoning variance merely underscored for Brennan the success of Penfield's exclusionary policies.

But the Burger Court did not invariably dismiss zoning challenges on standing grounds. At issue in *Village of Arlington Heights v. Metropolitan Housing Development Corp.* (1977) was a restrictive suburban zoning scheme very similar to the one at issue in *Warth*. Although ultimately rejecting constitutional and statutory challenges to the ordinance, the Court granted standing both to a developer seeking to construct a racially integrated low-income housing project and to one of its prospective tenants. The developer's project was contingent on its ability to obtain financing and qualify for federal subsidies. The Court thus easily could have concluded, as it had in *Warth*, that the impact of court-ordered rezoning upon the success of the proposed project was entirely too speculative to warrant a grant of standing. But since a specific proposed project was involved, the Court, speaking again through Justice Powell, found the case distinguishable from *Warth*.

The Court was more consistent in responding negatively to federal litigants who sought standing as "private attorneys general," claiming a right as citizens, voters, or taxpayers to judicial relief for injuries to the constitutional polity rather than for harms of a distinctly personal nature. Although occasionally straining, as in *SCRAP,* to find concrete personal injury in order to grant such plaintiffs standing, the Court's policy was one of opposition to public action lawsuits unless authorized by Congress and otherwise consistent with Article III's case or controversy requirements.

The Court's opposition to such suits was most clearly reflected in its decisions rejecting an expansive reading of the Warren Court's ruling in *Flast v. Cohen* (1968). As noted earlier, *Flast* relaxed the long-standing *Frothingham* rule against federal taxpayer suits, with Chief Justice Warren holding for the majority that taxpayers as taxpayers possessed the required personal stake in the outcome of a lawsuit if the federal law they challenged was an exercise of Congress's taxing and spending authority and was claimed to violate a specific constitutional limitation on that power. In a masterful *Flast* dissent, Justice Harlan pointed out that the conditions Warren had announced bore no relationship whatever to the degree of injury caused a particular taxpayer in a given case—the essence of the standing limit on access to the courts. The Court was simply—and improperly, in Harlan's judgment—embracing a right of litigants to file public interest suits without satisfying the traditional require-ment of discrete, personal injury to their interests.

Although it never formally overruled *Flast*, the Burger Court made clear that it would be limited largely to its facts. In *United States v. Richardson* (1974), a plain-tiff had sought standing as a citizen voter and taxpayer to challenge secret congres-sional funding of the CIA, a practice claimed to violate the provision of the Constitution requiring Congress to provide a periodic statement and account of con-gressional appropriations. Chief Justice Burger concluded for the majority that cre-ation and support of the CIA were not primarily exercises of Congress's taxing and spending powers; *Flast* was thus inapplicable. That day the chief justice took the same position in dismissing for lack of standing the long-established practice permit-ting members of Congress to serve in the military reserves, which challengers attacked as violating the Constitution's incompatibility clause, prohibiting them from holding other federal offices during their congressional tenure (*Schlesinger v. Reservists Committee to Stop the War* [1974]).

Burger was even less supportive of the litigants' claims to standing as citizen voters. In the CIA case, Richardson had claimed, for example, that secret funding of the agency made it more difficult for citizens to cast an intelligent vote in elections involving congressional incumbents seeking reelection. Rejecting such reasoning, Burger pointed out that federal courts historically had heard only disputes involving allegations of concrete personal injury; allowing plaintiffs to air abstract claims based only on the generalized interests of all citizens would unduly expand and distort the role of the courts, creating the potential for abuse of the judicial process. The plain-tiffs had argued that the practices at issue in the two cases could not be challenged without recognition of citizen or taxpayer standing; after all, no litigant could estab-lish direct, personal injury of the traditional sort in such cases. The chief justice had a ready response: "Our system of government leaves many crucial decisions to the political process" (p. 227).

Dissenters in both cases urged acceptance of a more flexible approach to stand-ing, and the ease with which the Court found traditional standing requirements satis-fied in the *SCRAP* case suggested that the difference between the "abstract" claims raised by public interest plaintiffs and the "concrete adverseness" alleged in tradi-tional suits might be more apparent than real. The majority's stance further reflected, however, the Burger Court's reluctance to expand litigant access to the judicial process.

Nor was its position limited to constitutional and prudential considerations. Although recognizing that Congress could confer standing in types of cases for which satisfaction of traditional standing requirements might be lacking, the Court often narrowly construed congressional statutes designed to broaden access to the federal judiciary. In *Eisen v. Carlisle* (1974), for example, it gave a restrictive interpretation to the rules governing class action damage suits in which plaintiffs seek relief for injuries not only to their own rights but also to those of all similarly situated persons (members of the plaintiffs' class). Plaintiffs filing class action damage suits in federal court, the justices held, must seek to contact each member of their class individually, not simply post general notices in newspapers and other places. The decision erected a significant barrier to such suits. Eisen's individual stake in his challenge to a surcharge brokers imposed on small stock purchases was only $70, but individual notice by mail to the 2.25 million members of his class would have cost him $225,000.

Separation of Powers

Burger Court decisions limiting access to the federal judiciary constricted the reach of national judicial power relative to the other branches and levels of government. The Court also handed down a number of other important pronouncements regarding the separation of powers among the branches of the national government and the nature of American federalism. Its best-known separation of powers ruling was undoubtedly *United States v. Nixon* (1974), the Watergate tapes decision that forced Richard M. Nixon to become the first president ever to resign from the nation's highest office. Attempting to conceal his involvement in the cover-up of the break-in at the Democratic National Committee headquarters in Washington's Watergate office complex, as well as related wrongdoing in connection with his 1972 reelection campaign, President Nixon repeatedly invoked the doctrine of executive privilege in an effort to avoid releasing to the courts and Congress tapes of conversations in the Oval Office and other incriminating evidence. In a suit brought by Watergate special prosecutor Leon Jaworski, the Supreme Court (with Justice Rehnquist, a former member of the Nixon Department of Justice, not participating) unanimously rejected the president's claims.

Presidents since Washington had withheld information from Congress and the judiciary, but the phrase "executive privilege" and its use in defending presidential confidentiality dated back only to the Eisenhower administration of the 1950s. Even so, lawyers for President Nixon contended that executive privilege was necessary to the effective functioning of the presidency and inherent in the doctrine of separation of powers; that presidential assertions of the privilege were absolute and unreviewable by courts; and that, even if subject to some degree of judicial limitation, the doctrine should prevail over special prosecutor Jaworski's subpoena of the Watergate evidence. For his part, Jaworski contended that courts are entitled to the best evidence available in a criminal prosecution (in this case, actual tapes of conversations rather than conflicting testimony about what was said) and that he was hardly on an indiscriminate "fishing expedition" into presidential papers. Instead, he could demonstrate the relevance of each item of evidence sought.

Consistent with long tradition permitting the chief justice to assign responsibility for drafting the Court's opinion in each case in which he is part of the majority, Chief Justice Burger assigned himself the *Nixon* opinion. The initial draft Burger prepared was extremely deferential to presidential authority—and unacceptable to his colleagues. As a result, the final product, though it carried Burger's name, was not the work of the chief justice so much as a multiauthored piece.

Even so, presidential authority received considerable deference in the Court's opinion. For the first time, the Supreme Court held that executive privilege, although stated nowhere in the Constitution, was implied in executive authority and the doctrine of separation of powers. Assertions of the privilege were to be presumed valid, moreover, yielding only in the face of a demonstrated, overriding need for information in a president's possession. Citing *Marbury v. Madison* (1803), however, the Court deemed every constitutional question, including disputes over executive privilege, potentially subject to judicial review, rejecting the president's contention to the contrary. Nor could it accept Nixon's claim to an absolute privilege, acceptance of which would unduly interfere with the powers and obligations of other parts of the government. In this case, the justices concluded, the president's claim to the privilege must yield to the special prosecutor's demonstrated need for particular evidence. The president was not seeking to withhold military or diplomatic secrets, over which assertions of confidentiality were obviously entitled to great respect. Nixon had merely asserted a general interest in confidentiality necessary, he claimed, to assure the frankness of aides and others from whom he sought information and opinion. The Watergate prosecutor's interest in securing the best evidence available for a criminal prosecution clearly outweighed, in the Court's judgment, the general need for candor in presidential conversations—especially since information divulged in such sessions was always vulnerable to leaks by those present.

U.S. district judge John Sirica, the trial judge, had stayed enforcement of a subpoena against the president pending expedited Supreme Court review of the case. Now, Chief Justice Burger instructed, Sirica was to review the evidence in his chambers, eliminate that which was irrelevant or otherwise inadmissible, and release the rest to the special prosecutor. "Presidential confidentiality," added the chief justice, was to be given "the greatest protection consistent with the fair administration of justice. The need for confidentiality even as to idle conversations with associates in which casual reference might be made concerning political leaders within the country or foreign statesmen is too obvious to call for further treatment" (p. 718).

President Nixon continued in his efforts to preserve the confidentiality of White House documents and tape recordings even after his ignoble resignation from office following the Court's rejection of his privilege claims. Under an agreement executed with the administrator of the General Services Administration (GSA), neither the former president nor the GSA could gain access to his presidential materials without the other's consent. After three years Nixon would be able to withdraw any materials from the collection except the tapes; after five years the GSA was to destroy whatever tapes the former president directed, and all the tapes were to be destroyed after ten years or at Nixon's death, whichever occurred first.

Not surprisingly, Congress soon passed, and President Ford signed into law, a bill to abrogate that agreement. Under provisions of the Presidential Recordings and Materials Preservation Act, the GSA administrator was to take custody of Nixon's presidential materials, have them screened by government archivists in order to return to the former president all items of a personal and private nature, and preserve those of historical value. The preserved materials were to be made available for judicial proceedings, subject to whatever legal claims Nixon or the government might raise; and the administrator was also to develop regulations governing eventual public access to portions of the collection.

The day after the statute became law, the ex-president challenged its constitutionality in a federal district court, contending that its provisions violated the principle of separation of powers, presidential privilege, Nixon's privacy interests, his First Amendment right of association, and the Constitution's bill of attainder clause, which prohibits legislative punishment of persons without a court trial. By a 7–2 vote, the Supreme Court, speaking through Justice Brennan, rejected each of Nixon's claims (*Nixon v. Adminstrator of General Services* [1977]). Noting that the branches of the national government were not intended to operate with absolute independence from each other, Brennan found nothing in the law unduly disruptive of executive power, especially since the GSA, an executive agency, retained full control over the collection and material could be released only if no executive privilege barred disclosure.

In rejecting the contention that the law unduly interfered with presidential confidentiality, Justice Brennan pointed to provisions preserving Nixon's right to raise privilege claims and requiring the return of purely private materials to the former president. The mere screening of the collection by government archivists, a task performed for other former chief executives without any suggestion of a breach of presidential privilege, would not interfere with presidential confidentiality or the candid expression of views by presidential advisers to any greater degree, asserted Brennan, than the judicial screening upheld in the Watergate case.

Nor, in the Court's judgment, did the statute encroach upon the former president's legitimate privacy expectations. Nixon, after all, had conceded that he had personally seen no more than 200,000 of the over 40 million items in the collection; and the law's sensitivity to legitimate privacy interests, the archivists' unblemished record for discretion, and further safeguards likely to be included in forthcoming public-access regulations made the possibility of encroachment on presidential privacy marginal at best. Compelling public interests in preserving the materials clearly outweighed, moreover, the speculative chill the statute might pose on the exercise of

First Amendment associational rights. Finally, Brennan observed, the statute's reference to Nixon by name did not amount to a forbidden bill of attainder. Not only was the law clearly nonpunitive, but since the papers of former presidents were already housed in libraries, the ex-president constituted a legitimate class of one.

Chief Justice Burger and Justice Rehnquist dissented separately. Burger argued that *United States v. Nixon* had permitted incursions on executive privilege only in the face of particularized demonstrations of overwhelming public need, while the invasion of privacy condoned by the current majority appeared virtually limitless. The prohibition against bills of attainder, he added, permitted no "class" or "class of one"; yet President Nixon was being subjected to regulations applicable to no other past or future president. For his part, Justice Rehnquist would have found little constitutional significance in the case had it only involved congressional authority to dispose of President Nixon's papers. By leaving all presidential papers vulnerable to control by Congress, however, the Court's decision "pose[d] a real threat to the ability of future Presidents to receive candid advice and to give candid instructions. This result, so at odds with our previous case law on the separation of powers, will daily stand as a veritable sword of Damocles over every succeeding President and his advisers" (p. 545).

Cases arising from the Watergate scandal were not the only separation of powers disputes generated by the Nixon administration. In 1982 the former president won a major victory when a 5–4 Court ruled that presidents are absolutely immune from damage suits for any conduct falling within the "outer perimeter" of their official responsibilities. In the last days of President Lyndon B. Johnson's administration, A. Ernest Fitzgerald, a civilian analyst with the air force, testified before a congressional subcommittee about cost overruns and unexpected technical difficulties in the development of the C-5A transport plane. In January 1970 Fitzgerald's job was eliminated, ostensibly as part of a departmental reorganization and reduction in force, but President Nixon boasted privately, as revealed in the Watergate tapes, that he had given the order to "get rid of the son of a bitch." Complaining that his separation was in retaliation for his whistle-blower congressional testimony, Fitzgerald filed a suit against various Defense Department officials, White House aides, and ultimately Nixon himself. In directing dismissal of the case against the president, the Court, speaking through Justice Powell, concluded that presidents were entitled to absolute immunity from such suits, even when they knowingly and willfully violate a person's legal rights. Immunity helped to assure, declared Powell, that presidents vigorously and courageously fulfilled the responsibilities of their unique office, free from fear of such suits and the distractions they create (*Nixon v. Fitzgerald* [1982]).

Joined by Justices Brennan, Marshall, and Blackmun, Justice White argued in dissent that absolute presidential immunity stood on no firmer ground than the absolute executive privilege rejected in the tapes case. In *Butz v. Economou* (1978),

White and the other *Fitzgerald* dissenters had helped to form a majority holding that a cabinet member was entitled only to qualified immunity from damage suits, while four members of the *Fitzgerald* majority had dissented in *Butz*, arguing for absolute immunity in such cases. Presidents, White contended in *Fitzgerald*, should also be vulnerable to suit for conduct they knew, or reasonably should have realized, was contrary to a statute or the Constitution. Attaching absolute immunity to the president's office, rather than to his specific conduct, White charged, placed the president "above the law" in "a reversion to the old notion that the King can do no wrong" (p. 766).

Two Nixon aides Fitzgerald sued were not as lucky as the president they had served. Extending *Butz* to senior presidential aides, Justice Powell held for an 8–1 majority that they, like cabinet officers, were shielded from liability only if they did not knowingly interfere with legal rights or could not reasonably have been expected to know their conduct was illegal. In a brief concurrence, Justice Rehnquist, a *Butz* dissenter, assured readers that he would join any future reexamination of that ruling "with alacrity" but thought *Butz* logically extended to presidential aides. In a lone dissent, Chief Justice Burger disagreed; noting that presidential aides worked more intimately on a daily basis with the president than did cabinet members, the chief justice contended that *Butz* was distinguishable (*Harlow v. Fitzgerald* [1982]).

The Burger Court limited most other administrators to qualified immunity as well. In *Wood v. Strickland* (1975), for example, the justices held subject to suit a high school principal who dismissed without any hearing a student suspected of spiking the punch bowl at a school dance. A recent case had ruled that students were entitled to notice and some sort of opportunity to defend themselves prior to suspension from school (*Goss v. Lopez* [1975]). The principal reasonably should have known, therefore, that his summary action violated the student's legal rights. In a suit growing out of the killing of student antiwar protesters by National Guardsmen at Kent State University in 1970, moreover, the Court even rejected absolute immunity for state governors (*Scheuer v. Rhodes* [1974]).

Like state legislators and members of Congress, however, judges stand on a different footing, as the Court made clear in the bizarre case of *Stump v. Sparkman* (1978). When an Indiana mother became concerned that her "somewhat retarded" fifteen-year-old daughter might become pregnant, an obliging state circuit judge signed an order for her sterilization. At the time of the surgery, the young woman was told that her appendix was being removed. When she learned the truth following her marriage, she and her husband sued her mother, the mother's attorney, her doctors, the hospital, and the judge. Drawing on early precedent (*Bradley v. Fisher* [1871]) and finding the judge's sterilization order within the broad scope of his official duties, a 6–3 Supreme Court majority found Judge Stump absolutely immune from liability. Complete immunity for judges, Justice White concluded for the majority, was necessary to guarantee judicial independence. In a cogent dissent, Justice Stewart conceded that judicial action is clothed with absolute immunity but scored the majority's conclusion that Stump's order fell within the scope of any reasonable conception of the judicial function. "[T]he conduct of a judge," declared Stewart, "surely does not become a judicial act merely on his own say-so. A judge is not free, like a loose cannon, to inflict indiscriminate damage whenever he announces that he is acting in his judicial capacity." Ordinarily, Stewart pointedly observed, a judge's errors can be corrected on appeal or through other channels of redress. But Judge Stump's action, of course, had assured there "could be no appeal" (pp. 367, 368).

A number of Burger Court separation of powers decisions involved the relationship between national executive and legislative authority. In November 1979, Iranians seized the U.S. embassy at Tehran, capturing U.S. diplomatic personnel and holding them hostage. Attempting to secure a bargaining chip for their release, President Jimmy Carter invoked the International Economic Emergency Powers Act (IEEPA) and froze all Iranian assets within U.S. jurisdiction. Treasury Department regulations issued to enforce the president's order protected the seized assets against judgment, decree, or attachment by the federal courts.

As part of the 1981 settlement ending the hostage crisis, the United States agreed to terminate all American lawsuits involving the frozen assets, submitting such disputes instead to a special Iran–U.S. Claims Tribunal, the judgments of which were to be final and enforceable in the courts of any nation. Executive orders implementing the arrangement, which President Carter issued and President Reagan confirmed, required banks holding Iranian assets to transfer them to the federal reserve bank in New York for eventual return to Iran, but with a small portion withheld for payment of claims tribunal judgments. Dames & Moore, a U.S. company involved in litigation to attach Iranian assets, filed suit against President Reagan's treasury secretary, claiming that the settlement provisions exceeded the president's constitutional and statutory powers. But the Supreme Court, speaking through Justice Rehnquist, upheld the arrangement (*Dames & Moore v. Regan* [1981]).

During the Korean War, a 6–3 majority had overturned President Truman's seizure of the nation's steel mills, a bold venture intended to avert a strike in an industry vital to the war effort. In his opinion for the Court in the *Steel Seizure Case* (*Youngstown Co. v. Sawyer* [1952]), Justice Black required only thirteen paragraphs to invalidate Truman's action. The president's power, if any, to seize the nation's steel mills, Black reasoned, must rest either on an act of Congress or the Constitution. No congressional statute authorized the action, nor did any constitutional provision. The president was commander-in-chief of the military forces, but the United States was hardly a theater of war, and the seizure of private property was a job for the nation's lawmakers, not its military authorities. The only legislative powers the Constitution conferred on the president were those of recommending and vetoing laws, while his constitutional authority as chief executive was precisely that—the power to execute laws. In seizing the steel mills, declared Black, President Truman had both made and executed law—action clearly contrary to the Constitution and laws.

In separate opinions most members of the *Steel Seizure* majority embraced a more flexible conception of executive authority than the textbook version of separation of powers Justice Black, a constitutional literalist, had adopted in his opinion. Justice Robert H. Jackson envisioned, for example, a range or spectrum of executive authority in which the president's power was greatest when his actions were based on an express constitutional or statutory grant and most vulnerable when he went against the will of Congress.

Opting essentially for the Jackson approach, Justice Rehnquist's opinion for the *Dames & Moore* Court rejected "over-simplified" interpretations of executive power, especially in cases involving presidential "responses to international crises the nature of which Congress [could] hardly have been expected to anticipate in any detail" (p. 669). Citing precedent upholding a broad reading of presidential authority in foreign affairs (*United States v. Curtiss-Wright Corp.* [1936], *United States v. Pink* [1942]) and straining to find congressional acquiescence in the Iranian settlement, Rehnquist concluded that the IEEPA empowered the president to nullify court orders attaching the Iranian assets and that the president also had authority to suspend claims filed in U.S. courts, even though no specific statute authorized such action. Underscoring the "narrowness" of its decision, Rehnquist stressed that the Court was not recognizing plenary presidential power to settle claims against foreign governments but concluded that "[w]here, as here, the settlement of claims has been determined to be a necessary incident to the resolution of a major foreign policy dispute between our country and another, and where, as here, we can conclude that Congress acquiesced in the President's action, we are not prepared to say that the President lacks the power to settle such claims" (p. 688).

The Court was not so flexible, however, in its reaction to the favorite device used by Congress to curb executive authority. Obviously unable to legislate on every detail of governmental operations, Congress has long delegated substantial lawmaking authority to the executive branch of government. Although giving lip service to the principle that Congress cannot constitutionally delegate its legislative powers to others without violating the principle of separation of powers, the Supreme Court has long upheld such delegations so long as they include guidelines limiting the scope of executive discretion. Nor need the guidelines be very specific and detailed. The Interstate Commerce Commission (ICC) was authorized, for example, to fix "just and reasonable" rates, and the FCC could grant licenses only in the "public convenience, interest, or necessity." The Supreme Court upheld each as a properly limited delegation of rule-making authority (*Interstate Commerce Commission v. Illinois Central* [1910], *Federal Radio Commission v. Nelson* [1933]).

To maintain ultimate control over such delegations, however, Congress also had long resorted to the legislative veto. Under the legislative veto arrangement, eventually incorporated into nearly 200 statutes, the president or an executive agency planning to exercise a delegated authority was obligated first to notify one or both houses of Congress or the appropriate congressional committee, depending on the veto requirement involved. If vetoed within a certain period of time, the proposed action could not be undertaken. In this way Congress could delegate powers to the executive yet prevent their exercise in particular circumstances.

One such scheme authorized the U.S. attorney general to suspend the deportation of aliens, subject to veto by a resolution passed by either house of Congress. Jaghish Rai Chadha, an East Indian who held a British passport, was subjected to deportation proceedings after his student visa expired. An immigration judge ordered his deportation suspended, and the attorney general recommended to Congress that Chadha be allowed to remain in the United States. When the House of Representatives vetoed the recommendation, Chadha filed suit, attacking the legislative veto as unconstitutional.

The Supreme Court, by a 7–2 vote, agreed. Speaking for the majority, Chief Justice Burger held that the legislative veto violated constitutional provisions requiring that laws be passed by both houses of the bicameral Congress, then presented to the president for his review and possible veto. Burger recognized the pragmatic appeal of the "convenient shortcut" the legislative veto provided but insisted there was

> no support in the Constitution or decisions of this Court for the proposition that the cumbersomeness and delays often encountered in complying with explicit constitutional standards may be avoided, either by the Congress or by the President. . . . With all the obvious flaws of delay, untidiness, and potential for abuse, we have not yet found a better way to preserve freedom than by making the exercise of power subject to the carefully crafted restraints spelled out in the Constitution. (*INS v. Chadha* [1983])

Justice Rehnquist dissented on narrow grounds, but Justice White filed an elaborate critique of the majority's rationale. The legislative veto, White declared, was a necessary ingredient of modern government; without it,

> Congress is faced with a Hobson's choice: either to refrain from delegating the necessary authority, leaving itself with a hopeless task of writing laws with the requisite specificity to cover endless special circumstances across the entire policy landscape, or in the alternative, to abdicate its law-making function to the Executive Branch and independent agencies. To choose the former leaves major national problems unresolved; to opt for the latter risks unaccountable policymaking by those not elected to fill that role. (p. 968)

Nor, in White's judgment, had Congress invoked the veto as a device for enlarging its own power at the expense of the other governmental branches; instead, the veto was a defensive mechanism by which the legislative branch could avoid surrendering undue control of the nation's destiny to the executive. The legislative veto provided, moreover, the same safeguards against the arbitrary exercise of governmental power as those stipulated in the Constitution's lawmaking provisions. Just as laws required the approval of both houses of Congress and submission to the president for his veto or approval, the legislative veto precluded the exercise of delegated authority over the objection of either legislative chamber or, of course, the executive.

White was especially alarmed by the broad basis of the Court's decision. Had it rested on an application of general separation of powers principles to the scheme at issue in the case, the status of other legislative veto arrangements would have been left undisturbed. By declaring the concept itself invalid, however, the Court, White asserted, had sounded the "death knell" for the many other veto provisions in federal law. The ruling was thus unusually significant and alarming.

Dissenting again three years later, White condemned as equally and "distressingly formalistic" the Court's treatment of separation of powers in *Bowsher v. Synar* (1986), overturning by a 7–2 vote the Balanced Budget and Emergency Deficit Control Act of 1985. Popularly known as the Gramm-Rudman-Hollings Act after its sponsors, the statute called for progressive annual cuts in the federal deficit, to be specified by the comptroller general if the Congress was unable to agree upon them.

Although appointed by the president from a list recommended by the Speaker of the House and president pro tem of the Senate and confirmed by the Senate, the comptroller general can be removed from office only on the initiative of Congress, by either impeachment or joint resolution. Traditionally, moreover, the post has been considered part of the legislative branch and subject to its control. The Court, speaking through Chief Justice Burger, concluded, however, that the comptroller general's duties under the challenged statute were clearly executive in nature and that authorizing Congress to remove such an official gave the legislative branch undue control over executive functions.

In a concurring opinion, Justice John Paul Stevens argued that the comptroller general's function under the statute was legislative rather than executive in nature. But he joined the majority on the ground that legislative action must be adopted by both houses of Congress and presented to the president for approval or veto. Calling the law at issue one of the most novel legislative responses to a national crisis since the New Deal, Justice White argued in dissent that the functions assigned by the statute were at least quasi-legislative and that the Court in the past had upheld the assignment of such tasks to officials subject to removal by the president only for cause established by Congress. White saw no meaningful distinction between such provisions and congressional power to remove the comptroller general directly. "The majority's contrary conclusion," he declared, rests on the rigid dogma that, outside of the impeachment process, any "direct congressional role in the removal of officers charged with the execution of the laws . . . is inconsistent with separation of powers." . . . Reliance on such an unyielding principle to strike down a statute posing no real danger of aggrandizement of congressional power is extremely misguided and insensitive to our constitutional roles. The wisdom of vesting "executive" powers in an officer removable by joint resolution may indeed by debatable . . . but such matters are for the most part to be worked out between the Congress and the President through the legislative process, which affords each branch ample opportunity to defend its interests. (p. 776)

Federalism

In addition to providing for a system of separation of powers among the branches of the national government, the Constitution embodies the principle of federalism, dividing governmental powers between the national and state governments and granting each level of government substantial authority. Underscoring the nation's federal character is the Tenth Amendment of the Bill of Rights, which reserves to the states or the people all powers not delegated by the Constitution to the national government nor denied to the states.

As with all other constitutional questions, disputes over federal-state relations are potentially subject to judicial review and final resolution in the Supreme Court. Under Article IV, the Constitution's supremacy clause, national law is supreme to state law. Thus, in cases of conflict between state law and a valid national law, the state must yield. Through the doctrine of "federal preemption," moreover, Congress can completely exclude state regulation in a field of government subject to national control. On occasion, in fact, the Supreme Court has declared an area of regulation to be limited exclusively to national control even when Congress has not specifically preempted the activity in question. In *Pennsylvania v. Nelson* (1956), for example, the Warren Court, drawing on earlier precedent, held that preemption is appropriate where extensive national legislation on the subject regulated indicates a congressional intent to fully occupy the field with national law, the matter is one of predominantly national concern, and efforts to enforce state laws on the subject have obstructed federal enforcement efforts. Applying those preemption criteria in the *Nelson* case, the Court held that protection against seditious speech directed at the national government was to be an exclusively national responsibility.

The Burger Court applied essentially the same standards in preemption cases. In one case utility companies challenged a California statute conditioning the construction of additional nuclear plants on the development of adequate storage and disposal facilities. The companies claimed that the federal Atomic Energy Act preempted such requirements. But citing the long history of dual federal-state regulation in the field of nuclear-powered electrical generation, as well as the limited conflict between federal and state regulatory efforts, the Court, speaking through Justice White, rejected the companies' contentions (*Pacific Gas & Electric Co. v. State Energy Resources Com'n* [1983]).

The Court also clarified the relationship of national courts to the state judiciary in the federal system. Under the doctrine of abstention, the Supreme Court, out of respect for state judges, will ordinarily refuse to decide federal legal issues raised in state cases if (1) criminal defendants failed to follow established state procedures in the trial and appeal of their cases, thereby indicating their disrespect for state law, or (2) the ultimate outcome of a state case would be based on an adequate and independent state law ground, rendering any Supreme Court ruling on federal issues raised in the case no more than legal advice. After the California Supreme Court struck down a state system of public school financing on the ground that it violated the equal protection guarantees of both the U.S. Constitution and the California constitution, for example, the Supreme Court refused to intervene (*Clowes v. Serrano* [1977]). It had previously upheld a similar Texas scheme against federal constitutional challenge (*San Antonio Independent School Dist. v. Rodriguez* [1973]), but extending that decision to the California case would have had no effect on the state supreme court's conclusion that its system of school financing violated the California constitution—an adequate and independent state law ground for the state court's decision.

The Supreme Court has traditionally also been reluctant to permit federal district courts to intervene in pending state judicial proceedings. In 1965 the Warren Court approved a district court's order enjoining further prosecution of civil rights activists under two Louisiana anti-Communist laws so vague and overbroad in scope that they had an inhibiting effect on the exercise of protected First Amendment rights of expression and freedom of association (*Dombrowski v. Pfister* [1965]). But the Burger Court in 1971 narrowly limited that decision in *Younger v. Harris* (1971). Harris, a California socialist, was charged with violating the state's criminal syndicalism statute, which made it a crime to advocate violence or other illegal means for fomenting political and social change. While the state prosecution was pending, Harris went to federal court, seeking a judgment that the statute was unconstitutional and an injunction ending the prosecution. The Supreme Court had upheld the challenged law in 1927 (*Whitney v. California* [1927]) but in 1969 struck down a virtually identical Ohio statute as an overly broad infringement on First Amendment freedoms (*Brandenburg v. Ohio* [1969]).

Arguing that the California statute chilled expression and associational rights, Harris secured an injunction stopping his prosecution. But the Supreme Court reversed. Drawing on earlier precedent, Justice Black concluded for the majority that federal courts must respect state judges and presume that they will be faithful to their oaths to support the U.S. Constitution and national laws. Absent a showing that a state prosecution was conducted in bad faith to harass defendants in their enjoyment of federal rights, federal courts had no business interfering with pending state proceedings. Such conduct, declared Black, offended "our federalism" and principles of comity requiring a proper respect for state courts.

Like its predecessors, the Burger Court was generally deferential as well to state laws regulating interstate commerce. The Constitution grants Congress the power to regulate commerce "among the several states," or interstate commerce. Under their "police powers"—that is, their authority to protect the public health, safety, and morals—states traditionally have been allowed, however, to impose regulations and taxes on interstate commerce, so long as the state measures serve a legitimate governmental interest, do not impose an undue or discriminatory burden on interstate commerce relative to local commerce, conflict with no valid congressional statute, and fall within no area preempted for exclusive federal control.

If such laws were not otherwise prohibited by federal law, the Burger Court was inclined to invalidate only those state regulations of interstate commerce that favored local businesses over interstate trade. In *City of Philadelphia v. New Jersey* (1978), for example, a 7–2 majority struck down as a forbidden protectionist measure a New Jersey statute prohibiting importation into the state of most solid or liquid waste brought in from outside its borders. And a 1981 decision (*Kassel v. Consolidated Freightways Corp.* [1981]) invalidated an Iowa law banning use of trucks longer than 60 feet on its interstate highways, not only because any safety advantage offered by the length restriction might be offset by the increased number of trucks on the highways but also because the statute contained exemptions giving Iowans many of the benefits of large trucks while placing on neighboring states many of the costs associated with their use. Under the law's "border cities" exemption, for example, Iowa cities adjacent to other states could adopt the neighboring state's policy allowing large trucks. This exemption offered the benefits of longer trucks to individuals and businesses in important border cities without burdening Iowa's highways with interstate through-traffic. Such provisions and their legislative history suggested, Justice Powell declared for a plurality in the case, that Iowa's statute was designed to discourage interstate truck traffic rather than eliminate dangerously long trucks.

Some members of the Court, most notably Justice Rehnquist, objected to even these uses of the "negative" commerce clause as a weapon against state regulations of interstate commerce. In *City of Philadelphia*, for example, Rehnquist first noted that the Court in the past had upheld state quarantine laws banning importation of diseased livestock and other immediate threats to the public health, then observed, "I do not see why a State may ban the importation of items whose movement risks contagion, and cannot ban the importation of items which, although they may be transported into the State without undue hazard, will then simply pile up in ever increasing danger to the public's health and safety" (pp. 632–633).

On occasion the Court also invoked the privileges and immunities clause of Article IV to invalidate regulations favoring a state's citizens over visitors from other states. Article IV guarantees to the citizens of each state all privileges and immunities of citizens in the other states. In practice that has been construed to mean that states cannot make unreasonable distinctions in their laws between their own citizens and citizens of other states. A state can justifiably exact a higher tuition from out-of-state students in its colleges and universities, limit voting and officeholding to its own citizens, and draw other reasonable lines between the two groups of citizens. In general, however, in-state and visiting citizens are entitled to substantially equal treatment in a state's laws and proceedings.

Cases under the privileges and immunities clause are rare. But in 1984 the Court, speaking through Justice Rehnquist, confronted a challenge to a Camden, New Jersey, city ordinance requiring at least 40 percent of the employees of contractors on city construction projects to be city residents (*United Building v. Camden* [1984]). Since the ordinance discriminated on the basis of municipal rather than state residence, the New Jersey Supreme Court held the privileges and immunities clause inapplicable. The U.S. Supreme Court reversed, finding no significance in the fact that the law disadvantaged citizens of other New Jersey communities as well as those of other states. The former, Justice Rehnquist observed, might have to look to the political process for relief, but out-of-state citizens were entitled to the protection of the privileges and immunities clause.

Since the case was remanded to the lower courts for review of that claim, the Court declined to review Camden's justification of the ordinance as an attempt to counteract grave economic and social ills, including chronic unemployment and a sharp decline in the city's population. The next year, though, the Court invoked the privileges and immunities clause to strike down a New Hampshire Supreme Court rule limiting bar admission to state residents. Although lawyers were indeed "officers of the Court," Justice Powell observed for the majority, they were not state officials in any political sense and thus were not covered by precedents allowing states to limit public officeholding to citizens alone. In attempting to justify the rule, New Hampshire officials argued that nonresidents were less likely than citizens to keep abreast of local rules and procedures, behave ethically, be available for court proceedings, do pro bono legal work, or engage in other volunteer services. Powell found none of these interests substantial nor the challenged rule narrowly tailored to meet such objectives (*Supreme Court of New Hampshire v. Piper* [1985]).

The Burger Court's most controversial federalism rulings, however, involved the Congress's use of its authority over commerce to impose regulations on state and local governments. From the 1880s to 1937, a laissez-faire majority generally dominated the Supreme Court, invalidating a large number of federal and state laws regulating the economy. When Congress used its commercial authority, or a related power, in an attempt to eliminate undesirable conditions in business and industry, the Old Court often balked, declaring that the statute at issue interfered in areas of authority reserved for state regulation under the Tenth Amendment. Giving the amendment a "dual federalism" interpretation, the Court demanded a strict division between national and state authority, refusing to uphold congressional statutes that regulated matters traditionally controlled by the states. In *Hammer v. Dagenhart* (1918), for example, the Court struck down the national Child Labor Act, which forbade interstate shipment of goods produced in violation of a federal ban on child labor. The problem of child labor in industry, the justices declared, affected interstate commerce only indirectly and thus was subject to regulation solely by the states under their police powers.

Through most of its history, the Tenth Amendment had not assumed such importance in the Court's decisions. In fact, Chief Justice John Marshall had made it clear in some of the Court's most significant early rulings that the regulatory powers of Congress were exceedingly broad and largely subject to restriction only through the political process, not via judicial intervention (*McCulloch v. Maryland* [1819], *Gibbons v. Ogden* [1824]). In 1937 and later, the Court rejected the Old Court's laissez-faire precedents and returned to those basic principles, refusing once again to view the Tenth Amendment as a limit on otherwise valid exercises of congressional power. Speaking for the Court in *United States v. Darby Lumber Co.* (1941), which upheld congressional imposition of minimum wage and maximum hour standards on local businesses, Justice Jackson dismissed the Tenth Amendment as only a "truism" placed in the Bill of Rights to make clear that the national government possessed only those powers delegated to it in the Constitution, and not to serve as a restriction on otherwise valid exercises of those powers. For nearly forty years, the Court adhered to that principle, refusing to invalidate a single federal regulatory measure on Tenth Amendment or state sovereignty grounds. Indeed, when Congress extended federal wage and hour benefits to state and local government employees, the Court, in *Maryland v. Wirtz* (1968), upheld the regulation as consistent with long precedent.

In 1976, however, a 5–4 Burger Court majority, speaking through Justice Rehnquist in *National League of Cities v. Usery*, overruled *Wirtz* and imposed limits on congressional controls over state and local governments and their employees. Federal regulation of traditional or integral state functions necessary to the states' effective functioning as sovereign entities conflicted, Rehnquist declared, with basic principles of federalism. In dissent, Justice Brennan, joined by Justices White and Marshall, scored the majority for choosing the bicentennial year of the Declaration of Independence as the occasion "to repudiate principles . . . settled since the time of Mr. Chief Justice John Marshall, discarding his postulate that the Constitution contemplates that restraints upon exercise by Congress of its plenary commerce power lie in the political process and not in the judicial process" (p. 857). Citing the long line of precedents upholding federal power over state and local governments, Brennan termed the majority's rationale a "transparent cover for invalidating a congressional judgment with which they disagree," and one consistent only with the repudiated constitutional doctrines of the Court's laissez-faire era (pp. 868–869). In a brief separate dissent, Justice Stevens questioned the wisdom of many of the federal controls to which state and local governments had been subjected but emphasized that such personal policy judgments could have no impact on his constitutional duty. Stevens could find no principled basis for distinguishing the challenged statute from many others he deemed "unquestionably permissible."

Justice Blackmun, the critical fifth vote for the *Usery* majority, indicated in a brief concurrence that he was "not untroubled by certain implications of the Court's opinion" (p. 856). Ultimately, Blackmun's doubts would lead to *Usery*'s demise. When lower courts experienced serious difficulties trying to determine to what federal regulations *Usery* did and did not apply, the justice reversed ground. Speaking for another 5–4 majority in *Garcia v. San Antonio Metropolitan Transit Authority* (1985), Justice Blackmun declared that *Usery* had proved unworkable and must be overruled. In the future, as through most of the nation's past, the political process was again to be the principal remedy against the excesses of Congress—in which, after all, every state enjoyed representation. The dissenters were not impressed. Justice Powell, joined by Chief Justice Burger and Justices Rehnquist and O'Connor, decried, for example, the Court's abrupt reversal of recent precedent and accused the majority of "barely acknowledg[ing] that the Tenth Amendment exists" (p. 574).

In a brief dissent, Justice Rehnquist expressed confidence that the principles of state sovereignty and federalism on which *Usery* was based would "in time again command the support of a majority of this Court" (p. 580). During his tenure as chief justice, his words would prove prophetic, as the Court again closely scrutinized congressional enactments claimed to interfere with federal principles. For the balance of Chief Justice Burger's tenure, however, the justices declined to resurrect the dual federalism rationale of the laissez-faire era.

The Framework of Civil Liberties

Although the Burger Court handed down a number of major decisions regarding the scope of governmental powers under the Constitution, the focus of its caseload was on individual rights. Like every other Court of the post-1937 era, moreover, its principal concern was with noneconomic freedoms rather than property rights. The laissez-faire Court of the late nineteenth and early twentieth centuries had given a broad substantive meaning to the Fifth and Fourteenth Amendment guarantees forbidding government to deprive persons of life, liberty, or property without due process of law.

Under its "substantive due process" interpretation of those fundamental guarantees, they became more than requirements of proper procedure. Instead, the Old Court frequently declared unconstitutional, as deprivations of due process, federal and state laws it considered to be unreasonable or arbitrary interferences with economic freedom. In the most notorious such ruling, *Lochner v. New York* (1905), a majority invalidated a maximum hour law for bakery employees on substantive due process grounds, thereby assuming what the Court's critics called a "super-legislative" role inconsistent with democratic principles of majority rule. As noted earlier, the laissez-faire Court also narrowly construed congressional authority over propertied interests.

In 1937, however, a new majority began dismantling the Old Court's precedents. Under a constitutional double standard established in that period (*United States v. Carolene Products Co.*, n.4 [1938]), the Court left the status of economic freedoms largely to the political arena and declared that economic regulations would be invalidated only if found to be totally lacking in any rational justifying basis. For the first time, though, the Court also subjected to close judicial scrutiny controls over fundamental safeguards of the Bill of Rights and other personal, noneconomic rights.

The Burger Court remained faithful to that double standard. Its justices did not invalidate a single economic regulation on substantive due process grounds, and in 1976 the Court rejected as unduly intrusive upon governmental power over propertied interests the one Warren-era precedent striking down a discriminatory economic control on Fourteenth Amendment equal protection grounds (*Morey v. Doud* [1957]). *New Orleans v. Dukes* upheld a city ordinance that banned pushcart vendors from the French Quarter but exempted longtime vendors from its coverage. The justices found the regulation and its grandfather clause rationally related to the city's interest in preserving the French Quarter's traditional appearance and customs.

The Court also gave the Constitution's few specific property rights guarantees a narrow reading. During the Rehnquist Court era, the Fifth Amendment takings clause, forbidding government to take private property for a public purpose without just compensation, would become a potent barrier to government regulation of private property, or what the Rehnquist Court has termed "regulatory takings." But the Burger Court, like its predecessors, gave the clause an interpretation very deferential to government. In 1978, for example, a divided Court even rejected a takings clause challenge to New York City's designation of the Grand Central railway station as a historic landmark and the city's refusal to permit the station's owner to build a high-rise office building atop the terminal (*Penn Central Transportation Co. v. New York City* [1978]).

Still, the Court's rejection of close scrutiny for economic regulations did not mean that the due process guarantee played a minor role in the jurisprudence of the Burger era. The Court reaffirmed the "incorporation" process through which most guarantees of the Bill of Rights have been made binding on the states. Early in the nation's history, the Court, speaking through Chief Justice Marshall, had held that the safeguards listed in the Bill of Rights were applicable only to the national government, not the states and local governments (*Barron v. Baltimore* [1833]). But the Fourteenth Amendment, adopted in 1868, forbids the states to deprive persons of life, liberty, or property without due process of law, just as the Fifth Amendment imposes an identical standard on the national government under the Bill of Rights. And beginning in the 1920s, the Court gradually incorporated Bill of Rights safeguards into the meaning of the Fourteenth Amendment due process clause, making them binding on the states (*Gitlow v. New York* [1925]).

Incorporation was initially confined to rights considered absolutely essential to liberty and justice, such as the First Amendment freedoms of religion, expression, and assembly (*Palko v. Connecticut* [1937]). In the 1960s, however, the Warren Court expanded the meaning of due process under the Fourteenth Amendment to include all Bill of Rights guarantees considered fundamental to the American scheme of liberty and justice. Since most Bill of Rights guarantees were widely required in the states, their application to all states via the incorporation process proceeded rapidly in the 1960s. In fact, through this process of "selective incorporation," the Court had applied all major provisions of the Bill of Rights except the Fifth Amendment's grand jury guarantee to the states by the end of Chief Justice Warren's tenure in 1969 (*Benton v. Maryland* [1969]).

Despite predictions that the Burger Court would reject major criminal justice rulings of the Warren era, including incorporation decisions in that field, the incorporation process easily survived the new chief justice and other Nixon-Ford appointees to the Court. By the vote of one justice, however, the Court did make clear in a trial by jury case that Bill of Rights safeguards would not necessarily be given the same application in federal and state cases. Although the Supreme Court had long construed due process to require fair and impartial jurors in state criminal cases, the Court did not *require* trial by jury in state cases until 1968, when the Warren Court held in *Duncan v. Louisiana* that defendants are entitled to jury trial in all serious state cases (those involving, that is, sentences of more than six months' imprisonment and a $500 fine).

The right to trial by jury in federal cases under the Sixth Amendment had long been interpreted to require a jury of twelve members. Two years after the *Duncan* decision, however, the Burger Court, in *Williams v. Florida* (1970), upheld a six-member state jury and indicated that twelve-member juries would no longer be required in federal trials either. Terming a "historical accident" the common-law requirement that juries number precisely twelve members, Justice White declared for the *Williams* Court that the requirement bore no relationship to the jury's principal historic function as "an inestimable safeguard against the corrupt or overzealous prosecutor and against the compliant, biased, or eccentric judge" (p. 100). White conceded that juries should be large enough to assure adequate group deliberation and the possibility for selection of a representative cross-section of the community on any jury; indeed, the Court would later invalidate a five-member jury on essentially those grounds (*Ballew v. Georgia* [1978]). But White doubted such goals were less likely to be achieved with a six-member jury than with one numbering twelve members.

The *Williams* ruling was consistent with the Court's conclusion in many earlier cases that incorporated rights be given the same application in federal and state cases. In fact, Justice Black, who had argued throughout his long career on the high bench that the Fourteenth Amendment's framers had intended its provisions to apply all Bill of Rights safeguards totally and fully to the states, concurred in the Court's judgment, contending that precedent cases mandating twelve-member federal juries had simply rested on an "improper interpretation" of the Sixth Amendment, the text of which, after all, required only trial by an "impartial jury," not a set number of jurors (p. 107).

Two years after *Williams*, however, the Court held in *Apodaca v. Oregon* and *Johnson v. Louisiana* that state juries need not render unanimous verdicts, while retaining the traditional rule requiring jury unanimity in federal cases. Justice White, joined by three colleagues, argued that neither the Sixth Amendment guarantee to trial by jury in federal cases nor general principles of due process to which states were subject under the Fourteenth Amendment, required unanimous verdicts. Due process had been construed to require proof of guilt beyond a reasonable doubt in criminal and related judicial proceedings (*In Re Winship* [1970]), observed White, but only those jurors necessary to render a verdict in a case were obliged to satisfy that standard, not all members of the jury.

White spoke, though, only for a plurality of justices. Justice Powell provided the critical fifth vote in the case, and Powell concluded that unanimous verdicts were mandatory in federal cases but not in state proceedings. In early decisions applying Bill of Rights safeguards to the states, the Court had initially suggested that incorporated rights could be given a more flexible meaning in state cases than in federal trials. Embracing that stance, Powell concluded on the basis of history and precedent that the Sixth Amendment required unanimity in federal cases but also declared that the Fourteenth Amendment due process clause did not incorporate all the elements of a Sixth Amendment jury within its meaning. For Powell, jury unanimity was not an essential ingredient of due process.

The *Apodaca* and *Johnson* rulings would remain the exception to the general rule that incorporated rights were to be given essentially identical treatment in federal and state cases. The incorporation doctrine itself also met surprisingly little opposition on the Burger Court. On occasion Justice Rehnquist disparaged the incorporation formula, terming it in one dissent a "mysterious process of transmogrification" and arguing—as the second Justice Harlan had often maintained in earlier years—that the Fourteenth Amendment due process clause obliged states only to accord people "fundamental fairness"; it did not bind them to the specific mandates of the Bill of Rights (*Carter v. Kentucky*, 309 [1981]). But Rehnquist stood virtually alone, and the Fourteenth Amendment continued to act as a sort of constitutional shorthand for most guarantees of the Bill of Rights.

The Burger Court was also hardly consistent in opposing constitutional recognition for rights mentioned nowhere in the Constitution's text; indeed, in at least certain respects it ventured far beyond the Warren Court in its recognition of unenumerated rights. Given the post-1937 Supreme Court's repudiation of precedents of the laissez-faire era, especially use of substantive due process to invalidate state and federal economic controls, it was naturally disinclined to resurrect due process as the basis for recognizing unenumerated noneconomic rights. In *Skinner v. Oklahoma* (1942), Justice Douglas suggested for the Court that the Constitution guarantees a "basic" right of procreation in striking down a state provision for the sterilization of habitual criminals. Since the law exempted certain classes of repeat offenders from its coverage, however, the decision could be rested on equal protection grounds, enabling the justices to avoid the controversial substantive due process formula.

In 1964 a Warren Court majority construed the Fifth Amendment due process clause to embody a right to international travel in striking down a statute denying passports to Communists (*Aptheker v. Secretary of State* [1964]). But that decision just as easily could have been based on enumerated First Amendment rights, as Justice Black pointed out in a concurring opinion. And when the Warren Court the next year recognized a general right to marital privacy, Justice Douglas attempted to tie the majority decision, however loosely, to specific constitutional safeguards. Speaking for a 7–2 majority in *Griswold v. Connecticut* (1965), which struck down a broad state ban on the use of contraceptives, Douglas found the right of privacy in the "penumbra" of several Bill of Rights guarantees and attempted to convince readers that the Court was not resurrecting the "super-legislative" substantive due process jurisprudence of the long-discredited laissez-faire era.

In separate concurrences, however, two members of the *Griswold* majority (Harlan and White) rested their positions squarely on substantive due process, while Justice Arthur Goldberg cited the Ninth Amendment as further support for constitutional recognition of unenumerated rights. The Ninth Amendment provides that "[e]numeration in the Constitution, of certain rights, shall not be construed to deny or disparage others retained by the people." The Court had never invoked the amendment to invalidate a single challenged statute, and it was generally viewed, like the Tenth Amendment, as simply underscoring the delegated character of national power and making clear that laws going beyond those delegated national powers would infringe upon the people's rights, whether enumerated in the Constitution or not. But as did a number of scholars and lower court judges, Justice Goldberg considered the Ninth Amendment evidence that the Constitution included unenumerated rights in its meaning, the nature and scope of which, like other constitutional issues, were subject to judicial resolution.

In dissent, Justice Black accused the majority justices, whatever their rhetoric, of simply engrafting onto the Constitution a right they considered important but the framers had neglected to include in the document. For Black, there was only one proper way to keep the Constitution abreast of the times and changing conceptions of individual liberty—the amendment process, not judicial usurpation of that enumerated mechanism for constitutional change.

Perhaps in an attempt to avoid such criticism and connection with doctrinal developments of the laissez-faire era, the Warren Court generally invoked equal protection rather than substantive due process or the penumbra doctrine as its tool of choice for extending constitutional protection to unenumerated rights. Developing a doctrine of "substantive equal protection," the justices held that discriminatory laws infringing upon "fundamental" rights or interests, including those not mentioned in the Constitution, were unconstitutional unless they were necessary to promote a compelling governmental interest and no means less restrictive of such rights were available to accomplish the government's objective. The Warren Court included among these fundamental safeguards the right to marry, the right to vote, rights flowing from intimate familial relationships, the right to interstate travel (said to be inherent in U.S. citizenship), and perhaps the rights to welfare benefits and an equal education. In *Harper v. Virginia Board of Elections* (1966), for example, the Court invoked such a rationale in striking down poll tax requirements for state elections, and *Shapiro v. Thompson* (1969) invalidated a one-year state residency requirement for welfare benefits on the ground it inhibited interstate travel.

The Burger Court readily applied, and at times even expanded, Warren Court equal protection precedents subjecting discriminatory interference with recognized fundamental rights to strict judicial scrutiny. Extending the privacy right recognized in the *Griswold* case to unmarried persons, for example, the Court, in *Eisenstadt v. Baird* (1972), struck down a statute making it illegal for single persons, but not married people, to obtain contraceptives. The statute, the Court concluded, was neither a health measure nor intended to deter premarital sex but based simply on a moral judgment unrelated to a legitimate governmental interest. "If the right of privacy means anything," Justice Brennan observed for the Court, "it is the right of the individual, married or single, to be free from unwanted governmental intrusion into matters so fundamentally affecting a person as the decision whether to bear or beget a child" (p. 453). In 1974, moreover, the Court invoked the right of interstate travel to strike down a one-year county residency requirement for receiving nonemergency hospitalization or medical care (*Memorial Hospital v. Maricopa County* [1974]). And *Zablocki v. Redhail* (1978) invalidated as an undue interference with the fundamental right to marriage a state statute requiring a court's approval before persons subject to child support court orders for children not in their custody could marry.

Shortly after Chief Justice Burger's appointment, however, the Court also began to curb the potentially limitless reach of substantive equal protection. In 1970 the Court rejected the claim that the Constitution included a fundamental right to welfare benefits and upheld a state-imposed family ceiling on such assistance, despite its impact on children of large families. Applying the lenient rational basis standard of judicial review extended to discriminatory economic controls, the Court found the welfare ceiling rationally related to the state's interests in encouraging work and equalizing the incomes of the working and welfare poor (*Dandridge v. Williams* [1970]).

In 1973 the Court went further. Speaking for the majority in *San Antonio Independent School District v. Rodriguez*, upholding a system of public school financing primarily through local property taxes, Justice Powell rejected the claim that the Constitution included a fundamental right to an equal education and held that henceforth the substantive equal protection doctrine would be limited to rights expressed or implied in the Constitution. Rejecting strict judicial review of the school finance scheme at issue in the case, Powell found it rationally related to the state's interest in promoting local control of public education. Later the Court also rejected the proposition that there is a fundamental right to public employment triggering strict judicial review of discriminatory laws in that field (*Massachusetts Bd. of Retirement v. Murgia* [1976]).

Ironically, however, while the Burger Court was seeking to curb further expansion of substantive equal protection, a majority resurrected substantive due process as the basis for recognizing the most controversial unenumerated right in the modern Court's history. In *Roe v. Wade* (1973), a 7–2 Court, speaking through Justice Blackmun, held that the liberty protected from government infringement by the Fourteenth Amendment due process clause (and its Fifth Amendment counterpart) included a right of privacy sufficiently broad to encompass a woman's decision to abort an unwanted pregnancy. Drawing on language employed in recent equal protection cases, Blackmun characterized abortion as a fundamental right subject to regulation only in furtherance of a compelling state interest. Dividing a pregnancy into three trimesters, the Court found no compelling interest justifying state interference with the abortion decision of a woman and her physician during the first three months of the pregnancy. Yet Blackmun agreed that the state's compelling interest in a pregnant woman's life and health would justify reasonable controls over abortion procedures during the second trimester, the period running from the end of the first trimester to the point at which the fetus becomes "viable," that is, capable of surviving independently of the woman's womb.

The Court rejected the contention that life in a legal or constitutional sense begins with conception, pointing out, among other things, that the law had traditionally confined legal personhood to postnatal beings and that any recognition of prenatal life for constitutional purposes would necessarily doom all abortions, whatever the circumstances. Justice Blackmun did hold for the majority, however, that during a woman's third trimester of pregnancy the state possessed a compelling interest not only in the life and health of the woman but also in the now viable fetus as a potential human life. In the third trimester, therefore, a state could regulate abortion procedures and even forbid abortions except where necessary, in the physician's judgment, to protect the life or health of the mother.

Since the Texas law at issue in *Roe* prohibited all abortions except to save the mother's life or in cases of rape and incest, it clearly violated the Court's newly announced abortion right. But in *Doe v. Bolton*, a companion case from Georgia, a more progressive abortion statute met the same fate. Again speaking through Justice Blackmun, the *Doe* Court struck down regulations requiring that abortions be conducted in a hospital, undertaken only after review by a hospital committee and confirmation by other physicians, and limited to Georgia residents. The residency requirement, Blackmun held, inhibited the right of interstate travel, while the other regulations were unduly broad restrictions on the abortion right, reaching first-trimester as well as later abortions and otherwise contrary to *Roe*'s trimester framework.

The Court invoked substantive due process to protect other procreative and sexual privacy rights as well. In 1977, for example, a 7–2 majority struck down a New York statute that forbade distribution of contraceptives to persons under age sixteen, required distribution to persons over sixteen only by a licensed physician, and prohibited their display or advertising (*Carey v. Population Services International* [1977]). Several Burger Court decisions further extended due process to procedural guarantees not mentioned in the Constitution's text. Not only was proof of guilt beyond a reasonable doubt held to be a fundamental requirement of procedural fairness implicit in due process (*In Re Winship* [1970]), but proceedings to revoke government benefits were also subjected to constitutional restrictions. *Goldberg v. Kelly* (1970) required an evidentiary hearing, for example, prior to termination of welfare benefits. The Court later made clear, however, that the degree of due process required in such cases would depend on the particular circumstances, holding in one case that no hearing was required prior to termination of Social Security disability benefits because the hardship imposed in such situations was usually less severe than that inflicted by the termination of welfare benefits and eligibility was not tied to need (*Mathews v. Eldridge* [1976]).

The Court's response to procedural due process claims in cases involving the discharge of public employees was equally mixed. Civil servants subject to removal only for cause were held to have a due process right to some sort of pretermination opportunity to respond to the allegations on which their discharge was to be based (e.g., *Cleveland Bd. of Education v. Loudermill* [1985]). College professors on annual appointments, in contrast, were not entitled to a hearing challenging the decision not to renew their contracts (*Board of Regents v. Roth* [1972]). Nor did the mere decision not to rehire a faculty member impose a stigma or other disability foreclosing further employment opportunities, in violation of the liberty protected by the due process guarantee.

For a time, the Burger Court subjected discriminatory laws to a form of strict judicial review under the due process guarantee via application of an "irrebuttable presumptions" doctrine. Under that formula, a law was held to violate due process if it treated classes of people differently based on a presumption that lacked universal, or nearly universal, validity, and persons subject to its provisions were given no opportunity to challenge the presumption on which the law was based. In one case the Court struck down a statute under which all unmarried fathers were presumed to be unfit parents and denied custody of their children, without any hearing on their fitness or proof of neglect, even though such proceedings were required in custody cases involving married or divorced parents and unmarried mothers (*Stanley v. Illinois* [1972]). Another ruling invalidated a statute under which college students who first enrolled as out-of-state students were irrebuttably presumed to retain that status (and be subject to higher tuition than their in-state counterparts) throughout their college careers (*Vlandis v. Kline* [1973]). And in *Cleveland Board of Education v. LaFleur* (1974), the Court struck down a mandatory leave requirement for pregnant teachers by rejecting the irrebuttable presumption they were invariably unfit for service after the relatively early leave date stipulated in school regulations.

Critics of the irrebuttable presumptions doctrine, most notably Justice Rehnquist, argued that it was contrary to the traditional notion of lawmaking through general but imperfect rules. And in *Weinberger v. Salfi*, Rehnquist spoke for a majority in upholding such a presumption and indicated that future regulations would be subjected to strict judicial review only if the presumption at issue affected recognized constitutional rights.

The Burger Court also proved reluctant to expand the scope of substantive liberties subject to the procedural protections of the due process guarantee. *Wisconsin v. Constantineau* (1971) invalidated that state's "posting law," under which liquor sales to persons designated excessive drinkers were prohibited and notices to that effect were posted in retail liquor outlets. "Where a person's good name, reputation, honor, or integrity is at stake because of what the government is doing to him," Justice Douglas concluded for the *Constantineau* Court, "notice and opportunity to be heard are essential" (p. 437).

Later, however, a majority gave *Constantineau* a narrow reading. The occasion was *Paul v. Davis* (1976). Police in the Louisville, Kentucky, area had circulated to about 800 merchants a five-page flyer containing mug shots of "active shoplifters." Police had circulated similar notices for fifteen years, including in the flyers many individuals who had never been convicted of any crime whatever and whose only "offense" was having been arrested for shoplifting. Among those identified in the most recent flyer was Edward Charles Davis III, whose photo and name appeared on the second page. Davis had been arrested by a store's security police, but his case had been put into an inactive file before the flyer's circulation, and shortly thereafter his case was dismissed.

In a federal court suit, Davis claimed that circulation of the flyer denied him due process by inhibiting him from entering businesses and seriously impairing his future job prospects. The trial court dismissed, but the court of appeals reversed, citing *Constantineau*. The Supreme Court, speaking through Justice Rehnquist, distinguished *Constantineau* and related cases and upheld the challenged practice against federal constitutional challenge, suggesting that Davis should seek relief in the Kentucky courts. The earlier cases had involved not only injury to reputation but also government action altering an individual's legal status, and Rehnquist rejected "the proposition that reputation alone, apart from some more tangible interests such as employment, is either 'liberty' or 'property' by itself sufficient to invoke the procedural protection of the Due Process Clause" (p. 701). Justice Brennan, joined by Justice Marshall and in part by Justice White, wrote a stinging dissent, characterizing "the enjoyment of one's good name and reputation" as "among the most cherished of rights" and scorning the Court's holding "that police officials, acting in their official capacities as law officers, may on their own initiative and without trial constitutionally condemn innocent individuals as criminals and thereby brand them with one of the most stigmatizing and debilitating labels in our society" (p. 714).

Paul v. Davis dealt primarily with the sort of procedural due process (such as notice and a hearing) that may be required when government interferes with liberty or property. But the Court's decision also reflected its reluctance to use due process as a device for expanding the scope of substantive rights not given specific mention in the Constitution's text. In *Kelley v. Johnson* (1976), decided the same year, the Court made clear that even those unenumerated rights included within the scope of due process will not always be given the protection accorded safeguards deemed fundamental to liberty and justice. The *Kelley* Court, in another opinion by Justice Rehnquist, upheld a New York county police department regulation banning beards, flared sideburns, and hair over the collar on uniformed police and requiring their hair to be neat, clean, trimmed, and well groomed. The Court, wrote Rehnquist, was willing to "assume" that citizens were entitled to "some sort of 'liberty' interest within the Fourteenth Amendment in matters of personal appearance" (p. 244). But the justice emphasized that government employees were subject to greater restrictions on their freedom than citizens in general and concluded that regulations relating to the organizational structure of police agencies were to be presumed valid and upheld unless totally lacking in any justifying rational basis. The challenged measure, he added, was rationally related to the legitimate goals of encouraging police esprit de corps and making police more easily recognizable to the public.

In a dissent joined by Justice Brennan, Justice Marshall contended that the exclusion of personal appearance from the scope of liberty protected by the Fourteenth Amendment was "fundamentally inconsistent with the values of privacy, self-identity, autonomy, and personal integrity" the Constitution was designed to protect (p. 251). Rejecting the finding of even a rational basis for the regulation, Marshall chided the majority's acceptance of the claim that the hair code was needed to make *uniformed* police more readily recognizable to the public. Since the president of a local police organization had brought the suit, and another police group had filed an amicus curiae (friend of the court) brief challenging the regulation, Marshall also seriously doubted that it had improved police esprit de corps.

During Chief Justice Burger's last term on the bench, a campaign for extension of substantive due process to encompass a right to homosexual privacy met a similar fate. An ancient Georgia statute, like the laws of about half the states, made sodomy (primarily oral or anal intercourse) a felony carrying a sentence of up to twenty years in prison. A police officer lawfully in the home of Michael Hardwick, a gay Atlanta bartender, to serve him with a warrant for failing to pay a fine in a public drunkenness case, discovered Hardwick performing oral sex on another man in his bedroom. After the district attorney decided not to take the case to the grand jury until further evidence was compiled, Hardwick and a heterosexual couple filed suit in a federal district court, contending that Georgia's sodomy law was unconstitutional to the extent it made consensual sodomy a crime.

In *Doe v. Commonwealth's Attorney* (1976), the Burger Court had summarily affirmed a federal court ruling sustaining Virginia's sodomy statute. Based on the *Doe* decision, the district court dismissed Hardwick's suit and also concluded that the heterosexual plaintiffs had no standing to sue since they had not been threatened with prosecution. A divided three-judge federal appeals court panel reversed, concluding that Georgia's sodomy statute violated fundamental privacy rights protected from state infringement by the Ninth Amendment and the due process guarantee. Especially since other federal appeals courts had reached a different conclusion on the issue, the Supreme Court agreed to review the case. Since the heterosexual couple had not contested the district court's dismissal of their suit on standing grounds, the Court limited its review and holding to the statute's impact on the rights of homosexuals, expressing no opinion on the constitutionality of the statute as applied to heterosexual conduct. So confined, a 5–4 majority, in *Bowers v. Hardwick* (1986), reversed the court of appeals and upheld the statute.

Speaking for the majority, Justice White distinguished the claim before the Court from earlier precedents recognizing a variety of privacy rights. Those cases, he declared, related to "family, marriage, and procreation" and thus bore no "resemblance to the claimed right of homosexuals to engage in acts of sodomy" (p. 190–191). Nor was the Court willing to extend those precedents. White conceded that a "legion" of earlier cases had given the due process guarantee a substantive content, even though its language appeared "to focus only on the processes by which life, liberty, or property is taken." He also agreed that among the guarantees so recognized were rights having "little or no textual support in the constitutional language" (p. 191). In an effort to assure that the justices did not impose their personal values on the other branches and levels of government, however, the Court had limited the scope of substantive due process to rights "deeply rooted in this Nation's history and tradition or 'implicit in the concept of ordered liberty.'" The asserted right to consensual homosexual sodomy was consistent, declared White, with neither of those standards. In fact, given the long history of criminal sanctions against such practices, he found the claim "at best, facetious" (p. 194).

The justice was equally scornful of the contention that homosexual conduct was at least entitled to protection when it occurred, as here, in the privacy of a person's home. In *Stanley v. Georgia* (1969), the Warren Court had upheld a person's right to possess adult pornography in the home. But White considered *Stanley* "firmly grounded in the First Amendment," a right stated in the Constitution, rather than in any privacy concept, and emphasized that "otherwise illegal conduct is not always immunized whenever it occurs in the home" (p. 195).

In a brief concurrence, Chief Justice Burger noted that he was writing separately to "underscore [his] view that in constitutional terms there is no such thing as a fundamental right to commit homosexual sodomy." Holding to the contrary, declared Burger, "would be to cast aside millennia of moral teaching" (pp. 196–197). A letter the chief justice wrote to Justice Powell while the case was pending was even more revealing of the depths of Burger's feelings. During the Court's discussion of the case in conference, Justice Powell had cited a Warren Court holding that criminal punishment of a person for the mere status of narcotics addiction violated the Eighth Amendment's guarantee against cruel and unusual punishments (*Robinson v. California* [1962]), then suggested that criminal prosecution of homosexual conduct might also amount to punishment based solely on "status." In his letter to his colleague, Burger asserted that he had "never heard of any responsible member (or even an 'avant-garde' member) of the psychiatric community"—a "breed of M.D.'s" about whom he was already "very skeptical"—"who recognized homosexuality as an 'addiction' in the sense of drug addiction. . . . In fact these homosexuals themselves proclaim this is a matter of sexual 'preference.' Moreover, even if homosexuality is somehow conditioned, the decision to commit an act of sodomy is a choice, pure and simple—maybe not so pure!" Acceptance of Powell's argument, contended Burger, "would swallow up centuries of criminal law since anyone who . . . has a psychological dependency would be entitled to carry out (at least in private or with a consenting partner) whatever is necessary to satisfy his cravings" (Warren E. Burger to Lewis F. Powell Jr., April 3, 1986, Lewis Powell Papers, School of Law, Washington and Lee University, Drawer 63).

In the margin at the top of Burger's letter, Justice Powell wrote, "There is both sense and nonsense in this letter—mostly the latter." He termed an "incredible statement," moreover, the chief justice's assertion elsewhere in the letter that *Bowers* posed "the most far reaching issue" of his thirty years on the bench. Powell eventually dropped his "status" rationale and joined the Court's decision rejecting Hardwick's substantive due process claim. In a brief concurring opinion, however, he made clear that "a prison sentence for such conduct—certainly a sentence of long duration—would create a serious Eighth Amendment issue" (*Bowers v. Hardwick*, p. 197). In 1990 the justice would tell a law school audience he "probably made a mistake" in joining the *Bowers* majority (Jeffries, p. 530).

The four *Bowers* dissenters had no doubt of the Court's error. Justice Blackmun, joined by Justices Brennan, Marshall, and Stevens, argued that the case was not about a right to engage in homosexual sodomy but rather involved "the fundamental interest all individuals have in controlling the nature of their intimate associations with others" (p. 206). Blackmun considered Georgia's sodomy law a flagrant affront to such constitutionally protected privacy interests. Since the Court had long excluded obscenity from First Amendment protection, he also disputed the majority's reading of *Stanley v. Georgia*, upholding the possession of pornography in the home, as essentially a First Amendment case. *Stanley*, the justice maintained, was based instead on "the right of an individual to conduct intimate relationships in the intimacy of his or her home"—a right at "the heart of the Constitution's protection of privacy" (p. 208) and central to Michael Hardwick's claim.

In a separate dissent joined by Brennan and Marshall, Justice Stevens noted that Georgia's sodomy law applied to heterosexual as well as homosexual conduct and that *Griswold* and other cases had upheld the rights of married and unmarried persons to engage in nonreproductive sexual relations, while denying government power to penalize behavior merely because it was considered immoral. The state thus bore a heavy burden of justifying selective enforcement of the challenged law against homosexual conduct alone. Georgia had to show, Stevens maintained, "a neutral and legitimate [justifying] interest—something more substantial than a habitual dislike for, or ignorance about, the disfavored group." Yet the challenged statute reflected only a judgment "that *all sodomy* is immoral and unacceptable," and its nonenforcement for several decades "belie[d]," in Stevens's judgment, the state's argument that it had important neutral reasons supporting selective enforcement.

The Intractable Abortion Issue

Even as *Bowers, Kelley v. Johnson,* and other cases demonstrated the Burger Court's general opposition to enlarging upon the number and reach of unenumerated rights accorded constitutional recognition, the Court's continued commitment to the reproductive safeguards announced in *Roe v. Wade* provoked an intense national debate. The two *Roe* dissenters, Justices White and Rehnquist, had accused the majority, despite Justice Blackmun's protests to the contrary, of resurrecting the substantive due process doctrine invoked so frequently by the justices of the laissez-faire era to rule on the wisdom of economic and social legislation. They were willing to concede that the Constitution included protection for unenumerated rights, but they found no basis in the document's text, the history surrounding the Fourteenth Amendment's adoption, or tradition for recognizing a woman's constitutional right to abort an unwanted pregnancy. If one existed, moreover, they faulted the majority for exaggerating its scope and minimizing state interests justifying its regulation. "During the period prior to the time the fetus becomes viable," Justice White, joined by Justice Rehnquist, declared, "the Constitution of the United States values the convenience, whim, or caprice of the pregnant woman more than the life or potential life of the fetus. . . . As an exercise of raw judicial power, the Court perhaps has authority to do what it does today; but in my view its judgment is an improvident and extravagant exercise of the power of judicial review" (p. 221–222). To the dissenters, abortion was a policy issue appropriate for resolution in the political branches of government, not the courts.

Extremist opponents of *Roe* went further, contending that life in a legal as well as moral sense begins at conception, equating abortion with murder, and comparing *Roe* to *Dred Scott v. Sandford* (1857), the discredited pre–Civil War Taney Court decision denying citizenship to African Americans. The "pro-life" movement became a formidable national political force, as did its "pro-choice" counterpart. Politicians and interest groups regularly raised the abortion issue to win elections and defeat opponents. Congress and state legislatures enacted legislation designed to obstruct *Roe*'s impact. *Roe*'s author, Justice Blackmun, became the frequent target of death threats, while Ronald Reagan adopted a pro-life stance as candidate and chief executive, even obliging George Bush to abandon his pro-choice position as a condition for joining the 1980 Republican presidential ticket. Each year on the anniversary of *Roe*, Reagan telephoned his support to antiabortion protesters gathered on the steps of the Supreme Court.

Despite the national controversy swirling around the abortion issue, the Court held firm to *Roe* and the trimester formula it applied to abortion restrictions. In 1976 a 6–3 majority struck down a Missouri regulation requiring a husband's written consent for abortions performed during the first twelve weeks of pregnancy, Justice Blackmun emphasizing for the justices that a state could not limit a woman's decision to secure abortion during the first trimester of pregnancy. A regulation requiring an unmarried woman under age eighteen to secure the consent of a parent met the same fate in the case, although the justices did concede that not every minor, regardless of age or maturity, could give effective consent for an abortion (*Planned Parenthood v.*

Danforth [1976]). Later the Court agreed that a state could involve a parent in a minor's abortion decision, but only if it also provided an alternative procedure to assure that the parent would not have an absolute veto over the minor's decision. In a 1983 case, for example, the justices upheld a parental consent requirement that included a judicial bypass procedure enabling a minor to convince a judge that she was sufficiently mature to make her own decisions or that an abortion was, in any event, in her best interests (*Planned Parenthood v. Ashcroft*). The Court was even more deferential to government in reviewing parental *notice* (rather than consent) requirements. *H. L. v. Matheson* (1981) thus upheld a law requiring physicians usually to notify parents of any minor before performing an abortion.

Restrictions on the abortion process rarely survived challenge. In *Akron v. Akron Center for Reproductive Health* (1983), the Court struck down as a significant obstacle to a woman's abortion decision a regulation requiring abortions after the first trimester to be performed in hospitals rather than outpatient clinics. Speaking for the majority, Justice Powell further concluded that a provision obliging patients to be given detailed information about abortions was actually designed to deter women from choosing abortion rather than to assure their informed consent to the procedure. A mandatory twenty-four-hour waiting period after a woman signed a consent form also fell, with Powell citing the increased cost of an additional trip to an abortion facility. In a 1986 case, the Court went further, striking down as unduly burdensome several reporting requirements and a provision obligating physicians to use the abortion technique providing the greatest protection to the fetus in postviability abortions as well as a second physician in such cases (*Thornburgh v. American Coll. of Obst. & Gyn.* [1986]). Earlier the justices nullified a law imposing criminal penalties when a doctor failed to follow a prescribed standard of care for viable fetuses or those reasonably believed to be viable (*Colautti v. Franklin* [1979]).

The Court refused to extend *Roe*, however, to funded abortions. Various states adopted provisions excluding most abortions from medical funding for poor women. Through a series of so-called Hyde amendments, sponsored by Illinois Republican congressman Henry Hyde and added to congressional appropriations bills, Congress also withheld Medicaid funds from most abortions, even though funding continued for medical costs connected with pregnancy and maternal care. In *Maher v. Roe* (1977), a 6–3 majority upheld a Connecticut restriction on abortion funding, and *Harris v. McRae* (1980) sustained a version of the Hyde amendment. Speaking for the *Harris* majority, Justice Stewart declared that

> [a]lthough the liberty protected by the Due Process Clause affords protection against unwarranted government interference with freedom of choice in the context of certain personal decisions, it does not confer an entitlement to such funds as may be necessary to realize all the advantages of that freedom. To hold other-

> wise would mark a drastic change in our understanding of the Constitution. It cannot be that because government may not prohibit the use of contraceptives, or prevent parents from sending their child to a private school, . . . government . . . has an affirmative constitutional obligation to ensure that all persons have the financial resources to obtain contraceptives or send their children to private schools. (pp. 317–318)

Dissenters argued that government should not be permitted to condition the enjoyment of a government benefit on the relinquishment of a constitutional right, citing as authority, among other cases, the Warren Court's ruling in *Sherbert v. Verner* (1963). *Sherbert* overturned on religious liberty grounds South Carolina's denial of unemployment benefits to a Seventh-Day Adventist unable to find employment not requiring work on Saturday, her day of worship. "The fundamental flaw in the [*Harris*] Court's due process analysis," asserted Justice Brennan, joined by Marshall and Blackmun, "is its failure to acknowledge that the discriminatory distribution of the benefits of government largesse can discourage the exercise of fundamental liberties just as effectively as can an outright denial of those rights through criminal and regulatory sanctions (p. 334)."

Equal Protection Doctrine

The Burger Court was no more consistent in curtailing expansive Warren Court constructions of the Constitution's equal protection guarantee than in limiting the scope of unenumerated rights recognized via substantive due process and related doctrines. Building on earlier precedents, the Warren Court had established a two-tiered approach to discriminatory laws claimed to violate the Fourteenth Amendment's prohibition on state denials of equal protection of the laws and the Fifth Amendment due process clause, which it interpreted to impose essentially the same limitations on national officials. Economic regulations and many other types of legislation were subjected to a lower, or "rational basis," tier of judicial review, under which the Court would uphold a discriminatory law if it was rationally related to a legitimate governmental purpose (such as protection of the public peace). Only one regulation subjected to that lenient rational basis, or "old" equal protection standard, as it was commonly known, met defeat in the Warren Court (*Morey v. Doud* [1957]). And the Burger Court, as we have seen, later overturned that precedent (*New Orleans v. Dukes* [1976]). But laws that discriminated on the basis of a "suspect" class or category, such as a person's race or color, or infringed upon a "fundamental right," were subjected to strict judicial scrutiny and struck down unless found to be the least restrictive means necessary to promote a compelling governmental interest. No discriminatory law subjected to this upper tier, or "new," equal protection standard survived challenge in the Warren Court.

The Burger Court, as noted earlier, limited the "fundamental rights" branch of the "new" equal protection test to rights expressly or implicitly guaranteed in the Constitution, rejecting, for example, claims that the document included in its scope rights to welfare benefits (*Dandridge v. Williams* [1970]) or an equal education (*San Antonio Indep. School Dist. v. Rodriguez* [1973]). The Court also appeared reluctant to expand upon the number of suspect classifications subject to strict judicial scrutiny under that branch of the "new" or substantive equal protection philosophy. Early in Chief Justice Burger's tenure, the justices did add alienage to the list of constitutional "suspects" and struck down a number of legal distinctions drawn between citizens and aliens, including lengthy residency requirements for receiving welfare benefits (*Graham v. Richardson* [1971]) as well as exclusion of aliens from state civil service positions (*Sugarman v. Dougall* [1973]) and admission to the bar (*In Re Griffiths* [1973]). But the Court also recognized the power of government to exclude aliens from elective office as well as important nonelective positions directly involved in the formulation, execution, or review of broad public policy, and a majority even included state troopers (*Foley v. Connelie* [1978]), though not notary publics (*Bernal v. Fainter* [1984]), in this "public function" exception to strict scrutiny for alienage classifications. The justices recognized, moreover, that overriding national interests might justify congressional controls over aliens that states would not be permitted to impose (*Hampton v. Mow Sun Wong* [1976]). A unanimous body upheld, for example, a Social Security regulation making aliens ineligible to participate in the Medicare supplemental medical insurance program unless they had been admitted for permanent residence and had also resided in the United States for at least five years (*Mathews v. Diaz* [1976]).

In a dissent from two of the Court's alienage rulings, Justice Rehnquist argued against strict judicial review of government classifications except those based on race or color. Rehnquist conceded that the "principal purpose" of the Fourteenth Amendment's drafters was "to prohibit the States from invidiously discriminating by reason of race" and that "because of this plainly manifested intent, classifications based on race [had] rightly been held 'suspect' under the Amendment." Emphasizing, however, that the amendment contained "no language concerning 'inherently suspect classifications,' or, for that matter, merely 'suspect classifications,'" he vigorously disputed the amendment's extension to "'discrete and insular minorities' other than racial minorities" (*Sugarman v. Dougall*, pp. 649–650). Alienage and other nonracial classifications should be upheld, contended Rehnquist, if they overcame the lenient, rational basis review under which economic and social regulations regularly withstood challenge.

Although unwilling fully to embrace Justice Rehnquist's position, a majority on the Court declined further additions to the list of constitutional suspects. In a 1976 case upholding a statute that imposed a mandatory retirement age of fifty on uniformed state police, for example, the Court refused to declare age a suspect basis of classification and sustained the challenged policy as a rational means for assuring physically fit police (*Massachusets Bd. of Retirement v. Murgia* [1976]). Other cases declined to extend suspect status to illegitimacy (*Labine v. Vincent* [1971]) and mental handicap (*City of Cleburne v. Cleburne Living Center* [1985]). Moreover, while several Warren Court decisions had subjected to strict scrutiny laws that drew lines based on individual wealth (e.g., *Harper v. Virginia Bd. of Elections* [1966]), the Burger Court refused to include poverty among the suspect classifications (*San Antonio Indep. School Dist. v. Rodriguez* [1973]).

The Burger Court's general refusal to expand the scope of the "suspect categories" and "fundamental rights" branches of the "new" equal protection doctrine did not mean, however, that discriminatory laws not included within the doctrine's reach would receive only the most lenient rational basis scrutiny and invariably be upheld against constitutional challenge. Instead, the Court subjected such classifications to varying degrees of meaningful review, upholding some and striking down others as violations of equal protection.

In certain cases the Court invoked the rational basis test but gave it a relatively strict application. A 1985 case struck down, for example, a city zoning ordinance limiting the location of group homes for the mentally retarded. Speaking for the majority, Justice White rejected the claim that classifications based on mental handicap should be given any stricter review than that normally accorded economic and social controls. At the same time, he found no rational basis for believing that a group home would pose any special threat to legitimate community interests and suggested that the city's policy rested instead on an irrational prejudice against the mentally retarded (*City of Cleburne v. Cleburne Living Center* [1985]). Had the Court been dealing with a purely economic measure, the ordinance would surely have withstood challenge under the rational basis test.

In other cases the Court extended meaningful protection to interests it had previously declined to characterize as fundamental rights. To sustain a district-to-district variation in per capita student funding for public schools, the Court in the *Rodriguez* case had rejected the contention that the Constitution includes a fundamental right to an equal education. In *Plyler v. Doe* (1982), it reaffirmed that position yet invalidated a Texas policy excluding illegal alien Mexican children from the state's public schools. Emphasizing the lifetime hardship the policy potentially inflicted on children hardly responsible for their situations, as well as the pivotal importance of education to the national interest, Justice Brennan concluded for the majority that the Court could properly consider such costs in evaluating a statute's rationality. Chief Justice Burger, joined by three colleagues, argued in dissent, however, that while it was indeed "senseless for an enlightened society to deprive any children . . . of an elementary education," the Texas policy interfered with no constitutional right. "If ever a court was guilty of an unabashedly result-oriented approach," he declared, "this case is a prime example" (pp. 242, 244).

Finally, and perhaps most significant, the Court subjected to varying degrees of intermediate judicial scrutiny forms of discrimination it considered to be based on "quasi-suspect" categories of classification. Classifications most clearly recognized as such were those based on sex or gender. The Supreme Court did not strike down a gender classification for the first time until 1971. Indeed, as late as 1961, the Warren Court had upheld a Florida law excluding women from jury duty unless they expressed a desire to serve (*Hoyt v. Florida*). Speaking for a unanimous body in *Reed v. Reed*, Chief Justice Burger declared unconstitutional a state law that gave males preference over equally qualified females in the appointment of administrators of estates. Burger purported to apply the lenient rational basis standard in the case. But he also recognized that the administrative convenience the challenged rule provided in reducing the workload of probate courts was "not without legitimacy" yet declared such "a mandatory preference to members of either sex over members of the other . . . the very kind of arbitrary legislative choice" the equal protection guarantee forbade (p. 76). The inference to be drawn was clear: Gender classifications were now subject to some degree of meaningful judicial oversight. But what sort?

Two years later a four-member plurality concluded that gender classifications, like those based on race or color, were inherently suspect, to be upheld against challenge only if found necessary to promote a compelling government interest. The case was *Frontiero v. Richardson*, invalidating a military regulation that automatically provided dependency allowances to married male members of the uniformed services but required females to establish that they were in fact responsible for over half their spouse's support. Announcing the Court's decision, Justice Brennan observed that the nation had experienced "a long and unfortunate history of sex [as well as racial] discrimination" (p. 684), that sex, like race, was an "accident of birth" bearing "no relationship to ability" or obligation (p. 686), and that Congress—a coequal branch of government entitled to respect—had implicitly concluded through its legislation "that classifications based on sex are inherently invidious" (p. 687). Based on such considerations, Brennan included gender among the constitutional suspects, subjected the dependency regulation to strict scrutiny, and found the claim of administrative convenience supporting the scheme inadequate to withstand that heavy burden of justification.

But Justice Brennan spoke only for himself and Justices Douglas, White, and Marshall. Justice Stewart joined the Court's judgment but not the Brennan rationale, citing the *Reed* decision. Justice Powell, joined by Burger and Blackmun, also based his vote on *Reed*, finding it unnecessary at that point to decide that sex was a suspect, especially since the proposed ERA was then pending in the state legislatures. The ERA provided that "[e]quality of rights under the law shall not be denied or abridged by the

United States or by any state on account of sex" and authorized Congress to enforce its provisions "by appropriate legislation." To Powell, therefore, Justice Brennan's "reaching out to preempt by judicial action a major political decision . . . currently in process of resolution [did] not reflect appropriate respect for duly prescribed legislative processes" (p. 692). The Court's final member, Justice Rehnquist, dissented, citing the lower court opinion in the case, which had upheld the challenged regulation as rationally related to the military's interest in administrative convenience.

Justice Brennan never secured a majority for his contention that gender classifications are inherently suspect. In 1976, however, he spoke for the Court, over the dissents of Chief Justice Burger and Justice Rehnquist, in announcing that gender-based laws must serve important governmental objectives and be substantially related to the achievement of those objectives. Struck down as a violation of equal protection in *Craig v. Boren* was an Oklahoma statute that permitted women to purchase 3.2 percent beer at age eighteen while requiring males to wait until age twenty-one. The state had cited data relating to the drunk-driving arrests and traffic injuries of young males in defending the law as a safety measure. Pointing out, among other things, that only .18 percent of females and 2 percent of males in the eighteen-to-twenty age group had been arrested for driving under the influence of liquor, Justice Brennan concluded that such statistical evidence was insufficient to justify the challenged law.

Under *Craig*, then, the Court treated sex in effect as quasi- (or semi-) suspect and subjected gender discrimination to an intermediate standard of judicial review more rigorous than the rational basis test required, yet less demanding than the strict review under which suspect classifications almost invariably met defeat. Applying such an approach in later cases, the Court upheld certain gender classifications while striking down others as a violation of equal protection. In 1982, for example, a majority overturned the refusal of the Mississippi University for Women to admit a male to its nursing program (*Mississippi University for Women v. Hogan* [1982]). But a year earlier, in *Rostker v. Goldberg*, a majority sustained, over the objections of Justices Brennan, White, and Marshall, a policy of male-only military draft registration. Emphasizing for the Court the considerable deference due congressional judgments, especially in the field of national security, Justice Rehnquist concluded that the decision of Congress was not based on gender stereotyping. Instead, all-male registration was based on the likely need, were the draft reactivated, for combat troops, from which women were excluded by statute or military policy—a policy the dissenters did not challenge. In another 1981 case, a 5–4 majority upheld a state statute punishing males, but not females, for statutory rape (sexual relations with an underaged person). The state could reasonably assume, Justice Rehnquist concluded for a plurality of justices, that fear of pregnancy would be an adequate deterrent to female promiscuity with young males (*Michael M. v. Superior Court*). And in 1979 the Court upheld a veterans' preference policy in state civil service recruitment against sex discrimination claims. Justice Stewart reasoned for the majority that the statute at issue preferred veterans of either sex over nonveterans, not men over women (*Personnel Administrator of Massachusetts v. Feeney* [1979]).

Although not in as clear-cut a fashion, the Court also treated illegitimacy as quasi-suspect, subjecting classifications based on status of birth to somewhat more meaningful scrutiny than the rational basis test required, even though at times purporting to apply the rationality standard. The Warren Court, in striking down several statutes that limited the inheritance rights of illegitimate children, suggested that the equal protection guarantee encompassed a right to intimate, familial relationships (e.g., *Levy v. Louisiana* [1971]). In *Labine v. Vincent* (1971), an early Burger Court ruling, Justice Black, who vehemently opposed use of the "vague generalities" of due process and equal protection as bases for the recognition of rights mentioned nowhere in the Constitution's text, spoke for a majority in ignoring the Warren Court's pronouncements, subjecting illegitimacy classifications to virtually no judicial scrutiny, and upholding a statute that barred an illegitimate child from sharing equally with legitimate children in the estate of their father. After Black's retirement and death, however, the Court made another partial about-face in *Weber v. Aetna Casualty Co.* (1972), striking down workmen's compensation statutes that denied equal recovery rights to dependent, unacknowledged illegitimate children. Speaking for the *Weber* majority, Justice Powell concluded that such classifications involved "sensitive and fundamental rights" requiring "stricter scrutiny" than the rationality standard imposed. Visiting society's condemnation of "irresponsible liaisons beyond the bonds of marriage . . . on the head of an infant," declared Powell, "is illogical and unjust" (p. 175). Following *Weber*, the Court upheld certain illegitimacy classifications while overturning others, applying a standard of scrutiny less stringent than that invoked in gender cases but more demanding than Justice Black had invoked in *Labine v. Vincent* (e.g., *Mathews v. Lucas* [1976], *Trimble v. Gordon* [1977], *Lalli v. Lalli* [1978], *Parham v. Hughes* [1979], *Mills v. Habluetzel* [1982]).

Clear-cut doctrinal standards were equally difficult to discern in other areas of Burger Court decision making in the equal protection field. Although the justices, as noted earlier, refused to include poverty among the constitutional suspects, a majority in *Boddie v. Connecticut* (1971) invoked the due process guarantee to invalidate a filing-fee requirement limiting access of the poor to divorce proceedings. But Justice Harlan's opinion for the *Boddie* Court was based on the importance of marriage to society and the state's monopoly over the means for its dissolution, and in a 1973 case the Court upheld imposition of a filing fee on those wishing to initiate bankruptcy proceedings. Justice Blackmun emphasized for the majority that there was no fundamental right to bankruptcy, and other means were available for resolving financial difficulties (*United States v. Kras* [1973]). Based on that reasoning, the Court also upheld a filing fee for persons seeking judicial review of a reduction in their welfare benefits (*Ortwein v. Schwab* [1973]). In *Sosna v. Iowa* (1975), moreover, a majority distinguished Warren and Burger Court decisions subjecting lengthy residency requirements to strict scrutiny on interstate travel grounds and upheld a one-year residency restriction on the filing of divorce actions. In dissent, Justice Marshall, joined by Justice Brennan, bemoaned the majority's failure to apply strict scrutiny in the case, especially given the critical importance of divorce relative to the interests at stake in certain of the earlier cases involving burdens on interstate travel.

What seemed clear, however, was that at least outside the racial sphere the Burger Court was unwilling to apply what a majority considered to be unduly rigid formulae to different categories of discrimination, preferring instead to tailor its opinions largely to the special circumstances of individual cases. In several dissenting opinions, Justice Marshall had urged the Court to adopt a flexible, balancing-of-interests approach to equal protection issues, under which "concentration [would] be placed upon the character of the classification in question, the relative importance to individuals in the class discriminated against of the government benefits that they do not receive, and the asserted state interests in support of the classification" (*Dandridge v. Williams*, pp. 520–521). Although never formally embracing Marshall's sliding scale approach, equal protection doctrine on the Burger Court clearly reflected the flexibility Marshall advocated, though often with results he and Justice Brennan vehemently opposed.

Equal Protection Issues

Of equal protection issues the Burger Court confronted, the most difficult and contentious, of course, involved race. In the last years of Chief Justice Warren's tenure, the Court had become increasingly impatient with southern resistance to school desegregation. State-mandated segregation in public education had been declared invalid in 1954, yet more than a decade later most southern school systems remained entirely or largely segregated. The progress in the desegregation field that began to occur in the late 1960s and early 1970s resulted primarily from the adoption of the 1964 Civil Rights Act, which included a provision authorizing the federal government to withhold funds from local schools that failed to desegregate. In 1968, however, the Warren Court had also assumed a more aggressive posture, declaring that any scheme of pupil placement that did not lead to meaningful change in the racial composition of public schools was unconstitutional (*Green v. New Kent County*). The next year the justices insisted that desegregation begin "at once" (*Alexander v. Holmes County Board of Education* [1969]).

Faithful to that stance and to growing congressional support of racial equality in a variety of fields, the Burger Court approved broad discretion on the part of federal trial judges to convert dual school systems into racially unitary institutions. Overcoming the doubts of Justice Black and Chief Justice Burger, among others, a unanimous body in *Swann v. Charlotte-Mecklenburg Board of Education* (1971) upheld the busing of students, the assignment of students and staff by race, and other measures to assure meaningful desegregation of school districts with a history of state-prescribed segregation. Speaking for the Court, the chief justice insisted that racial balance was not a long-term constitutional requirement and that the use of racial quotas in student-faculty placement was only a temporary desegregation tool. He also noted that consideration for the health of children might limit the permissible duration of court-ordered bus rides. In general, though, the ruling granted trial judges extraordinary authority to eliminate dual school systems.

The unanimity that had prevailed during the Warren era, however, soon collapsed. In 1972 a 5–4 majority prohibited the withdrawal of Emporia, Virginia, from its county school system, pointing out that there were fewer blacks in Emporia than in the surrounding county and that such realignments of school districts in an area with a history of state-enforced segregation would obstruct desegregation goals. Dissenters charged that the Court was seeking racial balance for its own sake rather than compliance with constitutional requirements (*Wright v. Emporia*).

The next year a more sizable majority extended desegregation principles to a school system with no history of segregation by law or state constitutional provision. In *Keyes v. School District*, the Court held that a finding of intentional segregation by officials in a meaningful portion of the Denver, Colorado, school system obliged school officials to prove that other segregated schools in the system were not also the result of such action. In a partial dissent, Justice Powell challenged the *Keyes* majority's assumption that the Constitution forbade only de jure segregation (that is, segregation promoted by law or other intentional governmental action) and not de facto segregation (resulting from segregated housing patterns and the placement of pupils in schools nearest their homes rather than from official misconduct). A Virginian, Powell realized that the nation's most segregated schools were now to be found outside the South, where the "*de facto/de jure* distinction . . . [was] accepted complacently by many of the same voices which denounced the evils of segregated schools" in his native region (pp. 218–219). Especially since the segregated housing patterns common in other parts of the country were themselves often a product of official design, Powell dismissed the de facto–de jure dichotomy as unrealistic and outmoded, favoring instead "constitutional principles of national rather than merely regional application" (p. 219).

In *Milliken v. Bradley* (1974), however, a 5–4 majority that included Justice Powell not only reaffirmed the de facto–de jure distinction but also imposed significant restrictions on the authority of federal courts to eliminate segregated schools in multidistrict metropolitan areas. After finding de jure segregation in the Detroit school system, a federal district judge attempted to effect meaningful racial change in the composition of its schools by imposing a cross-district desegregation order requiring the busing of students between Detroit's predominantly black system and largely white suburban districts. Speaking for the majority in overturning that order, Chief Justice Burger declared that desegregation must be confined to the area in which a constitutional violation had occurred. Forbidden de jure segregation existed only in the Detroit school system, and there was no evidence of interdistrict collusion to maintain the segregation of white and minority students. The trial court's order, declared Burger, had thus exceeded judicial authority and unduly interfered with local control over public education.

Accusing the majority of exalting administrative convenience over constitutional commands, Justice White, joined by Justices Douglas, Brennan, and Marshall, warned that the Court's approach would permit a state, "the entity at which the Fourteenth Amendment is directed," to avoid meaningful desegregation through the simple expedient of "vesting sufficient power over its public schools in its local school districts" (p. 763). White was

> mystified as to how the Court can ignore the legal reality that the constitutional violations, even if occurring locally, were committed by governmental entities for which the State is responsible and that it is the State that must respond to the command of the Fourteenth Amendment. An interdistrict remedy for the infringements that occurred in this case is well within the confines and powers of the State, which is the governmental entity ultimately responsible for desegregating its schools. (p. 770)

Echoing White's concerns, Justice Marshall, also joined by the other dissenters, expressed fear that

> [t]oday's holding . . . [was] more a reflection of a perceived public mood that we have gone far enough in enforcing the Constitution's guarantee of equal justice than it [was] the product of neutral principles of law. In the short run, it may seem to be the easier course to allow our great metropolitan areas to be divided up each into two cities—one white, the other black—but it is a course, I predict, our people will ultimately regret. (pp. 814–815)

Whatever *Milliken*'s impact on the rate of white flight to the suburbs, it was not to be the Burger Court's only decision limiting the authority of federal judges in school desegregation cases. In 1970 a federal judge had ordered the Pasadena, California, board of education to adopt a desegregation plan that included a provision stipulating that no school in the system would have a majority of any minority students. When the school system complied with the "no majority" rule the first year the order was in effect, but a number of schools were unable to comply in subsequent years as a result of population shifts in the system, the judge ordered annual adjustments in school attendance zones to achieve his objective. The Supreme Court, speaking through Justice Rehnquist, held that the lower court had exceeded its authority. Emphasizing that changes in the racial composition of schools in the system were the result of population shifts rather than official action designed to perpetuate segregation, Rehnquist concluded that a trial court could not continue indefinitely to impose racial quotas once a system had fulfilled, even briefly, its affirmative duty to desegregate (*Pasadena Bd. of Education v. Spangler* [1976]).

Nor was the Court's focus on intentional discrimination limited to school desegregation cases. In *Griggs v. Duke Power Co.* (1971), a unanimous body, with Justice Brennan not participating, upheld the anti–employment discrimination provisions of Title VII of the 1964 Civil Rights Act, as applied to a general intelligence test administered to job applicants and a requirement that they have a high school education. There was no showing that the test was adopted and administered with an invidious intent, but it had a racially disproportionate impact, and the Court, speaking through Chief Justice Burger, held that any employment requirement having such an effect was unlawful unless shown to bear "a demonstrable relationship to successful performance of the jobs for which it was used" (p. 431).

Although Congress was thus permitted to forbid by law practices with a racially disproportionate impact, however neutral their purpose, the Court required proof of invidious intent before striking down regulations on constitutional grounds. In the leading case on the issue, *Washington v. Davis* (1976), a 7–2 majority sustained a personnel test administered to applicants for jobs as police officers in Washington, D.C. A racially neutral requirement, declared Justice White, was not to be deemed unconstitutional merely because it had a disparate impact, whatever its relationship to actual job performance. The absence of discriminatory intent was significant in other cases as well. In 1971 a narrow majority upheld the decision of Jackson, Mississippi, officials to close the city's swimming pools rather than operate them on an integrated basis. Justice Black refused for the Court to find a discriminatory purpose in the city's decision, whatever psychological motives may have underlay its officials' decision (*Palmer v. Thompson* [1971]). *Mobile v. Bolden* (1980), moreover, upheld that city's at-large elections of city commissioners, even though the arrangement produced an all-white governing body. But in a 1982 case, a majority struck down a Georgia county's at-large election system on a finding that while racially neutral in origin, it was being maintained for invidious purposes (*Rogers v. Lodge*).

As *Griggs* indicated, the Court accorded Congress greater discretion in defining and enforcing civil rights under its various lawmaking powers than the justices allowed themselves or lower courts in their judicial interpretations of constitutional guarantees. Such a stance was consistent with the position the Warren Court had assumed. In 1959, for example, that Court had upheld fairly administered literacy tests for voting (*Lassiter v. Northampton Co. Bd. of Elections* [1959]). But when Congress outlawed such requirements in certain parts of the nation in the 1965 Voting Rights Act, based on evidence they were more often used to assure a white electorate than a literate one, the Court upheld the ban as a proper exercise of broad congressional power to enforce the Fifteenth Amendment's prohibition on racial discrimination in voting. The justices further concluded that congressional statutes need be only rationally related to carrying out one of Congress's lawmaking powers in order to withstand constitutional challenge (*South Carolina v. Katzenbach* [1959]). In 1968, moreover, the Warren Court upheld a provision of the 1866 Civil Rights Act, a Reconstruction-era measure giving all citizens the same rights as white citizens in the sale and rental of property. Declaring the law an appropriate exercise of Congress's power to enforce the Thirteenth Amendment's ban on slavery and involuntary servitude, Justice Stewart reasoned for the Court that the amendment empowered Congress to prohibit, as a badge or remnant of slavery, every form of racial discrimination, whether governmental or private in nature, despite numerous precedents giving the amendment a more restricted judicial construction (*Jones v. Alfred H. Mayer Co.*).

The Burger Court reaffirmed that broad construction of congressional authority in *Runyon v. McCrary* (1976). *Runyon* upheld a provision of the 1866 Civil Rights Act guaranteeing racial equality in contractual relationships, as applied to a commercially operated private school's refusal to admit black students. Later the Court sustained provisions of the 1965 Voting Rights Act obliging states and localities with a history of racial discrimination in the franchise to secure the approval (or "pre-clearance") of federal authorities before enacting new election laws—even when that requirement was used to deny pre-clearance to voting practices with only a racially disproportionate effect rather than an invidious purpose (*Rome v. United States* [1980]).

Still, at times the Court gave federal civil rights statutes a narrow interpretation. In *Grove City College v. Bell* (1984), a majority construed Title IX of 1972 civil rights legislation, forbidding gender discrimination in colleges and universities that received federal funds, to apply only to specific programs receiving such assistance, not to the entire institution. Recipients of federal funding could discriminate in their athletic programs, for example, so long as those programs received no federal money. The decision provoked considerable public outcry, and in 1987 Congress enacted, over President Reagan's veto, legislation applying Title IX to an entire institution if any of its programs received federal assistance.

Much of the Burger Court's nonracial equal protection caseload involved elections, voting, apportionment, and related issues. In a series of important reapportionment cases, the Warren Court had held that the districts from which members of the U.S. House of Representatives, both houses of state legislatures, and county commissions were elected must be substantially equal in population (e.g., *Wesberry v. Sanders* [1964], *Reynolds v. Sims* [1964], *Avery v. Midland Co.* [1968]). The Burger Court extended the reach of this one person, one vote principle to most governmental bodies whose members were elected by district (e.g., *Hadley v. Junior College Dist.* [1970]) but relaxed its application in cases involving state and local governing bodies. In one suit, for example, it upheld a Virginia state legislative districting scheme with a 16.4 percent population deviation, concluding that a state was justified in seeking to avoid cutting through county and city boundaries in fashioning districts (*Mahan v. Howell* [1973]). Deviations in population equality of up to 10 percent, the Court concluded in other cases, were so "relatively minor" they required no justification (*Gaffney v. Cummings* [1973], *White v. Register* [1973]). But a majority insisted that *congressional* districts adhere as closely as possible to mathematical equality of population (e.g., *Karcher v. Daggett* [1983]).

Other election and voting cases produced equally mixed results. The Court in 1970 struck down a statute restricting to property owners elections to approve general obligation bonds (*Phoenix v. Kolodziejsk*). Two years later it invalidated a one-year residency requirement for voting as an undue interference with fundamental voting rights (*Dunn v. Blumstein* [1972]), making clear later that thirty to fifty days were sufficient to assure the franchise was limited to bona fide residents (*Marston v. Lewis* [1973], *Burns v. Fortson* [1973]). But early in Chief Justice Burger's tenure, the Court upheld a state constitutional provision requiring voter approval for low-rent housing projects, ignoring the contention of dissenters that classifications based on poverty were constitutionally suspect (*James v. Valtierra* [1971]). The justices also permitted states considerable flexibility in limiting the eligible electorate for special-purpose governmental units. In a 1973 case, for example, a majority sustained an arrangement under which only landowners were allowed to vote for members of a water storage district's governing board and their votes were apportioned to the assessed value of their holdings (*Salyer Land Co. v. Water Storage Dist.* [1973]). That precedent was later extended to a "one acre, one vote" scheme for electing directors of a large Arizona water reclamation district (*Ball v. James* [1981]). Because of the specialized purposes of such governing bodies, the Court refused to subject them to the strict judicial scrutiny ordinarily given restrictions on voting rights.

Provisions for the disenfranchisement of voters were both upheld and struck down. A felony conviction is a common ground for the loss of voting rights. But in *Richardson v. Ramirez* (1974), a majority permitted a state to deny the vote even to ex-felons. The Fourteenth Amendment stipulated a reduction in congressional representation for states that denied adult males the vote but exempted states from that requirement for disenfranchisement of convicted felons. The amendment's framers, Justice Rehnquist reasoned for the *Ramirez* majority, thus could not have intended to forbid exclusion of felons, or ex-felons, from the franchise. In 1985, by contrast, a unanimous body declared unconstitutional a provision of the Alabama constitution disenfranchising persons convicted of crimes of moral turpitude, declaring that the enactment was motivated by a desire to deny the vote to blacks and had had a racially disproportionate impact since its adoption in 1901 (*Hunter v. Underwood* [1985]).

Other cases reviewed state restrictions on "raiding," the practice in which members of a political party temporarily cross party lines in an effort to secure another party's nomination of weak candidates for public office in a party primary. In 1973 the Court sustained a New York regulation requiring voters to register their party affiliation before a general election in order to be eligible to vote in the next year's party primary. The arrangement prevented changes in party affiliation for up to eleven months. Speaking for the majority, Justice Stewart emphasized that the regulation did not absolutely disenfranchise voters but merely imposed a time deadline that was not unreasonably long and thus did not unduly burden voting rights or the First-Fourteenth Amendment freedom of association (*Rosario v. Rockefeller* [1973]). The same year, though, a majority, again speaking through Justice Stewart, invalidated an Illinois law prohibiting persons from voting in a party's primary if they had participated in another party's primary in the past twenty-three months. The New York regulation, Justice Stewart explained, caused disenfranchisement only if a voter failed to change parties within the designated time limit, whereas the Illinois provision allowed voters to switch parties only by foregoing participation in any primary for nearly two years (*Kusper v. Pontikes* [1973]).

During Chief Justice Burger's last term, the Court also placed significant burdens on those challenging political gerrymandering, the practice of drawing legislative district lines with an eye toward favoring one political party or other group while disadvantaging others. In *Davis v. Bandemer* (1986), Democrats complained that Indiana's Republican-controlled legislature had drawn legislative district lines for partisan advantage. Speaking for a plurality, Justice White, joined by Brennan, Marshall, and Blackmun, required the challengers to produce evidence showing that a particular districting scheme caused "continued frustration of the will of the majority of the voters or effective denial to a minority of voters of a fair chance to influence the political process" over a significant number of elections (p. 133). The mere absence of party representation proportionate to party voting strength in the electorate was not sufficient. Although White spoke only for a plurality, three other justices concluded that partisan gerrymandering raised political questions that were inappropriate for judicial resolution.

By far the most troublesome equal protection issues facing the Burger Court, however, involved affirmative action programs created by public and private institutions in an effort to overcome the effects of past discrimination against minorities and women. Albeit varying considerably in form and rigor, such programs required special consideration for race and gender in employment, university admissions, and related competitive contexts. Their supporters cited the institutional advantages of diversity as well as the difficulties of eliminating covert forms of racial and gender discrimination without the imposition of affirmative obligations. The sooner the society became meaningfully integrated, defenders of affirmative action also maintained, the sooner racial and gender stereotypes, and the discrimination they fostered, would disappear. Critics contended that such programs constituted "reverse discrimination" every bit as offensive to the Constitution as discrimination against minorities and women, that they conflicted with the principle of advancement based on merit, aggravated racial and gender hostilities, and might even generate feelings of inferiority in those they were designed to help.

In his famous dissent from the Supreme Court's decision in *Plessy v. Ferguson* (1896), upholding state segregation laws, the first Justice John Marshall Harlan had declared that adoption of the Thirteenth, Fourteenth, and Fifteenth Amendments had created a "color-blind Constitution." Opponents of affirmative action argued that such programs violated that basic constitutional principle.

When the issue first reached the Court, a majority, as noted earlier, avoided a ruling on the issue by declaring the case moot (*DeFunis v. Odegaard* [1974]). In *Regents of the University of California v. Bakke* (1978), however, the Court struck down an arrangement under which sixteen of the 100 first-year seats at the University of California, Davis, medical school were set aside for minority applicants alone. In an opinion announcing the Court's judgment, Justice Powell concluded that such a racial quota violated the equal protection guarantee; four other justices (Burger, Stewart, Rehnquist, and Stevens) rested their votes to invalidate the program on statutory grounds, declaring that it violated Title VI of the 1964 Civil Rights Act, which forbade racial discrimination in federally funded institutions. Powell also asserted, however, that although all racial classifications were constitutionally suspect and subject to the most exacting judicial scrutiny, a state's interest in securing a diverse student body was sufficiently compelling to justify consideration of race and other nonacademic factors in university admissions decisions. Justices Brennan, White, Marshall, and Blackmun argued, moreover, that since affirmative action programs had no racially stigmatizing intent or effect, their constitutionality should be subjected to the less demanding intermediate standard of review then applied to gender and other quasi-suspect classifications, rather than to the exacting scrutiny the Court had previously reserved for discrimination motivated by racial hatred and prejudice. Under that standard, those justices considered the medical school's quota an acceptable means of correcting the effects of past discrimination against minorities. With Powell's position controlling, then, states were forbidden to impose racial quotas excluding other applicants from consideration. But race could be taken into account along with other nonmerit factors in admissions decisions.

The next year the Court decided its first affirmative action employment case. By agreement of union representatives and management, the Kaiser Aluminum Company established a plan to eliminate serious racial imbalances in its almost exclusively white craftwork positions. Under that plan Kaiser set aside 50 percent of its openings in craft training positions for black employees until the percentage of blacks in those jobs approximated the proportion of blacks in the local labor force. The Fourteenth Amendment equal protection guarantee applies only to state action, not private companies. But Brian Weber, a white production worker passed over for blacks with less seniority at Kaiser's Grammacy, Louisiana, plant, argued that the program violated Title VII of the 1964 Civil Rights Act, prohibiting racial discrimination in employment.

Reversing lower courts, a 5–2 Supreme Court, with Justices Powell and Stevens not participating, concluded that Title VII was not intended to forbid private, voluntary, race-conscious affirmative action programs. Citing an earlier Burger Court decision (*McDonald v. Santa Fe Trail Transportation Co.* [1976]), Justice Brennan conceded for the majority that Title VII protected whites as well as blacks from discrimination based on race or color. The legislative history underlying Title VII's adoption persuaded the majority, however, that the law forbade courts and enforcement agencies only from *requiring* companies to establish race-conscious hiring programs; it did not necessarily forbid all such voluntary arrangements. In dissent, though, Chief Justice Burger and Justice Rehnquist accused the majority of ignoring Title VII's clear language and rewriting the law to achieve what the majority regarded as a desirable result (*United Steelworkers v. Weber* [1979]).

Affirmative action in public employment bore a heavier burden of justification. In a 1986 case, for example, the Court overturned a teacher layoff arrangement that was based on seniority but also stipulated that at no time would a greater percentage of minority personnel be laid off than the percentage of minority teachers employed at the time of the layoff. Speaking for a four-member plurality, Justice Powell stressed that racial classifications were subject to strict scrutiny under the equal protection clause while also indicating that convincing evidence of prior discrimination was necessary to justify the use of racial classifications for remedial purposes (*Wygant v. Jackson Bd. of Education* [1986]). The Court also made clear, however, that Congress enjoyed broader discretion than the states and localities to impose race-conscious remedies. In 1980, for example, the Court upheld a congressional statute requiring at least 10 percent of federal funds granted for local public works projects to be set aside for services or supplies secured from minority businesses (*Fullilove v. Klutznick* [1980]). This double standard, subjecting federal affirmative action requirements to less rigorous review than their state and local counterparts, would persist until 1995, when the Rehnquist Court imposed the same strict standards on all such programs (*Adarand Constructors v. Pena* [1995]).

Freedom of Expression

The First Amendment provides, "Congress shall make no law respecting an establishment of religion, or prohibiting the free exercise thereof; or abridging the freedom of speech, or of the press; or the right of the people peaceably to assemble, and to petition the government for a redress of grievances." Through the incorporation process, as we have seen, these basic guarantees, like most other safeguards in the Bill of Rights, have been made binding on the states through the Supreme Court's interpretation of the Fourteenth Amendment due process clause. Given their importance to a free society, the modern Supreme Court has generally subjected governmental burdens on their enjoyment to close judicial scrutiny.

The Burger Court's impact on those provisions of the First Amendment safeguarding freedom of expression and association was significant but more subtle than fundamental, elaborating upon Warren-era and earlier precedents while both narrowing and expanding their scope. Like its modern predecessors, the Court imposed a heavier burden of justification on government impositions of prior restraints, or censorship of expression, than on its subsequent punishment through criminal prosecution or other sanctions. In *New York Times Co. v. United States* (1971), a 6–3 majority turned back perhaps the most alarming challenge to freedom of the press in the nation's history—the Nixon administration's attempt to secure court injunctions against the *Times* and *Washington Post* to prevent further publication of excerpts from a classified multivolume history of U.S. involvement in the Vietnam War, popularly known as *The Pentagon Papers*.

The brief per curiam opinion announcing the Court's decision simply indicated that the government had not met the "heavy burden" necessary to justify any prior restraint on the press, but every justice filed an opinion in the case. Embracing an absolutist interpretation of the First Amendment, Justices Black and Douglas opposed the imposition of any injunction against the press. Justice Brennan came close to adopting the Black-Douglas stance but suggested that he might vote to uphold an injunction against expression creating a clear and present danger to national security, such as a newspaper item identifying the routes of troop ships during wartime. Justice Marshall emphasized that Congress had twice declined to pass legislation giving the president the power President Nixon now wanted the courts to exercise, while Justice Stewart placed responsibility for international relations and national defense in the presidency, rejecting judicial authority to exercise such functions in the absence of specific laws and regulations. Justice White, like Marshall, stressed the absence of congressional authorization for prior restraints. Several of the majority justices questioned the president's assertion of an "inherent" national security power that had no basis in either a statute or the Constitution's text. But both Stewart and White, especially the latter, suggested that criminal proceedings under

existing laws could properly be brought against those responsible for leaking classified materials, including members of the press. (Ultimately, a criminal prosecution of
Daniel Ellsberg, the disillusioned Defense Department analyst who leaked the papers
to the press, collapsed as a result of violations of the defendant's constitutional
rights.)

The three dissenters vehemently protested the haste with which the case was
decided. For that reason, Chief Justice Burger declined to reach the First Amendment
issue, although supporting criminal prosecution of those guilty of violating security
statutes. Justice Harlan would have limited judicial review in such cases to a determination that the dispute lay within the broad scope of presidential power over foreign relations and that a department head had made the decision to classify the
material in question. Justice Blackmun, the third dissenter, concluded that the
national security interests at stake in the case outweighed the competing interest in
a free press.

Other prior restraints on expression failed to withstand challenge as well. The
same year the *Pentagon Papers* suit was decided, the Court struck down an injunction directed at a racially integrated citizens' organization's distribution of leaflets
critical of a real estate agency's use of "block-busting" techniques, rejecting as inadequate to support such a restraint on the organization's expression rights both the bro-
ker's privacy interests and any possible chilling effect the leafleting might have
imposed on its commercial activities (*Organization for a Better Austin v. Keefe*
[1971]). In 1975 the Court, over Justice Rehnquist's lone dissent, invalidated a statute
prohibiting media disclosure of the names of rape victims, Justice White asserting for
the majority that any privacy interests the law might protect must yield where information revealed in open court proceedings and available in court documents was
reported in the press (*Cox Broadcasting Corp. v. Cohn* [1975]). And in *Nebraska
Press Association v. Stuart* (1976), the Court struck down a state trial judge's gag
order forbidding the press to publish or broadcast confessions or other material
implicating a defendant in the murder of six members of a Nebraska farm family. In
his opinion for the Court, Chief Justice Burger reaffirmed the presumption against
prior restraints and faulted the trial judge for not exploring alternative means of
assuring the accused a trial by an impartial jury before imposing a gag on the press.
Given the limited territorial reach of the judge's jurisdiction and the likelihood that
events in a small community would travel rapidly by word of mouth, whatever the
media's conduct, Burger also questioned whether the gag would effectively protect
the defendant's fair trial rights. Despite the chief justice's opinion that a gag order
might be appropriate in certain cases, an inspection of concurring opinions filed in
the case offered little prospect that would occur. Although joining the Court's opinion, Justice White expressed "grave doubt" such an order "would ever be justifiable."
Justice Powell also joined the Court's opinion but wrote separately "to emphasize the

unique burden" on those seeking to justify a gag on the press. And Justice Brennan, joined by Stewart and Marshall, concluded that prior restraints were a "constitutionally impermissible means" for assuring a fair trial, declaring, "judges have at their disposal a broad spectrum of devices for ensuring that fundamental fairness is accorded the accused without necessitating so drastic an incursion on the equally fundamental and salutary constitutional mandate that discussion of public affairs in a free society cannot depend on the preliminary grace of judicial censors" (pp. 570, 571, 572–573).

Building on precedent, the Warren Court had applied a number of tests in determining whether particular regulations of expression were constitutional. Under the later Warren Court's version of the clear and present danger test, first enunciated by Justice Holmes in *Schenck v. United States* (1919), speech could be the basis for criminal prosecution only if it amounted to incitement of imminent, or immediate, lawless action very likely to occur as a result of that speech (*Brandenburg v. Ohio* [1969]). The Burger Court rarely invoked the clear and present danger test. In *Eaton v. City of Tulsa* (1974), however, the Court overturned the contempt of court conviction of a defendant who, while being cross-examined on the witness stand during his trial for another offense, had referred to an alleged assailant as "chicken shit." Applying the imminent danger test traditionally used in cases involving contempt citations issued against the press (e.g., *Bridges v. California* [1941]), the Court held that this isolated use of street vernacular, not directed at the judge or any officer of the court, did not create a clear and present danger to the administration of justice and thus could not be held a contempt of court. A year earlier, in overturning the disorderly conduct conviction of a campus demonstrator who had shouted, "We'll take the fucking street later," as police attempted to clear a street of protesters obstructing traffic, the Court had also found no clear and present danger justifying the conviction. Instead, the justices termed the defendant's remarks at worst merely the advocacy of illegal action at some indefinite future time (*Hess v. Indiana* [1973]).

Like its predecessors, the Burger Court also applied a variety of balancing-of-interest tests in expression and association cases. As in certain equal protection contexts, a law regulating the content of speech would be upheld only if found necessary to promote a legitimate and compelling governmental interest, and even then only if no less restrictive means were available to achieve the government's objective. Statutes not directed at the content of expression but at some legitimate governmental purpose, such as control of streets and sidewalks, withstood constitutional challenge if they furthered substantial governmental interests and were narrowly tailored to achieve those objectives.

Burger Court rulings invoked these and related tests, as well as two other staples of the Warren era, the vagueness and overbreadth tests. A law that is so vague in meaning that persons of reasonable intelligence must guess at its meaning violates due process because it provides inadequate notice of what it requires. To assure that laws do not become convenient weapons for the suppression of unpopular views, the Supreme Court has also long held the First Amendment to require that laws affecting expression must be very precisely written and construed by courts. Under the over-breadth test, laws that could be used to affect expression must be narrowly written and enforced, reaching only conduct within government's power to control rather than, because of their unduly broad sweep, constitutionally protected activities as well. In *Coates v. Cincinnati* (1971), the Court struck down on vagueness and over-breadth grounds a city ordinance that made it a crime for three or more persons to gather on sidewalks and engage in conduct "annoying" to passersby. Such a measure, the Court concluded, was so indefinite and sweeping in its scope that it could be used to punish protected speech (e.g., expression of "annoying" political ideas) as well as conduct clearly subject to government control (e.g., shoving passersby).

Relatively early in Chief Justice Burger's tenure, however, the Court imposed a potentially significant restriction on the overbreadth test. The Warren Court had fre-quently declared statutes unconstitutionally vague and overbroad "on their face," rather than as applied in a given case. The principal rationale for such an approach was that a vague and/or unduly broad law, by its very presence, imposed a chilling effect on those who wished to engage in protected expression but feared that the statute might be used to penalize their activities. On that ground the statute would be declared facially vague or overbroad, even if the behavior at issue were subject to regulation under a narrowly and clearly drafted law.

Yet such an approach appeared inconsistent with the traditional principle that courts should be limited to protecting the rights of specific litigants in a case rather than making general pronouncements on the constitutionality of laws. As a result, the Burger Court held in *Broadrick v. Oklahoma* (1973) and *Civil Service Com'n v. National Ass'n of Letter Carriers* (1973), reaffirming the power of government to reg-ulate the political activities of civil servants, that laws affecting expressive conduct and not merely speech alone could be declared overbroad on their face only if they suffered from "substantial" overbreadth. In such cases, Justice White declared for a 5–4 majority, "the overbreadth of a statute must not only be real, but substantial as well, judged in relation to [its] plainly legitimate sweep" (p. 615).

The Burger Court did not confine the scope of protected expression entirely to "pure speech," such as verbal or printed expression, motion pictures, and videotapes. Instead, as in the past, the justices also extended constitutional coverage to "speech-plus"—activities including elements of pure speech as well as other forms of conduct, such as picketing, marching, and demonstrations. But since such forms of expression were likely to interfere with vehicular and pedestrian traffic, they were subject to greater governmental control than pure speech. Government, for example, could impose permit requirements and other reasonable, nondiscriminatory regulations of time, place, and manner narrowly tailored to promote substantial governmental interests unrelated to the suppression of ideas. Not every form of public property, more-over, was held to constitute a "public forum" to which people had a right of access for purposes of expression. Streets, sidewalks, parks, and related areas had histori-cally served such purposes. But the state could deny access to public property (such as jails and courthouses) dedicated to functions inconsistent with its use for pur-poses of expression. As noted earlier, the Court also ultimately reversed precedents extending First Amendment obligations to shopping centers on the ground that they were not sufficiently similar to city business districts to constitute public property for purposes of expression. And even if government chose to convert property into a place of expression for certain purposes, creating a "limited public forum," it contin-ued to retain considerable control over its use. Similar considerations governed the right to "symbolic speech," or forms of nonverbal conduct designed to communicate ideas and feelings.

The relatively few symbolic-speech rulings in the Burger Court's record prima-rily involved statutes prohibiting flag misuse. In *United States v. O'Brien* (1968), upholding a congressional enactment preventing the destruction of military draft cards, as applied to the burning of draft cards during an antiwar demonstration, the Warren Court had concluded that conduct intended to communicate ideas or feelings was subject to governmental regulation that furthered an important interest unre-lated to the suppression of expression if the incidental restriction the regulation imposed on expression was no greater than essential to accomplish the government's objective. The Burger Court adhered to the *O'Brien* test but avoided deciding whether the First Amendment includes a right to burn a flag as a symbol of political protest, leaving that controversial issue for resolution, affirmatively, by a 5–4 Rehn-quist Court majority (*Texas v. Johnson* [1989], *United States v. Eichman* [1990]).

In *Smith v. Goguen* (1974), however, the Court, speaking through Justice Pow-ell, struck down as unduly vague a Massachusetts statute forbidding "contemptuous treatment" of the flag. Justice White concurred only in that judgment. At least as applied in *Goguen*, the flag statute presented no vagueness problems for White. Goguen had been convicted for wearing a small flag sewn to the seat of his trousers. Whatever the statute's ultimate scope, anyone should realize, White contended, that "sewing a flag on the seat of his pants is contemptuous of the flag" (p. 584). But it was also White's view that the Constitution protected expressive uses of the flag and that the challenged statute could be used to punish unconstitutionally the communication of "ideas about the flag unacceptable to the controlling majority in the legislature" (p. 588). Justice Blackmun, joined by Chief Justice Burger, argued in dissent that the flag law, as authoritatively construed in the Massachusetts courts, forbade only affronts to the flag's "physical integrity," not "speech—a communicative element" (p. 591). In a more elaborate dissent, Justice Rehnquist, also joined by the chief justice, assumed a similar stance. Applying the *O'Brien* formula for dealing with regulations of symbolic speech, Rehnquist concluded that the flag law furthered the state's substantial interest in safeguarding "the physical integrity of a unique national symbol which has been given content by generations of his and our forebears"—a position he would later assume as chief justice (p. 604).

That same year, Rehnquist, joined by Burger and White, adopted essentially the same stance in dissenting from the Court's disposition of *Spence v. Washington*, which overturned a statute forbidding the public display of a U.S. flag with any mark or symbol attached, as applied to a student protester who had suspended a flag bearing a peace symbol upside down from the window of his apartment. Emphasizing that the peace symbol was taped to the flag, which was thus not disfigured, the majority upheld the display as a protected form of expression. In dissent, however, Justice Rehnquist contended that the statute had simply "withdraw[n] a unique national symbol from the roster of materials that may be used as a background for communications" and observed that its enforcement did "not depend upon whether the flag is used for communicative or noncommunicative purposes; upon whether a particular message is deemed commercial or political; upon whether the use of the flag is respectful or contemptuous; or upon whether any particular segment of the State's citizenry might applaud or oppose the intended message" (pp. 422–423 [footnote omitted]).

Although the Burger Court's symbolic speech agenda was limited, the justices resolved many disputes dealing with government control over the use of public and private property for purposes of expression. During the 1971–1972 term, the Court applied equal protection standards to invalidate two ordinances that prohibited picketing near schools but exempted peaceful picketing of schools involved in a labor dispute (*Police Dept. v. Mosley* [1972], *Grayned v. City of Rockford* [1972]). Justice Marshall observed in his opinion for the Court in one of the cases that the significant interests justifying the regulation of picketing might even justify certain types of selective exclusions or distinctions among picketers. But he stressed that selective exclusions from a public forum could never be based on content alone. In one of the cases, however, the Court did reject a facial vagueness and overbreadth challenge to an antinoise ordinance that made it an offense to make a noise or distraction adjacent to a school building that disturbed the peace and good order of a school session. On its face, the Court concluded, the ordinance was narrowly tailored to further the community's compelling interest in assuring school sessions free of distraction and conducive to learning.

Those decisions produced no dissents. But in 1980 Justice Rehnquist, joined by Burger and Blackmun, objected when the Court struck down a statute that prohibited picketing of dwellings in residential neighborhoods but exempted peaceful picketing of businesses involved in a labor dispute (*Carey v. Brown* [1980]). The challenged law had been used to convict civil rights demonstrators who picketed the home of Chicago's mayor. Distinguishing the earlier rulings as involving exemptions based purely on the content of a picketer's message, Justice Rehnquist observed in dissent that the challenged statute allowed picketing at homes used for nonresidential purposes but not at homes used exclusively as residences. In his judgment government reasonably could impose such a distinction on the ground that owners of property utilized for business purposes had a more limited privacy interest in that property than those using their homes only as residences. "[T]he principal determinant of a person's right to picket a residence" under the challenged law, declared Rehnquist, was "not content, but rather the character of the residence to be picketed" (p. 474). The Court had long assured the states, he added, "that they may properly promote residential privacy even though free expression must be reduced" (p. 475).

Several decisions dealt with the reach of the public forum concept. As noted earlier, the Court ultimately refused to equate the premises of private shopping centers with public streets and sidewalks for expression purposes. But when the California Supreme Court interpreted that state's constitution to extend such obligations to shopping centers, the Court, speaking through Justice Rehnquist, refused to disturb the state court's decision. The U.S. Constitution, observed the justice, merely established a civil liberties floor below which individual rights could not be limited, not a ceiling on state authority to expand the scope of civil liberties beyond federal constitutional requirements (*Pruneyard Shopping Center v. Robins* [1980]).

In 1983 the justices struck down a statute prohibiting picketing in the Supreme Court's building and grounds, as applied to the public sidewalks bordering the property. Emphasizing the historic role of sidewalks in the communication of ideas, Justice White concluded for the Court that the statute's total ban on carrying a flag, banner, or device on the sidewalks surrounding the Court, as opposed to the building and grounds, did not serve the statute's purposes of maintaining law and order on the grounds and protecting the Court from outside influences or the appearance of such influence (*United States v. Grace* [1983]). The next year, however, the Court upheld a National Park Service regulation prohibiting camping in certain parks, as applied to demonstrators who wished to sleep in Washington's Lafayette Park and Mall area as a means of calling attention to the plight of the homeless (*Clark v. Community for Creative Non-Violence* [1984]). Assuming that the proposed encampment was expressive conduct entitled to some degree of constitutional protection, Justice White nevertheless concluded for the majority that the challenged regulation served the government's substantial interest in maintaining parks in the heart of the nation's capital in an attractive and intact condition, readily available to millions of annual visitors. Justice Marshall, joined in dissent by Justice Brennan, cited the absence of evidence that the proposed exercise in symbolic speech would cause substantial wear and tear to park property. Nor did Marshall agree that content-neutral measures such as the challenged regulation should always be subjected only to limited scrutiny, especially when government was balancing the interests of the general public against the First Amendment claims of the poor and politically powerless.

Other time, place, manner regulations drew mixed reactions from the Court. Over the partial dissents of four justices, it upheld a state rule prohibiting the sale or distribution on fairgrounds of any merchandise, including printed or written material, except from a fixed location. Against the First Amendment claims of members of the Hari Krishna sect, Justice White concluded that the rule promoted the substantial state interest in orderly crowd movement. Justice Brennan, joined by Marshall and Stevens, contended that the state had no interest sufficiently important to justify a restriction on the mere distribution of handbills but agreed that the remaining provisions were valid antifraud measures. Justice Blackmun joined Brennan's position on the distribution ban but concurred with White that the sales and solicitations restrictions were legitimate methods of promoting crowd control and public safety (*Heffron v. Intern. Soc. for Krishna Consciousness* [1981]).

Earlier the Court had upheld a city's refusal to accept political advertisements on its rapid transit system. Speaking for a plurality, Justice Blackmun declared that the advertising space on city transit vehicles did not constitute a public forum, while Justice Douglas, the fifth member of the majority, asserted that the political candidate who challenged the rule had no right to force his message upon a captive audience of riders using the transit system for transportation rather than as a place for discussion. Arguing that the city had created a public forum when it accepted and displayed commercial and public service advertisements on its transit vehicles, Justice Brennan contended for four dissenters that the city was barred from discriminating among the forum's users solely on the basis of the content of advertisers' messages (*Lehman v. City of Shaker Heights* [1974]). Brennan, joined by Marshall and Blackmun, also dissented when the Court upheld a Los Angeles ordinance prohibiting the posting of signs on public property, as applied to supporters of a political candidate. The Court cited the city's important aesthetic interests, but Brennan warned of the "unavoidable subjectivity of aesthetic judgments" and argued that such an objective should not "be pursued by arbitrarily discriminating against a form of speech that has the same aesthetic characteristics as other forms of speech that are also present in the community" (*Members of City Council v. Taxpayers for Vincent* [1984]).

What of the use of mail facilities for purposes of expression? In 1981 the Court upheld the power of the Postal Service to forbid the deposit of unstamped, mailable material in letterboxes (*U.S. Postal Service v. Council of Greenburgh* [1981]). Justice Rehnquist emphasized for the majority that the regulation was in no way content based and rejected the contention that a letterbox constituted a public forum. Justice Brennan characterized the latter conclusion as based on a disregard for "the historic role of the mails as a national medium of communication" (p. 135) but joined the Court's decision on the ground that the regulation advanced the government's significant interest in preventing the loss of mail revenue. Equating postage charges with user fees that the government as operator of the postal system could appropriately charge even for use only of mailboxes rather than the delivery system as well, Justice White also concurred in the Court's judgment. In dissent, however, Justice Marshall termed the letterbox an important public forum, and while Justice Stevens objected to this characterization, he, too, dissented, suggesting that boxholders should simply be permitted to decide whether or not to receive unstamped communications, with their wishes plainly indicated on their boxes, or obliged to replace overstuffed boxes with larger ones.

In another case a majority upheld a school system's collective bargaining agreement under which the union serving as the teachers' exclusive bargaining agent was given access to the system's interdistrict mail service and teacher mailboxes, while a rival union was denied access (*Perry Education Ass'n v. Local Educators Ass'n* [1983]). Rejecting the contention that school mail facilities were a limited public forum merely because they had been made available for periodic use by civic and church organizations, Justice White concluded for the Court that the regulation was reasonably related to the school district's legitimate interest in preserving school property for the use to which it was lawfully dedicated. White further noted that substantial alternative means were available for communication between the rival union and teachers and that, in any event, the challenged statute assured the rival union equal access to all modes of communication with the system's teachers when the election of a union to represent the teachers was in progress. Justice Brennan, joined by Marshall and Powell, argued in dissent that the regulation amounted to viewpoint discrimination that failed to advance any substantial state interest. "Once the government permits discussion of certain subject matter," declared Brennan, "it may not impose restrictions that discriminate among viewpoints on those subjects whether a nonpublic forum is involved or not" (p. 61 [footnote omitted]).

Restrictions on business mailings also attracted the Court's attention. When the state public service commission forbade Consolidated Edison Company to include inserts on controversial public policy issues in its monthly bills to the utility's customers, the Court, speaking through Justice Powell, invalidated the commission's order as a content-based regulation that served no substantial governmental interest (*Consolidated Edison Co. v. Public Service Com'n* [1980]). Since customers could simply toss objectionable material into a wastebasket, Powell observed, the order was not defensible as necessary to prevent Consolidated Edison from forcing its views on a captive audience. Nor could it be defended as safeguarding limited envelope space, no evidence having been presented to show that the inserts would prevent the company from also including in the billing envelope other material the commission might lawfully require the utility to send customers. Since the record of the case furnished no basis for assuming the utility could not exclude the costs of the inserts from its billing rates, the order also could not be justified as assuring customers would not be forced to subsidize the cost of the inserts.

Justice Blackmun, joined in part by Justice Rehnquist, asserted in dissent that given the company's monopoly status and rate structure, use of the inserts in effect forced utility customers to subsidize its speech in violation of their First Amendment rights. Blackmun suggested that in the future states might provide that utility company billing envelopes were the property of customers rather than the utility's shareholders, thereby enabling the state more easily to restrict their use. But when California required a gas and electric utility that had distributed a newsletter in its monthly billing statements for years periodically to share that space with a citizens' group, the Court declared the stipulation unconstitutional (*Pacific Gas & Electric v. P.U.C. of California* [1986]). Speaking for a plurality, Justice Powell observed that access was given only to persons or groups who disagreed with the utility's views and opposed the company in proceedings before the state utilities commission.

In a number of cases, the Court reviewed First Amendment challenges to restrictions on charitable solicitations. One measure invalidated prohibited door-to-door or street solicitations by any charitable organization not using at least 75 percent of its receipts for "charitable purposes." Striking the regulation down as unconstitutionally overbroad in a suit brought by an environmental protection group, Justice White asserted that financial solicitations were often intertwined with informative and persuasive speech and held for the Court that the government's asserted interests in preventing fraud and protecting public safety and residential privacy, while substantial, could be adequately served by means less destructive of the First Amendment freedoms of groups whose primary purpose was to collect and disseminate information and advocate positions on matters of public concern. In a lone dissent, Justice Rehnquist pointed out that the ordinance affected only door-to-door solicitations of financial contributions, left little or no discretion in the hands of authorities to censor unpopular causes, and was rationally related to the community's interest in assuring the public bestowed its contributions on organizations that were truly charitable (*Village of Schaumburg v. Citizens for a Better Environment* [1980]).

In 1984, however, a 5–4 majority struck down a state statute that prohibited charitable organizations from paying expenses exceeding 25 percent of the amount raised in a fundraising efforts but waived the limitation where it would effectively prevent an organization from raising contributions (*Secretary of State of Md. v. Joseph H. Munson Co.* [1984]). The next year, though, Rehnquist joined the Court in upholding a federal executive order excluding legal defense and political advocacy groups from participating in a charitable fundraising campaign directed at federal employees. Characterizing the campaign as a nonpublic forum, the Court, speaking through Justice O'Connor in a suit brought by the NAACP, held that the president could reasonably have concluded that money spent to provide food and shelter to the needy was more beneficial than that spent on litigation, and that the government's need to avoid the appearance of political favoritism justified the exclusion of political advocacy groups from the campaign. The majority agreed to remand the case to the lower courts for a decision on whether the Reagan administration impermissibly excluded such organizations because it disagreed with their views. By contrast, Justice Blackmun, joined by Justice Brennan, maintained in dissent that the campaign constituted a limited public forum created by the government from which litigation and advocacy groups had been excluded on the basis of unconstitutional viewpoint discrimination. Although doubtful of the value of the Court's efforts to distinguish types and degrees of public forums, Justice Stevens also contended in a separate dissent that the weakness of arguments supporting the order added strength to the inference that it was actually based on a subconscious bias against litigation and advocacy groups (*Cornelius v. NAACP Legal Def. & Educ. Fund* [1985]).

Several years earlier, the NAACP's organization of a boycott of white merchants in a Mississippi county had produced another Court pronouncement on the scope of constitutional protection for speech-related conduct. Launched to secure compliance with demands for equality and racial justice, the boycott, while generally peaceful, had been marred by a number of acts and threats of violence. When white merchants filed suit for injunctive relief and damages, a state court issued an injunction and held NAACP field secretary Charles Evers, brother of slain civil rights leader Medgar Evers, and other boycott leaders responsible for the merchants' lost earnings over a seven-year period. Based on evidence that some black citizens participated in the boycott out of fear of reprisal, the Mississippi Supreme Court held that the entire boycott was unlawful and affirmed the defendants' liability for all damages resulting from the boycott on the ground they had agreed to use force, violence, and threats to assure the boycott's success. Speaking through Justice Stevens, the Supreme Court reversed, reaffirming First Amendment coverage for peaceful political activity, limiting the merchants' recovery rights to losses caused by violent conduct, and faulting the "ambiguous findings" used by the state supreme court to condemn the entire boycott as unlawful. Justice Rehnquist concurred only in the Court's decision but filed no opinion. There were no dissents (*NAACP v. Claiborne Hardware Co.* [1982]).

Although government has relatively broad authority to control access to public and private property for purposes of expression, content-based regulations, as we have seen, are presumptively invalid, especially with respect to property traditionally used for the communication of ideas, such as streets, sidewalks, and parks. The Burger Court embraced that principle but played a relatively limited role in the most publicized case involving its application to come before the Court during Chief Justice Burger's tenure. When American Nazis announced plans to hold a march in Skokie, Illinois, a predominantly Jewish community with many Holocaust survivors among its residents, a state court issued an injunction forbidding members of the National Socialist Party to parade in Nazi uniforms, display the swastika symbol, and distribute literature promoting hatred of Jews or others based on their faith, ancestry, race, or religion. State appeals courts refused to stay enforcement of the injunction pending an appeal, and the Illinois Supreme Court declined expedited review of the case. When the organization sought a stay of the injunction from the U.S. Supreme Court, a 5–4 majority treated its petition as a petition for certiorari review of the case and summarily reversed the state supreme court's denial of a stay, based on precedent (*Freedman v. Maryland* [1965]) requiring strict procedural safeguards, including prompt appeal, in cases involving prior restraints on expression (*National Socialist Party v. Village of Skokie* [1977]). ·

The Illinois Supreme Court ultimately dissolved the injunction, but Skokie enacted three ordinances designed to block the Nazi demonstration. One prohibited public demonstrations by members of political parties wearing "military-style" uniforms; a second banned distribution of hate literature; a third established an elaborate permit requirement and obliged applicants to obtain $300,000 in public liability insurance and $50,000 coverage for property damage. In a suit brought by the Nazis and their current leader, a federal district court held the ordinances unconstitutional and an appeals court affirmed most of the lower court's ruling. With their rights so vindicated, the Nazis then dropped their plans for the Skokie march and held a rally in a Chicago park instead, with about twenty-five party members present for the July 9, 1978, event. That fall the Supreme Court declined to review the decision by the court of appeals (*Smith v. Collin* [1978]). But Justice Blackmun, joined by Justice White, dissented, declaring that review was necessary to resolve any conflict between the lower court ruling in the case and a 1952 Supreme Court decision upholding an Illinois group libel law that prohibited publications demeaning classes of citizens based on their race, color, creed, or religion (*Beauharnais v. Illinois* [1952]).

The Court did review, however, a number of cases involving the public use of offensive language. *Chaplinsky v. New Hampshire* (1942) had long ago denied First Amendment protection for "fighting words"—face-to-face verbal assaults likely to provoke violent retaliation. But *Chaplinsky* had raised more questions than it resolved, and a number of Burger Court rulings helped to clarify not only the fighting words exception to protected expression but the scope of constitutional protection accorded offensive speech generally. In *Cohen v. California* (1971), the first such ruling, a majority speaking through Justice Harlan overturned the breach-of-peace conviction of a young man who in the corridor of a courthouse wore a jacket bearing the words "Fuck the Draft." Harlan had initially favored a denial of review in the case, then voted at first to affirm Cohen's conviction. His opinion for the *Cohen* Court, however, would become one of his most frequently quoted opinions.

Harlan first emphasized what the case did not involve. Since Cohen had not directed his epithet at any person, his prosecution did not fall within the fighting words doctrine. Nor was he inciting others to disobey the draft laws, using language in an erotic and thus possibly obscene manner, interfering with the privacy of a captive audience (since those in the corridor could easily have averted their eyes), or being prosecuted under a narrowly drafted regulation of the time, place, and manner of expression. Harlan then observed that the sole issue in the case was whether a state could excise a particular offensive word from public discourse, either on the theory its use was inherently likely to provoke violence or on the more general assertion that the state, as guardian of public morality, could remove a scurrilous epithet from the public vocabulary. The Court rejected out of hand the notion that an expletive could be suppressed out of a mere general fear that its use alone, whatever the circumstances, would provoke violence. Harlan was hardly more patient with the claim that states could cleanse the public vocabulary. Such an approach not only seemed "inherently boundless" in its reach, but it also failed to recognize that "one man's vulgarity is another's lyric" (p. 25), that speech served important emotional as well as cognitive functions, and that state censorship of particular words could become a convenient pretext for banning the expression of unpopular views. Harlan did not speak, though, for a unanimous Court. Justice Blackmun, joined by the chief justice and Justice Black, saw "Cohen's absurd and immature antic . . . [as] mainly conduct" subject to state control and "little speech," well within the *Chaplinsky* exception to protected expression and government's broad authority over conduct in public buildings.

The *Cohen* Court had concluded that the speech at issue there was entitled to constitutional protection. In later cases a majority applied *Cohen*, the vagueness-overbreadth doctrines, and the clear and present danger test to reverse other convictions for the use of scurrilous speech. In *Gooding v. Wilson* (1972), for example, a majority overturned the conviction of an antiwar protester who cursed officers attempting to remove him and others from the entrance to a military induction center. Johnny Wilson's highly provocative language was probably subject to prosecution under a narrowly drafted law reaching fighting words. But the Georgia statute used to convict him punished those "who shall, without provocation, use to or of another, and in his presence, . . . opprobrious words or abusive language, tending to cause a breach of the peace." Speaking for the Court, Justice Brennan concluded that dictionary definitions and earlier state court interpretations of the law had given "opprobrious" and "abusive" a greater reach than fighting words. Brennan also spoke for the majority in a 1974 case overturning on overbreadth grounds a New Orleans ordinance making it a crime to revile police officers attempting to perform their duties (*Lewis v. City of New Orleans*).

Fighting words are not the only category of expression largely excluded from constitutional protection. The Supreme Court has long denied libel and obscenity full First Amendment coverage as well. Libel involves the defamation of a person's reputation through false publications and broadcasts, and slander is essentially libel's verbal counterpart. Out of regard for the constitutional commitment to robust debate on public issues and concern that an unduly broad libel control would impose a chilling effect on the exercise of protected expression, the Warren Court, in *New York Times v. Sullivan* (1964), imposed an important limitation on government's authority to penalize as libelous comments about the public actions of government officials. Under the *New York Times* libel rule, innocent errors, even if damaging to reputation, were constitutionally protected; only false statements about public officials made with "actual malice," that is, with knowledge that they were false or with reckless disregard for their truth or falsity, could be punished as libel. Soon the Warren Court had extended this "knowing or reckless falsehood" rule to comment about "public figures"—private citizens, such as entertainers, retired generals, and famous football coaches, who had thrust themselves into public controversies or enjoyed a status commanding wide public interest and attention. In one case, for example, the Court upheld a libel judgment against the *Saturday Evening Post* magazine accusing the former athletic director of the University of Georgia of giving his team's game plan to an opposing coach, but only after the justices concluded that the story displayed a reckless disregard for truth (*Curtis Publishing Co. v. Butts* [1967], *Associated Press v. Walker* [1967]).

For a time, it appeared that the Burger Court might apply the knowing or reckless falsehood rule to any comment on a matter of public or general interest, even that critical of private persons (*Rosenbloom v. Metromedia* [1971]). But in *Gertz v. Welch, Inc.* (1974), the Court limited the rule to public officials and public figures. Justice Powell emphasized for the majority that since private individuals had less opportunity to counter false statements and were thus more vulnerable to injury, they could recover damages for actual injury to their reputations under whatever standards the applicable statute imposed. *Gertz* did place on private persons wishing to recover punitive damages (awarded to punish the defendant rather than simply compensate for actual losses) the burden of establishing knowing or reckless falsity. In 1979, however, the Court, in a public figure suit brought by a Vietnam veteran who contended that he was libeled on a television program, held that plaintiffs must be permitted to question broadcasters about their thoughts, motivations, and internal editorial processes in establishing proof of malice (*Herbert v. Lando* [1979]).

Inevitably, the Burger Court also became heavily embroiled in the intractable obscenity issue, producing for the first time since 1957 (*Roth v. United States*) a majority definition of what constitutes obscenity. In *Miller v. California* (1973), a 5–4 Court, speaking through Chief Justice Burger and drawing on, yet also modifying, language in Warren Court opinions, ruled that the distribution of erotic material could be penalized under obscenity laws if (1) the average person, applying contemporary community standards, would find that the material taken as a whole appealed to a prurient (or lascivious) interest in sex; (2) the work depicted or described sexual conduct in a patently offensive way; and (3) it lacked serious literary, artistic, political, or scientific value. In judging a work's prurient appeal and patent offensiveness, added Burger, a jury could apply prevailing community standards rather than some conception of a national standard.

In *Paris Adult Theatre v. Slaton* (1973), the same 5–4 majority, again speaking through the chief justice, went further, upholding state power to forbid exhibition of obscene films in adults-only theaters. Distinguishing *Stanley v. Georgia* (1969), the Warren Court decision upholding the right of people to possess obscenity in their homes, Burger concluded that a commercial theater could not be equated with a private home. To the assertion that no scientific evidence conclusively demonstrated that exposure to obscenity would lead to antisocial behavior, the chief justice responded that laws are often based upon unprovable assumptions and that states could reasonably conclude that there is a relationship between obscenity and criminal behavior.

Dissenting in both cases, Justice Douglas argued, as he and Justice Black had often maintained during the Warren era, that the First Amendment's commands were absolute, permitting no censorship based on the content of expression. Justice Brennan, joined by Justices Stewart and Marshall, also dissented. Brennan had authored several important Warren-era opinions defining obscenity and excluding the commercial sale of obscene materials from First Amendment protection. Now, however, he concluded that no obscenity test could be devised that would be sufficiently clear to avoid the taint of vagueness yet narrow enough in reach to afford adequate protection to erotic expression. The inherent uncertainty of such standards, contended Brennan, not only provided inadequate notice of which erotic expression was obscene and inhibited the exercise of protected expression by those wishing to obey the law, but the tests had also created institutional stress for judges uncertain of how to apply them in individual cases. Brennan favored limiting governmental authority in the field to the protection of juveniles and unconsenting adults from exposure to erotica.

The next year the Court made clear that appellate courts, not trial juries and judges, had the final authority to determine whether material is obscene. Overturning the obscenity conviction of a Georgia man who exhibited the film *Carnal Knowledge* at his theater, Justice Rehnquist rejected any notion *Miller* might have given that juries had unbridled discretion to determine what films include patently offensive depictions of sexual conduct (*Jenkins v. Georgia* [1974]). In several cases the Court also refused to extend the right to possess obscene material recognized in the *Stanley* case beyond the confines of the home, prompting Justice Black to joke shortly before his death that perhaps in the future *Stanley* would "be recognized as good law only when a man writes a salacious book in his attic, prints it in his basement, and reads it in his living room" (*United States v. Thirty-Seven Photographs* [1971], p. 382; see also, e.g., *United States v. Twelve 200-Foot Reels* [1973]). Suggesting that sexual expression enjoys less constitutional protection than, for example, political debate, a majority also sustained the imposition of special zoning regulations on the location of adult establishments, including bookstores and theaters (*Young v. American Mini Theatres* [1976], *City of Renton v. Playtime Theatres* [1986]).

Consistent with a Warren Court decision upholding a ban on the sale to minors of erotic books and magazines not considered obscene for adults (*Ginsberg v. New York* [1968]), a unanimous Court in 1982 affirmed a statute proscribing sexual performances by minors below age sixteen, whether or not obscene under the *Miller* test (*New York v. Ferber*). But a 6–3 majority overturned a city's refusal to permit the performance of the controversial musical *Hair* in a city-leased auditorium, Justice Blackmun declaring for the majority that any system for licensing theatrical productions must conform to the strict procedural safeguards required of motion picture censorship schemes under another Warren Court decision (*Southeastern Promotions, Ltd. v. Conrad* [1975], *Freedman v. Maryland* [1965]). And in *Erznoznik v. City of Jacksonville* (1975), another 6–3 Court struck down as overly broad a city ordinance making it a public nuisance punishable as a crime for drive-in theaters to exhibit films depicting nudity on screens visible from a public street or other public place. Offended persons, Justice Powell declared for the majority, could simply avert their eyes. Also, the ordinance was not narrowly written to reach only sexually explicit nudity, and to the extent it was intended to prevent motorist distraction, it was grossly underinclusive in its reach, singling out movies containing nudity from all others likely to distract motorists. Dissenters accused the majority of exaggerating the First Amendment interests at stake in the case while minimizing government's authority to protect privacy interests.

In a 1942 case, the Supreme Court had also excluded commercial speech from First Amendment protection (*Valentine v. Chrestensen* [1942]), and in 1973 a 5–4 Burger Court majority reaffirmed that position in upholding a human-relations ordinance applied to forbid local newspapers from running advertisements in sex-designated help-wanted columns (*Pittsburgh Press Co. v. Pittsburgh Com'n on Human Relations* [1973]). But two years later a 7–2 Court partially eliminated the commercial speech exception to protected expression in overturning a state statute making it a misdemeanor to encourage or prompt abortions through the sale or circulation of a publication, as applied to a Virginia newspaper managing editor who ran an advertisement for a legal New York abortion service. As construed by the majority, speaking through Justice Blackmun, the earlier commercial speech cases had not completely stripped advertisements of all First Amendment protection. An advertisement containing information of potential interest and value to a diverse audience was constitutionally protected, declared Blackmun, and the state's asserted interest in shielding Virginians from information about activities outside its borders was entitled to little if any weight (*Bigelow v. Virginia* [1975]).

The next year the Court, again per Justice Blackmun, went further, extending the First Amendment to purely commercial advertising, applying a balancing-of-interests approach to government regulation of advertisements, and striking down a Virginia ban on the advertisement of prescription drug prices as little more than a way of keeping the public ignorant of the competitive prices pharmacists offered (*Virginia Bd. of Pharmacy v. Virginia Consumer Council* [1976]). Invalidating a state regulation completely banning all promotional advertising by an electric utility in a 1980 case, *Central Hudson Gas v. Public Service Commission*, the Court also laid down a four-part formula for court review of commercial speech regulations. Under the *Central Hudson* ruling, commercial speech was constitutionally protected only if it concerned lawful activity and was not misleading, and the regulation of such expression was valid only if it sought to promote a substantial government interest, directly advanced that interest, and was no more restrictive of expression than necessary to accomplish the government's objective.

In a lone dissent in the drug prescription case, Justice Rehnquist cited the important "societal interest against the promotion of drug use for every ill, real or imaginary" (p. 790) and warned that the Court's ruling would logically extend also to lawyers, doctors, and other professionals. Rehnquist's concern proved prophetic in 1977, when the Court struck down a state bar regulation forbidding all advertising by lawyers (*Bates v. State Bar of Arizona* [1977]). Later the justices invalidated a rule prohibiting certain types of lawyer advertising not shown to be misleading or fraudulent (*In Re R.M.J.* [1982]) but also upheld the disciplining of lawyers who directly and personally solicited clients for financial gain (*Ohralik v. Ohio State Bar Ass'n* [1978]), as well as those whose advertisements misled prospective clients regarding their obligations under contingent-fee arrangements (*Zauderer v. Office of Disciplinary Counsel* [1985]). Direct, personal solicitations, the justices declared, ran counter to the state's important interest, among others, in prohibiting lawyers from exerting undue influence over potential clients, and advertisements were subject to sanction when they misled prospective clients by failing to point out, for example, that while clients in contingent-fee cases were obliged to pay "legal fees" only if they won their case, they were responsible for paying "costs" whatever the outcome of the suit.

Other commercial speech cases produced mixed responses from the justices. A unanimous Court, for example, declared unconstitutional a township ordinance banning "For Sale" and "Sold" signs from residential property in an attempt to curb white flight from a racially integrated community (*Linmark Associates v. Township of Willingboro* [1977]). A 5–4 majority upheld Puerto Rico's law forbidding gambling casinos from advertising their facilities to local citizens while permitting advertising through media outside the commonwealth, but only because a Puerto Rican court had interpreted the law to allow local advertising directed at tourists even though it might also draw the attention of local residents. And the dissenters rejected entirely the notion that Puerto Rico could constitutionally suppress truthful commercial speech in order to discourage its residents from engaging in gambling, a lawful activity (*Posadas de Puerto Rico Ass'n v. Tourism Co.* [1986]). Although agreeing that a city's important interests in traffic safety and aesthetics would justify restrictions on billboards, another majority found exemptions in one city's regulations constitutionally fatal (*Metromedia, Inc. v. City of San Diego* [1981]).

Most Burger Court commercial speech cases dealt with advertising. The Court also extended corporations, however, more general First Amendment rights. In 1978, for example, a 5–4 majority struck down a Massachusetts criminal statute prohibiting business corporations from making contributions or expenditures to influence the outcome of votes on any question submitted to the electorate except those materially affecting a corporation's property, business, or assets (*First Nat'l. Bank of Boston v. Bellotti* [1978]). Justice Powell spoke for the Court in a suit brought by banks and business corporations wishing to publicize their opposition to a proposed state constitutional amendment referendum (later defeated by the voters) that would have authorized the state legislature to enact a graduated personal income tax. Powell rejected the claim that the law was needed to bolster the role of individual citizens in the election process and thus their confidence in government. Even if government could silence one group's political voice on a showing of an imminent danger to the electoral process, observed the justice, Massachusetts had not established that corporations exerted an overwhelming or even significant influence over state referenda measures or that public confidence in government was at risk. But in dissent, Justice White, joined by Brennan and Marshall, argued that the electoral process was "an arena in which the public interest in preventing corporate domination and the coerced support by shareholders of causes with which they disagree [was] at its weakest" (p. 821).

Justice Rehnquist also dissented, broadly rejecting First Amendment protection for corporate political expression. And in 1982 Rehnquist spoke for a unanimous Court in upholding a federal campaign finance regulation that prohibited corporations and labor unions from making contributions and expenditures in connection with federal elections but permitted them to establish segregated campaign funds subject to various restrictions, including a requirement that certain corporations could solicit contributions to a fund only from their members. At least as applied to the conservative National Right to Work Committee's solicitation of contributions from more than a quarter million persons, none of whom were its members, Rehnquist concluded that the government's interest in protecting against actual and apparent corruption of the election process overrode the committee's asserted associational rights (*Federal Election Com'n v. Nat'l Right to Work Comm.* [1982]).

Not all federal campaign finance regulations survived First Amendment challenges, however. *Buckley v. Valeo* (1976) upheld certain provisions of the Federal Election Campaign Act of 1971 and Federal Revenue Act of 1971, as amended in 1974, but declared other provisions invalid largely on free expression grounds. Among provisions held valid were regulations limiting contributions by individuals and organizations to candidates for federal office, providing for public funding of presidential campaigns, and establishing the Federal Election Commission (FEC) to oversee compliance with campaign finance regulations. Struck down as violations of free speech were portions of the legislation imposing, among other things, restrictions on independent expenditures by individuals and organizations in behalf of candidates. Direct contributions to candidates' campaigns could be limited, the Court reasoned, because of their potential for exerting an undue influence on candidates. But candidates presumably would be unaware of expenditures made in their behalf, so those restrictions on campaign spending were unconstitutional. In 1985 the Court went further, holding that restrictions on independent expenditures were invalid, even as applied to spending on behalf of presidential candidates who accepted public funds and thus were required by law to limit their campaign spending (*Federal Election Com'n v. National Conservative Political Action Comm.* [1985]).

Although never excluded entirely from First Amendment protection as commercial speech once appeared to be, broadcasting occupies a less favorable constitutional status than its newspaper and magazine counterparts. Since broadcast airwaves are limited in number, government allocation of channels and the licensing of broadcasters are necessary. That monopoly status in turn has been used to justify further regulation of broadcasting. At the end of the Warren era, for example, the Court, speaking through Justice White, applied such reasoning to uphold the "fairness doctrine," a set of FCC regulations requiring broadcasters to devote a reasonable amount of airtime to public issues and provide opportunities for the broadcast of contrasting points of view. White underscored, though, that broadcasting was to have the widest journalistic discretion, limited only by the minimum regulation necessary to assure the individual's right to receive information and society's interest in maintaining an informed electorate (*Red Lion Broadcasting Co. v. FCC* [1969]).

The Burger Court generally reaffirmed those principles but also sustained FCC authority to sanction broadcasters for "indecent" programming, at least during "family hours," when broadcasts are most readily accessible to children. When a child flipping the dial on his father's car radio tuned into a broadcast of comedian George Carlin's monologue on the "seven dirty words," the irate parent wrote the FCC a letter. The agency in turn filed the complaint and the radio station's response, informing the station that any additional complaints would prompt consideration of possible sanctions, including revocation of the station's license. Speaking partly for the Court and in part for a plurality of justices in upholding the FCC's action, Justice Stevens emphasized that broadcasting enjoyed the least protection of all forms of communication and that federal control over the content of broadcasts was not limited to obscenity but also extended to other forms of indecent speech (*Red Lion Broadcasting Co. v. FCC* [1969]).

The special characteristics of certain environments provided another justification for restrictions generally considered inappropriate burdens on expression. The Court's 1976 decision to uphold a hair code for police was based in part on special elements of police work permitting more extensive limitations on their enjoyment of constitutional freedoms than those applicable to citizens in general (*Kelley v. Johnson* [1976]). The rights of military personnel and others on military property were similarly conditioned. In *Flower v. United States* (1972), the justices summarily reversed the conviction of a civilian member of the American Friends Service Committee, an antiwar group, who had distributed leaflets on a military post. Previously barred from the post for attempting to distribute "unauthorized" literature, Flower was convicted under a federal statute making it a crime to reenter a military base after having been removed and ordered not to reenter. Noting that the post street on which the leaflets had been distributed was open to the public, the Court held that the military had "abandoned any claim that it had special interests in who walks, talks, or leaflets on the avenue" (p. 198). But in *Greer v. Spock* (1976), a 7–2 majority upheld military post regulations banning politically partisan speeches and demonstrations, as well as prohibiting the distribution of literature without the prior approval of post headquarters. Rejecting any notion that a military post is a public forum, the Court concluded that private citizens had no general constitutional right to make political speeches or distribute leaflets on its premises. Nor did the justices find any basis for concluding that military authorities applied the ban in a way that discriminated among candidates based on their supposed political views; instead, the Court, per Justice Stewart, concluded that it had been applied objectively and even-handedly to keep post military activities entirely free of entanglements with partisan political campaigns. Stewart recognized that the permit system used to screen requests to distribute literature could be applied in an arbitrary manner, but he pointed out that the challenged permit arrangement had been used only to exclude those who had previously distributed literature on the post without a permit.

Dissenters in *Spock* stressed that much of the post property was open to the public and that *Flower* should apply. In 1985, however, a 6–3 majority upheld the conviction of a man who reentered a military base after receiving a "bar letter" from the post commanding officer that excluded him from the base without written permission (*United States v. Albertini* [1985]). Vincent Albertini and several companions had returned to the base during its annual open house, where his companions engaged in a peaceful demonstration against the nuclear arms race while Albertini took photographs of displays at the open house. Albertini argued that the open house had converted the base into a temporary public forum. The Court, speaking through Justice O'Connor, rejected that contention but also concluded that in any event Albertini was excluded not because of expression but because he had violated an order denying him access to the post based on his previous unauthorized entry. Justice

Stevens, joined by Brennan and Marshall, dissented, however, arguing that the congressional statute providing for punishment in such cases was not intended to apply when circumstances, such as the open house, reasonably indicated that the visit was not prohibited but welcomed.

In 1974 the Court also highlighted the differences between the military and civilian communities while rejecting vagueness and overbreadth challenges to military regulations proscribing "conduct unbecoming an officer and a gentleman," as well as "all disorders and neglects to the prejudice of good order and discipline." *Parker v. Levy* involved the court-martial conviction of an army doctor who vocally opposed the Vietnam War and refused to teach medical skills to elite Green Beret troops. Dissenters condemned the regulations under which Levy was convicted as hopelessly vague. But Justice Rehnquist concluded for the majority that years of enforcement had given the provisions considerable specificity. (It had been established, for example, that sex with a chicken was "conduct unbecoming.") In rejecting the overbreadth challenge, Rehnquist stressed the need for discipline and obedience in a military setting and concluded that many forms of unprotected conduct fell within the regulations' legitimate reach; they could not be condemned, therefore, as substantially overbroad.

Toward the end of Chief Justice Burger's tenure, the Court also narrowly construed an important Warren-era ruling upholding the First Amendment rights of public school students. In *Tinker v. Des Moines Independent School District* (1969), a Warren Court majority addressed the rights of students suspended from school for wearing black armbands as a symbol of their opposition to U.S. involvement in the Vietnam War. Characterizing the armbands as a form of symbolic expression "closely akin" to "pure speech," Justice Fortas declared for the Court that school officials could curtail the speech of students (and teachers) only to the extent necessary to prevent substantial interferences with the educational process and school discipline. Since authorities had acted on the basis of general, undifferentiated fears rather than evidence of actual disruption, their conduct infringed upon the students' expression rights.

Although the Burger Court never overruled *Tinker*, it gradually developed a body of rulings making clear that controls over expression in public schools are subject to substantially less rigorous standards of judicial scrutiny than normally applied in First Amendment cases. In a 1972 case, the justices remanded for further hearings a case involving a state-supported college's refusal to grant campus recognition to a chapter of the controversial Students for a Democratic Society (SDS). Justice Powell emphasized that recognition could not be denied because of the campus group's philosophy; its relationship with the national SDS; or a general, unsupported fear of disruption. In an opinion concurring only in the Court's judgment, however, Justice Rehnquist maintained that "government as employer or school administrator may impose upon employees and students reasonable regulations that would be impermissible if imposed by the government upon all citizens" (*Healy v. James* [1972]).

The next year Chief Justice Burger and Justice Rehnquist, the latter joined by Justice Blackmun, filed vigorous dissents proceeding along the same lines when a majority summarily ordered reinstatement of a university graduate student suspended for campus distribution of a newspaper that contained a political cartoon depicting policemen raping the Statue of Liberty and the Goddess of Justice, as well as a headline story entitled "Motherfucker Acquitted," which discussed the trial of a member of an organization called Up Against the Wall, Motherfucker (*Papish v. Bd. of Curators* [1973]). Refusing to recognize a dual standard for the academic community with respect to the content of speech, the majority found neither the cartoon nor the story obscene or otherwise unprotected. But in dissent the chief justice characterized a university as "an institution where individuals learn to express themselves in acceptable, civil terms," while declaring it neither unreasonable nor unconstitutional for a college to take disciplinary action against students who distributed "obscene and infantile" publications (p. 672). Justice Rehnquist considered public use of the words at issue well within the fighting words exception to free speech.

Ultimately, Chief Justice Burger's position would prevail, at least in a high school setting. In *Bethel School District v. Fraser* (1986), a majority, per the chief justice, held *Tinker* inapplicable to a high school's disciplining of a student who resorted to graphic sexual imagery in his nominating speech for a fellow student seeking election to a school office. Observing that the rights of students are not coextensive with those of adults in other settings, Burger concluded that it was "[s]urely . . . a highly appropriate function of public school education to prohibit the use of vulgar and offensive terms in public discourse" (p. 683). Justice Brennan concurred in the Court's judgment, but only because he believed that school officials could reasonably have concluded that the speech in question was disruptive. Justice Marshall dissented because in his judgment the school had failed to establish that the speech was disruptive; Justice Stevens dissented as well, contending that the student had not received fair notice that such a speech would be considered disruptive.

It is no surprise, then, that the Court also refused to equate the First Amendment rights of prison inmates with those of the general public. In a 1974 case, a majority struck down as overly broad infringements on protected expression California prison regulations providing for the censorship of inmate mail. But as the Court's spokesperson, Justice Powell refused to cast the First Amendment issue in terms of prisoner rights. Instead, he concluded that the regulations violated the rights of persons wishing to correspond with prisoners and that any censorship arrangement must be accompanied by minimum procedural safeguards. Regulations narrowly written to further important governmental interests in internal order and discipline, institutional security, and prisoner rehabilitation would present no constitutional problems. But the challenged provisions, asserted Powell, had an unnecessarily broad sweep, authorizing censorship, for example, of statements that "unduly complain" or expressed "inflammatory political, racial, or religious, or other views" (*Procunier v. Martinez* [1974]).

Three members of the Court (Douglas, Marshall, and Brennan) reached the issue of inmate rights that the majority had avoided, each concluding, as Justice Marshall put it, that a "prisoner does not shed . . . basic First Amendment rights at the prison gate" (p. 422) and that the challenged censorship provisions were unconstitutional since the objectives they were said to serve could be furthered by means less restrictive of inmate rights. In a pair of later cases that term, the Court itself acknowledged that inmates possessed First Amendment rights yet upheld another California prison measure prohibiting news media interviews with specific inmates against claims raised by newspersons and prisoners. An inmate, Justice Stewart declared for the Court, retains only "those First Amendment rights that are not inconsistent with his status as a prisoner or with the legitimate penological objectives of the corrections system" (*Pell v. Procunier, Procunier v. Hillery*, p. 822 [1974]). Balancing inmate free speech interests against the state's interests in the deterrence of crime, rehabilitation, and security, Stewart struck the balance in favor of the state, pointing out that prisoners had ample alternative means of communication and that there was no evidence the regulation was being used to discriminate among inmates based on the likely content of interviews.

Finding media objections to the regulation even less persuasive than the inmate claims, Stewart rejected any notion that the Constitution requires government to accord the press special access to information not shared by the public in general. California gave the press greater access to inmates than the general public was permitted: The state conducted regular tours through its prisons for the benefit of interested citizens but permitted newspersons to enter the maximum and minimum security sections and speak to any inmate they encountered, as well as conduct interviews with inmates and corrections officials selected at random from the prison population. Under those circumstances, concluded Stewart, the challenged regulation did not interfere with the media's rights.

In *Saxbe v. Washington Post Co.* (1974), Justice Stewart employed essentially the same rationale in rejecting press challenges to a federal policy quite similar to the California measure. And in 1978 a 4–3 Court, with Brennan and Marshall not participating, largely sustained a county jail's refusal to allow a television crew to inspect and photograph a portion of the facility for an investigative report on jail conditions. A three-man plurality, speaking through Chief Justice Burger, rejected the contention that the press had a special right of access to government information or sources of information within the government's control—specifically, a right of access to a county jail over and above that of the general public, for the purpose of interviewing inmates and making recordings, films, and photographs for publication and broadcast. Justice Stewart concurred in the judgment, but in a separate opinion he urged flexibility and consideration for the media's special First Amendment interests in applying the concept of equal public-press access to government facilities (*Houchins v. KQED* [1978]).

The Burger Court rejected press privilege claims in other areas as well, but this time over the dissent of Justice Stewart, among others. In *Branzburg v. Hayes* (1972) and other cases, members of the media argued that they should be accorded a First Amendment privilege from testifying before grand jury hearings unless they were themselves suspects in a crime or possessed information available from no other source, and the societal interest in securing that evidence outweighed resulting burdens on freedom of expression. Such a privilege was necessary, it was claimed, to prevent a chilling effect on confidential news sources and thus assure the continued free flow of information. In rejecting the privilege for a 5–4 Court, Justice White characterized as highly speculative the newspersons' contention that their compelled appearance before grand jury proceedings would dry up confidential news sources, especially since the press had long thrived without a testimonial privilege. In White's judgment the privilege sought also posed significant enforcement problems, including difficult decisions regarding the categories of persons who would be entitled to its protection and the involvement of judges in the inappropriate task of deciding when the privilege would prevail and thus, in a sense, what criminal laws were most worthy of enforcement. Although agreeing that news gathering was entitled to some degree of constitutional protection, White concluded that it was more important to prosecute crimes than write about them.

In dissent, Justice Douglas embraced an absolute testimonial privilege for the press, while Justice Stewart, joined by Brennan and Marshall, supported adoption of the conditional privilege the media sought. More important, Justice Powell, the fifth member of the majority, appeared to advocate a balancing of competing governmental and free expression interests in each case to determine whether a journalist should be privileged from appearing before a grand jury—a position similar to that advocated by the media litigants and Justice Stewart but one more deferential to the societal interest in the effective prosecution of crimes.

In *Zurcher v. Stanford Daily* (1978), however, the Burger Court also foreclosed a meaningful case-by-case balancing of First Amendment and governmental interests when reporters claimed a limited privilege from searches of media offices. Lawyers for the Stanford student paper had argued that so-called third-party searches of a media office (that is, searches undertaken when no staff member was a suspect in a crime) should be permitted only under extraordinary circumstances where important evidence would otherwise be destroyed or removed from the jurisdiction; in other situations, police should be required to seek evidence through a subpoena issued by a judge to the media personnel involved. Speaking for the Court, Justice White rejected such a privilege on essentially the same grounds applied in the *Branzburg* case. The

Fourth Amendment's safeguards against unreasonable search and seizure, especially the warrant requirement, were adequate, concluded White, to protect the press against constitutional violations.

The next year the Court rejected a newspaper's challenge to court orders excluding the public and the press from a pretrial hearing on a motion to suppress allegedly involuntary confessions and physical evidence in a criminal case, Justice Stewart concluding that while the Sixth Amendment conferred on defendants a right of public trial, neither the press nor the public had a right to attend criminal proceedings (*Gannett Co. v. DePasquale* [1979]). In *Richmond Newspapers, Inc. v. Virginia* (1980), however, the Court distinguished the earlier case, holding that the public, and thus the press, enjoyed a constitutional right to attend criminal trials, absent some overriding interest justifying the public's exclusion from the proceedings. In a plurality opinion announcing the Court's decision, Chief Justice Burger stressed the historic role of public trials in assuring both justice and the appearance of justice and found the right to attend trials in the shadow of specific First Amendment safeguards. Finding no such right in the Constitution's language, Justice Rehnquist filed a lone dissent. But in later cases the Court extended the right to preliminary hearings held to determine whether adequate evidence (probable cause) existed for further proceedings against a suspect (*Press-Enterprise Co. v. Superior Court* [1986]) and to the voir dire examination of prospective jurors before trial (*Press-Enterprise Co. v. Superior Court* [1984]). In a somewhat related context, moreover, the Court had earlier held that the press could not be criminally punished for publishing truthful information regarding the closed proceedings of a judicial commission considering disciplinary action against a state judge (*Landmark Communications, Inc. v. Virginia* [1978]).

Whatever the public/media right of access to government, the Burger Court rejected a public right of access to the press. In 1973, for example, a seven-member majority upheld broadcaster programming discretion and rejected right-of-access claims in holding that neither the First Amendment nor FCC regulations required an FCC ruling that broadcasters accept paid editorial advertisements. Justices Brennan and Marshall argued in dissent that given government limits imposed on access to the airwaves, broadcasters had First Amendment obligations. Any interests served by an absolute broadcaster ban on editorial advertisements, they contended, were outweighed by the First Amendment interests in full discussion of public issues and self-expression by individuals and groups through the nation's most important modern forum for the expression of ideas (*CBS v. Democratic National Committee* [1973]).

When the forum moved from broadcasting to newsprint, however, a unanimous Court rejected right-of-access claims. Speaking through Chief Justice Burger in *Miami Herald Publishing Co. v. Tornillo* (1974), the justices invalidated Florida's "right-to-reply" statute under which newspapers were required to provide free space to political candidates wishing to respond to newspaper attacks on their personal character or political record. A responsible press was desirable, but the Constitution guaranteed only a free press, not a responsible media. By encouraging self-censorship and unduly interfering with journalistic discretion, concluded Burger, the challenged statute violated the First Amendment.

A host of other free expression cases involving a variety of issues also went before the Court during Chief Justice Burger's tenure. Among free association cases, for example, the Court overturned a law applied to require a controversial political party to disclose to the government the names and addresses of contributors and recipients of campaign funds (*Brown v. Socialist Workers* [1982]), protected public employees from discharge based solely on their political beliefs (*Branti v. Finkel* [1980]), and prohibited a teacher union from requiring teachers to contribute to the support of ideological causes with which they disagreed (*Abood v. Detroit Bd. of Education* [1977]). Yet the justices also upheld a requirement that public employees take an oath supporting their federal and state constitutions (*Cole v. Richardson* [1972]). A special tax on the cost of paper and ink products used in publications met defeat (*Minneapolis Star & Tribune Co. v. Minn. Com'n of Rev.* [1983]). But a television station's film coverage of the entire act of a "human cannonball," which lasted of course only a few seconds, was held to be a violation of copyright law (*Zacchini v. Scripps-Howard Broadcasting Co.* [1977]), as was a news magazine's unauthorized publication of verbatim quotations from President Ford's soon-to-be published memoirs (*Harper & Row Publishers v. Nation Enterprises* [1985]). In such cases, as well as others examined earlier in greater detail, the Court applied a particular standard of scrutiny based on the degree of First Amendment protection, if any, to which the expression at issue was entitled; the nature of the regulation (whether, for example, content based or content neutral); and related factors.

Freedom of Religion

The Constitution contains three clauses dealing with religion. The First Amendment forbids laws "respecting an establishment of religion" and those "prohibiting the free exercise thereof." Article VI forbids, moreover, the imposition of any religious test as a qualification for holding federal office. The establishment clause was incorporated into the meaning of the Fourteenth Amendment due process clause, making that provision applicable to the states, no later than 1947 (*Everson v. Bd. of Education*); the free exercise guarantee has been binding on the states via the same process at least since 1940 (*Cantwell v. Connecticut*). In 1961 the Court also concluded that the Constitution's ban on religious tests for public office was part of the liberty protected by the Fourteenth Amendment from state interference (*Torasco v. Watkins* [1961]). Although several members of the Burger Court invoked the religious-test clause as a basis for invalidating a Tennessee constitutional provision barring ministers and priests from public office (*McDaniel v. Paty* [1978]), the test clause has rarely been the subject of litigation. The modern Supreme Court has devoted much attention, however, to the reach and limits of the establishment and free exercise guarantees.

The establishment clause's framers probably intended it to serve primarily as a bar to the creation of an official national church in the new nation. But especially during the Warren era, the clause became a broad restriction on government contacts with religion. And in *Lemon v. Kurtzman* (1971), the Burger Court, building on earlier cases and speaking through the chief justice, announced a three-pronged test for determining whether laws and other government actions affecting religion violated the establishment clause. Under this *Lemon* test, such laws were to be held unconstitutional unless they (1) had a secular (or nonreligious) purpose, (2) had a neutral primary effect that neither advanced nor harmed religion, and (3) did not create an excessive entanglement between church and state.

Application of *Lemon* and related standards produced mixed results in Burger Court establishment cases. In a number of cases, the Court adopted and extended Warren Court precedents opposing state-sponsored religious exercises in the public schools. The Warren Court had prohibited state-directed prayer and Bible-reading programs based on the obviously religious purpose underlying such devotional exercises (*Engel v. Vitale* [1962], *School Dist. of Abington v. Schempp* [1963]). The Burger Court proscribed the posting of the Ten Commandments on the walls of public school classrooms, assigning no weight to the fact that the copies were provided from private funds and merely posted rather than read aloud (*Stone v. Graham* [1980]). In 1985, moreover, a 6–3 majority, speaking through Justice Stevens, overturned an Alabama statute setting aside a daily period of silence in that state's public schools for student meditation or voluntary prayer. Two members of the majority indicated that certain moment-of-silence laws might pass constitutional muster but concluded that the Alabama scheme was intended to promote prayer in the public schools and was thus unconstitutional (*Wallace v. Jaffree* [1985]).

Earlier, however, the Court held that a state university could not exclude religious student groups from facilities generally available for registered secular student organizations, basing its position on free speech/public forum grounds and rejecting the university's claim that equal access for religious and secular student groups would violate the establishment clause (*Widmar v. Vincent* [1981]). A majority also refused to extend the ban on state-sponsored devotional exercises in the public schools to legislative chambers. The provision of paid chaplains for legislative bodies would appear to be a clear violation of the secular purpose prong of the *Lemon* test. But the practice dated back to the first Congress, which drafted the Bill of Rights. Citing that history, Chief Justice Burger held for a 6–3 Court in *Marsh v. Chambers* (1983) that Nebraska's provision for a legislative chaplain did not conflict with the intent of the First Amendment's framers, even though a clergyman of only one denomination had served in the post for sixteen years and the prayers offered were in the Judeo-Christian tradition.

The equally time-honored practice of tax exemptions for churches also survived challenge. In dissent, Justice Douglas equated tax exemptions with a government subsidy of religion. But Chief Justice Burger emphasized that exemptions were extended to other beneficent institutions as well as churches, did not constitute government sponsorship of religion, and enabled the government to avoid the charge that it was interfering with religious liberty. All the Constitution required, declared Burger, was benevolent neutrality toward religion (*Walz v. Tax Commission* [1970]).

Other forms of government assistance to religious institutions did not always fare so well. In *Lemon* and a companion case, for example, the Court distinguished earlier cases upholding the reimbursement of parents for school transportation expenses (*Everson v. Bd. of Education* [1947]) and the loan of textbooks (*Bd. of Education v. Allen* [1968]) on the ground that such assistance had a secular purpose and only an incidental effect on religion. Speaking for the Court, the chief justice struck down a Pennsylvania program under which the state purchased certain secular educational services from nonpublic schools and a Rhode Island scheme supplementing the salaries of teachers of secular subjects in private schools. The surveillance required to assure that such funding was put only to secular uses, Burger reasoned, would create an excessive entanglement between church and state (*Lemon v. Kurtzman* [1971], *Robinson v. DiCenso* [1971]). Several 1973 decisions invalidated other assistance schemes on the ground that they had the impermissible primary effect of advancing religion. Struck down in one case were state grants to religious schools for the maintenance and repair of buildings, tuition reimbursement, and tax credits for parents failing to qualify for tuition support (*Committee for Public Education and Religious Liberty v. Nyquist* [1973]). Another salary supplement measure also met defeat (*Sloan v. Lemon* [1973]). And in a third case, the Court declared unconstitutional a program reimbursing nonpublic schools for costs connected with examinations and the maintenance of school records. Chief Justice Burger observed that such services could be put to religious ends (*Levitt v. Committee for Public Education and Religious Liberty* [1973]). On essentially the same ground, the justices struck down state funding of auxiliary services such as counseling, testing, and speech and hearing therapy (*Meek v. Pittinger* [1975]).

Ten years later the Court, in precedents later overruled by the Rehnquist Court (*Agostini v. Felton* [1997]), invalidated New York's practice of sending public school personnel into religious schools to provide remedial instruction as well as clinical and guidance services (*Aguilar v. Felton* [1985], *City of Grand Rapids v. Ball* [1985]). Upheld by varying votes earlier, however, was state provision of standardized testing and scoring; speech, hearing, and psychological diagnostic and therapeutic services; and guidance and remedial services. Such assistance, the justices concluded, was not likely to be used for religious purposes. But in the same case, the Court struck down grants for the purchase of instructional materials and equipment as well as transportation for field trips on the ground they could be used to advance religion (*Wolman v. Walter* [1977]). In *Mueller v. Allen* (1983), in contrast, a 5–4 majority sustained a state statute permitting taxpayers, in computing their state income tax, to deduct educational expenses, even if their children attended parochial schools. Emphasizing that parents of nonpublic school students, most of whom attended parochial schools, were the principal beneficiaries of the tax exemption since public schools charge no tuition, the dissenters contended that the scheme had the direct and immediate effect of advancing religion. But Justice Rehnquist observed for the majority that the exemption was available to all parents, promoted the state's secular interest in an educated citizenry and educational diversity, and did not "excessively entangle" the state in religion.

The Court also assumed a more accommodationist stance in dealing with government assistance to church-connected colleges and universities. Basing its position on the greater maturity of college students and the less sectarian atmosphere of religious colleges, in contrast to sectarian primary and secondary schools, the justices upheld various forms of secular aid to such institutions. *Tilton v. Richardson* (1971) sustained federal grants to church-related colleges for the construction of academic facilities but struck down a provision limiting to twenty years the period the facilities could not be used for religious purposes. In 1973 a 6–3 majority upheld a South Carolina scheme for issuance of revenue bonds to finance construction of secular facilities at a Baptist college (*Hunt v. McNair* [1973]). *Roemer v. Board of Public Works* (1976) upheld a statute providing annual grants to church colleges for secular uses. And when Washington state's highest court struck down state vocational rehabilitation assistance to a visually impaired student pursuing a Bible studies degree at a church college, the Court, speaking through Justice Marshall, reversed. The assistance appeared to be paid directly to the student rather than the school, created no special financial incentive to undertake a sectarian education, and was unlikely to significantly aid religious education, especially since there was no evidence that any other person had ever sought to finance a religious education under the program. For those reasons, Marshall rejected the contention that the assistance at issue would have the primary effect of advancing religion (*Witters v. Washington Dept. of Serv. for the Blind* [1986]).

Among other notable Burger Court establishment cases was *Lynch v. Donnelly* (1984), upholding the right of Pawtucket, Rhode Island, to include a nativity scene in the city's annual Christmas display at a park owned by a nonprofit organization and located in the heart of the city's shopping district. Given the presence in the city-owned display of secular symbols such as a Santa Claus house, reindeer, and a Christmas tree, Chief Justice Burger concluded for a 5–4 majority that the aggregation was most accurately to be considered a seasonal celebration of a national public holiday rather than a religious display. Justice Brennan, joined in dissent by Marshall, Blackmun, and Stevens, found nothing in the arrangement that "obscure[d] or diminishe[ed] the plain fact that Pawtucket's action amount[ed] to an impermissible governmental endorsement of a particular faith" (p. 695). Even so, the Rehnquist Court would later reaffirm what critics would call the *Lynch* majority's "interior decorator" approach to evaluating Christmas displays claimed to violate the establishment clause (*Allegheny County v. ACLU* [1989]). The Court struck down as a violation of the establishment clause, however, a state statute giving churches an effective veto over applications for liquor licenses by establishments located within a 500-foot radius of a church, the chief justice declaring that the challenged law had the primary or principal effect of advancing religion and also created the danger of divisiveness along political lines. The state's valid objective of protecting churches from the commotion associated with liquor outlets could readily be accomplished, added Burger, by other, less constitutionally suspect means (*Larkin v. Grendel's Den, Inc.* [1982]). A regulation giving worshipers an absolute, unqualified right not to work on their Sabbath, whatever the circumstances, met the same fate (*Estate of Thornton v. Caldor* [1985]). Such a requirement, the chief justice maintained, imposed on employers and other employees an absolute duty to conform their business practices to an employee's religious preferences. It thus had a primary effect that impermissibly advanced a particular religious practice.

Use of the *Lemon* test as the preferred formula for reviewing laws claimed to violate the establishment clause survived the Burger Court and, despite intense criticism, has not been officially overruled during Rehnquist's tenure in the Court's center seat. But it was controversial from the outset. In a *Lemon* dissent, Justice White charged that the three-pronged formula posed an "insoluble paradox" for government: "The State cannot finance secular instruction if it permits religion to be taught in the same classroom; but if it exacts a promise that religion not be taught . . . and enforces it [through surveillance techniques], it is then entangled in the 'no entanglement' aspect of the Court's Establishment Clause jurisprudence" (p. 668).

Justice Rehnquist delivered a more wide-ranging assault in *Wallace v. Jaffree*, the case invalidating Alabama's moment-of-silence law. Rehnquist's reading of the record surrounding the establishment clause's adoption and early history convinced him that it was intended to forbid only creation of a national church and governmental preference for particular sects or denominations; "it did not require government neutrality between religion and irreligion nor did it prohibit the Federal Government from providing nondiscriminatory aid to religion" (p. 106). The *Lemon* test clearly conflicted with Rehnquist's accommodationist interpretation of the establishment clause, and its "mercurial" character, in his judgment, had led to "unprincipled" and inconsistent rulings. Although not so outspokenly critical of *Lemon*, Justice O'Connor contended in a *Jaffree* concurrence that Lemon should be reexamined and refined. Later she argued that the Court should invalidate only those governmental actions intending "to convey a message of endorsement or disapproval of religion" (*Lynch v. Donnelly*, p. 691). In another *Jaffree* concurrence, Justice Powell defended the *Lemon* standards as a useful basis for analysis and the "only coherent" establishment test the Court had ever adopted, then expressed concern that "continued criticism of it could encourage other courts to feel free to decide Establishment Clause cases on an ad hoc basis" (*Wallace v. Jaffree*, p. 63). But Powell's words fell on deaf ears among *Lemon*'s critics.

The Burger Court's interpretation of the free exercise clause was largely consistent with Warren-era and earlier precedents. In *Reynolds v. United States* (1879), the Supreme Court drew a clear-cut distinction between religious belief and practices, held that the latter were subject to reasonable government regulation, and upheld the prosecution of a Mormon under a Utah territorial law prohibiting polygamy, even though the tenets of the Mormon faith encouraged multiple spouses. The Warren Court agreed that conduct based on religious beliefs was subject to some degree of government control, but only to further an overriding state interest through means least restrictive of religious liberty. In *Sherbert v. Verner* (1963), for example, the Court overturned South Carolina's refusal to provide unemployment benefits to a Seventh-Day Adventist unable to find a job not requiring work on Saturday, her Sabbath. The state's important interests in the prevention of fraud and protection of revenue, Justice Brennan declared for the Court, could be accomplished through means that would not burden the free exercise of religion. Justice Harlan argued in dissent, however, that requiring the state to carve out a special exception for persons refusing to work for religious reasons was contrary to the Court's broad interpretation of the establishment clause.

The Burger Court invoked the *Sherbert* approach in a variety of contexts. *Wisconsin v. Yoder* (1972) held that a state could not require Amish parents to comply with its compulsory high school education requirement, Chief Justice Burger pointing out for the Court that the Amish considered formal education beyond the eighth grade sinful and provided a meaningful alternative for their children through informal vocational training at home. In another case, the justices reaffirmed *Sherbert* in upholding the right to unemployment compensation of a Jehovah's Witness who quit his job with a foundry rather than accept a transfer to a department fabricating military tank turrets (*Thomas v. Review Board* [1981]). But the Court refused to exempt Amish employers from participating in the Social Security system, declaring that voluntary participation would undermine the program's stability (*United States v. Lee* [1982]). And when parents of a Native American child objected to the use of Social Security numbers in the federal food stamp and Aid to Families with Dependent Children (AFDC) programs, the Court rejected their free exercise claim, despite their sincere belief that use of the number would impair the child's spirit (*Bowen v. Ray* [1986]).

Speaking through Justice Rehnquist, a 5–4 majority also upheld an air force regulation preventing an Orthodox Jew and ordained rabbi from wearing a yarmulke while on duty and in uniform (*Goldman v. Weinberger* [1986]). Citing the deference extended military regulations challenged on First Amendment grounds, Rehnquist refused to subject the ban to the strict *Sherbert* standard of review. Instead, he concluded that it was a reasonable and evenhanded regulation designed to promote the military's perceived need for discipline and uniformity. The dissenters accused the majority, however, of subjecting the regulation to no scrutiny whatever. Justice Brennan charged, for example, that the air force had "failed utterly to furnish a credible explanation why an exception to the dress code [in the case was] . . . likely to interfere with its interest in discipline and uniformity" (p. 522).

In one case the Court invoked an important World War II–era precedent forbidding government to impose a particular orthodoxy on individuals without their consent. *West Virginia Board of Education v. Barnette* (1943) had held that Jehovah's Witness children could not be compelled to participate in public school flag exercises contrary to their religious beliefs. In *Wooley v. Maynard* (1977), the Burger Court, speaking through the chief justice, reaffirmed *Barnette* in upholding the right of a New Hampshire Jehovah's Witness couple to cover the state motto, "Live Free or Die," on their automobile license plate, a violation of state law. Only passenger vehicles, not commercial, trailer, or other vehicles, were required to display the motto, and New Hampshire argued that the requirement made it easier for police to determine whether passenger vehicles were carrying the proper plate. The state also claimed that the regulation promoted an appreciation of New Hampshire's history, individualism, and state pride. Chief Justice Burger concluded for the Court that the interest in identifying vehicles could be accomplished through means that did not interfere with individual freedom, while the other interests the regulation was claimed to serve were clearly outweighed by the Wooleys' right to avoid becoming couriers of state ideological messages. Justice Rehnquist, joined by Justice Blackmun, declared in dissent, however, that display of the state's motto on license plates was no more an affirmation of belief than the display of mottoes on coins and currency, which federal law forbade defacing. Persons wishing to make clear their opposition to whatever viewpoint the offensive motto might reflect, suggested Rehnquist, could simply place on their bumper a conspicuous sticker to that effect.

Rehnquist also dissented when the Court upheld the denial of tax-exempt status to racially discriminatory private religious schools, but on relatively narrow grounds. Until 1970 the IRS had granted tax-exempt status to private schools, without regard to their racial policies, under a provision of the internal revenue code providing exemptions for institutions operated exclusively for religious, charitable, or educational purposes. After a lower federal court issued an injunction prohibiting the IRS from granting tax-exempt status to racially discriminatory private schools in Mississippi, the agency modified its policy, denying such institutions tax exemptions as well as tax deductions for donor contributions. Bob Jones University in South Carolina and a Christian school in North Carolina challenged the new policy in court, contending, among other things, that it interfered with their religious liberty. The Supreme Court, per Chief Justice Burger, held that the IRS action was consistent with federal law and that the government's overriding interest in eradicating racial discrimination in education substantially outweighed whatever burden the denial of tax benefits had placed on the school's exercise of religious beliefs. But Justice Rehnquist argued in a strong dissent that while Congress had power to deny tax exemptions to discriminatory institutions, it had not authorized the IRS to take such action (*Bob Jones University v. United States* [1983]).

Criminal Justice

In the field of criminal justice, the Burger Court perhaps came closest to achieving the constitutional counterrevolution Warren Court critics hoped for and its supporters feared. Yet even here the retrenchment was more subtle than profound. The Burger Court faced a number of issues, moreover, that Warren Court justices were not obliged to confront.

The Constitution contains a large number of criminal procedure rights. Sections 9 and 10 of Article I prohibit the imposition of bills of attainders (legislative punishment of specified individuals or groups without benefit of judicial trial) and ex post facto laws (retroactively applied criminal laws that work to the detriment of the individual). Article III, Section 2, provides for trial by jury in all federal cases except impeachment proceedings (a guarantee also included in the Sixth Amendment of the Bill of Rights). Most specific criminal procedure guarantees are found, however, in the Fourth through the Eighth Amendments. The Fourth Amendment forbids unreasonable searches and seizures and imposes conditions on search and arrest warrants. The Fifth Amendment requires a formal charge or indictment by a grand jury before trial in all serious cases and also forbids compulsory self-incrimination and double jeopardy. The Sixth Amendment guarantees the accused in criminal prosecutions a speedy and public trial by an impartial jury, notice of the charges (and thus an opportunity to prepare a defense), the right to confront (and thus cross-examine) prosecution witnesses, a compulsory subpoena process for obtaining witnesses in the defendant's behalf, and the right to defense counsel. Amendment Seven grants the right of jury trial in most civil cases, and the Eighth Amendment forbids excessive bail, excessive fines, and cruel and unusual punishments.

Although these Bill of Rights guarantees are directly binding only on the national government, the Supreme Court, as discussed earlier in this chapter, has applied most of these rights to the states through the Fourteenth Amendment's due process clause and the process of selective incorporation. As noted previously, too, the Fifth and Fourteenth Amendment due process clauses have been construed to include within their meaning unenumerated procedural and substantive rights, such as the requirement that a person's guilt be established beyond a reasonable doubt in criminal cases. The Supreme Court has also used this general requirement of fundamentally fair proceedings implicit in due process to impose procedural requirements in juvenile cases. Although the Warren Court began this process (*In Re Gault* [1967]), the Burger Court applied the guarantee against double jeopardy to juveniles, holding in 1975 that minors could not first be tried in juvenile proceedings then in the regular courts for the same offense (*Breed v. Jones* [1975]). Like the Warren Court, however, the Burger Court made clear that not all procedural guarantees are applicable to juvenile proceedings; in 1971 it refused to extend the right of trial by jury to such cases (*McKeiver v. Pennsylvania* [1971]). Finally, like the Warren Court, the Burger Court on occasion invoked the equal protection guarantee to invalidate discriminatory civil and criminal procedures (e.g., *Williams v. Illinois* [1970], *Tate v. Short* [1970], *Boddie v. Connecticut* [1971]; but see also *United States v. Kras* [1973], *Ortwein v. Schwab* [1973]).

Probably because the rights against bills of attainder and ex post facto laws are truly rudimentary, their violation has rarely been a subject of litigation. In the dispute over control of the Nixon presidential papers, a Burger Court majority rejected the contention that the former president was being subjected to attainder, reasoning that he legitimately constituted a class of one, while dissenters argued that the enactment of legislation denying Nixon the custody over his papers other presidents enjoyed over theirs was precisely the sort of legislative punishment of a named individual the attainder clause was intended to prevent (*Nixon v. Administrator of General Services* [1977]). The Court also rejected an attainder challenge to a federal provision requiring all men applying for student financial aid to indicate that they had complied with military draft registration regulations (*Selective Service System v. Public Interest Research Group* [1984]). Under that law, declared Chief Justice Burger, any student wishing to apply for financial aid could do so at any time simply by registering for the draft. Nor did the law, in the Court's judgment, impose the sort of disabilities ordinarily associated with punishment.

Cases arising under the guarantee against ex post facto laws were equally rare, but the Court, speaking through Justice Marshall, in 1981 struck down Florida's retroactive application of new rules for computing a prison inmate's time off for good behavior to the disadvantage of a prisoner whose crime was committed before the rules were changed (*Weaver v. Graham* [1981]). But earlier the Court rejected the ex post facto claim of a Florida defendant sentenced to death under a statute not in effect when he brutally murdered two of his children. Although the death penalty statute in effect at the time of the murders had later been invalidated by Florida's supreme court, Justice Rehnquist reasoned that its existence had surely given the defendant clear warning of the possible punishment for such offenses—the sort of notice the ex post facto clause was adopted to assure (*Dobbert v. Florida* [1977]).

Criminal procedure claims relating to a number of Bill of Rights guarantees provided a large share of the Burger Court's caseload. Cases arising under the Fourth Amendment were particularly common. The Fourth Amendment provides, "The right of the people to be secure in their persons, houses, papers, and effects, against unreasonable searches and seizures, shall not be violated, and no warrants shall issue, but upon probable cause, supported by Oath or affirmation, and particularly describing the place to be searched, and the persons or things to be seized." The most intense Burger Court debates over this guarantee involved the exclusionary rule, under which unconstitutionally seized evidence is generally inadmissible as evidence in (or excluded from) criminal trials. The rule was first applied to federal trials in 1914 (*Weeks v. United States* [1914]), and in *Mapp v. Ohio* (1961), the Court extended the rule to state criminal cases, Justice Clark declaring for the *Mapp* Court that the exclusion of illegally seized evidence was implicit in the Fourth Amendment, made applicable to the states through the Fourteenth Amendment, as well as necessary to assure the integrity of the judicial process. But certain members of the Burger Court, especially the chief justice and Justice Rehnquist, were vocal critics of the rule. Chief Justice Burger argued, for example, that the rule was not required by the Fourth Amendment's language, did not meaningfully deter police misconduct, and exacted a terrible social cost through the exclusion of reliable, relevant evidence and the freeing of guilty defendants (see, e.g., Burger's dissent in *Bivens v. Six Unknown Named Agents* [1971]). Burger favored reserving the exclusionary rule for only the most egregious incidents of police misconduct and recommended alternative avenues (such as the development of remedies against the government for the misconduct of its officers) to assure compliance with the Fourth Amendment's requirements.

Burger was unable to convince a majority of his colleagues to discard the exclusionary rule. The Court did conclude, however, that the rule was not a constitutional requirement but merely a judicially created device to deter police from Fourth Amendment violations. Under that approach, application of the rule was held to depend on whether it served to promote its deterrent purpose, and on that ground the Court refused to extend the rule to certain types of situations. In *United States v. Calandra* (1974), for example, a 6–3 majority refused to prohibit questioning of grand jury witnesses based on illegal evidence, Justice Powell concluding for the Court that exclusion of the evidence in a defendant's later trial would serve as a sufficient deterrent to police misconduct. A 1976 ruling held the exclusionary rule inapplicable to civil proceedings involving a government agency (*United States v. Janis* [1976]). In *Stone v. Powell* (1976), a 6–3 majority, speaking through Justice Powell, held that defendants challenging their state convictions in a federal habeas corpus proceeding (to determine whether they were unconstitutionally convicted and thus illegally in prison) could not raise an illegal search and seizure claim if they had been given a full and fair opportunity to raise such claims in the state courts. Extension of exclusionary rule claims to such proceedings, asserted Powell, would have only a minimal additional deterrent effect on police compared with the substantial costs further extension of the rule would inflict on society.

In dissent, Justice Brennan, joined by Justice Marshall, contended that the rule was "part and parcel of the Fourth Amendment's prohibition of unreasonable searches and seizures" (p. 502) and should not be subjected to the sort of cost-benefit analysis the majority was using to justify its selective application. But Justice White, the third dissenter, indicated that he would happily join four other justices in "substantially limiting" the rule's reach, and Chief Justice Burger filed a concurrence calling for rejection of the rule even in the absence of other remedies against police misconduct.

Further dilution of the exclusionary rule continued in later cases. In 1984 the Court adopted the "inevitable discovery" exception to the rule, under which illegally seized evidence was nevertheless admissible if police would inevitably have discovered it anyway (*Nix v. Williams* [1984]). That same year, moreover, the Court announced a potentially sweeping "good faith" exception to the rule. In his dissent in the *Stone* case, Justice White had argued that the rule should be inapplicable in cases in which police illegally seized evidence in a reasonable but mistaken belief their conduct was lawful. In *United States v. Leon*, White spoke for a 6–3 majority in upholding the use at trial of evidence seized with a defective warrant by officers acting in a reasonable, good-faith belief the warrant was valid. Since police had relied on a warrant they believed to be legitimate, issued by a detached and neutral magistrate, exclusion of the evidence under such circumstances, concluded White, would serve no deterrent purpose. Dissenters contended that the Fourth Amendment required suppression of all illegally seized evidence and cited the difficulty of distinguishing innocent and willful violations of the guarantee against unreasonable searches and seizures. But the Rehnquist Court would later extend the good-faith exception to other contexts, including police seizure of evidence based on a statute authorizing warrantless administrative searches that was later found to be unconstitutional (*Illinois v. Krull* [1987]).

The Burger Court also expanded the circumstances under which warrantless searches are permissible. The Supreme Court has never required warrants for all arrests and searches. Arrests without a warrant based upon probable cause (or reasonable belief the person arrested has committed a crime) are allowed in public places, although the Burger Court, citing the importance of the home as a place of privacy, required a warrant for routine arrests of people in their homes (*Payton v. New York* [1980]). The Warren Court required search warrants except under a number of limited, exceptional circumstances, but the Burger Court substantially enlarged upon the scope of permissible warrantless searches. Searches without a warrant based on free and voluntary consent have traditionally been allowed, and in 1973 a 6–3 majority held that suspects need not be informed of their right not to consent to a warrantless search (*Schneckloth v. Bustamonte* [1973]). Instead, Justice Stewart declared for the Court, the voluntariness of a consent search was to be determined by an examination of the totality of the surrounding circumstances; no evidence that suspects explicitly waived their right not to be searched was required. Such knowing and intelligent waivers were largely reserved, asserted Stewart, only for those rights necessary to preserve the accused's right to a fair trial, such as the guarantee against compulsory self-incrimination and the right to counsel. Whether reliable evidence was improperly seized had nothing to do with assuring the fair determination of the truth in a criminal trial.

Dissenters were amazed at the Court's conclusion, as Justice Brennan put it, "that an individual can effectively waive [his right not to consent to a search] even though he is totally ignorant of the fact that, in the absence of his consent, such invasions of his privacy would be constitutionally prohibited" (p. 277). When the Court later held that any person jointly occupying premises with other persons can give consent for its search, not merely the suspect, Justice Brennan again dissented. In that case a woman sharing a bedroom in her parents' house with a man arrested in the front yard had given police consent to search the bedroom. Absent evidence the woman had been aware of her right to refuse consent, Brennan, joined by Marshall, would have held the search invalid (*United States v. Matlock* [1974]).

The Warren Court had also upheld warrantless searches incident to a valid arrest but had limited such searches to the suspect's body and the immediate area within the suspect's reach for weapons and evidence that could be easily destroyed, thereby tying such searches to the important interests in the safety of police and the protection of evidence. In two 1973 cases, however, a Burger Court majority sustained a full-body search incident to arrest where suspects were arrested for petty traffic offenses and arresting officers had no reason to believe they were armed or carrying contraband. The arrest, Justice Rehnquist reasoned for the Court, provided authority for the search, and no other justification was necessary. Justice Marshall, joined by Justices Douglas and Brennan, contended in dissent, however, that the reasonableness of a search should turn on the particular circumstances of each case and that the scope of searches incident to arrest should be limited to that reasonably necessary to protect officers from harm and prevent escape (*United States v. Robinson* [1973], *Gustafson v. Florida* [1973]).

There was also the danger, of course, that officers would use an arrest for a minor offense as a mere pretext for searching a person suspected of a more serious crime, such as drug-dealing. The Burger Court was not always willing, however, to uphold warrantless searches incident to arrest. In 1971, for example, the Court rejected the claim that an arrest outside a house justified a search of the arrestee's automobile outside on the driveway, especially when it was not actually searched until two days later, after being seized and taken to the police station (*Coolidge v. New Hampshire* [1971]).

The Burger Court expanded, too, the circumstances under which police could conduct a warrantless stop and frisk of suspects for weapons. In *Terry v. Ohio* (1968), the Warren Court, per the chief justice, upheld a limited pat-down search of the outer clothing of two men a veteran police officer had reason to believe were armed and planning to rob a store. Applying a balancing-of-interests approach to the officer's conduct, Warren concluded that the interest in public safety outweighed the limited intrusion on the suspects' privacy and that the search was thus reasonable, even though the officer lacked the probable cause required for a full search. The Burger Court in 1972 approved such searches even when the tip of an anonymous, reliable informer rather than an officer's direct knowledge provided the basis for the officer's belief a suspect was armed and dangerous. The majority, per Justice Rehnquist, further concluded that discovery of a weapon during a pat-down search justified a full search that might yield other evidence (e.g., drugs) as well as weapons. Dissenters argued that *Terry* pat-downs should be allowed only to protect the safety of police (*Adams v. Williams* [1972]).

Not surprisingly, given the mobility of vehicles, the Supreme Court held long ago (*Carroll v. United States* [1925]) that police could conduct warrantless searches of automobiles and other vehicles, based on probable cause that they contained evidence of a crime, had been used in the commission of a crime, or contained persons who had committed crimes. The Burger Court enlarged this vehicle exception to the warrant requirement in a number of ways, permitting such searches to include containers or packages found in a car (*United States v. Ross* [1982]), even if there was no independent basis for concluding they contained contraband, as well as mobile homes parked in public places (*California v. Carney* [1985]) and impounded automobiles of arrested persons (*Chambers v. Maroney* [1970]). To protect against charges of theft, officers were also allowed to inventory impounded vehicles—and seize any evidence discovered during the inventory (*South Dakota v. Opperman* [1976]). The Court invalidated, however, random automobile stops by police to check the validity of drivers' licenses and vehicle registrations (*Delaware v. Prouse* [1979]).

Warrantless searches at international borders have traditionally been considered beyond the Fourth Amendment's reach. But the Burger Court rendered mixed decisions regarding the use of roving patrols in an effort to reduce the rate of illegal Mexican immigration into the United States. In several cases the Court invalidated the search of vehicles without warrant or probable cause (*Almeida-Sanchez v. United States* [1973]); forbade the stopping of vehicles to question occupants unless there was a reasonable basis for suspecting they were aliens (*United States v. Brignoni-Ponce* [1975]); and, in *United States v. Ortiz* (1975), prohibited use of fixed checkpoints for the same purpose. But in 1976 the Court overruled *Ortiz*, holding that vehicles could be stopped at fixed checkpoints for brief questioning of occupants regarding their citizenship, without a warrant or reasonable suspicion they were illegal aliens. Certain motorists could also be referred to an inspection area for further questioning, even if such referrals might be made largely on the basis of apparent Mexican ancestry (*United States v. Martinez-Fuerte* [1976]).

Another exception to the warrant requirement permits police to search and seize evidence in plain view if officers are lawfully in a place where the evidence is spotted, it is obvious that the item observed is evidence of a crime, and police have probable cause for that belief. In 1982, for example, the Court upheld the plain-sight seizure of drug contraband from a university student by a policeman who lawfully accompanied the student to his dormitory room following his arrest for underage drinking (*Washington v. Chrisman* [1982]). Along similar lines police have a right to seize without a warrant evidence people have openly revealed to the public, thereby surrendering any reasonable expectation of privacy over the items so exposed. Thus, in a 1986 case, the Court upheld a warrantless police flight over a private home from which marijuana was spotted growing in a fenced backyard. A photograph taken during the flight was used to secure a warrant to search the property, and dissenters contended that the defendant had not relinquished his expectation of privacy from the viewing of those flying over the area. But the majority, speaking through Chief Justice Burger, disagreed, concluding that anyone flying over the property could have seen everything the police spotted (*California v. Ciraolo* [1986]).

The Burger Court also approved warrantless searches based on probable cause and exigent circumstances justifying prompt action by police. In *Cupp v. Murphy* (1973), police seized skin scrapings from beneath the fingernails of a murder suspect who went voluntarily to the police station for questioning. The police had secured no search warrant, and the suspect had not been arrested. But there was probable cause to believe he had committed the crime and an obvious need for quick action to preserve evidence that could easily disappear. In another case firefighters and police were permitted to enter a burning building without a warrant and remain there a reasonable period of time to investigate the cause of the blaze. But the emergency could not be used indefinitely, the Court held, to justify an exhaustive, warrantless search for evidence not in plain view (*Michigan v. Tyler* [1978]).

Searches by government officials other than police are subject to less stringent requirements than those governing police investigations of crime. The Burger Court made clear in a 1985 case, for example, that public school personnel have broad authority to search students when the act is reasonably related to maintaining discipline and furthering other legitimate school objectives. In *New Jersey v. T.L.O.*, an assistant principal opened the purse of a student suspected of smoking in a school lavatory in violation of school rules. When he opened the purse, he spotted not only a pack of cigarettes but also a package of rolling papers commonly associated with the use of marijuana. That discovery prompted a thorough search of the purse, where he found marijuana and other evidence implicating the student in drug use and dealing. The Burger Court found each stage of the search reasonable, upheld use of the evidence in delinquency proceedings, and concluded that the important interests of public school officials in maintaining an atmosphere conducive to learning justified some easing of the restrictions to which searches by government authorities were usually subjected. In a partial dissent, Justice Brennan, joined by Marshall, agreed that school officials not acting as agents of police did not ordinarily require a warrant to search a student but argued that the rolling papers alone had not been an adequate justification for a full search of the student's purse. In a separate dissent, Justice Stevens contended that since smoking was neither unlawful nor significantly disruptive of school order or the educational process, the opening of the purse was itself unjustified. Administrative inspections of homes or businesses were held to require a warrant, but magistrates could issue such administrative warrants if the inspection in question was authorized by law; probable cause was not required (*Marshall v. Barlow's* [1978]). No warrant at all was required, moreover, for types of businesses with a history of extensive government oversight, such as the liquor and firearms industries (*Colonnade Catering Corp. v. United States* [1970], *United States v. Biswell* [1972]).

Although declining to hold that prison inmates have no Fourth Amendment rights, the Court also made it clear that prisoners have limited expectations of privacy. In *Hudson v. Palmer* (1984), for example, Chief Justice Burger, speaking for a 5–4 majority, invoked the states' interests in prison security and discipline to sustain shakedown searches of prison cells. Declaring that inmates had no reasonable expectation of privacy from cell searches, the Court overturned a court of appeals ruling limiting searches to those based on an established plan of random searches or a reasonable belief that an inmate possessed contraband. But Justice Stevens, joined by Brennan, Marshall, and Blackmun, emphasized in dissent that a prison guard had seized only noncontraband personal items (letters and personal effects) that obviously posed no threat to prison security or discipline. Inmates, asserted Stevens, were constitutionally entitled to protection from such harassment.

Rejecting the rationale of earlier precedent that the Fourth Amendment applied only to the seizure of tangible objects, not words (*Olmstead v. United States* [1928]), the Warren Court had held in 1967 that police must secure a warrant before engaging in electronic eavesdropping (*Katz v. United States* [1967]). The Burger Court also embraced that position. When President Nixon's first attorney general, John Mitchell, concluded that a provision of the federal Crime Control and Safe Streets Act of 1968 requiring warrants for electronic surveillance was not applicable to "national security" investigations, the Court unanimously rejected that reading of the statute, at least in cases involving persons suspected of domestic subversion. A portion of the law stipulating that none of its provisions should be construed to limit the president's "constitutional" power to protect the nation's security, declared Justice Powell for the Court, meant simply that—the president's authority must conform to the Constitution's requirements, including the Fourth Amendment's warrant provisions.

The Court reserved a ruling, however, on the scope of presidential power to authorize surveillance of foreign agents within or outside the United States (*United States v. U.S. District Court* [1972]). And in a later case (*Smith v. Maryland* [1979]), a 5–3 majority held that use of a pen register, a device that records telephone numbers dialed but not the content of calls, was not a search within the Fourth Amendment's meaning and thus was not subject to the warrant requirement. Speaking for the Court, Justice Blackmun concluded that callers have no reasonable expectation of privacy in the numbers they dial. But the three dissenters rejected the notion that telephone numbers, unlike conversations, were lacking in content; they could be used, after all, to reveal the identities of persons called and thus intimate details of a caller's life.

Like its predecessors, the Burger Court generally approved of the warrantless use of undercover agents to secure incriminating statements from suspects. In 1971, for example, the Court upheld use of a transmitter concealed on an informant's body to broadcast a suspect's incriminating statements to nearby agents (*United States v. White* [1971]). In such cases a suspect was talking freely, if unwittingly, and had surrendered his reasonable expectation of privacy; there was thus no violation of the Fourth Amendment or the Fifth Amendment's guarantee against compulsory self-incrimination.

The Burger Court also reaffirmed the traditional narrow constitutional definition of entrapment. Government violates due process if its officials entrap a person into committing a crime. To establish entrapment, however, it is not sufficient merely to show that the government assisted or encouraged a defendant to commit a crime. Instead, police must have lured otherwise innocent persons into an offense they had no predisposition to commit. In 1973, for example, a 5–4 majority upheld a defendant's drug conviction against an entrapment claim. The record indicated that an undercover narcotics agent had provided the accused with an ingredient essential to the manufacture of an illicit drug and difficult to obtain. But Justice Rehnquist observed for the Court that the defendant had conceded a possible predisposition to commit the crime (*United States v. Russell* [1973]).

The Burger Court's approach to self-incrimination claims was similar to the pattern of its Fourth Amendment rulings, largely though not invariably restricting the reach of individual rights. The Fifth Amendment, applied to the states through the Fourteenth Amendment, provides that no person "shall be compelled in any criminal case to be a witness against himself." Under this guarantee, defendants cannot be compelled to testify in their own defense, and the Warren Court in 1965 forbade prosecutors and judges to call to a jury's attention the accused's refusal to take the witness stand (*Griffin v. California* [1965]). Over the objections of Justice Rehnquist, the Burger Court also embraced that position and further held that at a defendant's request, the trial judge must instruct jurors they can draw no adverse inferences from the defendant's failure to testify (*Carter v. Kentucky* [1981]).

But the Burger Court also reaffirmed the distinction traditionally drawn between physical and testimonial evidence, prohibiting only the compulsion of the latter from suspects under the self-incrimination clause. In 1973, for example, the Court upheld a court order requiring a person to make a voice recording for comparison by a federal grand jury with a legally intercepted telephone conversation (*United States v. Dionisio* [1973]). And in *Kastigar v. United States* (1972), a majority attached a narrow interpretation to the sort of immunity from prosecution suspects must be given in exchange for being compelled to testify. Under federal and state immunity statutes, judges are authorized to grant immunity to suspects who are then obliged to provide otherwise incriminating statements to grand juries, courts, and other bodies, usually as part of an effort to secure evidence against top figures in a criminal enterprise. Such laws traditionally granted complete or "transactional" immunity, preventing the suspect's prosecution at all for crimes revealed under the immunity grant. The *Kastigar* majority held, however, that the Fifth Amendment required only "use" immunity, that is, immunity solely from the use of statements made by the suspect or evidence derived from those statements. If an independent case could be developed that did not rely, directly or indirectly, on immunized statements, a suspect given use immunity could be prosecuted for crimes confessed to under immunity.

Burger Court justices were most critical of the rules established by the Warren Court for custodial interrogation of suspects. The due process guarantee had long been construed to forbid the use in court of confessions secured through torture or other forms of physical or psychological coercion. In an effort to provide more clear-cut safeguards against coerced confessions, a 5–4 Warren Court majority held in *Miranda v. Arizona* (1966) that suspects in police custody could be questioned only after being informed that they had a right to remain silent and not submit to questioning, that they had the right to the presence of counsel if they waived their right to silence, that counsel would be appointed for indigent suspects, and that anything said during interrogation would be recorded and might be used against them in court. Any statements obtained in violation of these requirements were held inadmissible in court. Such warnings were necessary, Chief Justice Warren asserted for the Court, to eliminate the inherently coercive pressures of the custodial interrogation process and to assure that suspects were aware both of their rights and of police willingness to honor them. Dissenters complained, however, that the Constitution was intended to prevent only undue pressures on suspects and charged that the ruling would result in the virtual elimination of confessions as an important investigatory tool, as well as the freeing of murderers, rapists, and other guilty defendants.

The Burger Court did not overrule *Miranda* and, in fact, extended its reach in certain cases. A unanimous Court held in 1981, for example, that the warnings were applicable prior to in-custody court-ordered psychiatric examinations to determine a defendant's competency to stand trial (*Estelle v. Smith* [1981]). Another case forbade police to continue to interrogate a suspect who had asked for an attorney (*Edwards v. Arizona* [1981]). As with the Fourth Amendment exclusionary rule, however, several justices vehemently attacked *Miranda*, and a majority, viewing the *Miranda* warnings as judicially created safeguards against coerced confessions rather than a constitutional requirement, recognized numerous exceptions to their application.

The Court held, for example, that confessions secured in violation of *Miranda* could be used to impeach or challenge the truthfulness of a defendant's trial testimony (*Harris v. New York* [1971]) and to secure other evidence against the accused, such as the name of a prosecution witness (*Michigan v. Tucker* [1974]). Rejecting the view that grand jury hearings are inherently coercive proceedings, the Court also held that witnesses could be required to appear before grand juries without counsel, even if a target of investigation, although they could of course refuse to answer particular questions on self-incrimination grounds, like all witnesses before governmental bodies (*United States v. Mandujano* [1976]). The Court emphasized, too, that *Miranda* applied only to custodial interrogation, not questioning to which persons not in custody voluntarily submit (*Oregon v. Mathiason* [1977]). And in 1984 a majority recognized a public safety exception to *Miranda*. In that case, the Court upheld admission into evidence of a gun police retrieved from behind empty cartons in a supermarket, even though they were directed there by a suspect questioned before being given the required warnings. *Miranda*, Justice Rehnquist concluded for the Court, was not intended to apply to police questioning prompted by an immediate concern for public safety (*New York v. Quarles* [1984]).

Burger Court decisions regarding the Sixth and Fourteenth Amendment right of defendants to the assistance of counsel both extended and narrowed the reach of Warren Court counsel rulings. The Sixth Amendment had been construed to require a court-appointed lawyer for indigent defendants in most federal cases since 1938 (*Johnson v. Zerbst*), and in *Gideon v. Wainwright* (1963) the Warren Court, in an important incorporation decision, held that the right to appointed counsel was a fundamental Bill of Rights safeguard required in serious state cases via the Fourteenth Amendment's due process clause. The Burger Court extended that requirement to any case in which a jail sentence, regardless of length, was imposed (*Argersinger v. Hamlin* [1972]), yet it later made clear that counsel is required only in prosecutions that actually lead to imprisonment, not to every case carrying a potential jail term (*Scott v. Illinois* [1979]).

Just as the Warren Court had required the appointment of counsel for poor persons not merely at trial but during all critical stages of the truth-determining process, so, too, did the Burger Court, holding, for example, that a lawyer was required for preliminary hearings in which a judge determines whether there is probable cause for further proceedings against a suspect (*Coleman v. Alabama* [1970]). The Court refused, though, to extend to preindictment lineups a Warren Court decision requiring counsel for lineups conducted after indictment (*Kirby v. Illinois* [1972], *United States v. Wade* [1967]). And in 1975 a divided Court held in *Faretta v. California* that mentally competent defendants can make a voluntary, knowing, and intelligent waiver of their right to counsel and represent themselves at trial.

At times, of course, issues of counsel and interrogation merge. In *Brewer v. Williams* (1977), a 5–4 majority, speaking through Justice Stewart, overturned the conviction of an escaped mental patient charged with the murder of a ten-year-old girl in Des Moines, Iowa. Williams was arrested in Davenport, Iowa, booked for the crime, and given the *Miranda* warnings before a return trip with police to Des Moines. Before leaving Davenport, the police agreed they would not question Williams until he had been given an opportunity to speak with his lawyer in Des Moines. During the trip, however, a detective aware that the suspect was deeply religious began to lament the possibility that a snowfall could cover the child's body, denying her a "Christian burial." Williams soon directed the police to the body, but the Supreme Court held that the detective's speech amounted to impermissible interrogation outside the presence of counsel. The Court sustained Williams's second trial and conviction, though, on the ground that the pattern police had followed in a search for the body would inevitably have led to its discovery, even without Williams's assistance (*Nix v. Williams* [1984]).

The Court made clear in another case that what constitutes interrogation turns on the specific circumstances of a particular case. In *Rhode Island v. Innis* (1980), police arrested an armed robbery suspect believed to have discarded his sawed-off shotgun near a school for handicapped children. On the drive to the police station, two of three officers in the squad car with the suspect engaged in a conversation about the missing weapon, with one stating, "God forbid one [of the children] might find a weapon with shells and . . . hurt themselves." Innis then took the officers to the weapon "to get the gun out of the way . . . of the kids in the area in the school." In upholding his later conviction, the Court, again speaking through Justice Stewart, held that the officers' remarks constituted neither questioning nor its functional equivalent, particularly since there was nothing in the record to suggest the defendant would be especially susceptible to an appeal to his conscience based on concern for the safety of handicapped children. But in dissent Justice Marshall ridiculed the view that the "conversation" was not intended to elicit a response from the suspect. "The notion that such an appeal could not be expected to have any effect unless the suspect were known to have some special interest in handicapped children," he added, "verges on the ludicrous" (p. 306).

Other Burger Court decisions involved a variety of additional criminal justice safeguards. In cases involving the Fifth Amendment guarantee against being "subject for the same offense to be twice put in jeopardy of life or limb," the Court held that a defendant was placed in jeopardy the moment a jury was empaneled (*Crist v. Bretz* [1978]) and further concluded that "same offense" meant "same evidence" in the double jeopardy context (*Ashe v. Swenson* [1970]). Whether a defendant could be tried more than once for various offenses growing out of the same criminal activity would depend, in other words, on whether different evidence was necessary for conviction in each trial. In taking this position, the Court absorbed into the double jeopardy provision the doctrine of "collateral estoppel," under which once an issue of ultimate fact (such as the identity of the one robber of several poker players) has been finally determined in one case, the issue cannot again be litigated between the same parties in another trial. Dissenting, however, Justice Brennan argued that the standard should be "same transaction" rather than same evidence. Given the potential for prosecutorial abuse of power inherent in multiple trials, Brennan would have required all charges against a defendant growing out of the same criminal transaction to be tried in the same proceeding.

In another case, however, the Court narrowed the reach of the "separate sovereignties" doctrine under which the federal and state governments had traditionally each been permitted to try a person once for an offense that violated both federal and state law. In 1970 the Court held that a defendant convicted in a municipal court for violation of a city ordinance could not then be tried by the state on charges based on the same act. Local governments, after all, were merely creatures of their state governments, not independent sovereign bodies (*Waller v. Florida* [1970]).

Among the most controversial of Burger Court criminal justice rulings, however, were those involving the Eighth Amendment guarantee against cruel and unusual punishments, particularly the Court's evolving stance regarding the constitutional status of the death penalty. In general, the Eighth Amendment has been construed to forbid barbaric forms of punishment, those grossly disproportionate to the seriousness of the offense, and those that served no legitimate purpose of criminal justice. Especially outside the death penalty arena, the Burger Court was reluctant to second-guess legislatures and trial courts with respect to the proportionality of a criminal sentence. In *Rummel v. Estelle* (1980), for example, a 5–4 majority, per Justice Rehnquist, upheld a mandatory life sentence imposed under a Texas recidivism statute on a defendant following his third felony conviction for obtaining $120.75 by false pretenses. Rummel's previous convictions had involved nonviolent property crimes (fraudulent use of a credit card and passing a forged check) totaling $108.36, and the dissenters, speaking through Justice Powell, found the mandatory life sentence grossly disproportionate to Rummel's offenses. But Justice Rehnquist cited the state's important interest in dealing harshly with those who had shown through repeat offenses that they were incapable of conforming to society's norms.

Two years later the Court sustained a sentence of forty years' imprisonment and a $20,000 fine imposed on a defendant convicted of possession with intent to distribute and distribution of marijuana (*Hutto v. Davis* [1982]). Justice Powell concurred in the Court's judgment, but solely on the strength of the *Rummel* precedent, which he argued should be overruled. The three other *Rummel* dissenters again dissented on proportionality grounds. When the Court confronted a habitual offender statute that imposed a mandatory life sentence without possibility of parole, however, Justice Blackmun joined the *Rummel* dissenters in overturning the sentence of a defendant convicted of passing a $100 bad check after three prior convictions for third-degree burglary, one for obtaining money under false pretenses, one for grand larceny, and one for drunk driving. In dissent, Chief Justice Burger, joined by White, Rehnquist, and O'Connor, faulted the majority for "blithely discard[ing] any concept of *stare decisis*." Pointing out that Rummel received a life sentence after only a third nonviolent felony conviction, while the defendant then before the Court had amassed seven felony convictions, Burger termed Rummel, whose sentence had been upheld, a "relatively 'model citizen'" by comparison (*Solem v. Helm* [1982], p. 304).

In the death penalty field, the Burger Court did not enlarge upon or narrow the reach of Warren Court decisions but moved instead through a virtually uncharted course. In 1968 the Warren Court had held that jurors could not be excluded from capital cases merely because they harbored constitutional scruples against the death penalty; only those prospective jurors who would be unable to render a guilty verdict because of their opposition to capital punishment could be denied a place in the jury box (*Witherspoon v. Illinois* [1968]). But the Warren Court avoided a direct ruling on the constitutionality per se of capital punishment, and as late as 1971 the Burger Court upheld state statutes leaving imposition of a death sentence to the jury's absolute discretion (*McGautha v. California* [1971], *Crampton v. Ohio* [1971]). In *Furman v. Georgia* (1972), however, a 5–4 majority concluded that such a death penalty statute constituted cruel and unusual punishment.

Furman, though, was hardly a clear-cut repudiation of the death penalty. The majority justices were so divided in their reasoning that the Court's decision, declaring imposition of the death penalty under Georgia's statute cruel and unusual punishment, was announced in a one-paragraph per curiam opinion, and each justice filed a separate opinion. Of the five members of the majority, only Justices Brennan and Marshall contended that capital punishment was per se unconstitutional, whatever the offense or circumstances. Capital punishment, they contended, served no function a life sentence would not serve, was inherently arbitrary, rejected the ultimate humanity of all human beings, and conflicted with fundamental standards of decency in a modern, civilized society. Other majority justices assumed less rigid stances. Justice Douglas emphasized capital punishment's history of irregular and discriminatory application, Justice Stewart found its freakishly arbitrary imposition comparable to being struck by lightning, and Justice White cited the comparative rarity of executions as evidence that the death sentence was arbitrarily inflicted. For their part, the dissenters stressed, among other things, the death penalty's long history, acceptance in the language of the Constitution, and public opinion polls indicating popular support for its use.

In the wake of *Furman*, state legislatures and Congress drafted new death penalty statutes designed to reduce the arbitrariness that appeared central to Justices Stewart's and White's rejection of Georgia's capital punishment scheme. Some jurisdictions adopted mandatory death sentences on the theory that would eliminate the concerns of key members of the *Furman* majority, but most imposed controls designed to limit rather than eliminate jury discretion in capital cases. In several 1976 cases, the Court rejected mandatory death sentence statutes as themselves arbitrary in that they eliminated the opportunity for the consideration of mitigating factors that might justify a life sentence rather than execution in individual cases (e.g., *Woodson v. North Carolina* [1976]). But in *Gregg v. Georgia*, the Court upheld that state's revised death penalty law and rejected the contention that capital punishment is per se unconstitutional in first-degree murder cases.

Justice Douglas was no longer on the Court when the 1976 cases were decided, and only Brennan and Marshall dissented in *Gregg*. Speaking for himself and Justices Powell and Stevens, Justice Stewart found the death penalty for murder consistent with the Constitution's text (which, for example, forbade the taking of life, but only *without* due process of law), the intent of the framers, long tradition, and the state's important interests in deterrence and retribution. Stewart recognized that statistical studies had produced mixed conclusions with respect to capital punishment's deterrent effect, but he concluded that a legislature could reasonably determine that under certain circumstances fear of a death sentence would serve as a greater deterrent to murder than a life sentence. He also considered death a fair form of retribution for those found guilty of willful murder. Under Georgia's revised law, separate guilt and penalty hearings were required in capital cases, and a jury could not recommend death unless one or more of several specified aggravating circumstances about the crime were present in a case. There was also to be an automatic appeal of every death sentence to the state supreme court, and Georgia's high court was to reverse death sentences in any case in which it found no aggravating circumstances or determined that the sentence was harsher than usually imposed in such cases. Stewart was convinced such features of the new law would eliminate the caprice inherent in the statute struck down in *Furman*.

Chief Justice Burger and Justices White, Blackmun, and Rehnquist would have gone further, rejecting challenges to mandatory death-sentencing statutes as well. But only Justice Rehnquist would remain consistently supportive of death penalty schemes. In 1977 White and Blackmun parted company with the chief justice and Rehnquist when the Court struck down as disproportionate to the gravity of the offense the death sentence for rape of an adult woman (*Coker v. Georgia* [1977]). White spoke for himself, Stewart, Blackmun, and Stevens in defending that position; Brennan and Marshall reaffirmed their opposition to all death sentences, and Justice Powell found the punishment disproportionate to the penalty only because the crime at issue had not been excessively brutal and the victim sustained neither serious nor lasting injury. The next year a majority, with the chief justice speaking in part for the Court and partly for a plurality, struck down a statute limiting the types of mitigating circumstances a jury could consider in determining whether to recommend death or a life sentence (*Lockett v. Ohio* [1978]). Ohio's refusal to allow consideration of all mitigating factors, Burger and three other justices asserted, created the risk that defendants would be executed even though they deserved a lighter sentence. Justice White contended in a partial dissent, however, that allowing jurors to consider whatever mitigating factors they wished essentially reinstated the very unbridled jury discretion *Furman* had condemned.

4

Legacy and Impact

R ichard Nixon had ample opportunity to make a lasting impact on our nation's highest tribunal, adding not only a chief justice but three associate justices to the bench well before the end of his first term. Like so many presidents before and since, however, Nixon was hardly a perfect prophet. The Burger Court did not produce the constitutional counterrevolution he and other critics of the Warren Court had hoped for—and its supporters had dreaded. Of Nixon's four appointees to the Court, only Chief Justice Burger and Justice Rehnquist seemed inclined toward a dramatic break with Warren Court precedent, and only Rehnquist consistently so. Justice Blackmun did not long remain Burger's conservative "Minnesota twin," and the moderate Lewis Powell was never a predictable conservative vote in civil liberties cases. Justices Brennan and Marshall, two of the most liberal members of the Warren Court, remained on the bench throughout Burger's tenure and well into the Rehnquist era, and William O. Douglas, perhaps the most liberal justice of any era, continued on the Court for the first six terms of Burger's tenure. Although something of a maverick, John Paul Stevens, Douglas's replacement and President Ford's only selection to the high bench, regularly voted with Brennan, Marshall, and Blackmun. And while Justice O'Connor, President Reagan's only Burger Court nominee, assumed a conservative stance on a variety of civil liberties issues and federal-state conflicts, she was hardly so consistently deferential to government in civil liberties litigation as the Reagan administration no doubt would have preferred.

As we saw in Chapter Three, however, the Burger Court definitely left its mark on the fabric of American law, making a significant impact on constitutional doctrine in a variety of fields and directions. This chapter underscores major Burger Court doctrinal contributions and assesses the Court and its chief justice.

Judicial Power

Albeit with notable exceptions, Burger Court majorities substantially restricted access to the federal judiciary. Although occasionally reaching out to grant standing to sue to litigants whose claims to injury seemed marginal at best (e.g., *United States v. SCRAP* [1973]), the justices generally invoked a strict version of the standing doctrine. A majority narrowly limited if it did not formally reject, for example, the Warren Court decision in *Flast v. Cohen* (1968), granting federal taxpayers as taxpayers standing to challenge federal spending programs claimed to violate constitutional limitations on congressional taxing and spending powers (e.g., *United States v. Richardson* [1974]). Justice Powell, among others, also warned of the dangers of judicial overreaching inherent in the *Flast* doctrine and other expansive interpretations of the standing limitations on access to the federal courts. The Court's obvious aversion to federal taxpayer suits and generally narrow reading of the standing doctrine (e.g., in *Warth v. Seldin* [1975]) had an inhibiting effect on litigants otherwise inclined to assert innovative claims to standing, especially in environmental and other lawsuits involving essentially public interest issues rather than traditional disputes in which the parties had no difficulty establishing discrete and substantial injury to their personal legal rights. Such suits became a rarity in the Burger and Rehnquist Courts. The Court also limited litigant use of class action suits under which plaintiffs could sue not only in their own interests but also in behalf of all similarly situated persons (that is, members of their class), securing a much broader grant of relief than possible via the claims of a single plaintiff. As we saw in Chapter Three, for example, *Eisen v. Carlisle* (1974) erected a formidable obstacle against the filing of class action damage suits by plaintiffs with little individual financial stake in the outcome of a case.

The Burger Court's restrictive conception of the "state action" doctrine further limited access to judicial relief in the federal courts. A majority narrowly construed (*Lloyd Corporation v. Tanner* [1972]) then overturned (*Hudgens v. NLRB* [1976]), the Warren Court's *Logan Valley* decision equating the premises of a shopping center with the business district of a town and imposing First Amendment obligations on such facilities. An unduly expansive conception of the "public forum," the Burger Court declared, would infringe upon rights of private property secured by the due process clauses and other constitutional guarantees. In other cases a majority rejected contentions that extensive governmental regulation of private entities transformed their activities into state action subject to constitutional obligations. Thus, a majority refused to reach constitutional challenges to a private club licensed to serve liquor that refused to serve the black guest of a member (*Moose Lodge v. Irvis* [1972]) and a utility company that cut off service to a delinquent customer without notice and a hearing (*Jackson v. Metropolitan Edison Co.* [1974]). As a result of such rulings, few innovative state action claims later came to the Burger and Rehnquist Courts.

Separation of Powers

Some of the most important Burger Court decisions, as we saw in Chapter Three, involved relations among the branches of the national government. In its most publicized ruling, *United States v. Nixon* (1974), the justices recognized a president's constitutionally implied executive privilege to withhold evidence from other branches of the government and declared its exercise presumptively valid (that is, ordinarily to be upheld by courts). But the Court also rejected the president's claim that assertions of the privilege were absolute and unreviewable in the courts, holding instead that the privilege must yield in particular cases to an overriding and demonstrated need of a coordinate branch of government for documents in the president's possession. The *Nixon* decision remains the Supreme Court's major pronouncement on the executive privilege doctrine. In *Nixon v. Administrator of General Services* (1977), moreover, the Court upheld a federal statute under which the GSA obtained substantial control over the former president's papers, rejecting Nixon's claims that the law violated separation of powers, presidential privilege, his privacy and associational rights, and the ban on legislative punishment of persons without trial stipulated in the bill of attainder clause.

In a number of other issue areas, however, the Burger Court supported an expansive construction of the separation of powers doctrine. Although holding that cabinet officers (*Butz v. Economou* [1978]), presidential aides (*Harlow v. Fitzgerald* [1982]), and most other administrators (e.g., *Wood v. Strickland* [1975]) were entitled only to qualified immunity from damage suits, the Court conferred absolute immunity on Nixon and other presidents from suits growing out of their official conduct—even willful violations of legal rights—on the ground that such a privilege was necessary to assure the president's courageous performance of his at times controversial duties and insulate him from the distractions of litigation (*Nixon v. Fitzgerald* [1982]). On essentially the same rationale, the Court in *Stump v. Sparkman* (1978) reaffirmed the absolute immunity from damage suits long accorded judges.

In cases involving executive-legislative relations, the Court also generally assumed a resolutely separationist position. To uphold President Carter's conclusion of the 1981 agreement that ended the Iranian hostage crisis, Justice Rehnquist, it will be recalled, strained to find congressional acquiescence in the arrangement, even though no statute authorized certain parts of the agreement. He also emphasized precedents upholding broad presidential authority in foreign affairs and rejected "over-simplified" interpretations of the president's power to respond to international crises (*Dames & Moore v. Regan* [1981]).

In several significant rulings, however, the Court invoked a textbook version of separation of powers doctrine. Congress had long resorted to the legislative veto as a means of delegating necessary discretion to the executive while also retaining power to disapprove proposed exercises of that delegated authority. But in the *Chadha* case, as discussed in Chapter Three, a majority concluded that it was the job of the president, not Congress, to veto proposed policies. Justice White, in a cogent dissent to *Chadha*, chided the Court for its artificial conception of separation of powers and contended that the legislative veto provided precisely the same safeguards against arbitrary government as those stipulated in the Constitution's lawmaking provisions (that is, prevention of action by objection of either house of Congress or the executive). Again over White's dissent, the Court also overturned a provision of the Gramm-Rudman-Hollings deficit control statute on the ground it assigned executive functions to the comptroller general, a legislative officer (*Bowsher v. Synar* [1986]). Earlier a provision of the 1974 Federal Election Campaign Act giving congressional leaders a role in the selection of Federal Election Commission members met the same fate in *Buckley v. Valeo* (1976). Not since *Youngstown Co. v. Sawyer* (1952), rejecting President Truman's seizure of the nation's steel mills during the Korean War, had the Court given separation of powers such a broad construction.

Federalism

The Burger Court's potentially most significant decision with respect to federal-state relations did not, of course, survive its chief justice's tenure. In the *Usery* case, a 5–4 majority in 1976 struck down on state sovereignty grounds a congressional statute requiring state and local governments to conform to federal wage and hour standards. Even in the exercise of its admittedly broad authority over interstate commerce, Justice Rehnquist declared for the majority, Congress could not interfere with "integral" or "traditional" state functions. From the outset, Justice Blackmun, the fifth *Usery* vote, was uncomfortable with the Court's decision, rationale, and departure from long precedent leaving the correction of alleged congressional excesses in the exercise of its powers over the states largely to the political arena. In 1985 Blackmun spoke for the *Garcia* Court in overruling *Usery*. Later, however, Justices Rehnquist and O'Connor, who vigorously dissented in the *Garcia* case, provided the nucleus for a narrow Rehnquist Court majority striking down a number of congressional statutes on state sovereignty grounds. The growing Rehnquist Court defense of state power against federal oversight arguably had its roots, therefore, in the *Usery* majority opinion and the *Garcia* dissents.

The Burger Court also demonstrated considerable solicitude for state courts in resolving issues of judicial federalism. In *Younger v. Harris* (1971) and other cases, for example, a majority narrowly construed a Warren-era decision and reaffirmed the Court's traditional opposition to federal district court intervention in pending state judicial proceedings, absent special circumstances, such as a state court's bad-faith enforcement of an unconstitutional law. Adhering to another aspect of this abstention doctrine, the Court, despite its generally conservative bent, declined to review state court decisions giving civil liberties guaranteed in a state constitution a broader construction than the Court was willing to assign their federal constitutional counterparts. In *Pruneyard Shopping Center v. Robins* (1980), for example, the Court refused to disturb a state court decision upholding a state constitutional right to freedom of expression on a shopping center's property, even though earlier, of course, it had rejected a First Amendment right of access to such property for purposes of expression. In *Michigan v. Long* (1983), however, a majority required a clear statement in a state court's opinion that its decision rested primarily on state rather than federal constitutional grounds before the Court would decline to reach federal issues raised in a state case. Such precedents remain in force on the Rehnquist Court.

Indeed, the Burger Court's general influence on Rehnquist Court federalism trends has been substantial in a variety of issue areas. Despite the Burger Court's rejection of *Usery* in the *Garcia* case, the Rehnquist Court's increasing deference to state authority in federal-state disputes—a deference reflected, among other ways, in its invalidation of congressional statutes on state sovereignty grounds and expansive interpretation of state sovereign immunity from lawsuit, even in cases involving the refusal of states to comply with valid congressional enactments—arguably had its roots in the Burger era.

Framework of Civil Liberties

A number of Burger Court decisions made important contributions to the developing law on the general scope and reach of constitutional rights. During the laissez-faire era of the late nineteenth and early twentieth centuries, the Supreme Court had regularly invoked substantive due process and, to a lesser degree, the equal protection clause in striking down a variety of federal and state controls over business and industry, while giving little attention to noneconomic personal liberties. The post-1936 Supreme Court largely repudiated that era. Property rights are now enjoying something of a rebirth in the Rehnquist Court via its expansive interpretations of the Fifth Amendment guarantee against government taking of private property for a public use without just compensation. The Burger Court kept faith, however, with the double standard the post-1936 Court embraced, according relatively significant protection to noneconomic liberties yet leaving the safeguarding of property interests largely to the political arena. Indeed, in *New Orleans v. Dukes* (1976), it will be recalled, the justices rejected as unduly intrusive upon state power the only precedent of the post-1936 period (a 1957 ruling) invalidating an economic regulation on equal protection grounds.

The Court also largely declined to disturb Warren-era and earlier precedents incorporating Bill of Rights guarantees into the Fourteenth Amendment due process clause, thus making them applicable to the states and their localities as well as the national government. In *Apodaca v. Oregon* (1972), the Court, with Justice Powell providing the critical vote, did hold that state juries were not constitutionally required to render unanimous verdicts but reaffirmed earlier decisions mandating jury unanimity in federal cases. But that was the only area in which the Burger Court approved the application of different Bill of Rights standards in state and federal cases. The Court's willingness to keep faith with incorporation throughout Chief Justice Burger's seventeen-year tenure made it virtually impossible for the Rehnquist Court to dismantle the Warren Court's incorporation precedents, even though Chief Justice Rehnquist was an early opponent of incorporation in his years as an associate justice.

In its willingness to grant constitutional standing via substantive due process to rights enumerated nowhere in the Constitution's text, the Burger Court, ironically enough, went well beyond the more liberal Warren Court. Justice Douglas's opinion for the Warren Court in *Griswold v. Connecticut* (1965) attempted to tie the right of marital privacy recognized there largely, if loosely, to specific guarantees of the Bill of Rights, although Justices Harlan and White openly embraced substantive due process in their concurrences and Justice Goldberg rested his concurrence on the Ninth Amendment's reference to other rights retained by the people in addition to those enumerated in the Constitution. The Warren Court also declined opportunities to rule on the constitutional status of abortions. The Burger Court, in contrast, not only invoked the equal protection guarantee to extend the right of sexual privacy recognized in *Griswold* to unmarried as well as married couples (*Eisenstadt v. Baird* [1972]) but also embraced an invigorated and expansive modern version of substantive due process as the basis for its decision in *Roe v. Wade*. And while the Court refused to extend the right of privacy to homosexual sodomy in *Bowers v. Hardwick* (1986), at the end of Chief Justice Burger's tenure, the vote in that case was 5–4 and Justice Powell later stated that he probably erred in siding with the *Bowers* majority.

The modern Supreme Court's use of due process to recognize unenumerated procedural rights guarantees was also much more evident in the Burger than Warren era. The Burger Court's acceptance of such claims varied from context to context. In *Goldberg v. Kelly* (1970), for example, a majority held that welfare recipients were entitled to a hearing before termination of their benefits, while *Mathews v. Eldridge* (1976) held that a post-termination hearing satisfied due process when Social Security disability payments were ended, with Justice Powell reasoning for the *Mathews* majority that disability benefits, unlike welfare benefits, were not tied to financial need and their termination was thus less likely to pose a significant hardship for recipients. But it was principally the Burger Court rather than the Warren Court that developed a significant body of case law regarding the varying degrees of procedural due process required when government terminates benefits, public employment, or other services. Such procedural requirements, unlike the Bill of Rights guarantees associated with criminal prosecutions, were stated nowhere in the Constitution but instead were held to be implicit in due process. Albeit more rarely, the Burger Court also found certain standards of criminal procedure implicit in due process, including the requirement that a defendant's guilt be established beyond a reasonable doubt in criminal and related cases (*In Re Winship* [1970]).

Although initially appearing to curtail significantly Warren Court expansion of equal protection doctrine, the Burger Court proved equally flexible in the standards of judicial scrutiny to which it subjected discriminatory laws. Early in Burger's tenure, as seen in Chapter Three, a majority imposed restrictions on the "suspect categories" and "fundamental rights" branches of modern equal protection doctrine. A majority refused to consider poverty, age, illegitimacy, or gender among the constitutional suspects. And while the Court agreed that classifications based on alienage were suspect, it granted government considerable latitude to exclude noncitizens from elective office as well as many appointive positions involved in the formulation or execution of public policy, broadly construing the latter to include even state troopers in its scope. The Court concluded in the *Rodriguez* case, moreover, that fundamental rights entitled to strictest judicial protection from discriminatory legislation under the compelling interest standard were to be limited to those explicitly or implicitly guaranteed in the Constitution, and a majority refused to include welfare benefits or the right to an equal education among implicit rights triggering strict scrutiny.

Ultimately, however, the Court proved to be neither rigid nor consistently narrow in its interpretation of equal protection. On occasion, when purporting to apply the lenient, rational basis equal protection formula under which economic regulations regularly withstood challenge, a majority struck down the statute at issue, giving the rationality standard a relatively strict application. Thus, in *City of Cleburne v. Cleburne Living Center* (1985), it will be recalled, the Court invalidated an ordinance limiting the location of group homes for the mentally retarded, finding no rational basis for believing they posed any special threat to legitimate community interests. Even where the Court declined to recognize an interest as a fundamental right, moreover, a majority at times accorded it meaningful judicial protection, as in *Plyler v. Doe* (1982), which struck down the Texas policy excluding illegal alien Mexican children from the state's public schools yet reaffirmed its refusal to recognize a fundamental right to an equal education. While generally unwilling, therefore, to expand on the number of unenumerated rights subject to strictest judicial solicitude in discrimination cases, the Burger Court hardly denied other interests all meaningful protection. Instead, it required varying degrees of justification for laws impinging on such interests, substantially adopting in substance, though not form, Justice Marshall's proposal that the Court balance competing governmental and individual interests in such cases.

Even more important, perhaps, the Court accorded varying degrees of heightened scrutiny to classifications it refused to label suspect. Most notable among such "quasi-suspect" forms of discrimination, it will be remembered, were those based on sex or gender. A minority of justices argued in the *Frontiero* case that gender classifications, like those based on race or color, should be condemned as constitutionally suspect and subjected to the strict, compelling interest standard of review applied to such discrimination. Although a majority never embraced that position, the Court did hold in *Craig v. Boren* that gender-based laws were unconstitutional unless they furthered important governmental objectives through means substantially related to those goals. Certain forms of discrimination (e.g., male-only draft registration and prosecution of males alone for statutory rape) survived that intermediate standard of scrutiny, while others (e.g., the gender discrimination with respect to beer purchases at issue in *Craig*) did not.

Equal Protection Issues

The Burger Court also left its mark in a variety of other equal protection issue areas. In school desegregation cases, the unanimity that had prevailed in the Warren years soon collapsed. A unanimous *Swann* Court did uphold broad remedial powers for trial judges in desegregation cases, including the busing of students and the imposition of racial quotas in the assignment of students and staff. Even in *Swann*, however, Chief Justice Burger emphasized that racial balance was not a constitutional requirement but only a temporary means for converting school systems with a history of racial segregation rooted in law into unitary systems. And in *Wright v. Emporia* (1972), only a 5–4 majority supported a decision preventing a town's withdrawal from its county school system as a result of the disruptive effect of such a move on desegregation; dissenters complained that the majority was seeking racial balance for its own sake rather than the system's compliance with the Constitution.

The next year, as noted in Chapter Three, a larger majority held that a finding of official, or de jure, segregation in a substantial portion of a school system justified a systemwide desegregation order. But in *Milliken v. Bradley* (1974), a 5–4 Court drew a sharp distinction between de jure and de facto segregation, holding only the former to constitutional obligations and overturning a Detroit metropolitan area desegregation decree that had required the busing of students between the predominantly black Detroit school system and predominantly white suburban districts. Only the Detroit schools had a history of de jure segregation, Chief Justice Burger observed for the majority, and any desegregation order must be confined to the area in which a constitutional violation had occurred; desegregation for the purpose of racial balance alone exceeded the reach of federal court authority. *Pasadena Board of Education v.*

Spangler (1976) further limited the remedial powers of trial judges in desegregation cases. Once a school system had fulfilled, even briefly, its affirmative duty to deseg- regate, Justice Rehnquist concluded for the *Spangler* Court, the judge had no author- ity to continue imposing racial quotas indefinitely merely to assure racial balance.

As seen in Chapter Three, the Court's insistence that civil rights decrees be lim- ited largely to intentional discrimination was not confined to school desegregation cases. *Griggs v. Duke Power Co.* (1971) did hold that Congress could forbid private employment practices with a racially disproportionate effect or impact, striking down under that standard an employment test that was unrelated to the successful performance of the jobs for which it was used. Before invalidating challenged gov- ernmental practices on constitutional grounds, however, the justices required a showing of discriminatory intent. A majority upheld on that ground, for example, a southern city's decision to close its swimming pools rather than operate them on a desegregated basis (*Palmer v. Thompson* [1971]), a personnel test for police appli- cants that disqualified more blacks than whites (*Washington v. Davis* [1976]), and a southern city's at-large elections of city commissioners under which no black candi- dates had ever been elected (*Mobile v. Bolden* [1980]).

The Court recognized broader remedial power for Congress than the judiciary in other fields as well. A Warren Court majority had upheld a congressional ban on literacy tests for voting despite its earlier ruling that fairly administered literacy tests were consistent with the Constitution. Congress needed only a rational basis, the jus- tices declared, for concluding that a particular voter registration requirement was racially discriminatory. Later, in *Jones v. Alfred H. Mayer Co.* (1968), the Warren Court expansively construed congressional power to enforce the Thirteenth Amend- ment's ban on slavery and involuntary servitude, permitting Congress to prohibit, as remnants of slavery, every form of racial discrimination and upholding as a valid exer- cise of that power a Reconstruction statute forbidding discrimination in property transactions. The Burger Court in *Runyon v. McCrary* (1976), it will be recalled, reaf- firmed *Jones*, sustaining another provision of the same law giving all citizens the same contractual rights as whites. *Rome v. United States* (1980) upheld, moreover, federal voting rights provisions requiring states and localities with a history of voting discrimination to secure the "pre-clearance" of federal authorities before enacting new election laws, even when used to deny preclearance to voting practices that had only a racially disparate effect rather than an invidious intent.

Although extending Congress wide latitude in the exercise of its authority to protect civil rights, however, the Court did not always give congressional statutes a broad interpretation. *Grove City College v. Bell* (1984), for example, construed Title IX of a 1972 statute forbidding gender discrimination in colleges and universities that received federal funds to apply only to the specific programs so underwritten rather than to the entire institution. But Congress later overturned the Court's construction, amending Title IX to authorize the denial of funds to an entire school if one or more of its programs engaged in gender discrimination.

As might be expected given the wide variety of issues confronting the justices, the Burger Court established a mixed record in nonracial equal protection cases involving elections, voting, apportionment, and related matters. By extending states considerable discretion to deviate from population equality in the creation of districts from which state and local officials were elected, the Court limited the ultimate impact of the reapportionment revolution the Warren Court had spawned. The justices also sustained state power to restrict the eligible electorate for special-purpose governmental units, approving, among other schemes, an arrangement in which only landowners were allowed to vote for members of a water storage district's governing board and the weight of their votes was tied to the assessed value of their property (*Salyer Land Co. v. Water Storage District* [1973]). And *Davis v. Bandemer* (1986) placed significant burdens on those challenging political gerrymandering. A plurality required a showing of protracted frustration of majority will or what amounted to the denial to an electoral minority of the opportunity to affect the political process over a significant number of elections as a condition for establishing that a districting scheme was unconstitutional, while other justices concluded that political gerrymandering raised political questions inappropriate for judicial intervention.

The Court's response to affirmative action disputes, the most troublesome equal protection issues confronting the justices during Burger's tenure, was equally complex. As seen in Chapter Three, Justice Powell provided the classic pivotal vote in the *Bakke* case, where he joined four colleagues to reject the use of racial quotas in state university admissions and four other justices in permitting universities to take race as well as other nonmerit factors into account in furthering their compelling interest in attracting a diverse student body. Thus, *Bakke* was hardly the victory critics of affirmative action would have preferred. The next year, of course, the Court in the *Weber* case declined a literal reading of the antiemployment discrimination provisions of the 1964 Civil Rights Act, concluding instead that Congress had not intended to prohibit affirmative action quotas that a private company voluntarily chose to establish, as opposed to those required by a court's decree.

Affirmative action in public employment bore a heavier burden of justification. In one case, for example, the justices overturned a teacher layoff arrangement that was based on seniority but limited the percentage of minority staff who could be laid off in a personnel cutback (*Wygant v. Jackson Board of Education* [1986]). Justice Powell emphasized for a plurality in that case, it will be recalled, that all racial classifications were subject to strict scrutiny and that convincing evidence of prior discrimination was necessary to justify even benign classifications based on a person's color.

But the Court, as we have seen, also applied a double standard in affirmative action cases, granting considerably greater latitude to Congress than to states and localities in such litigation. In *Fullilove v. Klutznick* (1980), the justices sustained a congressional statute requiring that at least 10 percent of federal funds granted for local public works projects be set aside for minority businesses, according congressional authority a deference not extended the states that would remain in force until the Rehnquist Court's 1995 decision in *Adarand Constructors v. Pena*.

In resolving equal protection issues, then, the Burger Court was no more rigid than in most other fields of litigation. Although refusing to impose any constitutional obligations on de facto segregation, it accorded trial judges extensive authority to eliminate segregated public schools of the de jure variety. While insisting on proof of invidious intent in cases involving constitutional challenges to discriminatory regulations, it recognized congressional power to forbid public and private policies having only a racially disparate effect. In nonracial cases involving elections, voting, apportionment, and related matters, a majority was as likely to accept as to reject constitutional claims. And its affirmative action precedents were sufficiently flexible to justify rulings supporting or striking down particular programs, particularly those established in federal law.

Free Expression

In free expression and association cases, the Burger Court largely elaborated on Warren-era precedents rather than forging entirely new doctrine. Even so, it made a number of important contributions to that element of First Amendment law. First, a number of Burger-era decisions clarified the Court's position regarding prior restraints on the press. The brief per curiam opinion announcing the Court's decision in the *Pentagon Papers Cases* merely noted that prior restraints bore a "heavy burden" of justification that the government had failed to satisfy. In *Nebraska Press Association v. Stuart* (1976), however, Chief Justice Burger emphasized that courts must explore alternative means of satisfying governmental objectives before imposing a gag on the press in criminal proceedings and also make certain that such a prior restraint will actually be effective in furthering its objectives. In *Stuart* and *Cox Broadcasting Corp. v. Cohn* (1975), which struck down a statute prohibiting media disclosure of rape victims' names, the Court made clear, moreover, its firm opposition to restrictions on the publication or broadcast of information available to the public in court records.

A majority also significantly curtailed Warren Court precedents invalidating statutes on facial overbreadth grounds. Ordinarily, only a litigant whose own legal rights are being violated has standing to challenge the constitutionality of a law, and a law is declared invalid only as applied in a particular case. The Warren Court held, however, that litigants could challenge as unconstitutional on their face laws claimed to be so overly broad or sweeping in their scope that they could be used to interfere with protected expression as well as conduct subject to governmental control, even if the litigants' own conduct were subject to regulation under a valid law.

Declaring a statute unconstitutional on its face and forbidding its enforcement even against persons whose conduct was not protected by the First Amendment was strong medicine indeed. Early in Chief Justice Burger's tenure, it will be recalled, a majority struck down as facially broad and vague a city ordinance that made "annoying" public conduct a crime (*Coates v. Cincinnati* [1971]). *Gooding v. Wilson* (1972) overturned the conviction of an antiwar protester under a statute that prohibited the use of "opprobrious words or abusive language." The challenged law, Justice Brennan held for the Court, had a more sweeping reach than the face-to-face verbal assaults government traditionally had been empowered to punish as "fighting words." In *Lewis v. City of New Orleans* (1974), Brennan spoke for another majority in striking down on overbreadth grounds a city ordinance making it a crime to revile police attempting to perform their duties. The previous year, however, the Court had limited application of the overbreadth doctrine in cases involving speech-related conduct rather than speech alone. *Civil Service Commission v. National Association of Letter Carriers* and *Broadrick v. Oklahoma* sustained federal and state laws regulating the political activities of civil servants against overbreadth claims. Laws affecting expressive conduct rather than pure speech, Justice White concluded for the majority, could be struck down on their face only if they suffered from "substantial" overbreadth. Following these rulings, the number of facial overbreadth rulings declined significantly.

The Court also made a number of elaborations on the "public forum" concept. Warren-era decisions had permitted government to make jail grounds and certain other public property off-limits for First Amendment purposes on the ground that such property was dedicated to functions inconsistent with its use as a forum for expression. The Burger Court did not disturb such decisions. Refusing to equate shopping centers with community business districts, it also overturned, as we have seen, the Warren Court's *Logan Valley* precedent and held that shopping centers were private property with no First Amendment obligations. The Burger Court made clear, moreover, that even if a government chose to convert public property into a place of expression for certain purposes, thereby creating a "limited public forum," it retained considerable control over its use. Along such lines a majority upheld a city's refusal to accept political advertisements, as opposed to commercial ads, on its rapid transit system (*Lehman v. City of Shaker Heights* [1974]), as well as the authority of the U.S. Postal Service to forbid the deposit of unstamped material in letterboxes (*U.S. Postal Service v. Council of Greenburgh* [1981]) and a school system's selective grant of access to its teachers' mailboxes by rival teacher unions (*Perry Education Association v. Local Educators Association* [1983]).

The Court was hardly unanimous, of course, in its public forum rulings; in fact, Justice Stevens even doubted the wisdom of the majority's efforts to distinguish types and degrees of public forums. In *Cornelius v. NAACP Legal Defense and Educational Fund* (1985), the Court upheld a federal executive order excluding legal defense and political advocacy groups from participation in a charity fundraising campaign directed at federal employees. Speaking for the majority, Justice O'Connor characterized the effort as a nonpublic forum. In dissent, Justice Stevens raised concerns about such classifications and suggested that weaknesses in the arguments supporting the ban bolstered the suspicion it was really based on bias against litigation and advocacy groups.

Several Burger Court decisions helped to clarify the scope of governmental authority over fighting words and other forms of offensive speech. In *Chaplinsky v. New Hampshire* (1942), the Stone Court had denied constitutional protection to face-to-face verbal assaults likely to provoke a violent reaction. But *Chaplinsky* raised more questions than it resolved, some of which the Burger Court was obliged to confront. *Cohen v. California* (1971), overturning the breach-of-peace conviction of a young man who in a courtroom corridor wore a jacket bearing an offensive epithet, made clear that government had no power to cleanse the public vocabulary of offensive expression and that speech could be penalized under the fighting words doctrine only if directed at specific persons. The *Cohen* majority also emphasized that offensive speech could be punished as obscenity only if it had an erotic connotation; that the state's power to protect a captive audience from unwanted exposure to offensive epithets did not extend to expression from which those offended could easily avert their eyes; that the clear and present danger standard permitted government to prosecute only those who advocated imminent lawless action; and that controls over the time, place, and manner of expression must be enforced through laws directed specifically at such objectives rather than via a general statute forbidding breaches of the peace, whatever the location. *Gooding v. Wilson* (1972) and other fighting words cases stressed, moreover, that such speech can be prosecuted exclusively under clearly and narrowly drafted laws that reached only such speech rather than protected forms of provocative expression.

Although the modern law of libel had its roots in the Warren Court's decision and opinion in *New York Times v. Sullivan* (1964), the Burger Court, it will be recalled, also had an impact on that element of free expression doctrine. The Warren Court had concluded that comments about public officials or public figures could be penalized as libelous only if made with knowledge they were false or with reckless disregard for their truth or falsity. In *Rosenbloom v. Metromedia* (1971), a Burger Court plurality favored extending the knowing or reckless falsehood rule to all comment on matters of public or general interest, even that critical of private persons. The rule had been established, after all, to assure uninhibited and robust debate about public issues; its extension to comment about all such issues, not merely those involving public officials and public figures, seemed eminently logical. Speaking for the Court in *Gertz v. Welch, Inc.* (1974), however, Justice Powell declined further expansion of the knowing or reckless falsehood doctrine. Private persons had less opportunity to counter false statements and thus were more vulnerable to the injury they inflicted; consequently, they could recover damages for actual injury to their reputations, declared Powell, under whatever libel standards the applicable statute provided. Only if they sought punitive damages would they be obliged to establish knowing or reckless falsity. The *Gertz* restriction on the scope of protected expression continues in force.

Burger Court restrictions on Warren-era precedents in the field of erotic expression have also survived attack. The Warren Court could muster no majority behind a definition of obscenity after *Roth v. United States* (1957). But in *Memoirs v. Massachusetts* (1966), a plurality concluded that erotica could be suppressed as obscene only if it was utterly lacking in any social value; those justices, joined by Black and Douglas, who rejected all obscenity controls, formed a majority willing to extend First Amendment protection to virtually all forms of erotic material and their distribution to consenting adults, at least absent evidence of pandering in their marketing to potential customers. *Stanley v. Georgia* (1969) recognized, moreover, a right of people to possess obscenity in the privacy of the home.

As shown in Chapter Three, a narrow Burger Court majority modified such rulings in a variety of significant ways. In the *Miller* case, a 5–4 majority concluded that prurient, offensive erotica could be considered obscene unless it possessed serious literary, artistic, political, or scientific value, thus rejecting the *Memoirs* plurality's standard of utter lack of value. Resolving an inconclusive Warren Court debate over whether national or local standards should be used to determine whether material was prurient and offensive, the *Miller* majority also opted for a local-standards approach under which the obscenity of a particular book, film, or photograph might vary somewhat from jurisdiction to jurisdiction. Other cases narrowly limited to the home the right to possess obscenity that the Warren Court had announced in the *Stanley* case, sustaining governmental authority to penalize those who import obscenity in their luggage, transport it interstate in their automobiles for personal use, or view it in an adults-only theater. In a *Miller* dissent, Justice Douglas advocated absolute protection for erotic expression. The other three dissenters, speaking through Justice Brennan, author of *Roth* and the *Memoirs* plurality opinion, concluded that no definition of obscenity could be established that would be both free of vagueness and sufficiently solicitous of expression to withstand constitutional challenge; in their judgment, therefore, government's power in the field should be limited to protecting minors and unconsenting adults from exposure to such material. But the Burger Court stood by the *Miller* standard while also recognizing broad governmental authority to prevent the use of minors in sexual performances. Although the Rehnquist Court has made a number of additions to obscenity doctrine—rejecting, for example, extension of *Stanley* to the possession of child pornography in the home (*Osborne v. Ohio* [1990])—standards largely developed in the Burger era remain prevailing law.

While expanding government's power over obscenity and libel, however, the Burger Court also extended constitutional protection for the first time to commercial speech. In *Pittsburgh Press Co. v. Pittsburgh Commission on Human Relations* (1973), a 5–4 majority reaffirmed *Valentine v. Chrestensen*, the 1942 decision excluding advertisements from the First Amendment's coverage, and upheld a Pittsburgh human-relations ordinance applied to prevent local newspapers from carrying sex-designated help-wanted columns. But two years later, it will be recalled, *Bigelow v. Virginia* (1975) lifted the exception for advertisements that contained information of potential interest and value to a diverse audience. In *Virginia Board of Pharmacy v. Virginia Consumer Council* (1976), the Court extended the First Amendment to purely commercial advertising; the 1980 *Central Hudson* ruling held, moreover, that commercial speech was protected if it concerned lawful activity and was not misleading, while regulation of such expression was valid only if it sought to promote a substantial government interest, directly advanced that interest, and restricted expression only to the extent necessary to accomplish the government's goals.

The Burger Court established enduring precedents in other expression areas as well. While upholding congressional authority to limit contributions to federal election campaigns in *Buckley v. Valeo* (1976), the Court struck down restrictions on independent expenditures by individuals and organizations in behalf of federal candidates, basing its ruling on the doubtful logic that candidates would be aware of, and perhaps improperly influenced by, direct contributions to their campaigns but unaware of independent expenditures (even in huge amounts) in their behalf. A 1985 decision extended *Buckley* to invalidate limits on independent expenditures even in behalf of those candidates who accepted public funds and were thus obliged by law to limit their own campaign spending. Such decisions remain prevailing law with respect to free expression and campaign finance regulations. Although of more limited application, the Court's support of federal authority to sanction broadcasters for "indecent" programming, at least during family hours, when broadcasts are most accessible to children (*FCC v. Pacifica Foundation* [1978]), still stands as well. By that decision the Burger Court went beyond a Warren-era precedent approving the FCC's "fairness doctrine" and accepted federal power to review programming judgments relating to the "decency" of broadcast content.

Burger Court precedents regarding the scope of protected expression in special environments, including the military, police, public schools, and prisons, also remain in force. *Greer v. Spock* (1976) and other cases, it will be remembered, rejected the contention that military posts generally constitute public forums for expression and upheld restrictions on leafleting and speechmaking that would not survive scrutiny as applied to public streets and sidewalks. Acknowledging the special discipline, security, and morale needs of the military, the Court applied more lenient vagueness, overbreadth, and related constitutional standards to military regulations (*Parker v. Levy* [1974]).

In cases involving expression in the public schools, the justices ultimately curbed the rights extended students in the *Tinker* case. While a majority refused to recognize a dual standard for the college community with respect to control over the content of publications (*Papish v. Board of Curators* [1973]), the Court accorded greater latitude to high school officials, holding *Tinker* inapplicable to a school's disciplining of a student who used graphic sexual imagery in a school election campaign speech (*Bethel School District v. Fraser* [1986]). As seen in Chapter Three, the Court also recognized broad authority of prison officials to regulate media interviews with prison inmates and press access to facilities not open to the public.

Press privilege claims met defeat in other areas as well. *Branzburg v. Hayes* (1972) rejected a testimonial privilege for newspersons called before grand juries, with Justice White observing in the principal opinion that the media are not entitled to special First Amendment privileges (although legislatures were obviously free to enact shield laws for journalists if they wished), that it was more important to prosecute crimes than to write about them, and that the free flow of information obtained from confidential press informants had flourished for years without such a privilege. Nor would a majority privilege the press from searches of news offices. Instead, *Zurcher v. Stanford Daily* (1978) rebuffed the contention that evidence ordinarily should be sought from the press through subpoenas rather than searches and the latter allowed only when newspersons were themselves suspects or the evidence at issue was available from no other source. In 1980 a majority, as we have seen, did hold that the public, and therefore the press, enjoyed a constitutional right to attend criminal trials in the absence of an overriding interest justifying closed proceedings, with Chief Justice Burger emphasizing in a plurality opinion the importance of public trials in assuring both the appearance and reality of justice (*Richmond Newspapers, Inc. v. Virginia* [1980]). But the press was given that right of access only because newspersons were part of the public.

In precedents that also remain in place, as we have seen, the Burger Court rejected claims of a public right of access to the press. A seven-member Court held in 1973 that neither the First Amendment nor FCC regulations required broadcasters to accept paid editorial advertisements, with only Brennan and Marshall arguing in dissent that government-imposed limits on access to the airwaves, as well as First Amendment interests in full discussion of public issues and self-expression by individuals and groups, placed some constitutional obligations on those broadcasters favored with licenses (*CBS v. Democratic National Committee* [1973]). When newsprint rather than broadcasting was the medium of communication, moreover, the Court was unanimous in its rejection of right-of-access claims underlying the Florida right-of-reply statute struck down in *Miami Herald Publishing Co. v. Tornillo* (1974). Speaking for the *Tornillo* Court, it will be recalled, the chief justice declared that requiring newspapers to provide free reply space to candidates they criticized fostered self-censorship and hindered journalistic editorial discretion. The First Amendment, added Burger, guaranteed a free press, not a responsible one.

Religious Liberty

Burger Court decisions applying the First Amendment's religious establishment and free exercise clauses reflected both continuity with Warren era doctrine and a more accommodationist stance in certain establishment fields. Drawing on Warren Court precedents and its own opinion in *Walz v. Tax Commission* (1970), the Burger Court embraced the three-part *Lemon* test under which laws affecting religion could withstand establishment clause challenge only if they had a secular purpose, exerted a primary effect that neither advanced nor harmed religion, and created no excessive entanglement between church and state (*Lemon v. Kurtzman* [1971]). A majority rigorously applied the *Lemon* standards to state-directed religion in the public schools, invalidating the posting of the Ten Commandments on the walls of classrooms (*Stone v. Graham* [1980]) and a state law setting aside a daily period of silence for student meditation or silent prayer (*Wallace v. Jaffree* [1985]).

Largely on free speech/public forum grounds, however, the Court held that a state university could not exclude religious student groups from facilities available to secular student organizations, dismissing the university's concern that permitting such use of its facilities would violate the establishment clause (*Widmar v. Vincent* [1981]). Relying on long tradition dating back to the first Congress, it will be recalled, Chief Justice Burger also spoke for a 6–3 Court in sustaining a state's provision for paid legislative chaplains (*Marsh v. Chambers* [1983]). Tax exemptions for religious property survived attack on essentially the same ground and because they not only were also extended to secular beneficent institutions but allowed governments to avoid the charge they were imposing an undue financial burden on religious liberty (*Walz v. Tax Commission* [1970]).

Other forms of government assistance to religious institutions received a mixed reception in the Burger Court. *Lemon* and a companion case struck down state purchases of secular educational services from primary and secondary religious schools as well as salary supplements for teachers of secular subjects in such schools, while later cases invalidated, among other forms of assistance, state repair and maintenance grants, tuition reimbursements, tax credits for parochial school parents who failed to qualify for tuition support, reimbursements to religious schools for costs connected with examinations and record-keeping, and the provision of public school personnel for remedial instruction in public schools (a precedent the Rehnquist Court eventually overturned in *Agostini v. Felton* [1997]).

But majorities upheld state provision of standardized testing and scoring; speech, hearing, and psychological diagnostic and therapeutic services; guidance and remedial services; and, in *Mueller v. Allen* (1983), a state income tax provision permitting taxpayers to deduct educational expenses from gross income, even though the parents of private school students were its primary beneficiaries. In cases involving aid to church-affiliated colleges and universities, the Court assumed an even more accommodationist stance, approving construction grants, annual student grants, and other assistance so long as it was used only for secular purposes, basing such deference on the assumption college students were less vulnerable to sectarian influence, and colleges less religious in atmosphere, than their primary and secondary school counterparts (e.g., *Tilton v. Richardson* [1971]).

During the Burger era, the Court also confronted for the first time a constitutional challenge to religious displays on public property. Although a nativity scene would appear to have a clearly religious purpose and thus to violate the first prong of the *Lemon* test, Chief Justice Burger spoke for a 5–4 majority in upholding a Rhode Island community's inclusion of such a scene in its annual Christmas display and concluding that the presence of a Santa Claus house and other secular accouterments gave the display essentially a seasonal rather than religious character. For the dissenters, however, the aggregation was nothing less than an impermissible governmental endorsement of a particular faith that its secular features in no way obscured (*Lynch v. Donnelly* [1984]).

The Burger Court not only gave *Lemon* a mixed application, but, as seen in Chapter Three, the *Lemon* standards were themselves controversial from the beginning. In striking down the state assistance at issue there, the *Lemon* majority concluded that it would have the forbidden primary effect of advancing religion, while government surveillance to assure that the challenged aid served only secular purposes would in fact create an excessive entanglement of the church with the state. In dissent, Justice White complained of the "insoluble paradox" *Lemon* created for government: Granting assistance without oversight to confine it to secular uses would risk a primary effect supportive of religion, while surveillance to protect against violation of *Lemon*'s effects prong would conflict with its prohibition against excessive church-state entanglements.

Justice Rehnquist's dissent in *Wallace v. Jaffree* went further, contending that the establishment guarantee forbade only creation of a national church and government preference for particular sects; it did not require, in Rehnquist's judgment, government neutrality between religion and irreligion or prohibit nondiscriminatory aid to religion. Urging in a *Jaffree* concurrence that *Lemon* be reexamined and refined, Justice O'Connor later argued in the Rhode Island crèche case that the establishment clause should invalidate only those government actions endorsing or disapproving of religion. Justice Powell defended *Lemon* in his *Jaffree* concurrence, terming it the "only coherent" establishment test the Court had yet adopted and expressing fear that his colleagues' criticisms of *Lemon* might encourage lower courts simply to decide establishment issues on a purely ad hoc basis. But criticism of *Lemon* mounted over the years, and though it has not yet been officially overruled, the Rehnquist Court has adopted a more flexible establishment formula incorporating to some degree Justice O'Connor's endorsement standard and other elements according government greater deference in such cases.

In the religious free exercise field, however, it would be the Rehnquist Court rather than its predecessor that would embark upon a potentially significant departure from Warren-era doctrine. In *Sherbert v. Verner* (1963) and other cases, Warren Court majorities held that conduct based on religious belief was protected from governmental interference except where necessary to promote a compelling interest not amenable to solution through means less restrictive of religious liberty. The Burger Court declined to apply the *Sherbert* formula in *Goldman v. Weinberger* (1986), where a 5–4 majority, emphasizing the deference traditionally accorded military authority in the First Amendment field, upheld an air force regulation prohibiting a rabbi from wearing a yarmulke while on duty and in uniform. But a majority adhered to the strict *Sherbert* standard in other areas. In *Wisconsin v. Yoder* (1972), for example, the justices exempted Amish parents from an obligation to obey the state's compulsory high school education requirement, with Chief Justice Burger declaring for the Court that a state's interest in an educated citizenry, while obviously important, was inadequate to offset the burden compulsory high school placed on Amish religious tenets, especially since the Amish provided home training as a reasonable alternative to high school education for their children.

While stopping short of overturning such precedents, the Rehnquist Court held in *Employment Division, Dept. of Human Resources of Oregon v. Smith* (1990), involving the ritual use of peyote, that people were obliged to conform their religious practices to valid, religiously neutral laws, whether or not their application to a particular religious practice served a compelling governmental interest. When Congress attempted to revive the *Sherbert* standard for such cases in the Religious Freedom Restoration Act (1993), the Court rebuffed that effort, emphasizing that the judiciary, not Congress, had the final authority to construe the meaning of the free exercise clause and other constitutional provisions (*City of Boerne v. Flores* [1997]).

The Rehnquist Court has not disturbed, however, two other significant Burger Court religious precedents. *Wooley v. Maynard* (1977) reaffirmed the Stone Court's ruling in *West Virginia Board of Education v. Barnette* (1943), which had struck down compulsory flag salute programs in public schools and declared that government had no business imposing a particular religious or political orthodoxy on people against their beliefs. The *Wooley* Court, speaking through Chief Justice Burger, extended *Barnette* in upholding the right of a Jehovah's Witness couple to cover what they considered to be an objectionable state motto ("Live Free or Die") on their automobile license plate. And in *Bob Jones University v. United States* (1983), the Court, over Justice Rehnquist's lone dissent, upheld the authority of the Internal Revenue Service to deny tax-exempt status to racially discriminatory private religious schools, with Chief Justice Burger declaring for the majority that the government's overriding interest in eradicating racial discrimination in education outweighed any burden the denial of an exemption placed on a school's religious beliefs. In his dissent, Justice Rehnquist did not question congressional power to deny tax exemptions to discriminatory private institutions; he simply argued that Congress had not authorized the IRS to take such action.

Criminal Justice

In most constitutional fields, as we have seen, the Burger Court failed to produce the counterrevolution Warren Court critics had expected. Indeed, a majority expanded Warren-era civil liberties precedents in a variety of areas. The Court came closest, however, to mirroring the retrenchment its predecessor's opponents had anticipated in cases involving the rights of criminal suspects and defendants, although even there it produced a mixed record.

Among Burger Court precedents most restrictive of criminal procedure rights were those relating to search and seizure and police interrogation of suspects. Although refusing to overturn the Fourth Amendment exclusionary rule outright or retain it only for the most egregious cases, as Chief Justice Burger and Justice Rehnquist urged, a majority rejected Warren Court opinions declaring the rule a constitutional requirement, held that it was simply a judicially created device designed to deter police misconduct, and limited its application to contexts in which its use would meaningfully enhance that deterrence objective. Following such a rationale, as indicated in Chapter Three, Burger Court majorities held the exclusionary rule inapplicable to grand jury proceedings (*United States v. Calandra* [1974]), civil cases involving a government agency (*United States v. Janis* [1976]), and habeas corpus proceedings in which state prisoners had previously been given a full and fair opportunity to raise their search and seizure claims in the state courts (*Stone v. Powell* [1976]), while *United States v. Leon* (1984) sustained the admission of evidence seized by police in a good-faith reliance on an unconstitutional warrant.

Although it required a warrant for routine home arrests of suspects (*Payton v. New York* [1980]), the Court also substantially expanded the conditions under which police were permitted to conduct a search without a warrant. Warrantless searches based on voluntary consent had traditionally been allowed, but a Burger Court majority held in 1973 that suspects need not be informed of their right not to consent and that the decision whether a consent search was actually voluntary would depend on the totality of the circumstances (*Schneckloth v. Bustamonte* [1973]).

Enlarging upon police authority to conduct a warrantless search incident to a valid arrest, the Court upheld full-body searches even of suspects arrested only for petty traffic offenses, even though the nature of such an arrest afforded no basis for suspicion that the person arrested was armed or concealing contraband (*United States v. Robinson* [1973]; *Gustafson v. Florida* [1973]). Also expanded was the stop-and-frisk for weapons sustained by the Warren Court in *Terry v. Ohio* (1968), with Justice Rehnquist holding for a majority in *Adams v. Williams* (1972) that the tip of an anonymous, reliable informer rather than an officer's personal observations could also provide sufficient justification for a weapons pat-down. Precedents recognizing the authority of police to conduct warrantless, probable-cause searches of vehicles were also reaffirmed and enlarged; as seen in Chapter Three, for example, the Court upheld the search of closed containers and packages found in a car, even absent an independent basis for believing they contained evidence; mobile homes parked in public places; and the impounded automobiles of arrested persons, as well as the inventory of any impounded vehicle and seizure of evidence uncovered during an inventory (*South Dakota v. Opperman* [1976]).

Other Burger Court decisions upholding warrantless searches also remain in force. Majorities not only reaffirmed the traditional principle that searches at international borders are beyond the Fourth Amendment's reach, but also ultimately sustained use of roving patrols to reduce the entry of illegal Mexican immigrants into the United States (*United States v. Martinez-Fuerte* [1976]). The Court reaffirmed the plain-view exception to the warrant requirement as well and, along similar lines, upheld use of an aerial photograph of a marijuana crop in a fenced backyard to obtain a warrant for search of the property, Chief Justice Burger reasoning for the majority that people had no reasonable expectation of privacy from the observations of those flying over an area visible from the sky. As sort of a catchall exception to the warrant requirement, the Court also sustained any warrantless search based on probable cause and exigent circumstances justifying quick action by police, upholding on that basis in *Cupp v. Murphy* (1973), for example, police seizure of skin scrapings from beneath a murder suspect's fingernails.

Although declining to require the same strict standards for administrative searches as those imposed on police, the Warren Court had refused to exempt such searches entirely from the warrant requirement. The Burger Court was more deferential to administrative officials, sustaining, for example, each stage of an assistant principal's increasingly intrusive warrantless search of the purse of a student initially suspected only of violating a regulation against cigarette smoking in school lavatories (*New Jersey v. T.L.O.* [1985]) and concluding in *Hudson v. Palmer* (1984), which sustained shakedown searches of cells, that inmates have limited expectations of privacy in a prison. While it reaffirmed Warren Court rulings subjecting electronic surveillance to Fourth Amendment requirements and refused to read federal law to permit warrantless eavesdropping in domestic national security cases, the Court reserved judgment on surveillance of foreign agents (*United States v. U.S. District Court* [1972]) and rejected the claim that police use of a pen register to record the telephone numbers suspects dial, rather than their conversations, amounted to a search subject to constitutional requirements (*Smith v. Maryland* [1979]). Like its predecessor, moreover, the Burger Court rejected Fourth Amendment and self-incrimination claims against the use of undercover agents, even those armed with recording or transmitter devices, to obtain incriminating statements from a suspect, while also narrowly construing the entrapment defense to apply only on proof that police placed the predisposition to commit a crime into the defendant's mind, rather than merely providing encouragement and assistance (*United States v. Russell* [1973]).

In a variety of other ways, the Burger Court further limited the reach of the self-incrimination guarantee. Enlarging upon a 1965 Warren Court ruling, the justices did require trial judges, at a defendant's request, to instruct jurors that they could draw no adverse inferences from the accused's failure to testify (*Carter v. Kentucky* [1981]). But the Burger Court also reasoned that suspects given immunity from prosecution and compelled under pain of a contempt of court citation to testify need only be extended immunity from any use of their statements to secure their conviction for offenses mentioned under immunity, not complete or transactional immunity from any prosecution for such offenses (*Kastigar v. United States* [1972]).

As with the Fourth Amendment exclusionary rule, as we have seen, the Court also restricted application of the *Miranda* doctrine. While extending the *Miranda* warnings to psychiatric examinations of defendants (*Estelle v. Smith* [1981]), a majority held that they, like the Fourth Amendment rule, were merely judicially created safeguards against coerced confessions, extension of which to particular situations was subject to judicial discretion. On that basis, majorities permitted use of *Miranda*-tainted confessions to impeach a defendant's trial testimony (*Harris v. New York* [1971]) or secure other prosecution evidence (*Michigan v. Tucker* [1974]) and also held *Miranda* inapplicable to grand jury proceedings (*United States v. Mandujano* [1976]), noncustodial questioning of suspects (*Oregon v. Mathiason* [1977]), and interrogation intended to avert an imminent threat to public safety (*New York v. Quarles* [1984]).

As demonstrated in Chapter Three, the Court's decisions in counsel and related cases both enlarged upon and curtailed Warren-era precedents. While extending the right of appointed counsel recognized by the Warren Court in the *Gideon* case to all state prosecutions in which any jail sentence was imposed (*Argersinger v. Hamlin* [1972]), a majority later limited that precedent to those cases actually leading to imprisonment rather than all prosecutions carrying a potential jail term. Like the Warren Court, a Burger Court majority also extended the right to counsel beyond the trial to other critical stages in a criminal case, including the preliminary hearing to determine whether there is probable cause for further proceedings against a suspect (*Coleman v. Alabama* [1970]), but refused to require a lawyer for preindictment lineups or where a defendant voluntarily, knowingly, and intelligently waived the right to trial counsel (*Faretta v. California* [1975]). In cases implicating the right to counsel and the *Miranda* doctrine, moreover, a majority both sustained (*Brewer v. Williams* [1977]) and rejected (*Rhode Island v. Innis* [1980]) claims that police "conversations" with or in the company of a suspect amounted to interrogation without a waiver of counsel.

Among other Burger Court criminal procedure rulings that remain substantially intact are a number involving the double jeopardy guarantee. One limited the "separate sovereignties" doctrine to federal and state trials of a defendant for an offense violative of both national and state law and refused to extend the doctrine to state and local trials for the same offense on the ground that local governments are merely creatures of the state rather than independent sovereigns (*Waller v. Florida* [1970]). In *Ashe v. Swenson* (1970), moreover, a majority held that a defendant could be tried in separate proceedings for multiple offenses growing out of the same criminal transaction, so long as different evidence was necessary to prove each charge, as required by the rule of collateral estoppel.

Some of the most significant, groundbreaking, controversial, and enduring Burger Court criminal justice precedents were those involving the Eighth Amendment right against cruel and unusual punishments, particularly its death penalty rulings. In a number of cases, the Court cited the important societal interest in curbing recidivism to uphold mandatory life sentences for habitual offenders, even those convicted only of minor, nonviolent property crimes. A majority struck down such a statute only when the life sentences at issue carried no possibility of parole (*Solem v. Helm* [1983]).

Shifting majorities established a number of important guidelines for evaluating the constitutionality of capital punishment statutes. First, the Court held that the death penalty was not per se unconstitutional for first-degree murder, since it was consistent with the Constitution's language, long practice, and prevailing public opinion reflected primarily in the actions of legislative bodies, while also serving legitimate societal interests in deterrence and retribution (*Gregg v. Georgia* [1976]). Second, mandatory imposition of the death sentence following conviction for a capital crime without consideration of possible mitigating circumstances was unconstitutionally arbitrary (*Woodson v. North Carolina* [1976]), as were capital punishment provisions leaving the decision entirely to the discretion of jurors and judges (*Furman v. Georgia* [1972]). Third, capital punishment statutes requiring a separate penalty hearing following conviction, consideration of aggravating and mitigating circumstances before sentencing, imposition of the death penalty only on a finding of one or more aggravating circumstances stipulated in statute, and automatic appeal of all death sentences, among other features, were considered adequate safeguards against arbitrary sentencing (*Gregg v. Georgia*). Fourth, the death sentence for rape of an adult was held to be disproportionate to the gravity of the offense (*Coker v. Georgia* [1977]). Finally, a statute limiting the types of mitigating circumstances considered during the penalty phase of a case created a constitutionally unacceptable risk of arbitrariness (*Lockett v. Ohio* [1978]). Several justices favored greater deference to government in death penalty cases, but only Justices Brennan and Marshall of Burger Court jurists argued that the death penalty was inherently arbitrary cruel and unusual punishment, whatever the crime or death penalty provision at issue.

The Chief Justice and His Court

Warren Burger will probably never be ranked as a great or near great chief justice—certainly not in comparison with his immediate predecessor, Earl Warren, or even his successor, William Rehnquist. He wrote workmanlike opinions, looked the part of a chief justice, and worked tirelessly and productively to improve the quality of judicial administration and effective workload management. But Burger lacked the considerable interpersonal skills of Warren and Rehnquist; found it difficult to suppress his personal preferences in behalf of compromise and a collegial, united Court; and wasted valuable goodwill early in his tenure by his preoccupation with Court ritual and the appearance of the Court's building and grounds, as well as his inadequate appreciation for the Court's deeply rooted decisional and related traditions. His clumsy and disruptive attempt first to delay the Court's decision in *Roe v. Wade* and then to rest the ruling on narrow vagueness grounds with little precedential impact was but one example of his shortcomings as a leader; his colleagues' co-optation of his opinion for the Court in *United States v. Nixon* (1974), the Watergate tapes case, another. Nor, of course, was he able to produce the constitutional counterrevolution he and President Nixon no doubt envisioned when he took the Court's center seat.

As we also have seen, however, Chief Justice Burger presided over an important period in the Court's history—arguably more significant, in fact, than developments during Chief Justice Rehnquist's tenure to date, at least with the exception of those relating to issues of federal-state authority and property rights claims. It was the Burger Court, after all, that rendered major decisions regarding executive privilege, the legislative veto, and comparable separation of powers issues, while also dramatically curtailing access to the federal courts through restrictive constructions of the state action doctrine, the rule of standing, and related, largely prudential limitations on judicial authority.

Burger Court majorities also enlarged as well as narrowed the scope of civil liberties. Rejecting the constitutional underpinnings of the Fourth Amendment exclusionary rule and its *Miranda* counterpart, the Court recognized numerous exceptions to their application while substantially increasing the circumstances under which police were permitted to conduct warrantless evidence searches. Modern death penalty law had its origins in the Burger era, as did affirmative action doctrine. The Court significantly curtailed the First Amendment, privacy, and procedural rights of persons in special environments, including schools, prisons, and military bases. Yet modern abortion law also had its beginnings and major development in *Roe* and other Burger Court precedents. Although generally declining to expand the suspect categories and fundamental rights branches of modern equal protection doctrine, moreover, majorities subjected to heightened judicial scrutiny discrimination based on gender and other quasi-suspect classifications, as well as that interfering with important nonconstitutional interests. And while broadening governmental authority over erotic expression, the Court also substantially eliminated the commercial speech exception to the First Amendment's scope.

The Rehnquist Court, in contrast, for the most part has simply built on Burger Court precedents in many constitutional fields. Whether invoking obscenity and commercial speech doctrine, the variety of standards now applied in equal protection cases, limits on access to the courts, restrictions on the Fourth Amendment exclusionary rule and *Miranda* doctrine, or any number of other legal principles, the current Court has relied heavily on rulings of the Burger era.

In short, whatever the weaknesses of its chief justice, the Burger Court was no mere bridge from the Warren to Rehnquist eras. Instead, it left an enduring—and to date largely permanent—imprint on virtually every element of constitutional law. That it moved in less consistent and predictable directions than its predecessor in no way diminishes that record or the Burger Court's important place in the modern Court's history.

PART TWO

Reference Materials

Key People, Laws, and Events

American Bar Association, Committee on Federal Judiciary

In 1945–1946 the American Bar Association, the nation's most influential organization of lawyers, established a committee to review and rate nominees and prospective nominees to the federal courts. Composed of fifteen members (one from each of the eleven numbered federal court of appeals circuits and a second member from the West Coast's large Ninth Circuit, one from the District of Columbia circuit, one from the nationwide Federal Circuit, and a chairperson), the Committee on Federal Judiciary generally conducts a six- to eight-week investigation and makes an evaluation. Under the current rating system, lower court candidates are ranked as "well qualified," "qualified," or "not qualified," and a similar system is used to rate Supreme Court nominees. Traditionally, the committee was made aware of nominees only when their names were submitted to the Senate for confirmation. For a time, the Nixon administration permitted the ABA to screen potential nominees before submission of their names to the Senate. Following leaks of the ABA's ratings of potential nominees for Supreme Court seats left vacant by the retirements of Justice Black and the second Justice Harlan, President Nixon reverted to the traditional practice for the balance of his tenure. President Ford and Attorney General Edward Levi restored the practice of giving the association advance notice of candidates under consideration when a search began in the fall of 1975 for a nominee to replace Justice Douglas; the nominee selected–Levi's close friend John Paul Stevens—received the ABA's highest rating. The Reagan administration submitted the names of its nominees directly to the Senate, but Presidents Bush and Clinton resumed the practice of submitting the names of prospective nominees to the association. The ABA's judiciary committee has no formal role in the selection of nominees or their confirmation by the Senate. But ABA opposition never bodes well for a nominee's chances in the confirmation process.

Balanced Budget and Emergency Deficit Control Act (1985)

This statute was a response to soaring federal budget deficits during the administration of President Reagan. Popularly known as the Gramm-Rudman-Hollings Act after its sponsors, the law established maximum annual permissible deficits with the goal of reducing the deficit to zero by the 1991 fiscal year. If necessary to keep the deficit within the maximum annual limits, the statute required across-the-board budget cuts, half in defense programs and half in other budget areas. Under the law, the directors of the Office of Management and Budget (OMB) and the Congressional Budget Office (CBO) were required to make an independent estimate of the likely federal budget deficit for the next year. If the estimates exceeded the deficit reduction target for that year, they were to calculate the program-by-program budget cuts required to meet the target and submit a joint report of their calculations to the comptroller general, the official within the legislative branch responsible for overseeing federal expenditures. The comptroller general was required to make an independent judgment regarding the directors' estimates and report his conclusions to the president. The president was then to issue an order putting those reductions into effect unless Congress, within a specified period, met the deficit goal in other ways. In *Bowsher v. Synar* (1986), the Supreme Court concluded that the law unconstitutionally vested executive powers in the comptroller general, a legislative officer selected by the president from three nominees chosen by the presiding officers of the House of Representatives and Senate and subject to removal not only by impeachment but also by a joint resolution of Congress.

Bell, Griffin B.

An attorney general (1977–1979) in the administration of President Carter, Griffin B. Bell was born in Americus, Georgia, in 1918 and received his law degree from Mercer University following army service in World War II. A partner in the prominent Atlanta firm of King and Spalding, Bell was closely associated with segregationist Georgia governor S. Ernest Vandiver, in whose administration he served as chief of staff from 1959 to 1961. But as a member of the U.S. Court of Appeals for the Fifth Circuit, to which President Kennedy appointed him in 1961, Bell developed a moderate record in racial cases. In 1976 Bell resigned from the court of appeals to become legal adviser to Carter in his successful presidential campaign. Following Carter's election, Bell was chosen as attorney general, winning Senate confirmation by a comfortable 75–21 vote, but only after six days of committee hearings and a day of floor debate in which the nominee's commitment to civil rights, especially in view of his membership in segregated Atlanta and Savannah social clubs, was a major source of concern. As attorney general, Bell named women and blacks, including Solicitor General Wade McCree, to important Justice Department posts. He also played a major role in the Carter administration's creation of a system of merit selection of federal court of appeals judges from nominees selected by blue-ribbon commissions composed of lawyers and laypersons. Critics attacked the administration's insistence that the commissions also take race, gender, and related diversity factors into consideration, and Reagan abandoned the arrangement on assuming the presidency. But supporters considered the plan a laudable attempt to improve the professional credentials of the federal judiciary.

Bork, Robert H.

A solicitor general in the Nixon and Ford administrations and defeated Reagan nominee to the Supreme Court, Robert H. Bork was born in Pittsburgh in 1927 and received his undergraduate and law degrees from the University of Chicago in 1948 and 1953. He was a partner in the prominent Kirkland, Ellis law firm as well as a distinguished member of the Yale law faculty; he served as acting attorney general from 1973 to 1974 and as solicitor general from 1973 to 1977. As solicitor general, he earned the enduring enmity of President Nixon's critics when he complied with the president's order to fire Watergate special prosecutor Archibald Cox after Attorney General Elliot Richardson and his deputy attorney general resigned their positions rather than do Nixon's bidding. President Reagan named Bork to a seat on the U.S. Court of Appeals for the District of Columbia in 1982, but Reagan's 1987 nomination of the outspoken conservative to replace Justice Lewis Powell on the Supreme Court met defeat in the Senate. A well-orchestrated opposition feared that Bork, an avowed opponent of *Roe v. Wade*, would provide the fifth vote on the Rehnquist Court necessary to scuttle *Roe* as well as a number of other important civil liberties and civil rights precedents. The nominee's appearance before the Senate Judiciary Committee, where he opposed not only *Roe* but other less controversial privacy rulings as well and projected a professorial, somewhat condescending image to committee members and the public alike, was no help to his cause either. After a protracted hearing, the Judiciary Committee rejected his nomination 9–5, and the full Senate concurred by a vote of 58–42. The next year Bork resigned his circuit court seat, becoming, in assorted books, articles, lectures, and media interviews, a vehement critic of judicial activism and what he considers the decline of American civilization.

Budget and Impounding Control Act (1974)

This measure, one of several adopted by Congress to restrict presidential authority during the latter days of the Nixon administration, limited the president's ability to defer or forbid the expenditure of congressional appropriations. Presidents had invoked this impoundment power since the days of George Washington, although the Constitution included no explicit provision for its exercise. But President Nixon had been particularly aggressive, impounding funds in an effort to kill legal services, environmental protection, and other programs he opposed. In its first impoundment case, *Train v. City of New York* (1975), the Burger Court overturned President Nixon's use of the power on statutory grounds, holding that an appropriations provision that specified that certain sums "shall be allotted" did not permit the administration to withhold any of those funds, even though congressional authorization of the expenditure elsewhere in the statute was for sums "not to exceed" the specified amounts. Under the Budget and Impounding Control Act, moreover, the president could defer an expenditure unless overruled by a resolution of either house of Congress but could refuse to spend the funds entirely only if both houses approved the proposed impoundment within forty-five days.

Carswell, G. Harrold

A defeated Nixon Supreme Court nominee born in Georgia in 1919, G. Harrold Carswell received his law degree from Mercer and served another five years as U.S. attorney before being appointed by President Eisenhower in 1958 to the U.S. District Court for the Northern District of Florida. Six months after elevating him to a seat on the Court of Appeals for the Fifth Circuit, President Nixon nominated Carswell to the Supreme Court vacancy created by the resignation of Justice Abe Fortas, following the Senate's rejection of Clement Haynsworth, Nixon's first nominee to the position. Carswell not only had a mediocre district court record, but opponents quickly uncovered a prosegregationist speech he made in 1948 while running for a seat in the Georgia legislature, his condescending treatment of African Americans in his courtroom, and his involvement while U.S. attorney in the transfer of a municipally owned Tallahassee golf course (built with federal funds) to a private, segregated club. The Senate rejected Carswell 51–45. Resigning from the circuit bench two weeks later, he made an unsuccessful primary bid for the Republican nomination to a U.S. Senate seat, then returned to Tallahassee to practice law.

Carter, James Earl (Jimmy)

The first Deep South president since the Civil War, Jimmy Carter was born in Plains, Georgia, in 1924. Following graduation from the U.S. Naval Academy, he embarked upon a career in the navy, entering its nuclear submarine program in 1952 as an aide to Admiral Hyman Rickover. When his father died in 1953, Carter left the navy to take over the family peanut business. He also became active in politics, winning a seat in the state senate and serving as Georgia's governor from 1971 to 1975. In 1976 Carter won the Democratic presidential nomination and defeated President Ford in the fall elections. On his first full day in office, Carter pardoned all Vietnam War draft evaders. He also played a major role in peace negotiations between Israel and Egypt, and when the Soviet Union invaded Afghanistan he imposed a grain embargo and forbade U.S. participation in the Moscow Olympic Games. But the Carter administration was plagued by spiraling inflation, fueled in large part by dramatic increases in the price of foreign oil. The November 1979 seizure of the U.S. embassy in Tehran by Iranian student militants and efforts to secure the safe release of embassy staff were a major administration preoccupation for the balance of his term and contributed greatly to his 1980 defeat for reelection by Reagan. Carter's efforts to end the crisis were ultimately successful, but it was not until Reagan's inauguration that the hostages were released—an event, some evidence suggests, that the new president's aides may have orchestrated to coincide with Reagan's assumption of office. In *Dames & Moore v. Regan* (1981), the Burger Court upheld retaliatory economic measures taken by the Carter administration to end the hostage crisis. In *Goldwater v. Carter* (1979), moreover, the Court summarily set aside lower court decisions on the constitutionality of President Carter's termination, without Senate involvement, of U.S. treaty agreements with Taiwan, Justice Rehnquist concluding for a plurality that the case presented a nonjusticiable political question and Justice Powell, the pivotal vote, declaring that the case was not yet ripe for decision.

Civil Rights Act of 1866

This Reconstruction-era statute provided, among other things, that "all persons" would have the "same right . . . as is enjoyed by white citizens" to "make and enforce contracts" and to "inherit, purchase, lease, sell, hold, and convey real and personal property." In *Jones v. Alfred H. Mayer Co.* (1968), the Warren Court held that the provision regarding equal enjoyment of property rights could be applied against the discriminatory practices of a real estate company and upheld the power of Congress, under its constitutional authority to enforce the Thirteenth Amendment, to eliminate, as a badge or remnant of slavery, virtually all racial discrimination, whether state-enforced or private. In *Runyon v. McCrary* (1976), the Burger Court reaffirmed *Mayer* in upholding the provision of the law granting an equal right to make and enforce contracts, at least as applied to a commercially operated, nonsectarian private school with racially discriminatory admission policies.

Civil Rights Act of 1964

This omnibus legislation was intended to outlaw discrimination based on race and related factors in several areas of American life. Enlarging upon the voting rights provisions of 1957 and 1960 civil rights legislation, the 1964 statute prohibited various voter registration practices (such as disqualification of voter applicants for misspellings or other irrelevant errors on application forms) used in the past to discriminate on the basis of race or national origin. It also authorized the national government to bring desegregation suits, extended the life and increased the authority of the U.S.

Commission on Civil Rights, and created the Equal Employment Opportunity Commission (EEOC) to investigate disputes over private employment discrimination (a jurisdiction later enlarged to cover federal employment, administration of federal equal pay regulations, and employment discrimination based on age or handicap). Its most important provisions, however, were Title II, which barred discrimination in theaters, restaurants, hotels, and other places of "public accommodation" that affected interstate commerce (in that a substantial share of their customers or products had moved interstate); Title VI, which authorized the cutoff of federal funds to schools and other institutions that practiced discrimination (and proved to be the major weapon against school systems that refused to desegregate their facilities); and Title VII, which forbade employment discrimination based on race, color, religion, national origin, or sex.

Civiletti, Benjamin

Attorney general (1979–1981) in the administration of President Carter, Benjamin Civiletti was born in Peekskill, New York, in 1935. He received his undergraduate degree from Johns Hopkins in 1957 and law degree from the University of Maryland in 1961. After clerking for a federal district judge in Maryland, Civiletti became an assistant U.S. attorney in Baltimore, devoting most of his attention to the prosecution of fraud cases during his two-year tenure. In 1964 he entered private practice with a major Baltimore firm, where he soon became partner and head of its litigation division. Work with one of his cases led to Civiletti's association with Charles H. Kirbo, a close adviser to Georgia governor Jimmy Carter. At Kirbo's suggestion, Civiletti was named in 1977 to head the criminal division in the Carter Justice Department. Later that year President Carter, on the recommendation of Attorney General Griffin Bell, appointed Civiletti to fill a vacancy in the post of deputy attorney general, the second highest-ranking position in the Justice Department. When Bell resigned in 1975, Civiletti replaced him as attorney general, winning Senate confirmation by a 94–1 vote. During the balance of President Carter's tenure, the new attorney general was involved in a variety of controversial issues, including the Iranian hostage crisis. In protest against the seizure of the U.S. embassy in Tehran, he initiated deportation proceedings against Iranians illegally in the United States, an action a federal district judge declared unconstitutional in *Narenji v. Civiletti* (1979). But the Court of Appeals for the District of Columbia reinstated the proceedings, citing the considerable deference traditionally extended the executive in foreign affairs. The Supreme Court declined review.

Committee on the Judiciary, U.S. Senate

All presidential nominees to the Supreme Court, as well as other federal judgeships, must be confirmed or approved by a simple majority vote of the Senate. The Senate

Judiciary Committee plays the principal role in the confirmation process, investigating the nominee's background and credentials and typically conducting a hearing before which the nominee and other witnesses appear for questioning. At times, as with the nomination of Chief Justice Burger and Justice Powell, the hearings are brief, perfunctory affairs; on other occasions the proceedings become meaningful inquiries into a nominee's fitness for judicial office. As a candidate for both associate and chief justice, Rehnquist faced considerable probing with respect to his civil rights views, role in the Nixon administration, and partisan political activities. Pro-life witnesses appeared before the committee to attack what they considered 1981 Reagan nominee O'Connor's ambivalent stance as a state legislator on the abortion issue. Once the committee completes its work, members vote on the nomination. Floor debate and a final vote follow in the full Senate. Most nominees have won confirmation, but the Senate has rejected or declined to act upon 28 of 145 Supreme Court nominations submitted to it since adoption of the Constitution.

Courts of Appeals, U.S.

First created in 1891, the courts of appeals are the intermediate appellate tribunals of the federal judiciary. The United States is divided into eleven numbered regional circuits with a court of appeals in each, and the District of Columbia constitutes a twelfth circuit. These courts hear appeals from U.S. district courts, federal territorial courts, and the decisions of certain federal administrative agencies. They vary greatly in number of judges but ordinarily hear cases in three-judge panels, although an entire court will sit en banc to decide cases of major importance or in which different three-judge panels have rendered conflicting rulings in similar cases. In 1982 Congress also created the Court of Appeals for the Federal Circuit with a nationwide jurisdiction over appeals in a variety of business-related cases from other courts and certain administrative agencies. Composed of twelve judges appointed by the president for life terms, the Court of Appeals for the Federal Circuit, like the regional appeals courts, usually hears cases in three-judge panels but sometimes sits en banc.

Cox, Archibald

The first special prosecutor selected to investigate the Watergate scandal in the Nixon administration, Archibald Cox was born in Plainfield, New Jersey, in 1912. Long a professor of law at Harvard, where he received his undergraduate and law degrees in 1934 and 1937, Cox served as U.S. solicitor general in the administrations of Presidents John F. Kennedy (1961–1963) and Lyndon B. Johnson (1963–1969). In 1973 President Nixon's attorney general Elliot Richardson appointed Cox as special prosecutor, with broad authority and independence to investigate the alleged presidential cover-up of the break-in at the Democratic National Committee headquarters in Washington's Watergate office complex, as well as other illegal activity relating to the 1972 presidential campaign. When the existence of secret tape recordings of communications in President Nixon's White House office was revealed, Cox demanded to hear specific tapes. When the president refused, Cox filed a federal court suit. Rejecting Nixon's claims to executive privilege, a federal district judge and the Court of Appeals for the District of Columbia ordered the tapes turned over to Cox. When the special prosecutor declined as unacceptable the president's offer to provide him with verified, edited transcripts instead, Nixon ordered Cox fired. Attorney General Elliot Richardson and his deputy attorney general resigned rather than comply. But Nixon's solicitor general Robert H. Bork, as acting attorney general, carried out the president's directive. Those events (popularly known as the "Saturday Night Massacre") provoked an intense public outcry, leading to the appointment of a new special prosecutor, Leon Jaworski, who secured a Supreme Court rejection of the president's confidentiality claims in *United States v. Nixon* (1974). In August following that decision, Nixon resigned the presidency.

District Courts, U.S.

First created by Congress in 1789, the federal district courts are the general trial courts of the federal judiciary, presiding over federal criminal prosecutions and a wide variety of civil cases. From one to four district courts sit in each state and vary widely in number of judges. Ordinarily, a single judge sits to hear a case, but federal law provides for three-judge panels (generally composed of one court of appeals judge and two district judges) to hear certain types of cases (such as litigation dealing with the enforcement of federal voting rights laws). Federal magistrate judges, appointed by the district judges for eight-year terms, assist the district judges with their work. In recent years the magistrate's role has grown substantially. With the consent of all parties, for example, a magistrate judge can conduct all proceedings in a civil case and with the defendant's consent try minor criminal cases.

Eastland, James O.

Chairman of the Senate Judiciary Committee through much of the Burger Court era, James O. Eastland was born in Mississippi in 1904 and raised in Scott County, near the state capital in Jackson. Eastland was admitted to the Mississippi bar in 1927 and elected to the state legislature the next year. First appointed to the Senate in 1941 to fill an unexpired term, he won election to a full term in 1942 and became chairman of the Judiciary Committee in the 1950s. Operator of a large Mississippi plantation and one of the South's most powerful segregationists, Eastland was an ardent foe of civil rights and a ready ally in President Nixon's efforts to place conservative justices on the Supreme Court. When a prosegregation memorandum William Rehnquist wrote while clerking for Justice Robert H. Jackson surfaced after Judiciary Committee proceedings on Rehnquist's confirmation as associate justice had concluded, Eastland rebuffed efforts to reopen the hearing. Eastland retired from the Senate in 1978.

Equal Rights Amendment (ERA)

The proposed Equal Rights Amendment provided, "Equality of rights under the law shall not be denied or abridged by the United States or by any State on account of sex." Congress submitted the proposal to the states in March 1972 with the usual stipulation for modern amendment proposals that it must be ratified by the required three-fourths of the state legislatures within seven years. When it appeared certain the ERA would not be ratified within the seven-year limit, Congress extended the period for ratification until June 30, 1982, but to no avail. Only thirty-five of the thirty-eight states required for ratification approved the proposal. Proponents and opponents differed vigorously over the ERA's likely scope, had it been adopted. Presumably, the courts would have treated discrimination based on sex, like racial classifications, as inherently suspect and to be struck down as unconstitutional unless found necessary to promote a compelling governmental interest through means least restrictive of individual rights. In part because the ERA was pending in the state legislatures, a Supreme Court majority refused in 1973 to equate sex with race and subject gender classifications to the strictest judicial scrutiny reserved for racial and related forms of discrimination under the Fourteenth Amendment's equal protection guarantee. In *Craig v. Boren* (1976) and later cases, however, the Court, viewing gender classifications as quasi-suspect, subjected them to intermediate, or heightened review, holding that they must be closely related to a substantial governmental interest to withstand challenge. Under that approach, certain forms of sex discrimination have been struck down, while others have been upheld.

Federal Election Campaign Act
(1974, and as amended)

Adopted in the wake of the Watergate scandal that ultimately drove President Nixon from office, this statute and the 1971 Federal Revenue Act imposed several important restrictions on the financing of federal election campaigns. First, individuals could contribute no more than $3,000 (a maximum of $1,000 for each campaign) to a federal candidate in a given year, with an overall annual contribution limit of $25,000 to all federal candidates. Political organizations could contribute no more than $15,000 (a maximum of $5,000 for each campaign), albeit with no overall limit. Second, the same restrictions were imposed on individual and organizational expenditures in behalf of a candidate. Third, presidential campaigns were to be financed in part from public funds. Fourth, limits were imposed on overall expenditures by candidates personally, as well as through their campaign organizations. Finally, the law established the Federal Election Commission to supervise compliance with federal campaign finance regulations and require periodic financial reports from candidates and their committees. In *Buckley v. Valeo* (1976), the Burger Court upheld the restrictions on contributions, the public funding provisions, and creation of the FEC, although it invalidated a provision permitting Congress to choose a majority of the FEC's voting members on the ground that arrangement interfered with the president's appointive powers (Congress rewrote portions of the law to eliminate that objection). Essentially on free speech grounds, however, the Court struck down the provisions limiting the amounts individuals and organizations could spend in behalf of candidates, as well as restrictions on how much candidates could spend from their own or family funds. Congress could have reasonably concluded that large contributions directly to candidates might unduly influence their actions once in office, the Court reasoned, but candidates would be unaware of funds spent independently in their behalf. In *Federal Election Commission v. National Conservative Political Action Committee* (1983), moreover, the Court struck down restrictions on independent expenditures even in behalf of presidential candidates who accepted public campaign funds and thus were required to limit their spending.

Ford, Gerald R.

The future president was born in Omaha, Nebraska, in 1913. At age two, following his parents' divorce, he moved with his mother to Grand Rapids, Michigan. There she married Gerald R. Ford, who formally adopted her child, giving him his own name. After completing an undergraduate degree at the University of Michigan and a Yale law degree in 1941, Ford began practice in Grand Rapids. During World War II, he served with the navy in the Pacific, becoming a lieutenant commander. In 1949 he began a twenty-five-year tenure in the U.S. House of Representatives, eight as Republican House leader. Following the resignation in disgrace of Vice-President Spiro Agnew in 1973, President Nixon became the first president to invoke the succession provisions of the Twenty-fifth Amendment, appointing Ford to replace Agnew with the approval of a simple majority in each house of Congress. When Nixon resigned the presidency on August 9, 1974, in the wake of the Supreme Court's ruling in *United States v. Nixon* (1974) and subsequent revelations of the president's involvement in the Watergate scandal, Ford became president. A month later he granted the former president a full pardon for any federal crimes Nixon may have committed during his White House tenure. Perhaps in part as a result of his pardoning the former president, Ford lost a 1976 election bid to Democrat Jimmy Carter. He thus became the only person in the nation's history to date to hold the offices of both the presidency and vice-presidency without winning election to either office.

Fortas, Abe

A prominent Washington lawyer, Supreme Court justice, and nominee for the Court's center seat, Abe Fortas was born in Memphis, Tennessee, in 1910, the son of immigrant Jews. Following undergraduate education at Southwestern College in Memphis and law school at Yale, where he became a disciple of legal realism and served as editor in chief of the law review, Fortas joined President Franklin D. Roosevelt's New Deal administration, serving first in the Agricultural Adjustment Administration and then in the Department of the Interior. As Interior undersecretary during World War II, he opposed the imposition of martial law in Hawaii and the internment of Japanese Americans on the West Coast. Following the war, Fortas established a Washington law firm with his former Yale professor Thurmond Arnold and Paul Porter. The firm attracted a clientele of lucrative corporate interests, but Fortas was also a vigorous defender of the victims of postwar McCarthyism and successfully argued a number of landmark civil liberties cases, most notably *Gideon v. Wainwright* (1963), in which the Supreme Court recognized the right of indigent state defendants to court-appointed counsel. In 1965 President Johnson, to whom Fortas had become a trusted adviser, nominated his longtime friend to a seat on the Supreme Court. A virtually certain vote for Warren Court decisions expanding the scope of civil liberties, Fortas authored a number of important opinions of that era, including *In Re Gault* (1967), extending due process safeguards to juvenile proceedings, and *Tinker v. Des Moines Independent School District* (1969), recognizing the free speech rights of public school students. To the dismay of his colleagues, however, Fortas also continued to serve as adviser to President Johnson, becoming intimately involved in a variety of foreign and domestic policy issues. When Johnson nominated his friend to replace Chief Justice Earl Warren in 1968, critics charged that Fortas had violated the constitutional principle of separation of powers, and the president, who had decided not to seek reelection, could do little to assure Fortas's confirmation. When conflict-of-interest charges also surfaced, Johnson withdrew the nomination at the justice's request. The following year, press reports revealed that Fortas had accepted a $20,000 honorarium from a foundation headed by a twice-indicted former client, Louis Wolfson. Amid the outcry that followed, particularly among congressional Republicans, Fortas resigned his seat in May 1969, giving President Nixon a second seat to fill on the Court.

Griswold, Erwin N.

Solicitor general during the Johnson and Nixon administrations, Erwin N. Griswold was born in Ohio in 1904. He received undergraduate and master's degrees from Oberlin and a law degree from Harvard in 1928. Although admitted to the Ohio bar and to practice with his father's Cleveland firm in 1929, Griswold, on the recommendation of his former Harvard professor and future Supreme Court justice Felix Frankfurter, became an attorney in the U.S. solicitor general's office that same year. He served in that capacity until 1934, when he became a member of the Harvard law faculty. He became dean of the law school in 1946, and in 1967 President Johnson appointed Griswold, a moderate Republican, to the post of solicitor general—a position he retained in the Nixon administration. In that capacity Griswold defended the White House position in the 1971 *Pentagon Papers Cases*, filing a brief with the Court in which he declared that publication of the papers would cause immediate and irreparable harm to the nation's security. Privately, however, he had advised against the suit to enjoin further publication of the papers and, based on the judgment of Defense Department and other officials, concluded that political embarrassment would be the only harm that might flow from the papers' publication. The Supreme Court, by a 6–3 vote, refused to enjoin publication of any part of the papers.

Haynsworth, Clement F., Jr.

A defeated Nixon nominee to the Supreme Court born in Greenville, South Carolina, in 1912, Clement F. Haynsworth graduated from Furman in 1933 and received a law degree from Harvard in 1936. He then joined his father's Greenville practice; after World War II service in the naval reserves, he was made a senior partner in 1946. Under Haynsworth's direction, the firm became South Carolina's largest and wealthiest, with many major corporate interests among its clients. A southern Democrat disenchanted with the national party, Haynsworth supported Republican Dwight Eisenhower's successful 1952 and 1956 presidential bids. In 1957 Eisenhower chose Haynsworth for a seat on the U.S. Court of Appeals for the Fourth Circuit, where in 1964 he became that court's senior jurist in terms of service and thus its chief judge. His circuit court record, not surprisingly, was moderately conservative. In 1968, for example, the Supreme Court reversed his ruling upholding a "freedom of choice" school desegregation plan that had produced virtually no change in the racial patterns of public schools. He was also decidedly probusiness in labor-management cases. His votes in racial and labor litigation hardly endeared him to union or civil rights leaders. But the Nixon administration considered the Fourth Circuit jurist ideally suited to its "southern strategy" for luring dissident white southerners into the Republican Party. When Justice Abe Fortas resigned his seat on the Supreme Court in the spring of 1969, Haynsworth quickly emerged as a leading candidate for the vacancy. On August 18 President Nixon submitted his name to the Senate. Even before his nomination was announced, however, the president's choice was generating the same sorts of ethical concerns that had led to Justice Fortas's resignation the previous May. Opponents initially charged that the nominee should have recused or disqualified himself from participating in a case involving Darlington Manufacturing, since he was a director and one-seventh owner of a vending machine firm that did business with Darlington's parent company, South Carolina industrial giant Dearing Milliken. A judicial ethics specialist told the Senate Judiciary Committee that recusal was unwarranted in the case. But Haynsworth's opponents then revealed he had purchased stock in the Brunswick Corporation after participating in a decision involving that firm but before the ruling was announced. And while the ABA's judiciary committee assigned the nominee a positive rating and sixteen past ABA presidents supported the nomination as well, concerns over the nominee's sensitivity to ethical propriety persisted. The Senate Judiciary Committee recommended confirmation by a 10–7 vote. But a growing number of Republican senators, including several who had led the fight against President Johnson's 1968 nomination of Justice Fortas as chief justice, announced their opposition to Haynsworth also. In November the Senate rejected the nominee by a vote of 55–45. Haynsworth remained on the circuit bench, becoming a senior judge in 1981. He died in 1989, twenty years and a day after his rejection by the Senate.

Hruska, Roman Lee

Senate floor manager of G. Harrold Carswell's abortive Supreme Court appointment, Roman Hruska was born in Nebraska in 1904, the son of a Bohemian immigrant brought to the United States as an infant. Following study at the University of Omaha and two years at the University of Chicago Law School, he obtained a law degree in 1929 at Omaha's Creighton University. From 1929 to 1952, Hruska developed a thriving Omaha law practice and participated in a variety of Republican Party and civic activities, also serving as a county commissioner. In 1952 he won election to the U.S. House of Representatives. Two years later, following the death of one of Nebraska's senators, he won election to the Senate, siding with the minority early in his tenure when that chamber voted to censure controversial Republican Wisconsin senator Joseph McCarthy. Senator Hruska's most enduring—and dubious—claim to fame would be his laughable effort to convert G. Harrold Carswell's mediocrity into an asset during Senate confirmation proceedings on the Carswell nomination. "Even if he is mediocre," declared the senator, "there are a lot of mediocre judges and people and lawyers. They are entitled to a little representation, aren't they . . . ? We can't have all Brandeises, Cardozos, and Frankfurters, and stuff like that there."

Hyde Amendment

Named for Henry J. Hyde, a Republican member of the U.S. House of Representatives from Illinois vigorously opposed to abortion, this term is used to refer to amendments added to congressional appropriations bills that forbid the use of federal Medicaid funds for most abortions. Congress adopted the initial version of the Hyde amendment in 1976. The provision upheld by the Supreme Court in *Harris v. McRae* (1980) stipulated that "none of the funds provided . . . shall be used to perform abortions except where the life of the mother would be endangered if the fetus were carried to term; or except for such medical procedures necessary for the victims of rape or incest when such rape or incest has been reported promptly to a law enforcement agency or public health service." Earlier versions had been more or less restrictive; the original provision, for example, had not included the "rape or incest" exception, but others had allowed the use of Medicaid funds if, in the judgment of two physicians, carrying a pregnancy to term would result in "severe and long-lasting physical health damage to the mother."

Iranian Hostage Crisis

On November 4, 1979, militant Iranian followers of conservative Muslim religious leader Ayatollah Khomeini seized the U.S. embassy in Tehran and took hostages, including sixty-two Americans. Despite criticism by the international community and a variety of U.S. strategies, such as the seizure of Iranian assets in U.S. banks, deportation of Iranians illegally in the United States, and an abortive air rescue attempt, the crisis continued for the balance of President Jimmy Carter's White House tenure, seriously impeding the administration's work on a variety of policy fronts and significantly contributing to Carter's defeat by Ronald Reagan in his 1980 reelection bid. But an accord President Carter crafted, Reagan affirmed, and the Burger Court upheld in *Dames & Moore v. Regan* (1981) resulted in release of the hostages on January 20, 1981, Reagan's inauguration day.

Jackson, Robert H.

A Franklin D. Roosevelt Supreme Court appointee, Robert H. Jackson was born in Pennsylvania in 1892 but spent most of his youth in rural New York. Following a year at Albany Law School and clerkship in the law office of a prominent area Democrat, Jackson won admission to the New York bar in 1913, thereby becoming the last Supreme Court justice to secure his legal education by reading law in a law office rather than attending law school. While engaged in a thriving legal practice in Jamestown, New York, for twenty years, Jackson developed close ties with Franklin Roosevelt. Following Roosevelt's 1932 election to the presidency, he held a variety of administration posts, becoming solicitor general in 1938 and attorney general in 1940. The next year Roosevelt named Jackson to the Supreme Court, on which he served until his death in 1954. Although moderately conservative and restraintist in his reaction to civil liberties claims, he spoke for the Court in *West Virginia Board of Education v. Barnette* (1943), overturning compulsory school flag programs, and shortly before his death, despite deep personal concerns about federal court intrusion into local education, joined the Court's unanimous opinion in *Brown v. Board of Education* (1954), outlawing state-mandated racial segregation in public schools. While clerking for Jackson in 1952 and 1953, William H. Rehnquist drafted memoranda opposing reversal of *Plessy v. Ferguson*, the 1896 decision endorsing the "separate but equal" doctrine. The memoranda did not surface until the Senate Judiciary Committee proceedings on his confirmation as associate justice had concluded, and Senator James Eastland, the committee chair, refused to reopen the hearing. During 1986 hearings on his confirmation as chief justice, however, Rehnquist suggested variously that the memoranda expressed the justice's views or the segregationist position rather than the nominee's personal feelings. The phrasing of the memoranda and other evidence raised doubts about Rehnquist's veracity.

Jaworski, Leon

The second special prosecutor in the Watergate proceedings, Leon Jaworski was born in Waco, Texas, in 1905, the son of immigrant parents. He received his law degree from Baylor University in 1925 and an LL.M. from George Washington University the following year before returning to Waco to practice law. In 1930 Jaworski joined a Houston firm, then moved to another firm (later known as Fulbright and Jaworski) the next year, becoming a partner in 1935 and managing partner in 1948. At his death in 1982, his firm was among the largest in the nation, with offices in Washington and London as well as several Texas cities. A leader in his profession, Jaworski was president of the ABA from 1971 to 1972. Long active in politics and public service and closely associated with fellow Texan Lyndon B. Johnson, Jaworski would be best remembered as the second head of the Watergate special prosecution force. Appointed with expanded authority by President Nixon after the president's firing of the first special prosecutor, Archibald Cox, had provoked a national furor, Jaworski argued *United States v. Nixon* (1974), winning a unanimous decision (with Justice Rehnquist, a former member of the Nixon Justice Department, not participating) that rejected President Nixon's claims of executive privilege to withhold from the Watergate grand jury and the courts tape recordings and other evidence relevant to the inquiry. Although agreeing that executive privilege was a presidential prerogative implicit in the Constitution, the Court concluded, as Jaworski had contended, that assertions of the privilege must yield to a demonstrated and overriding need of criminal justice.

Johnson, Lyndon B.

Born in Stonewall, Texas, in 1908, Lyndon B. Johnson graduated from Southeast Texas State Teachers College in 1930. After teaching in the Houston public schools for a time, Johnson became secretary to a Texas congressman, then won a special election to the U.S. House of Representatives held to fill a vacancy left by the death of a member of the Texas delegation. In 1938 he was elected to a full term. Following four terms in the House and World War II service with the navy in the Pacific, Johnson was elected to the Senate in 1948. Reelected in 1954, the year following his selection as Senate Democratic leader, Johnson became the most powerful figure in Congress. Vice-president in the Kennedy administration, he assumed the presidency upon Kennedy's assassination on November 22, 1963, and won election to a full term in 1964. Pursuing an aggressive domestic program known as the Great Society, Johnson won congressional passage of major civil rights, antipoverty, education, and health-care legislation. But his escalation of the Vietnam War and the antiwar protest movement it provoked soon overshadowed his legislative accomplishments. Faced with intense political division at home and repeated frustration in the conduct of the war abroad, President Johnson decided not to seek reelection in 1968. His lame-duck status and questionable reliance on longtime friend Abe Fortas as a presidential adviser even after Fortas's 1965 appointment as an associate justice no doubt contributed to the failure of Johnson's efforts to elevate Fortas to the Court's center seat.

Kleindienst, Richard G.

The second of four attorneys general in the Nixon administration, Richard G. Kleindienst was born near Winslow, Arizona, in 1923. When called into military service during World War II, he was a student at the University of Arizona. After the war, Kleindienst graduated with honors from Harvard in 1947 and obtained a law degree there in 1950. From 1950 to 1969, he practiced law in his native state, becoming a senior partner in a major Phoenix firm in 1958. Long active in Republican politics, he played a major role in Richard M. Nixon's successful 1968 presidential bid and became deputy attorney general in the Nixon Justice Department, taking along with him to Washington his longtime friend William H. Rehnquist, who served as assistant attorney general in charge of the Office of Legal Counsel until his appointment to the Supreme Court. As deputy attorney general, Kleindienst was a major figure in the selection of Nixon nominees to the federal judiciary, including Rehnquist and two choices rejected by the Senate, Clement Haynsworth and G. Harrold Carswell. When President Nixon's first attorney general, John Mitchell, resigned in 1972 to direct the president's reelection campaign, the president nominated Kleindienst to replace Mitchell. Lengthy Senate Judiciary Committee proceedings raised questions, among other matters, about the nominee's involvement in the Justice Department's out-of-court settlement of an antitrust suit against the International Telephone and Telegraph Company (ITT) and its possible connection to a $400,000 ITT guarantee to help finance the 1972 Republican national convention. He won confirmation, but a year after Nixon's landslide reelection, Kleindienst became one of the casualties of the Watergate scandal, forced to resign, along with Nixon's top White House aides, in a futile effort to prevent the president's impeachment or resignation.

Lee, Rex

A solicitor general in the Reagan administration, Rex Lee received his undergraduate degree in 1960 from Brigham Young and law degree from the University of Chicago in 1963. After law school, Lee clerked for Supreme Court justice Byron R. White, then engaged in private practice and served as dean of the Brigham Young Law School from 1972 to 1981, when he became solicitor general. As chief representative of the United States and federal law before the Supreme Court, Lee developed an impressive won-loss record. Critics complained, however, that he was not pressing the conservative constitutional agenda of the Reagan White House on such issues as abortion, school desegregation, and criminal procedure rights with sufficient zeal. In 1985 Lee resigned from the position, explaining that a return to private practice was necessary to finance his children's college education. But he was also concerned that an unduly aggressive stance might damage his credibility with the Court. He told one interviewer he was the solicitor general, not the pamphleteer general, of the United States. Lee's successor, Harvard law professor Charles Fried, aggressively pressed Reagan policy positions before the Court but partially relented when his tactics irritated a number of justices.

Legislative Veto

The Constitution, of course, delegates lawmaking power to the Congress. In the modern administrative state, however, Congress has been obliged to delegate rule-making authority to the executive, allowing the president and other officials to "fill in the details" of broad policy embodied in congressional statutes. The Supreme Court, with few exceptions, has upheld such delegations where Congress has attached guidelines limiting executive discretion, thereby avoiding an undue congressional delegation of its lawmaking power to the president. The Court has been exceedingly deferential to Congress, moreover, in its review of challenges to such delegations. To maintain ultimate control over the executive, however, Congress also incorporated a legislative veto into many such arrangements. Under the legislative veto, a proposed executive action was voided if vetoed by, depending on the particular law in question, both congressional chambers, one house, or even a congressional committee. The legislative veto had its beginnings in the 1930s, when Congress approved a grant of authority to the president for reorganization of the executive branch only on the condition that either house could disapprove a proposed reorganization by adoption of a veto resolution. By the early 1980s, Congress had enacted nearly 200 legislative veto provisions. But in *INS v. Chadha* (1983), a Supreme Court majority struck down the legislative veto as a violation of the constitutional provisions requiring all proposed laws to be passed by both houses of Congress and submitted to the president for approval or veto. Since *Chadha*, though, Congress has continued to enact legislative veto schemes—an additional fifty-three, according to one source, between the Court's ruling and the adjournment of that session of Congress. Technically, at least, they have simply been of a more advisory or informal nature.

Levi, Edward H.

An attorney general during the Ford administration, Edward H. Levi was born in Chicago in 1911. He received his undergraduate and law degrees from the University of Chicago in 1932 and 1935. Following further study at Yale, he joined the Chicago law faculty. He took a leave of absence from his teaching position in 1940 to serve as a special assistant to Attorneys General Robert H. Jackson and Francis Biddle in the U.S. Department of Justice. In 1945 he returned to the University of Chicago, where he became an outstanding scholar in antitrust law. Increasingly concerned with nuclear energy and its control, Levi was an adviser to the Chicago physicists engaged in atomic energy research during and after World War II. In 1950 he became dean of the law school, a position he held until 1962; he was also the university's provost beginning in 1961. As provost and later as undergraduate dean, he played major roles in curricular innovations and creation of the university's Center for Policy Analysis. In 1968 Levi became the University of Chicago's eighth president. President Ford appointed him to head the Department of Justice in 1975. As attorney general, Levi was probably instrumental in the selection of his longtime friend John Paul Stevens to replace Justice Douglas on the Supreme Court.

McCree, Wade H., Jr.

The second African American appointed U.S. solicitor general (the first was Thurgood Marshall, who in 1967 became the first African American Supreme Court justice), Wade H. McCree was born in Des Moines, Iowa, in 1920. He received his undergraduate degree from Fisk University in 1941 and a law degree from Harvard in 1944. Admitted to the Michigan bar in 1948, he practiced law in Detroit until 1952, when he became a member of the state's workmen's compensation commission. From 1952 to 1954, he sat on the state circuit court bench in Detroit. In 1961 President Kennedy selected McCree for a federal district judgeship. Five years later President Johnson appointed him to the Court of Appeals for the Sixth Circuit, where he remained until his selection as solicitor general by President Carter in 1977—a position he retained throughout the Carter presidency. By all accounts an excellent solicitor general who placed the law above White House policy preferences, McCree once commented that the briefs filed with the Supreme Court by President Reagan's second solicitor general, Harvard law professor Charles Fried, were less "dispassionate" and "objective" than those the solicitor's office had traditionally submitted. Two other former solicitors general raised the same sorts of concerns.

Meese, Edwin, III

Presidential counselor and later attorney general in the Reagan administration, Edwin Meese III was born in Oakland, California, in 1931. Meese obtained an undergraduate degree from Yale in 1953 and a law degree in 1958 from the University of California at Berkeley, which he entered following two years in army intelligence. During eight years as an Alameda County deputy district attorney, he became deeply interested in the work of police, spending much of his free time riding with officers on patrol. Meese's conservative reputation, including his vigorous support of the death penalty, brought him to Reagan's attention. When Reagan won election as California's governor, he named Meese his secretary in charge of clemency and extradition matters. In 1969 he was also the governor's chief representative in dealing with antiwar demonstrations at Berkeley and San Francisco State College, persuading Reagan to declare a state of emergency there. During Reagan's second gubernatorial term, Meese was named chief of staff, becoming in effect California's deputy governor. After playing a major role in Reagan's 1980 presidential election, he was appointed to the newly created position of counselor to the president, while James A. Baker, who had supported George Bush for the Republican presidential nomination, became Reagan's chief of staff. Although probably miffed at Baker's selection, Meese agreed to accept the post of presidential counselor, but only after being promised he would enjoy cabinet rank and have control over a number of White House agencies. Whatever his formal title, Meese became one of the top three power brokers in the Reagan White House. In 1985 he became attorney general, replacing William French Smith. In that capacity he was a vocal critic of Warren and Burger Court decisions expanding the procedural safeguards of suspects and defendants in criminal cases, recognizing abortion rights, requiring church-state separation, and imposing Bill of Rights guarantees on the states via the Fourteenth Amendment's due process clause and the incorporation process. Part of the "sleaze factor" that by late 1986 had prompted more than 100 members of the Reagan administration to leave office under allegations of wrongdoing, Meese was the target of several criminal investigations, although none led to his indictment. In 1988 he resigned his post as attorney general, replaced by Richard Thornburgh.

Mitchell, John N.

John N. Mitchell was born in Detroit, Michigan, in 1913; his family moved to Long Island, New York, a few years later. Mitchell graduated from a Queens high school in 1931, then did undergraduate work at Fordham and obtained a law degree there in 1938. That same year he became an associate with a New York firm, in which he became a partner in 1942. After World War II service with the navy, he returned to his firm, which now carried his name and specialized in state and municipal bond practice. Over the years Mitchell also figured prominently in the creation of state housing, college, and hospital programs financed through bond issues for which his firm was retained as bond counsel. In 1967 Mitchell's firm merged with a larger one in which Nixon was a senior partner, and the two soon became close friends. Late that year Mitchell agreed to manage Nixon's 1968 presidential bid, and following the election the new president-elect named Mitchell to the post of attorney general, despite the widespread misgivings of civil rights leaders. Their concerns were well founded: Mitchell figured prominently in President Nixon's harsh policy toward antiwar protesters and his efforts to remold the Supreme Court into a more conservative image. In early 1972 Mitchell resigned his post as attorney general to head President Nixon's reelection campaign. In June, shortly after the break-in at the offices of the Democratic National Committee in Washington's Watergate office complex, he resigned from the reelection committee to return to his law practice. In 1974 he was acquitted in New York on federal charges of perjury and conspiracy to obstruct justice in connection with a secret cash contribution to Nixon's 1972 campaign. But on January 5, 1975, Mitchell was convicted on conspiracy and other charges growing out of the Watergate break-in and cover-up. After exhausting his appeal efforts, he entered prison in 1977 to begin serving a sentence of two to eight years. That sentence was later reduced, and he was paroled in 1979, after serving nineteen months. Disbarred from law practice, Mitchell became a business consultant. He died in 1988.

National Court of Appeals

Each year the Supreme Court grants a writ of certiorari (instructing a lower court to send up a case for review) in relatively few of the thousands of suits brought before it. Concern that the justices devote an inordinate portion of their limited time to this screening function rather than to the merits of those cases considered worthy of review has led to a variety of suggested remedies, including proposals for placing the screening process largely in the hands of an intermediate tribunal situated between the Supreme Court and lower tribunals. In 1972, for example, a study group on Supreme Court caseload headed by Harvard law professor Paul Freund and convened by the Federal Judicial Center proposed creation of a seven-member national court of appeals, composed initially of judges assigned on a rotating basis from the federal courts of appeals for staggered, three-year terms. The proposed court was annually to review all petitions for writs of certiorari, forward approximately 10 percent to the Supreme Court for further screening and review, and dismiss the rest. To assure a nationally uniform response to legal issues, the proposed court was also to decide cases reflecting conflicts among court of appeals circuits regarding the appropriate resolution of a legal issue not sent on to the Supreme Court for possible review and decision. A number of justices, including John Paul Stevens, went on record in support of such a proposal as a means of giving the Court more time for review of cases it agreed to decide. But other justices, most notably William J. Brennan, opposed the Freund committee's report and similar proposals. Critics contended, among other things, that such arrangements would violate the Constitution's provision in Article III for "one" Supreme Court and that the Court's screening and decisional functions were inextricably linked. Congress to date has declined to create a "junior Supreme Court."

Nixon, Richard M.

Born in Yorba Linda, California, in 1913, Richard M. Nixon graduated from Whittier College in 1934 and obtained a law degree from Duke University in 1937. Following graduation, Nixon practiced law in Whittier, worked briefly in 1942 with the federal Office of Price Administration, and saw World War II service with the navy in the Pacific. In 1946 and 1948, he won election on the California Republican ticket to a seat in the U.S. House of Representatives, achieving national notoriety as a member of the House Committee on Un-American Activities. Elected to the Senate in 1950, he became Eisenhower's vice-presidential running mate in 1952. In the wake of charges he had benefited personally and illegally from a fund raised by wealthy supporters, and the demand of some that he withdraw from the ticket, he instead made an aggressive and politically effective televised defense against the charges in his famous "Checkers" speech. The Eisenhower-Nixon ticket won election by a decisive margin that year and again in 1956. As a 1960 presidential candidate, Nixon lost a close contest with Democrat John F. Kennedy. Two years later, after also losing a California gubernatorial bid, he bitterly announced his retirement from politics. In 1968, however, Nixon was back in the national arena, winning a close election against Democrat Hubert H. Humphrey. During the campaign he vowed to appoint to the federal bench "strict constructionists"—judges who would interpret the Constitution's meaning rather than "create" rights under the guise of judicial interpretation, especially in cases involving the claims of criminal suspects and defendants. In his first term, Nixon had the opportunity not only to select Warren Burger as the Supreme Court's chief justice but also to fill three additional vacancies on the high bench. When Nixon asserted executive privilege in refusing to disclose tape recordings and other evidence of his cover-up of presidential involvement in the 1972 Watergate break-in, the Supreme Court held that the president's general claim to confidentiality must yield to the Watergate special prosecutor's demonstrated need for the evidence sought. Facing certain impeachment and conviction in the Congress in the wake of his compliance with the Court's ruling, on August 9, 1974, Nixon became the first president in the nation's history to resign from that office. In subsequent years he was gradually able to restore his reputation to a degree, becoming something of an elder statesman. He died in 1994.

Office of Legal Counsel

The U.S. Justice Department's Office of Legal Counsel, headed by an assistant attorney general, advises the president and attorney general with respect to constitutional and other questions confronting the president's administration. Rehnquist was in charge of that office in the Nixon administration until his appointment to the Supreme Court. As a result, he was a prominent proponent before congressional committees of administration policies claimed to violate civil liberties, including military surveillance of persons present at antiwar demonstrations.

Presidential Recordings and Materials
Preservation Act (1975)

Following his resignation from the presidency under threat of impeachment, Nixon entered into an agreement with the federal administrator of general services that provided for storage near his California home of an estimated 42 million pages of documents and 880 tape recordings from his years in the White House. Under the agreement, neither Nixon nor the General Services Administration could gain access to the materials without the other's consent. For a three-year period, the ex-president could not withdraw any original writing but could make and withdraw copies of materials in the collection. After that initial three years, he would have been permitted to withdraw any material except tape recordings. Nixon further agreed that he would not withdraw any original tape recordings for five years and make copies of tapes only with the consent of the GSA administrator. After the five-year period lapsed, the administrator would have been allowed to destroy whatever tapes the former president designated, and all the tapes were to be destroyed at Nixon's death or after ten years, whichever occurred first. Shortly after the agreement became public, Congress adopted and President Ford signed into law the Presidential Recordings and Materials Preservation Act. That statute directed the GSA administrator to take custody of the Nixon presidential materials for screening by government archivists. Material of a personal and private nature was to be returned to the ex-president. The rest was to be preserved and made available for use in judicial proceedings, subject to whatever legal claims the government or "any person" might invoke. The GSA administrator was also to promulgate regulations governing public access to some of the materials, and those provisions were to take into consideration seven guidelines, including the need to protect any person's opportunity to assert legal or constitutional rights or privileges and to return private and personal family materials to the former president. In *Nixon v. Administrator of General Services* (1977), the Supreme Court, over the dissents of Chief Justice Burger and Justice Rehnquist, rejected Nixon's claims that the statute violated the separation of powers doctrine or presidential privilege, infringed on his privacy and First Amendment associational rights, and constituted a bill of attainder (that is, legislative punishment without benefit of a trial).

Reagan, Ronald W.

One of the most popular yet controversial presidents of the modern era, Ronald W. Reagan was born in Tampico, Illinois, in 1911. Following graduation from Eureka College in 1932, he worked as a sports announcer in Des Moines, Iowa, then in 1937 began a lengthy career in motion pictures. A liberal Democrat during most of his Hollywood years, Reagan served as president of the Screen Actors Guild in 1947–1952 and 1959–1960. Never able to gain more than second-lead status in major productions, he saw his entertainment career decline precipitously in the 1950s, when he was reduced largely to lead roles in westerns and other minor titles, a job as host for the low-budget western television series *Death Valley Days*, and a mercifully brief stint in a Las Vegas lounge act with a former film costar—a chimpanzee. The General Electric corporation came to his rescue, offering Reagan the opportunity to host its popular *GE Theater* television series and serve as national spokesman for the company, its products, and a "free-enterprise" philosophy. Remolding himself into a conservative, Reagan proved to be not only an effective pitchman for conservative corporate causes but a promising prospect for elective office. Elected California's governor in 1966 and 1970, he won a landslide victory over incumbent president Jimmy Carter in the 1980 presidential election. Easily reelected in 1984, Reagan primarily pursued a policy of tax cuts, cutbacks in government social programs, and a major build-up in defense spending. The tax reductions were expected to produce increased spending, earnings, and thus larger tax revenues. But although the nation was enjoying its sixth consecutive year of economic prosperity when Reagan left office, the tax cuts also produced massive increases in the federal deficit during his White House years—a trend that would not end until the Clinton administration. During his administration Reagan was able to name nearly half of all federal judges, including Chief Justice Rehnquist and three associate justices, among them O'Connor, appointed in 1981, during Chief Justice Burger's tenure. More aggressively than any of his predecessors, he also pursued an intense but only partially successful campaign to secure the reversal or weakening of Warren and Burger Court civil liberties precedents. More than 100 Reagan administration officials left office amid allegations of criminal wrongdoing. The president and his top aides faced a major crisis in 1986–1987, moreover, when it was revealed that the United States secretly and illegally sold weapons to Iran in exchange for the release of U.S. hostages in Lebanon, then used some of the proceeds from the arms sales to aid, again illegally, the Contra rebellion against the government of Nicaragua. The popular and aging president escaped impeachment proceedings, but a number of his top aides were forced to resign and face criminal prosecution for their part in the Iran-Contra scandal. At this writing the former president is in the advanced stages of Alzheimer's disease, symptoms of which apparently first appeared while he was still in the White House.

Reynolds, William Bradford

The assistant attorney general in charge of the Reagan Justice Department's civil rights division, William Bradford Reynolds was born in Bridgeport, Connecticut, in 1942. His mother was a member of the Du Pont family, and his father was head of the Du Pont Company's patent and trademark division. After prep school at Phillips Academy, Reynolds attended Yale University, graduating in 1964. He received a law degree from Vanderbilt in 1967 and became an associate with Sullivan and Cromwell in New York, one of the nation's most prestigious firms. In 1970 he joined the staff of U.S. solicitor general Erwin N. Griswold, remaining in that position until 1973, when he joined a prominent Washington firm specializing in commercial litigation. Soon interested in returning to government, Reynolds made an unsuccessful bid for a job in the Justice Department's civil rights division during the Carter administration. When other candidates for the post of assistant attorney general for civil rights in the Reagan Justice Department proved too controversial, Reynolds got the position. The civil rights division is responsible for enforcing federal statutes and executive orders forbidding discrimination in voting, education, employment, housing, credit, public accommodations, and public facilities, as well as in institutions and programs receiving federal funds. Like President Reagan's first and second attorneys general, William French Smith and Edwin Meese III, Reynolds from the beginning vigorously opposed racial quotas in hiring and university admissions, as well as court-ordered busing to achieve school desegregation. He played a key role, moreover, in the administration's decision to reverse an eleven-year-old Internal Revenue Service policy and reinstate tax exemptions for racially discriminatory private schools, based on the argument that the IRS lacked statutory authority to deny tax-exempt status to otherwise eligible schools merely because of their discriminatory admissions and related policies. But more than 200 civil rights division employees, including well over half its lawyers, signed a letter of protest to Reynolds, and the Supreme Court, over Justice Rehnquist's lone dissent, upheld the IRS's action. When Congress was considering a twenty-year extension of the 1965 Voting Rights Act, including a provision forbidding any state or county election practice that resulted in the denial or dilution of the right to vote on account of race or color, Reynolds spoke for the administration in opposing the measure before a Senate subcommittee. Only practices with a discriminatory intent, he argued, should be prohibited. A compromise bill was eventually adopted, but disputes over its meaning and constitutional validity have continued in a variety of voting rights suits. Congressional critics regularly complained, moreover, of the slow pace with which the division pursued voting rights claims. As late as two years into Reagan's first term, the Justice Department also had not filed a single school desegregation suit, and the sizable number of division staff lawyers who resigned in protest charged, among other things, that Reynolds had no program for enforcing laws to end discrimination against women or protect the rights of institutionalized persons, including mental patients. Reynolds was also drawn into the Iran-Contra scandal. When he delayed several days in alerting the FBI and the Justice Department's criminal division about a memorandum he found indicating that proceeds from the administration's illegal arms sales to Iran had been illegally diverted to Contra rebels in Nicaragua, Reynolds's critics suggested that his lag might have been calculated to give Lieutenant Colonel Oliver North and others involved in the conspiracy time to destroy relevant documents. Earlier, when Edwin Meese replaced William French Smith as attorney general, President Reagan, at Meese's suggestion, nominated Reynolds for the position of associate attorney general, with authority over all divisions dealing with noncriminal matters. But the Senate Judiciary Committee refused to recommend Reynolds's confirmation by a vote of 10–8 after the nominee was obliged on four occasions to apologize to the committee for giving inaccurate or misleading testimony with respect to his civil rights record. In 1987 Reynolds became counselor to Attorney General Meese. In that capacity he played a major role in the abortive efforts to secure Senate approval for President Reagan's nominations of Robert H. Bork and Douglas Ginsburg to the Supreme Court. Particularly since Meese was obliged to devote considerable attention to defending himself against possible criminal indictments, Reynolds was also in many ways the real head of the department during the latter days of Meese's tenure.

Richardson, Elliot L.

Appointed to several cabinet posts during the Nixon administration, Elliot L. Richardson would be best known for his decision to resign as Richard M. Nixon's attorney general rather than comply with the president's directive to fire Archibald Cox, the first special prosecutor appointed to investigate the Watergate scandal. Richardson, a descendant of early New England settlers, was born in Boston in 1920, the son of an eminent physician and Harvard medical school professor. He received his undergraduate degree from Harvard in 1941, but after a short time in law school there entered the army for World War II service. During the war he took part in the Normandy landing and developed an impressive military record, earning a Bronze Star and two Purple Hearts. Returning to Harvard in 1945 to complete his law studies, Richardson became editor of the law review and graduated with honors. Following clerkships with federal appeals court judge Learned Hand and Supreme Court justice Felix Frankfurter, he joined a venerable Boston firm but would devote much of his career to public service. After a year as aide to a Massachusetts senator in 1953–1954, he returned to private practice again, but in 1957 President Eisenhower made him an assistant secretary in the Department of Health, Education, and Welfare (HEW). He remained in that position until 1959, when Eisenhower named him U.S. attorney for Massachusetts, a post in which he earned a reputation as a vigorous prosecutor. In 1962, a year after returning yet again to his Boston firm, he lost a bid to become the Republican candidate for state attorney general. But in 1964 he was elected lieutenant governor of Massachusetts, taking an active role in assisting the governor to coordinate the state's health, education, and welfare programs. In 1969 he became undersecretary of state in the Nixon administration, where he was soon the department's most influential voice at the White House. As HEW secretary, which Nixon named him the next year, he was an articulate advocate for the administration's proposal to establish a guaranteed minimum family income. But while the plan passed in the House, filibusters prevented its coming to a vote in the Senate. In 1973 Richardson served briefly as secretary of defense before being appointed attorney general later that year, replacing Richard G. Kleindienst, a casualty of the Watergate investigation. When Watergate special prosecutor Archibald Cox secured a court order requiring President Nixon to make tape recordings and other documents available to the Watergate grand jury, the president ordered Richardson to fire Cox. Rather than comply, Richardson resigned as attorney general, thereby distancing himself from the developing scandal that would eventually drive Nixon from office.

Saxbe, William B.

William B. Saxbe became the Nixon administration's fourth attorney general. Born in Ohio in 1916, Saxbe received an undergraduate degree from Ohio State University in 1940. During service with the armed forces in World War II and the Korean conflict, he achieved the rank of colonel. While studying law at Ohio State, from which he graduated in 1948, Saxbe was elected to the first of four terms in the state house of representatives, the last as house speaker. After several years in private practice and as owner of a cattle farm, he won election as Ohio's attorney general, serving in that capacity for eight years. Although a Republican, he enjoyed the support of organized labor, based on his opposition to "right to work" laws. Although sympathetic to a number of Warren Court rulings, including decisions expanding the right to counsel, Saxbe generally assumed a conservative stance on capital punishment and other criminal justice issues as Ohio's chief law enforcement officer. In 1968 he won election to the U.S. Senate against a liberal Democrat. Although something of a maverick, his Senate voting record was largely conservative; he opposed the cut-off of funds for the Vietnam War, for example, and supported authority for police to conduct "no knock" searches.

Saxbe was a frequent critic of the Nixon administration, including the president and his top aides. But Nixon selected Saxbe to replace Attorney General Richardson, and Saxbe promised senators during confirmation proceedings that he would not attempt to interfere with court or impeachment proceedings growing out of the president's involvement in the Watergate scandal. Following Nixon's resignation, Saxbe continued briefly as attorney general under President Gerald R. Ford but was soon replaced by Edward Levi, who held the position for the balance of President Ford's tenure.

Smith, William French

President Ronald Reagan's first attorney general was born in New Hampshire in 1917. Smith was raised in Boston, where the main offices of the telephone company his father headed were located. When William was six, his father died. Traveling extensively with his mother in his youth, Smith developed an attraction for California. After completing an undergraduate degree at Berkeley in 1939 and a Harvard law degree in 1942, Smith served with the naval reserves during World War II, then joined an influential Los Angeles firm with a lucrative corporate clientele, ultimately becoming a senior partner and head of its labor department. Smith remained with the firm thirty-four years. In 1963 he met Ronald Reagan. Like many other wealthy Californians, he was impressed with Reagan's message of support for private enterprise and concerns about the growing concentration of power in Washington, particularly federal intrusion on business and industry. When Reagan made his successful bid for governor in 1966, Smith was one of his principal advisers and fundraisers. As a member and chair of the University of California system's board of regents, to which the governor appointed him in 1968, he took a strong stance against campus antiwar demonstrators, supported Reagan's efforts to cut the university's budget, and resisted demands it divorce itself from nuclear weapons research and connections with corporations doing business with the proapartheid government of South Africa. He also played a major role in Reagan's abortive 1976 bid for the Republican presidential nomination, as well as his successful 1980 campaign. As attorney general, Smith developed an extensive program of legislative proposals and administrative regulations to increase crime control, restrict the influx of illegal aliens, and relax enforcement of antitrust law. He also pushed unsuccessfully for repeal of provisions of the 1978 Ethics in Government Act, which authorized a panel of federal judges to select special prosecutors to investigate criminal charges against high-ranking executive officials, including the president, and which the Supreme Court upheld in *Morrison v. Olson* (1988). Like the administration he served, he also vigorously opposed racial hiring and university admissions quotas, court-ordered busing to achieve school desegregation, and an IRS policy denying tax exemptions to racially discriminatory private schools, which the Supreme Court upheld in *Bob Jones University v. United States* (1983).

Solicitor General

The position of solicitor general was first created in 1870, when Congress established the Department of Justice. Third in rank among Justice Department officials after the attorney general and deputy attorney general, the solicitor general is the chief representative of the government and federal law before the Supreme Court, maintaining offices at both the Court and Justice Department. Early solicitors general occasionally tried cases. Kentuckian Benjamin Bristow, the first to hold the office, prosecuted members of the Ku Klux Klan, for example, in highly publicized litigation. For many years, however, the solicitor general has been concerned primarily with government appeals, especially to the Supreme Court. Solicitors have traditionally sought the Court's review only of those cases believed most worthy of consideration. For that reason, the Court has generally been much more likely to grant review in cases the solicitors have brought to the justices than in the average suit—approximately 80 percent of their certiorari petitions, in contrast to only 3 percent submitted by other litigants. Widely viewed as the representatives ultimately of federal law rather than a particular presidential administration's agenda, solicitors general are expected to file a confession of error with the Supreme Court if they conclude that the government won a case in a lower court through error. Administration pressure to pursue its social agenda more aggressively in the Court prompted the resignation of Rex Lee, President Reagan's first solicitor general. Lee's successor, Harvard law professor Charles Fried, was initially a more vigorous advocate for the administration's positions but reverted to the more traditional stance when his early zeal irritated a number of justices.

Thurmond, Strom

The ranking minority member of the Senate Judiciary Committee through the first decade of Chief Justice Burger's tenure, South Carolina Republican Strom Thurmond became the committee's chairman when the Republicans gained control of the Senate in 1981. Thurmond was born in 1902 in Edgefield County, South Carolina. He received a degree in agricultural science and English from Clemson, then taught agriculture and coached athletics at South Carolina high schools for eight years. In 1930, after studying law privately at night under his father's supervision, he passed the state bar examination and joined his father's Edgefield firm. Thurmond served as city and county attorney and in 1933 was elected to the South Carolina senate. In 1938 the state legislature elected him to a circuit judgeship. Serving with the army in Europe and the Pacific during World War II, he took part in the Normandy invasion and earned five battle stars and other service medals. At the time of his discharge in 1946, he held the rank of lieutenant colonel. He retired from the military reserves in 1960 with the rank of major general. The year of his discharge from World War II service,

Thurmond ran a populist campaign against the state's long-entrenched political machine, winning the Democratic nomination for governor in a field of eleven primary opponents, tantamount to election in South Carolina at that time. Initially pursuing a liberal course, the state's new chief executive secured increased funds for health and education, including African American schools; led a successful campaign to abolish the poll tax; and backed a fair minimum wage. But when President Harry S. Truman integrated the armed forces and pushed for federal antilynching legislation, an end to the poll tax as a voter requirement, and a ban on employment discrimination, Thurmond became the presidential candidate of the States' Rights, or Dixiecrat, Party, carrying four Deep South states in the 1948 election. In 1950 he challenged incumbent U.S. senator Olin D. Johnston for the Democratic nomination, with the candidates stooping to new lows in demagogic campaign rhetoric in attempting to convince white voters of their zeal for segregation. He lost that race, but when South Carolina's other senator, Burnet R. Maybank, died in 1954 and the state Democratic Party denied Thurmond the nomination, Thurmond mounted a vigorous and victorious write-in campaign for the Senate. In 1956 he resigned his seat to run for a full six-year term without, as he had promised, the advantage of incumbency. He won that election handily and repeated reelections by large margins. For years, Senator Thurmond was an aggressive opponent of civil rights legislation, establishing the dubious record in one of those battles for the most long-winded filibuster in the Senate's history (twenty-four hours, eighteen minutes). Largely on the basis of his opposition to the civil rights policies of the national Democrats, he broke with the party in 1964, becoming a Republican and supporter of conservative Arizona senator Barry M. Goldwater's futile presidential campaign that year. With the passage of the 1965 Voting Rights Act and substantial increases in black voter registration, however, Thurmond gradually began to moderate his racial image. In 1978, for example, he backed a constitutional amendment that, had it passed, would have given predominantly African American Washington, D.C., full representation in Congress. He also supported establishment of a national holiday in honor of slain civil rights leader Martin Luther King Jr. In 1968, moreover, he had endorsed the more moderate Richard M. Nixon over conservative Ronald Reagan for the Republican presidential nomination and also actively opposed the third-party candidacy that year of segregationist Alabama governor George C. Wallace. In 1980 he threw his support to John Connally of Texas rather than Governor Reagan. A longtime member of the Senate Judiciary Committee, Thurmond became committee chair in 1981, following the Republican takeover of the Senate and White House in the 1980 elections. On the committee he was a strong proponent of the death penalty and frequent critic of Supreme Court rulings, especially those expanding the rights of criminal suspects and defendants—a stance regularly reflected in his interrogation of judicial nominees.

Vietnam War

Vietnam in Southeast Asia was the principal site for the most protracted and frustrating military campaign in U.S. history. At the end of World War II, Communist guerrillas under Ho Chi Minh overthrew a Japanese-sponsored regime in Vietnam headed by Bao Dai. For nearly a decade after the war, France sought to regain its former colonial control over the region but met a final defeat at Dienbienphu in 1954. Under the terms of the cease-fire agreement, France withdrew from North Vietnam, with the Communists gaining control of that territory and establishing a capital at Hanoi, while Ngo Dinh Diem became president of the government of South Vietnam in Saigon. But beginning as early as 1954, North Vietnam attempted to win control of the south. By 1964 North Vietnamese forces, with Soviet and Chinese arms support, were making an intensive effort, and northern forces were stationed along the South Vietnamese border in Laos and Cambodia. The previous year, moreover, a military coup had toppled the Diem regime, and in 1964 the United States began air strikes against North Vietnam. The next year the raids escalated, and U.S. troops began taking part in ground combat. U.S. troop strength reached over half a million by 1969. President Nixon ordered a series of reductions in force beginning in June of that year. But U.S. bombings were resumed and intensified in 1972–1973. Representatives of North and South Vietnam and the United States signed a cease-fire in 1973. It was never implemented, and in the spring of 1975 the Saigon regime surrendered to the North Vietnamese. Critics contended that in the absence of a formal congressional declaration of war, U.S. involvement in the conflict was unconstitutional. But the Supreme Court persistently avoided a ruling on the issue, and lower courts either dismissed such claims as political questions inappropriate for judicial resolution or found legislative endorsement of the war in various congressional statutes and resolutions.

Voting Rights Act (1965, as amended)

Acting under its power to enforce through appropriate legislation the Fifteenth Amendment's ban on racial discrimination in the suffrage, Congress in this statute significantly strengthened previous federal voting rights legislation. One provision of the 1965 Voting Rights Act suspended all literacy and related voter tests in states or counties with low voter registration or voting rates in the 1964 presidential election. The officials of such areas were presumed guilty of discrimination in voter registration but could reinstate their election tests if they convinced the U.S. District Court for the District of Columbia the regulations had not been used for discriminatory purposes. Another provision of the law permitted the appointment of federal voter registrars to add to the voting rolls of such areas the names of persons who met the qualifications required of white applicants but might otherwise be denied registration on account of race. Under its most controversial section, areas with a past history of voter discrimination were forbidden to adopt new election laws without first securing approval, or "pre-clearance," from the U.S. attorney general or the federal district court in Washington. Even though the Warren Court had upheld a validly administered literacy test in 1959, a majority in *South Carolina v. Katzenbach* (1966) sustained the ban on voter tests and all other provisions of the Voting Rights Act, emphasizing the broad authority of Congress within the scope of its lawmaking powers. In *Mobile v. Bolden* (1980), the Burger Court limited the law to intentional discrimination rather than applying it also to regulations that had a racially disparate effect, upholding a city's system of at-large elections of city commissioners even though it resulted in an all-white commission. In its 1982 extension of the Voting Rights Act, Congress adopted an effects standard for reviewing alleged violations of the law, partially overturning the Court's interpretation of the law.

War Powers Act (1973)

The Constitution confers on Congress the power to declare war but also provides that the president shall be commander in chief of U.S. military forces, thereby embodying the principle of civilian control of the military. In their capacity as commander in chief, presidents traditionally have assumed authority to commit troops to combat in the absence of congressional authorization. Through repeated military appropriations and resolutions, Congress arguably demonstrated its support of presidential war making during the Vietnam War. But as the nation became increasingly weary of that protracted, costly, and seemingly hopeless conflict, Congress attempted to assert its own military prerogatives. In the War Powers Act (actually a joint resolution), Congress required the president to consult with Congress if at all "possible" before deploying forces abroad. Within forty-eight hours after a deployment and periodically thereafter, the president was to submit to Congress a report of the circumstances and likely duration of a troop commitment, then terminate the deployment within sixty days unless Congress specifically approved the action or the president requested a thirty-day extension to protect the safety of the forces involved. Congress could also direct withdrawal of troops at any time through adoption of a concurrent resolution that would not be subject to presidential veto. Presidents, with the exception of Jimmy Carter, have complained that the act interferes with presidential war powers in violation of the separation of powers doctrine; other critics have charged that the act, whatever its intended purpose, actually delegates congressional military powers unconstitutionally to the executive. Particularly as a result of numerous loopholes in its provisions, the act's enforcement has been weak. On the grounds that the matter is a political question, lower courts have declined to review alleged violations of its provisions, and the Supreme Court has yet to confront the issue.

Warren, Earl

Chief justice (1953–1969) during one of the most liberal-activist and controversial periods in the Supreme Court's history, Earl Warren was born in Los Angeles in 1891 but raised in Bakersfield, where his father was a mechanic on the Southern Pacific Railroad. After undergraduate work and law school at the University of California at Berkeley, followed by army service in World War I, Warren began an eighteen-year tenure in the Alameda County district attorney's office, thirteen as district attorney. In that capacity he developed a reputation as a tough prosecutor but also secured a public defender for indigent defendants and appeared genuinely concerned about the rights of the accused. Warren won election as California's attorney general in 1942. His tenure in that post will be marked mainly, and unfortunately, by his demands for the World War II evacuation of Japanese Americans from the West Coast. But he was a popular, three-term governor and in 1948 was the Republican vice-presidential candidate on the losing Dewey ticket. More conservative state Republicans, including Nixon and California senator William F. Knowland, were anxious to see the popular, politically moderate Warren out of California politics. When Eisenhower won the White House for the GOP in 1952, with Nixon as his running mate, Warren was destined for a position in the new administration. Chief Justice Fred M. Vinson died in 1953, and the new president, with some misgivings, named Warren to the Court's center seat. After Warren and another Ike appointee, New Jersey Democrat William J. Brennan, forged liberal records on the Court, Eisenhower complained that their appointments were among the worst mistakes of his presidency. Whatever the president's feelings, however, Warren and his Court must count among the most influential in the nation's history. The Warren Court had a profound impact on the scope of constitutional liberties in virtually every field, especially during the last seven years of Warren's tenure. He died in 1974, five years after his retirement and President Nixon's appointment of the more conservative Warren Burger as chief justice.

Watergate Scandal

The Watergate scandal amounted to the most serious violation of public trust by a presidential administration in the nation's history. Named for the 1972 White House–directed break-in at the Democratic National Committee headquarters in the Watergate office complex in Washington, D.C., the scandal also involved efforts by President Nixon and top members of his administration to cover-up presidential involvement in the break-in; bribe-taking; the payment of hush money; misuse of the FBI and other agencies for illegal partisan purposes; income tax fraud; an organized campaign of "dirty tricks" against political opponents; illegal campaign contributions; and use of legitimate campaign funds for illegal purposes, among other egregious violations of law and ethical propriety. Following the Supreme Court's ruling in *United*

States v. Nixon (1974) that President Nixon would have to release to the Watergate grand jury and courts tape recordings and other documents relevant to the president's involvement in the affair, Nixon became the first president to resign from office. Earlier Spiro T. Agnew, Nixon's first vice-president, had been forced to accept a plea bargain in which he agreed to plead no contest to a minor income tax count and resign from his office in exchange for escaping prosecution and jail time on more serious charges. Many cabinet officers, presidential assistants, and other Nixon administration officials were also convicted on criminal charges growing out of the scandal. President Gerald R. Ford's decision, one month after Nixon's resignation, to grant the former president a full and absolute pardon for any and all federal crimes he may have committed during his presidential tenure contributed, moreover, to Ford's defeat in the 1976 election. As a result of the scandal, Congress also enacted meaningful campaign finance regulations. In *Buckley v. Valeo* (1976), however, the Supreme Court invalidated several key provisions of the legislation on First Amendment and other grounds.

Chronology

1969   Appointment of Warren Burger by President Richard M. Nixon to replace Earl Warren as chief justice of the Supreme Court.

1970   Nomination of Clement Haynsworth of South Carolina by President Nixon to replace Justice Abe Fortas; confirmation defeated in the Senate.

Nomination of G. Harrold Carswell of Florida by President Nixon to replace Justice Fortas; confirmation defeated in the Senate.

Angry announcement by President Nixon that the Senate would never confirm a southern nominee and that he would have to look elsewhere for his next nomination.

Nomination of Harry A. Blackmun of Minnesota, Chief Justice Burger's childhood friend, to replace Justice Fortas; confirmation by the Senate.

Dandridge v. Williams, upholding a family ceiling on welfare benefits and rejecting the claim, suggested in a Warren Court ruling, that the Constitution includes a fundamental right to the necessities of life, government discrimination in access to which would be subjected to strict judicial review.

Hadley v. Junior College District, holding that districts from which local governing bodies are elected must be nearly equal in population to satisfy the requirements of equal protection.

In Re Winship, holding proof of guilt beyond a reasonable doubt in criminal cases, including juvenile proceedings, to be a requirement of fundamental fairness implicit in due process.

Williams v. Florida, rejecting the claim that a twelve-member jury is required by due process or the Constitution's guarantee to trial by an impartial jury.

1971   Nomination of Lewis F. Powell by President Nixon to replace Justice Hugo L. Black; confirmation by the Senate.

Nomination of William H. Rehnquist by President Nixon to replace Justice John Marshall Harlan; confirmation by the Senate.

Cohen v. California, overturning on First Amendment grounds criminal prosecution for the mere public use of an offensive epithet.

Graham v. Richardson, declaring classifications based on alienage inherently suspect and striking down a law limiting welfare benefits to citizens.

Griggs v. Duke Power Co., upholding employment discrimination provisions of Title VII of the 1964 Civil Rights Act, as amended, that forbade employment practices with a racially disparate impact, even without a showing of invidious intent, if the practice in question (in this case a test for job applicants) was irrelevant to job performance.

Harris v. New York, holding that confessions secured in violation of the warnings police are required to give suspects prior to custodial questioning under *Miranda v. Arizona* (1966) could be used to impeach or challenge the accused's trial testimony.

Lemon v. Kurtzman, overturning government assistance to religious schools and holding that in order to withstand challenge under the establishment clause, a law affecting religion must have a secular purpose and primary effect that neither advances nor inhibits religion, while also avoiding an excessive entanglement between church and state.

New York Times Co. v. United States, subjecting prior restraints on the press to a heavy burden of justification and overturning the Nixon administration's efforts to secure an injunction against further publication of *The Pentagon Papers*.

Palmer v. Thompson, rejecting equal protection challenges to the decision of Jackson, Mississippi, to close all its swimming pools rather than comply with a court's desegregation order, the majority concluding that the city had no constitutional obligation to operate swimming pools and refusing to probe the underlying psychological motives that may have prompted the city's decision to close its pools.

Reed v. Reed, overturning a gender classification for the first time and declaring a violation of equal protection a law giving men preference over women in being selected to administer the estates of deceased persons.

Swann v. Charlotte-Mecklenburg Board of Education, affirming broad authority for trial judges to convert school systems with a history of de jure (or official) segregation into unitary systems, including the power to order the busing of students and impose racial quotas for the placement of students and staff as an appropriate means of beginning the desegregation process.

Tilton v. Richardson, upholding federal grants to religious colleges and universities for the construction of secular facilities and extending greater deference to such assistance than to that for primary and secondary religious schools on the ground that religious colleges are less sectarian, and their students less impressionable, than their primary and secondary counterparts.

Wyman v. James, holding that welfare home visits did not constitute searches subject to the Constitution's ban on unreasonable search and seizure.

1972   *Apodaca v. Oregon*, upholding nonunanimous jury verdicts in state criminal cases while reaffirming precedents requiring unanimous federal verdicts.

Argersinger v. Hamlin, extending the right of indigent defendants to court-appointed trial counsel to any criminal case in which a jail sentence of any length is imposed.

Branzburg v. Hayes, rejecting the First Amendment claim of newspersons to a testimonial privilege from grand jury appearances on the ground that the impact of such testimony on their confidential informants and the free flow of news was entirely too speculative to support such a claim, that the press had thrived in the past without a testimonial privilege, and that the prosecution of crime was more important than its coverage by the press.

Eisenstadt v. Baird, overturning on equal protection and privacy grounds a law forbidding single, but not married, persons to obtain contraceptives.

Furman v. Georgia, invalidating on cruel and unusual punishment and due process grounds a state statute that left imposition of the death penalty to the unbridled discretion of judges and juries.

Gravel v. United States, extending legislative aides the free expression rights granted members of Congress by the Constitution's speech and debate clause but refusing to include a senator's private publication of *The Pentagon Papers* within the legislative functions protected under the clause.

Kirby v. Illinois, rejecting the presence of counsel for suspects at preindictment lineups, thus narrowing an earlier ruling requiring a lawyer at postindictment lineups.

Moose Lodge v. Irvis, rejecting the claim that a private club's refusal to serve a member's guest at its bar amounted to unconstitutional "state action," even though the club had a state liquor license and was subject to other regulations.

Wisconsin v. Yoder, exempting Amish children from compulsory high school education on the ground Amish parents considered high school a serious threat to their faith, were willing to send their children through eight grades of formal schooling, and provided an adequate alternative to high school through home training for their children.

1973   *Broadrick v. Oklahoma*, upholding restrictions on the political activities of civil servants and concluding that laws affecting expressive conduct could be struck down on their face only if they suffered from "substantial overbreadth."

Cupp v. Murphy, sustaining the warrantless seizure of evidence (in this case, skin scrapings beneath the suspect's fingernails) based on probable cause and exigent circumstances justifying quick police action.

Doe v. Bolton, striking down a statute requiring all abortions to be performed in hospitals, approved by a hospital committee and other physicians, and available only to Georgia residents.

Frontiero v. Richardson, invalidating a military regulation granting married servicemen an automatic spouse dependency allowance while requiring married servicewomen to establish their spouse's dependency, with a plurality contending that gender classifications, like those based on race or color, were constitutionally "suspect" and subject to strict judicial scrutiny.

Keyes v. School District, sustaining a desegregation order covering an entire school district even though de jure (or official) segregation was found only in a portion of the district.

Miller v. California, enlarging governmental authority over the distribution of obscenity, which the Court defined as material that appealed to a prurient interest in sex, depicted or described sexual conduct in a patently offensive manner, and lacked serious literary, artistic, political, or scientific value, though the Court also permitted local judges and juries to draw on local community standards in reaching a decision in obscenity cases.

Paris Adult Theatre v. Slaton, upholding criminal penalties for the exhibition of obscene films in adults-only theaters as rationally related to the prevention of sex crimes and other legitimate governmental interests.

Roe v. Wade, holding for the first time that the right of privacy implicit in the liberty protected by the Constitution's due process guarantee encompasses a woman's decision with her physician to abort a pregnancy, that this fundamental right could be restricted only to further a compelling state interest, that no such interest justified abortion controls during the first trimester (roughly three months) of a pregnancy, that the state's important interest in the mother's health justified reasonable regulation of abortion procedures in the second trimester, and that the compelling interest in protecting the potential life of a viable fetus (that is, a fetus capable of surviving independently of the mother's womb) empowered the state to prohibit nontherapeutic (or non-health-related) abortions during the last trimester of the pregnancy.

San Antonio Indep. School Dist. v. Rodriguez, upholding a state scheme for financing public schools largely through local property taxes, despite substantial disparities in per pupil expenditures from district to district; subjecting discriminatory laws claimed to interfere with fundamental rights to strict judicial review only if they infringed upon a right expressly or implicitly guaranteed in the Constitution; and rejecting the claim of a fundamental right to an equal education.

Schneckloth v. Bustamonte, holding that the voluntariness of a suspect's consent to a warrantless police search was to be determined through a review of the totality of the circumstances in which the search took place, that a suspect's ignorance of the right to refuse consent was merely one factor to be considered, and that suspects were not entitled to be informed by police of their right to decline consent.

United States v. Robinson, sustaining warrantless searches of persons incident to their arrest, even for traffic violations or other petty offenses.

1974   *Cleveland Bd. of Education v. LaFleur,* striking down on due process grounds an early mandatory unpaid leave requirement for pregnant public school teachers, based on an irrebuttable presumption they were unable to perform their duties effectively after the designated date.

DeFunis v. Odegaard, dismissing as moot (that is, already resolved by circumstances) a challenge to an affirmative action law school admissions program on the ground that the white petitioner had been ordered admitted by a lower court and was in his final term when the Supreme Court reviewed his claim.

Eaton v. City of Tulsa, overturning a defendant's contempt of court conviction on the ground that his conversational use of a vulgarity during his trial had created no clear and imminent danger to the orderly administration of justice.

Gertz v. Welch, Inc., refusing to extend the knowing or reckless falsehood libel rule, first announced in *New York Times v. Sullivan* (1964), beyond public officials and public figures to suits for compensatory (as opposed to punitive) damages brought by private persons involved in issues of public interest.

Jenkins v. Georgia, overturning a theater manager's obscenity conviction and emphasizing that the judiciary had the final authority to determine whether erotic expression possessed sufficient literary, artistic, political, or scientific value to escape the obscenity label.

Lehman v. City of Shaker Heights, rejecting the claim that municipal buses were "public forums" with First Amendment obligations and upholding a transit system's refusal to sell advertising space on its buses to a political candidate.

Memorial Hospital v. Maricopa County, striking down a one-year residency requirement for nonemergency medical services on the ground the regulation inhibited the fundamental right to interstate travel.

Miami Herald Publishing Co. v. Tornillo, invalidating a state statute requiring newspapers to provide free and equal reply space to politicians they criticized, with the Court declaring that the law imposed a chilling effect on protected expression and interfered unduly with editorial discretion.

Michigan v. Tucker, holding that statements secured by police from suspects through interrogation conducted in violation of *Miranda v. Arizona* (1966) could nevertheless be used to obtain other evidence against a suspect, such as the name of a prosecution witness.

Milliken v. Bradley, striking down a federal district court's interdistrict school desegregation decree ordering the busing of students between the predominantly African American Detroit school district, which had a history of de jure (or official) segregation, and predominantly white suburban districts in which only de facto segregation was present, the majority concluding that desegregation orders must be confined to the area in which the constitutional violation had occurred, absent evidence of collusion among the districts to maintain segregation.

Parker v. Levy, emphasizing that the First Amendment has a decidedly more limited reach in the military than in the civilian community and sustaining the application of several vaguely worded military regulations to an army officer who urged soldiers to refuse to take part in the Vietnam War.

Pell v. Procunier and *Saxbe v. Washington Post Co.*, denying the media a right to face-to-face interviews with prison inmates of their choice.

Richardson v. Ramirez, sustaining the authority of states to deny the vote to ex-felons as well as current ones, based on the Court's interpretation of a provision of the Fourteenth Amendment providing for reduction in congressional representation for states denying the right to vote to male citizens, except those who had participated "in rebellion, or other crime."

Smith v. Goguen, holding unconstitutionally vague and overbroad a statute prohibiting "contemptuous" treatment of the flag, as applied to a youth who wore a small flag on the seat of his pants.

Spence v. Washington, overturning the conviction for improper flag use of a college student who, at the time of the Cambodian invasion during the Vietnam War, suspended a flag upside down from his window with a peace symbol attached.

United States v. Calandra, holding that the Fourth Amendment exclusionary rule is a judicially created device for deterring police misconduct rather than a constitutional requirement and concluding that the rule's extension to grand jury proceedings would not appreciably enhance its impact as a deterrent.

United States v. Nixon, holding that the doctrine of executive privilege, under which presidents seek to withhold materials from Congress and the courts, is implied in the Constitution and presumptively valid but is not an absolute presidential prerogative and thus must yield in particular cases to overriding competing claims, such as the interest of the courts and special prosecutor in securing presidential tape recordings and other documents relating to the Watergate affair.

United States v. Richardson, narrowly construing the Warren Court ruling in *Flast v. Cohen* (1968) and refusing to grant federal taxpayer or citizen voter standing to a litigant challenging secret congressional funding of the CIA.

1975   Nomination of John Paul Stevens by President Gerald Ford to replace Justice William O. Douglas; confirmation by the Senate.

Bigelow v. Virginia, striking down a state law prohibiting the advertising of abortion services, as applied to an advertisement for a legal New York abortion service, and holding that commercial speech is entitled to First Amendment protection, at least if it conveys information of potential interest to a diverse audience.

Breed v. Jones, extending the guarantee against double jeopardy to juvenile proceedings and reaffirming that juveniles are entitled to fundamentally fair proceedings, although not all the rights enjoyed by the accused in criminal cases.

Cox Broadcasting Corp. v. Cohn, overturning on First Amendment grounds a state statute forbidding publication or broadcast of the names of rape victims even if they appeared in judicial records open to the public.

Erznoznik v. City of Jacksonville, invalidating as unduly broad an ordinance forbidding drive-in theaters with screens visible from public places to display films depicting nudity.

Faretta v. California, upholding the right of defendants to waive their right to counsel and defend themselves at trial, so long as the waiver was intelligently, voluntarily, and knowingly made.

Goss v. Lopez, striking down on due process grounds the suspension of students from school without some sort of hearing.

Train v. City of New York, overturning on statutory grounds President Nixon's use of the impoundment power to limit federal funding for municipal sewers and sewage treatment facilities.

United States v. Brignoni-Ponce, forbidding roving border patrols to stop automobiles for questioning of occupants without reasonable suspicion they were aliens.

Wood v. Strickland, denying a school principal qualified immunity from a damage suit on the ground that he knew, or reasonably should have known, his suspension of a student without a hearing violated due process.

1976   *Buckley v. Valeo,* upholding, among other provisions, sections of the 1974 Federal Election Campaign Act limiting contributions to federal candidates and establishing the Federal Election Commission to oversee compliance with federal campaign finance regulations, while striking down as violations of free speech those provisions of the law limiting independent expenditures in behalf of a candidate and overall expenditures by candidates and their campaigns.

Craig v. Boren, declaring gender classifications quasi-suspect and thus subject to heightened judicial scrutiny and applying that intermediate standard of review to strike down as a denial of equal protection an Oklahoma statute permitting young women to purchase beer at age eighteen while setting twenty-one as the minimum drinking age for males.

Gregg v. Georgia, upholding against cruel and unusual punishment and due process challenge a state death penalty statute for murder that sought to eliminate arbitrariness in the infliction of death sentences by, among other things, provision for separate guilt and penalty hearings, a requirement that a jury or judge find one or more statutorily specified aggravating circumstances in a case before imposing the death penalty, and automatic appeal of all death sentences to the state supreme court, which was obliged to overturn a sentence if that court failed to find an aggravating circumstance or concluded that the punishment inflicted was disproportionate to the sentence ordinarily imposed in such cases.

Hudgens v. NLRB, reversing earlier cases and holding that shopping centers did not constitute "public forums" with First Amendment obligations.

Kelley v. Johnson, assuming some degree of constitutional protection for personal appearance but holding that the freedom accorded police is much more limited than that afforded civilians and sustaining a hair code for police as rationally related to the promotion of morale and making officers more readily identifiable to the public.

Massachusetts Bd. of Retirement v. Murgia, rejecting the claim that age classifications were constitutionally suspect and upholding a requirement that uniformed state police retire at age fifty as rationally related to the state's legitimate interest in assuring the physical preparedness of its uniformed officers.

National League of Cities v. Usery, holding, in a decision overruled in the 1985 *Garcia* case, that a congressional statute extending federal wage and hour regulations to state and local governments and their employees violated principles of federalism, if applied to agencies exercising traditional or integral state functions.

Nebraska Press Association v. Stuart, overturning a trial judge's gag order forbidding publication or broadcast of information implicating the defendant in the crime as an impermissible prior restraint on the press and citing, among other things, the judge's failure to explore less drastic alternative avenues for assuring the accused a fair trial by an impartial jury.

New Orleans v. Dukes, upholding against equal protection challenge an ordinance that banned pushcart vendors from the New Orleans French Quarter but exempted veteran vendors from its coverage, the Court declaring that the discrimination against more recent vendors was rationally related to the city's interest in maintaining the Quarter's traditional atmosphere and emphasizing that economic classifications were entitled to substantial, if not absolute, judicial deference.

Pasadena Bd. of Education v. Spangler, emphasizing that federal courts must lift desegregation decrees once the conversion of dual school systems into unitary systems has been substantially achieved.

Paul v. Davis, rejecting a challenge to police circulation of a list of "known shoplifters" by a person included in the list, although he was never convicted and the charges against him were eventually dismissed, the Court declaring that the police conduct at issue did not constitute sufficient interference with reputational rights to warrant federal court relief.

Planned Parenthood v. Danforth, invalidating an abortion law requiring married women to secure their spouse's consent and giving parents an absolute veto over abortions for unmarried minor daughters.

Roemer v. Board of Public Works, upholding annual state grants for secular purposes to religious colleges and universities.

Runyon v. McCrary, upholding provisions of an 1866 Civil Rights Act granting all persons the same rights as white citizens in contract transactions, as applied to a commercially operated private school that refused to admit minority students.

South Dakota v. Opperman, upholding police authority to inventory impounded vehicles as a means of avoiding theft complaints and to use at trial any evidence discovered during a vehicle inventory.

Stone v. Powell, refusing to extend the Fourth Amendment exclusionary rule to federal habeas corpus proceedings brought by state defendants who had a full and fair opportunity to raise their illegal search and seizure claims at trial and on direct appeal of their convictions.

United States v. Janis, holding that the Fourth Amendment exclusionary rule did not extend to civil trials, even those in which the government was a party.

United States v. Mandujano, holding that the requirements of *Miranda v. Arizona* (1966) did not extend to grand jury proceedings and thus grand jury witnesses, even those who were suspects, were not entitled to the presence of counsel and could not refuse to be questioned during a grand jury hearing, although they could invoke their privilege against compulsory self-incrimination in declining to answer specific questions.

United States v. Martinez-Fuerte, sustaining the stopping of automobiles at fixed checkpoints for brief questioning of occupants about their citizenship, without a warrant or reasonable suspicion they were illegal aliens.

Virginia Bd. of Pharmacy v. Virginia Consumer Council, extending First Amendment protection to commercial speech, absent an overriding justifying interest unrelated to the suppression of expression, and overturning a state law forbidding the advertisement of prescription drug prices.

Washington v. Davis, sustaining against a due process/equal protection challenge a job test for prospective police officers on which minority applicants generally had lower scores than white applicants, the Court holding that an invidious intent, not merely a racially disparate impact, was necessary to establish a constitutional violation.

Woodson v. North Carolina, striking down on cruel and unusual punishment and due process grounds a state statute imposing a mandatory death sentence on defendants convicted of capital crimes, the Court concluding that such a scheme did not allow for consideration of mitigating factors that might justify a lesser sentence for certain defendants and thus was inherently arbitrary.

Young v. American Mini Theatres, upholding an ordinance imposing special zoning requirements on adult bookstores, theaters, and related establishments, the Court emphasizing that the law did not forbid or criminally prosecute such businesses and that such fare was entitled to less constitutional protection than other forms of expression.

1977   *Arlington Heights v. Metropolitan Housing Development Corp.*, sustaining restrictive zoning requirements that limited available housing for low-income persons, the Court declaring that such regulations had not been shown to have a racially invidious intent and thus were not subject to strict judicial review under the equal protection guarantee.

Brewer v. Williams, overturning a defendant's rape/murder conviction on the ground that a policeman's comments about the need to give the victim a "Christian burial," prompting the suspect to lead officers to her body, had amounted to forbidden interrogation in the absence of counsel.

Carey v. Population Services International, overturning on privacy grounds a law forbidding distribution of contraceptives to minors and the advertisement of nonprescription birth control devices.

Coker v. Georgia, striking down the death penalty for rape of an adult as disproportionate to the gravity of the offense.

Linmark Associates v. Township of Willingboro, invalidating an ordinance prohibiting real estate "For Sale" and "Sold" signs as an undue restriction on commercial speech.

Maher v. Roe, holding that indigent women have no more right to government-funded abortions than people generally have a right to funds for the exercise of other constitutional rights, and upholding a state law excluding most abortions from government funding.

Nixon v. Administrator of General Services, sustaining a statute giving the government control over Richard M. Nixon's presidential papers, agreeing that the former president constituted a legitimate class of one whose papers could be subjected to greater control than those of other presidents, and rejecting Nixon's privacy, bill of attainder, separation of powers, and related challenges to the law at issue.

Wolman v. Walter, upholding against establishment clause claims state assistance to religious schools, including textbook loans; the provision of standardized tests; speech, hearing, and psychological services; and guidance and remedial services for religious primary and secondary schools, while striking down their use of public money to purchase instructional materials and equipment, as well as transportation for field trips.

Wooley v. Maynard, overturning on free speech grounds New Hampshire's attempt to require a Jehovah's Witness couple to display the state motto, "Live Free or Die," on their automobile license plate.

1978   *Ballew v. Georgia*, holding that a five-member jury was of insufficient size to assure compliance with the Constitution's requirement of trial by an impartial jury and the due process guarantee.

Butz v. Economou, declaring that cabinet officers are entitled only to qualified rather than absolute immunity from damage suits for misconduct connected with their official duties and thus can be sued if they knowingly violate a person's legal rights or reasonably should have known their conduct was illegal.

FCC v. Pacifica Foundation, sustaining threatened FCC sanctions against a radio station that broadcast a comic monologue, "The Seven Filthy Words," during the day, basing its ruling largely on the easy access of young people to broadcasts.

First Nat. Bank of Boston v. Bellotti, extending free expression rights to corporations that wish to influence votes on election issues not substantially related to the corporation's property, business, or assets.

Foley v. Connelie, upholding a state law limiting service in the state police to citizens, one of a number of rulings creating a public function exception to the Court's holding in *Graham v. Richardson* (1971) that alienage classifications are inherently suspect and subject to strict judicial scrutiny.

Lockett v. Ohio, overturning a state statute limiting the sorts of mitigating factors a jury or judge could consider in deciding whether to impose a death sentence in a given case, the Court concluding that such a restriction was inherently arbitrary.

Marshall v. Barlow's, requiring administrative warrants for health and safety inspectors to search employers' premises.

Regents of the University of California v. Bakke, overturning a medical school's use of a racial quota in admissions but also holding that universities could consider race and other nonmerit factors to further their compelling interest in attracting a diverse student body.

Stump v. Sparkman, reaffirming the absolute immunity from damage suits traditionally accorded judges acting within the scope of their official duties, even for a judge who ordered a young woman's sterilization without her knowledge, at her mother's request.

Zurcher v. Stanford Daily, rejecting press claims to a privilege from police searches of media offices, with the Court essentially citing the reasons used to deny a testimonial privilege in the *Branzburg* case.

1979   *Gannett Co. v. DePasquale*, upholding exclusion of the press from a pretrial hearing on a motion to suppress evidence in a criminal case.

United Steelworkers v. Weber, construing employment discrimination provisions of the 1964 Civil Rights Act to permit a private company, in negotiation with union representatives, to establish a racial hiring quota as a means of correcting the effects of prior employment discrimination in the area.

1980   *Central Hudson Gas v. Public Service Com'n*, announcing that commercial speech enjoys First Amendment protection if it makes a legal offer and is subject to regulation only in furtherance of important governmental interests unrelated to the suppression of expression.

Fullilove v. Klutznick, upholding a federal statute requiring that at least 10 percent of federal funds granted for local public works projects be used to procure services or supplies from minority businesses, with the Court emphasizing that federal affirmative action programs are entitled to considerable judicial deference given broad congressional authority to enforce the Fourteenth Amendment.

Harris v. McRae, sustaining the Hyde amendment to congressional Medicaid appropriations that denied the use of federal funds for most abortions.

Payton v. New York, holding that warrantless arrests based on probable cause are permissible in public places but a warrant is required for routine arrests in the home.

Pruneyard Shopping Center v. Robins, refusing to overturn a state court ruling imposing public forum obligations on shopping centers under its state constitution's First Amendment counterpart, even though the Supreme Court had ultimately rejected such a construction of the First Amendment, with the Court emphasizing that the U.S. Constitution merely established a floor below which individual rights could not be restricted rather than a ceiling on the scope of rights a state could protect under its own constitution.

Rhode Island v. Innis, holding that police expressions of hope that a suspect's discarded gun could be found before handicapped children in the area discovered it, which had prompted the suspect to lead officers to the weapon, did not constitute impermissible interrogation without counsel.

Richmond Newspapers, Inc. v. Virginia, holding that absent a demonstrated overriding interest in closing the proceedings, the people, including the press, had a First Amendment related right to attend criminal trials as a means of assuring both justice and the appearance of justice in the courts.

Stone v. Graham, declaring that the posting of privately financed copies of the Ten Commandments on public school walls constituted state support of religion forbidden by the establishment clause.

1981   Nomination of Sandra Day O'Connor by President Ronald Reagan to replace Justice Potter Stewart; confirmation by the Senate.

Carter v. Kentucky, holding that a trial judge, at the accused's request, must inform jurors that they may draw no adverse inferences of guilt from the defendant's refusal to take the witness stand at trial.

Dames & Moore v. Regan, upholding steps taken by President Jimmy Carter to end the Iranian hostage crisis.

Estelle v. Smith, declaring that the warnings police are required to give suspects prior to custodial questioning under *Miranda v. Arizona* (1966) must also be administered prior to a psychiatric evaluation of an accused.

H. L. v. Matheson, sustaining a law requiring a doctor to inform parents of a minor female before performing an abortion.

Michael M. v. Superior Court, upholding a statutory rape law applicable to males only, based on the rationale that males, unlike females, are unable to become pregnant and thus need the threat of criminal prosecution to inhibit them from having sex with young women.

Rostker v. Goldberg, sustaining male-only registration for the military draft on the ground Congress could reasonably have concluded that males would be more likely than females to be capable of combat.

Thomas v. Review Board, striking down on religious liberty grounds a state's denial of unemployment compensation to a person who quit his job with a manufacturing concern rather than accept transfer to its weapons division.

1982   *Harlow v. Fitzgerald*, holding that presidential aides, unlike presidents, were entitled only to qualified immunity from damage suits for misconduct in the performance of their official duties and thus could be sued if they knowingly violated a person's legal rights or reasonably should have known they were engaging in illegal conduct.

Larkin v. Grendel's Den, Inc., striking down a state law giving churches a veto over issuance of liquor licenses to premises located within 500 feet of their property.

Mississippi University for Women v. Hogan, striking down on equal protection grounds a state university's restriction of its program in nursing to women students only.

New York v. Ferber, upholding state authority to forbid use of minors in sexual performances, whether or not obscene in nature.

Nixon v. Fitzgerald, holding that presidents are absolutely immune from damage suits for misconduct falling within the broad reach of their official duties and basing that judgment largely on the need to assure that presidents will not be inhibited from courageously and aggressively performing the responsibilities of their office, nor distracted from their duties by time-consuming lawsuits.

Plyler v. Doe, striking down a state's denial of schooling to the minor children of illegal alien immigrants.

United States v. Lee, upholding against religious liberty claims federal authority to require Amish employers to pay Social Security and unemployment taxes despite their belief that the payment of taxes was a sin.

United States v. Ross, holding that police can conduct warrantless searches of closed containers in vehicles based on probable cause the vehicle contains evidence of crime.

1983   *Akron v. Akron Center for Reproductive Health*, reaffirming *Roe v. Wade* (1973) and declaring unconstitutional abortion regulations requiring a twenty-four-hour waiting period, performance of all abortions in a hospital after the first three months of a pregnancy, and a doctor's explanation to women seeking abortions of possible adverse physical and emotional consequences.

Bob Jones University v. United States, upholding IRS regulations construed to deny tax-exempt status (and thus tax deductions for donors) to private schools and universities with racially discriminatory admissions and other policies.

INS v. Chadha, holding that the legislative veto, under which the president and other executive branch officials were authorized to issue regulations or take other action subject to a congressional veto, violated provisions of the Constitution requiring laws to be enacted by each house of Congress, then submitted to the president for review and possible veto.

Marsh v. Chambers, rejecting a First Amendment establishment clause challenge to a state's provision of paid legislative chaplains, with the Court emphasizing long acceptance of such practices going back to the earliest days of the republic.

Michigan v. Long, holding that the Supreme Court would abstain from deciding federal constitutional questions raised in an appeal of a state court decision only if the state court's ruling clearly rested on state rather than federal law grounds.

Mueller v. Allen, rejecting an establishment clause challenge to a state's grant of tax deductions for educational expenses to parents of children enrolled in religious as well as public and other private schools.

Planned Parenthood v. Ashcroft, sustaining a requirement of parental consent, or approval by a judge through a judicial bypass arrangement, before an abortion could be performed on a pregnant minor.

Solem v. Helm, striking down as cruel and unusual punishment disproportionate to the offense the imposition of a life sentence without possibility of parole on a defendant under a state recidivism statute for a bad check conviction and six prior convictions for nonviolent offenses, thereby limiting earlier precedents upholding such sentences where the defendant was eligible for parole.

United States v. Grace, upholding a federal statute prohibiting picketing, distributing leaflets, and demonstrating on the grounds of the Supreme Court but striking down application of the law to the sidewalks around the Court.

1984   *Firefighters v. Stotts*, holding that a court order protecting minorities hired under an affirmative action program from being laid off before more senior employees exceeded judicial power under Title VII of the 1964 Civil Rights Act.

Grove City College v. Bell, construing federal civil rights legislation to permit the cutoff of federal funds only to those programs in a federally financed institution (such as its athletic department) that practiced discrimination, not to the entire institution, a construction of the law later overturned by congressional statute.

Hudson v. Palmer, holding that prison inmates had no reasonable expectation of privacy from shakedown searches of their cells, even those conducted without probable cause or reasonable grounds to suspect violation of prison regulations.

Lynch v. Donnelly, upholding against an establishment clause challenge a city's display of a nativity scene on the ground the presence of secular Christmas symbols in the aggregation made the display seasonal rather than religious in character.

New York v. Quarles, holding that the warnings police are required to give suspects prior to custodial questioning under *Miranda v. Arizona* (1966) are unnecessary when officers in the field question a suspect about the whereabouts of a discarded weapon in order to prevent an imminent threat to public safety.

Nix v. Williams, declaring that evidence (the body of a victim) found by police based on unlawful custodial interrogation of a suspect was nevertheless admissible in court if police (given the pattern of their search) inevitably would have discovered that evidence even without the accused's assistance.

United States v. Leon, upholding the admissibility of evidence seized by police in reasonable, good-faith reliance on an invalid warrant, with the Court concluding that application of the exclusionary rule in such circumstances would be unlikely to deter future police misconduct.

1985   *Aguilar v. Felton* and *City of Grand Rapids v. Ball*, invalidating on establishment clause grounds state provision of public school teachers for religious schools, a precedent overturned by the Rehnquist Court in *Agostini v. Felton* (1997).

Garcia v. San Antonio Metropolitan Transit Auth., reversing the *Usery* precedent and upholding congressional power to require state and local governments to obey federal wage and hour standards, with the majority emphasizing that the appropriate remedy for such legislation lay with the political process, not the courts.

New Jersey v. T.L.O., upholding the use in a delinquency proceeding of drug evidence seized during a principal's warrantless search of the purse of a student suspected of smoking in the school lavatory, the Court deciding that the presence of rolling papers (typically associated with marijuana smoking) in the purse's open compartment justified the principal's continuing his search into other compartments, where he discovered drug evidence.

Supreme Court of New Hampshire v. Piper, striking down as a violation of the Article IV privileges and immunities clause's ban on unreasonable state discrimination against citizens of other states a law limiting bar admission to state residents, as applied to a woman who lived 400 yards from the New Hampshire border and had passed the state's bar examination.

Wallace v. Jaffree, invalidating on establishment grounds an Alabama law setting aside a moment of silence for prayer and meditation in the public schools, with several justices indicating they would have no constitutional concern about a law that did not earmark the period of silence for religious purposes.

1986   *Bethel School District v. Fraser*, upholding against free expression claims a school's disciplining of a student who employed sexual innuendo in his speech supporting a candidate for a student government office, the Court emphasizing that people enjoy more limited First Amendment rights in schools and other special environments than elsewhere.

Bowers v. Hardwick, sustaining the authority of states to penalize homosexual sodomy and limiting the scope of privacy and other unenumerated constitutional guarantees to rights deeply rooted in the nation's history and tradition.

Bowsher v. Synar, invalidating provisions of the Balanced Budget and Emergency Deficit Control Act of 1985 assigning executive functions to the comptroller general, a legislative branch officer.

California v. Ciraolo, concluding that homeowners have no reasonable expectation of privacy from those flying over their property and upholding the use of an aerial photograph of a backyard marijuana crop as the basis for a warrant to search the premises.

Davis v. Bandemer, holding that political gerrymandering of legislative districts constitutes unconstitutional discrimination only when it substantially disadvantages certain groups of voters over a substantial period of time.

Goldman v. Weinberger, upholding the disciplining of an orthodox Jew for wearing his yarmulke in violation of an air force regulation forbidding the wearing of headgear indoors, the Court emphasizing the extensive deference accorded the military in First Amendment contexts.

Thornburgh v. American Coll. of Obst. & Gyn., reaffirming *Roe v. Wade* (1973) and invalidating abortion regulations much like those struck down earlier in the *Akron* case.

Wygant v. Jackson Bd. of Education, barring layoffs of white teachers with more seniority than African American teachers, absent evidence the latter were victims of past racial discrimination.

Table of Cases

Eastland v. Servicemen's Fund, 421 U.S. 491 (1975)

Eaton v. City of Tulsa, 415 U.S. 697 (1974)

Edwards v. Arizona, 451 U.S. 477 (1981)

Eisen v. Carlisle, 417 U.S. 156 (1974)

Eisenstadt v. Baird, 405 U.S. 438 (1972)

Ellis v. Dyson, 421 U.S. 426 (1975)

Employment Division, Dept. of Human Resources of Oregon v. Smith, 494 U.S. 872 (1990)

Engel v. Vitale, 370 U.S. 421 (1962)

Erznoznik v. City of Jacksonville, 422 U.S. 205 (1975)

Estate of Thornton v. Caldor, 472 U.S. 703 (1985)

Estelle v. Smith, 451 U.S. 454 (1981)

Everson v. Bd. of Education, 330 U.S. 1 (1947)

Faretta v. California, 422 U.S. 806 (1975)

FCC v. Pacifica Foundation, 438 U.S. 726 (1978)

Federal Election Com'n v. National Conservative Political Action Committee, 470 U.S. 480 (1985)

Federal Election Com'n v. Nat. Right to Work Comm., 459 U.S. 197 (1982)

Federal Energy Regulatory Com'n. v. Mississippi, 456 U.S. 742 (1982)

Federal Radio Commission v. Nelson Bros., 289 U.S. 266 (1933)

Firefighters v. Stotts, 467 U.S. 561 (1984)

First Nat. Bank of Boston v. Bellotti, 435 U.S. 765 (1978)

Flast v. Cohen, 392 U.S. 83 (1968)

Flower v. United States, 407 U.S. 197 (1972)

Foley v. Connelie, 435 U.S. 291 (1978)

Freedman v. Maryland, 380 U.S. 51 (1965)

Frontiero v. Richardson, 411 U.S. 677 (1973)

Frothingham v. Mellon, 262 U.S. 447 (1923)

Fullilove v. Klutznick, 448 U.S. 448 (1980)

Furman v. Georgia, 408 U.S. 238 (1972)

Gaffney v. Cummings, 412 U.S. 735 (1973)

Gannett Co. v. DePasquale, 443 U.S. 368 (1979)

Garcia v. San Antonio Metropolitan Transit Authority, 469 U.S. 528 (1985)

Gault, In Re, 387 U.S. 1 (1967)

Gertz v. Welch, Inc., 418 U.S. 323 (1974)

Gibbons v. Ogden, 9 Wheat. 1 (1824)

Gideon v. Wainwright, 372 U.S. 335 (1963)

Gillette v. United States, 401 U.S. 437 (1971)

Ginsberg v. New York, 390 U.S. 629 (1968)

Gitlow v. New York, 268 U.S. 652 (1925)

Hunter v. Underwood, 471 U.S. 222 (1985)

Hutchinson v. Proxmire, 443 U.S. 111 (1979)

Hutto v. Davis, 454 U.S. 370 (1982)

Illinois v. Krull, 480 U.S. 340 (1987)

INS v. Chadha, 462 U.S. 919 (1983)

Interstate Commerce Commission v. Illinois Central, 215 U.S. 452 (1910)

Jackson v. Metropolitan Edison Co., 419 U.S. 345 (1974)

James v. Valtierra, 402 U.S. 137 (1971)

Jenkins v. Georgia, 418 U.S. 153 (1974)

Johnson v. Louisiana, 406 U.S. 356 (1972)

Johnson v. Zerbst, 304 U.S. 458 (1938)

Jones v. Alfred H. Mayer Co., 392 U.S. 409 (1968)

Jones v. Opelika, 316 U.S. 584 (1942)

Karcher v. Daggett, 462 U.S. 725 (1983)

Kassel v. Consolidated Freightways Corp., 450 U.S. 662 (1981)

Kastigar v. United States, 406 U.S. 441 (1972)

Katz v. United States, 389 U.S. 347 (1967)

Katzenbach v. Morgan, 384 U.S. 641 (1966)

Kelley v. Johnson, 425 U.S. 238 (1976)

Keyes v. School District, 413 U.S. 189 (1973)

Keyishian v. Board of Regents, 385 U.S. 589 (1967)

Kirby v. Illinois, 406 U.S. 682 (1972)

Kirkpatrick v. Preisler, 394 U.S. 526 (1969)

Korematsu v. United States (1944)

Kusper v. Pontikes, 414 U.S. 51 (1973)

Labine v. Vincent, 401 U.S. 532 (1971)

Laird v. Tatum, 408 U.S. 1 (1972)

Lalli v. Lalli, 439 U.S. 259 (1978)

Landmark Communications, Inc. v. Virginia, 435 U.S. 829 (1978)

Larkin v. Grendel's Den, Inc., 459 U.S. 116 (1982)

Lassiter v. Northhampton Co. Bd. of Education, 360 U.S. 45 (1959)

Lehman v. City of Shaker Heights, 418 U.S. 298 (1974)

Lemon v. Kurtzman, 403 U.S. 602 (1971)

Levitt v. Committee for Public Education and Religious Liberty, 413 U.S. 472
    (1973)

Levy v. Louisiana, 391 U.S. 68 (1968)

Lewis v. City of New Orleans, 414 U.S. 130 (1974)

Linda R. S. v. Richard D., 410 U.S. 614 (1973)

Linmark Associates v. Township of Willingboro, 431 U.S. 85 (1977)

Lloyd Corporation v. Tanner, 407 U.S. 551 (1972)

Mobile v. Bolden (1980)

Moose Lodge v. Irvis, 407 U.S. 163 (1972)

Morey v. Doud, 354 U.S. 439 (1957)

Morrison v. Olson, 487 U.S. 654 (1988)

Mueller v. Allen, 463 U.S. 388 (1983)

NAACP v. Alabama, 357 U.S. 449 (1958)

NAACP v. Claiborne Hardware Co., 458 U.S. 886 (1982)

Narenji v. Civiletti, 481 F. Supp. 1132 (D.D.C. 1979)

National League of Cities v. Usery, 426 U.S. 833 (1976)

National Socialist Party v. Village of Skokie, 432 U.S. 43 (1977)

Nebraska Press Ass'n v. Stuart, 427 U.S. 539 (1976)

New Jersey v. T.L.O., 469 U.S. 325 (1985)

New Orleans v. Dukes, 427 U.S. 297 (1976)

New York v. Ferber, 458 U.S. 747 (1982)

New York v. Quarles, 467 U.S. 649 (1984)

New York Times v. Sullivan, 376 U.S. 254 (1964)

New York Times Co. v. United States, 403 U.S. 713 (1971)

Nix v. Williams, 467 U.S. 431 (1984)

Nixon v. Administrator of General Services, 433 U.S. 425 (1977)

Nixon v. Fitzgerald, 457 U.S. 731 (1982)

Ohralik v. Ohio State Bar Ass'n, 436 U.S. 447 (1978)

Olmstead v. United States, 277 U.S. 438 (1928)

Oregon v. Mathiason, 429 U.S. 711 (1977)

Organization for a Better Austin v. Keefe, 402 U.S. 415 (1971)

Ortwein v. Schwab, 410 U.S. 656 (1973)

Osborne v. Ohio, 495 U.S. 103 (1990)

Pacific Gas & Electric v. P.U.C. of California, 475 U.S. 1 (1986)

Pacific Gas & Electric Co. v. State Energy Resources Comm'n, 461 U.S. 190 (1983)

Palko v. Connecticut, 302 U.S. 319 (1937)

Palmer v. Thompson, 403 U.S. 217 (1971)

Papish v. Bd. of Curators, 410 U.S. 667 (1973)

Parham v. Hughes, 441 U.S. 347 (1979)

Paris Adult Theatre v. Slaton, 413 U.S. 49 (1973)

Parker v. Levy, 417 U.S. 733 (1974)

Pasadena Bd. of Education v. Spangler, 427 U.S. 424 (1976)

Paul v. Davis, 424 U.S. 693 (1976)

Payton v. New York, 445 U.S. 573 (1980)

Pell v. Procunier, 417 U.S. 817 (1974)

Penn Central Transportation Co. v. New York City, 438 U.S. 104 (1978)

Pennsylvania v. Nelson, 350 U.S. 497 (1956)

Rosenbloom v. Metromedia, 403 U.S. 29 (1971)

Rostker v. Goldberg, 453 U.S. 57 (1981)

Roth v. United States, 354 U.S. 476 (1957)

Rummel v. Estelle, 445 U.S. 263 (1980)

Runyon v. McCrary, 427 U.S. 160 (1976)

Salyer Land Co. v. Water Storage Dist., 410 U.S. 719 (1973)

San Antonio Indep. School Dist. v. Rodriguez, 411 U.S. 1 (1973)

Sarnoff v. Shultz, 409 U.S. 929 (1972)

Saxbe v. Washington Post Co., 417 U.S. 843 (1974)

Scales v. United States, 367 U.S. 203 (1961)

Schaumburg, Village of v. Citizens for a Better Environment, 444 U.S. 620 (1980)

Schenck v. United States, 249 U.S. 47 (1919)

Scheuer v. Rhodes, 416 U.S. 232 (1974)

Schlesinger v. Reservists Committee to Stop the War, 418 U.S. 208 (1974)

Schmerber v. California, 384 U.S. 757 (1966)

Schneckloth v. Bustamonte, 412 U.S. 218 (1973)

School District of Abington v. Schempp, 374 U.S. 203 (1963)

Scott v. Illinois, 440 U.S. 367 (1979)

Secretary of State of Md. v. Joseph H. Munson Co., 467 U.S. 947 (1984)

Selective Service System v. Public Interest Research Group, 468 U.S. 841 (1984)

Shapiro v. Thompson, 394 U.S. 618 (1969)

Sherbert v. Verner, 374 U.S. 398 (1963)

Sierra Club v. Morton, 405 U.S. 727 (1972)

Skinner v. Oklahoma, 316 U.S. 535 (1942)

Sloan v. Lemon, 413 U.S. 825 (1973)

Smith v. Collin, 439 U.S. 916 (1978)

Smith v. Goguen, 415 U.S. 566 (1974)

Smith v. Maryland, 442 U.S. 735 (1979)

Smith v. United States (1977)

Solem v. Helm, 463 U.S. 277 (1983)

Sosna v. Iowa, 419 U.S. 393 (1975)

South Carolina v. Katzenbach, 392 U.S. 409 (1966)

South Dakota v. Opperman, 428 U.S. 364 (1976)

Southeastern Promotions, Ltd. v. Conrad, 420 U.S. 546 (1975)

Southern Pacific Co. v. Arizona, 325 U.S. 761 (1945)

Spence v. Washington, 418 U.S. 405 (1974)

Stanley v. Georgia, 394 U.S. 557 (1969)

Stanley v. Illinois, 405 U.S. 645 (1972)

Stone v. Graham, 449 U.S. 39 (1980)

Stone v. Powell, 428 U.S. 465 (1976)

Glossary

absolutism, First Amendment The view, vigorously defended by Justice Hugo L. Black but never accepted by a Supreme Court majority, that the rights of the First Amendment are absolutely protected from governmental interference.

abstention, District Court The doctrine under which federal district courts, out of respect for state judges, are expected ordinarily to abstain from issuing an injunction against, or otherwise interfering in, a pending state court proceeding.

abstention, Supreme Court The doctrine under which the Supreme Court will ordinarily refuse to decide federal legal issues raised in a case if the petitioner failed to follow state procedures in raising the claim or if the ultimate outcome of the case would depend on an adequate and independent state law ground, regardless of how the Court decided the federal issues raised in the case.

affirmative action The name for programs under which minorities and women are given some degree of preference in job applications, university admissions, and other competitive contexts.

amicus curiae (lit., "friend of the court") An individual or organization given permission by a court to file a brief and, on rare occasions, participate in other ways in behalf of a party in a case.

***Central Hudson* test** The standard under which commercial speech enjoys First Amendment protection if it is truthful and not misleading and the state can show no substantial interest justifying its regulation.

cert pool The arrangement, begun during Chief Justice Warren Burger's tenure, under which the clerks for most justices save time and energy by pooling their review of petitions for writs of certiorari.

certiorari, writ of The procedure under which cases are brought to the Supreme Court for decision if four or more justices consider the issues raised worthy of review.

chilling effect The concept under which laws will be declared a violation of the

307

First Amendment if they are so unduly vague or broad in their scope that they could exert an inhibiting, or "chilling," effect on the exercise of protected expression.

class action A lawsuit brought by plaintiffs in a case not only for themselves but also in behalf of all other persons similarly situated (that is, all members of their class), so that any relief granted by the court extends to members of the class as well as the plaintiffs.

clear and present danger test The First Amendment test under which courts will allow speech to be regulated only if the speaker incites imminent lawless action that is likely to occur as a result of the speech at issue.

common law The name for a body of judge-made rules initially established by English courts beginning in the twelfth century and later made part of American law.

compelling interest test The rule under which laws that interfere with fundamental constitutional rights or discriminate against suspect classes are considered unconstitutional unless found necessary to the furtherance of a major governmental concern.

conference The closed meeting of Supreme Court justices in which they discuss and decide cases as well as transact other business of the Court.

constructionists, strict Judges said to interpret the Constitution as written or consistent with the framers' intent rather than according to their personal moral, ethical, or social preferences.

de facto segregation Racial separation in public schools and other facilities that exists in fact but is not caused or perpetuated by laws or other official actions and thus does not violate the constitutional guarantee forbidding government to deny persons equal protection of the laws.

de jure segregation Racial separation in public schools and other facilities that is based on laws or other actions of government officials.

disenfranchisement The withdrawal of voting rights from a person based on a felony conviction or other grounds for disqualification established by law.

double standard The post-1936 Supreme Court's subjection of laws interfering with noneconomic personal rights to close judicial scrutiny while leaving the regulation of property rights almost entirely to the discretion of Congress and state legislatures.

dual federalism The doctrine holding that otherwise valid acts of Congress violate the Tenth Amendment or state sovereignty if they interfere with matters traditionally subject to regulation by the states under their police powers.

due process, procedural The concept that the Constitution's due process clauses require government to follow fundamentally fair procedures when interfering with a person's life, liberty, or property, including procedural rights mentioned nowhere in the Constitution's text.

due process, substantive   The concept that due process forbids laws that unreasonably interfere with a person's life, liberty, or property, including privacy and other unenumerated rights.

entrapment   The due process doctrine forbidding police tactics that provoke a person with no predisposition to criminal conduct to commit a crime.

equal protection, substantive (or "new")   The doctrine holding that discriminatory laws that are based on inherently suspect classifications or interfere with fundamental rights are to be declared invalid unless found necessary to promote a compelling governmental interest.

ex post facto law   A retroactively applied criminal law that works to the disadvantage of the individual, forbidden by Article I, Sections 9 and 10, of the Constitution.

exclusionary rule   The rule forbidding use of unconstitutionally seized evidence against an accused in a criminal case.

executive privilege   The doctrine permitting presidents and certain other executive officials to withhold evidence from the courts and Congress unless the latter can establish an overriding interest (such as the effective prosecution of a crime) justifying disclosure.

federal preemption   The doctrine holding that Congress can entirely preclude the states from regulating a matter over which the national government has been delegated authority.

federalism   The division of power between the national government and the states, as provided for in the Tenth Amendment.

gag order   A court order forbidding officers of the court or others to engage in out-of-court discussion of a pending case; largely designed to protect the accused's right to a fair trial by an impartial jury, gag orders against the media, like other prior restraints on the press, are strongly disfavored and bear a heavy burden of justification.

gerrymandering   The practice of drawing governmental election district boundaries in such a way as to favor one political party (or other group) over others.

"good faith" exception   An exception to the Fourth Amendment exclusionary rule permitting use in court of evidence seized unconstitutionally by police acting in the honest belief that the search warrant on which they relied was valid.

habeas corpus, writ of A court order requiring the release of persons from unconstitutional or otherwise illegal imprisonment.

habitual offender statute A statute providing for harsher punishment of repeat offenders as a way of discouraging recidivism, although the imposition of a life sentence without possibility of parole under a habitual offender law has been held to be cruel and unusual punishment.

Hughes Court The Supreme Court during the chief justiceship of Charles Evans Hughes (1930–1941).

Hyde amendment A series of amendments to congressional appropriations statutes forbidding use of federal funds for most abortions; named for their chief sponsor, Republican representative Henry Hyde of Illinois.

immunity, official The protection from damage lawsuits enjoyed by most public officials, with presidents, legislators, judges, and certain other officials entitled to absolute or complete immunity from suit for conduct within the scope of their official duties, and most other officials extended conditional immunity, under which they are subject to suit only if they knowingly violate a person's legal rights or reasonably should have known their conduct was illegal.

immunity, sovereign The protection of the national and state governments (as opposed to individual officials) from damage lawsuits without their consent.

immunity statutes Laws authorizing courts to grant persons exemption from prosecution and require them to make otherwise incriminating statements to police, with a grant of transactional immunity protecting persons entirely from prosecution for crimes confessed to under immunity, and use immunity insulating them only from having what is said used directly or indirectly against them in court but not forbidding prosecution based on evidence gathered independently of the immunized statements.

impoundment power The power long asserted by presidents to delay or forbid the expenditure of congressional appropriations by federal agencies, an authority significantly curtailed by Congress in the Budgeting and Impounding Act of 1974.

incorporation, selective The doctrine long embraced by a Supreme Court majority that holds that the Fourteenth Amendment due process clause includes (or incorporates) within its meaning, and thus makes binding on the states, those rights of the federal Bill of Rights that the Court considers fundamental to the American scheme of liberty and justice.

incorporation, total The contention of the first Justice John Marshall Harlan and Justice Hugo L. Black, among others, that the framers of the Fourteenth Amendment intended it to include (or incorporate) within its meaning all the guarantees of the Bill of Rights, thereby making them totally binding on the states.

incorporation-plus The contention that the Fourteenth Amendment due process guarantee includes (or incorporates) within its meaning not only some or all of the explicit rights of the Bill of Rights but other, unenumerated fundamental rights as well.

intermediate scrutiny The concept holding that discrimination based on gender or other quasi-suspect classifications is unconstitutional unless closely related to the promotion of legitimate and substantial governmental interests.

irrebuttable presumptions doctrine The concept that holds that laws violate due process if they are based on assumptions about human conduct (for example, that all pregnant teachers are unable to perform their duties after a certain relatively early date in a pregnancy) that are not universally valid or substantially so, yet are not subject to challenge.

judicial activism The perception of a judge's function holding that constitutional commands are generally clear and judges have a duty aggressively to apply those standards in the exercise of judicial review over the acts of other government officials.

judicial bypass A provision in certain laws permitting a minor to secure an abortion without notice to or approval of her parents if a court authorizes the procedure.

judicial review The power of a court, in an appropriate case, to declare null and void any law, procedure, or other official action found to conflict with the Constitution.

judicial self-restraint The perception of the judicial function holding that judges should be reluctant to exercise the power of judicial review since that principle is inconsistent with majoritarian democratic principles and the meaning of most constitutional provisions is subject to reasonable debate.

jurisprudence, interpretivist The belief held by legal positivists that judges should interpret the Constitution largely on the basis of its language and the original intent or meaning of its framers, rather than in a way designed to produce what they consider to be the most socially desirable or just result.

jurisprudence, noninterpretivist The belief that since the language and intent of the framers of constitutional provisions are rarely clear and may be irrelevant to the needs of modern society, judges should construe the Constitution based largely on contemporary conceptions of justice and social utility.

knowing or reckless falsehood libel rule The doctrine permitting media and other defamatory comment about public officials or public figures to be penalized as libel only if made with "actual malice," that is, with knowledge that the comment is false or with reckless disregard for its truth or falsity.

laissez-faire era The period in the late nineteenth and early twentieth centuries when the Supreme Court was largely dominated by judges opposed to federal or state government regulation of business and industry; the era came to a rather abrupt end in 1937.

law clerk An outstanding law school graduate selected to assist a jurist with research and the preparation of memoranda and judicial opinions.

least restrictive means test The doctrine holding that a law furthering legitimate and compelling governmental interests is nonetheless invalid if it interferes with First Amendment or other fundamental constitutional rights and means less restrictive of those rights are available for promoting the important interests the law serves.

***Lemon* test** The controversial test under which the Supreme Court held a law that affects religion a violation of the First Amendment establishment clause unless it had a secular purpose, a primary effect neither advancing nor harming religion, and did not create an excessive entanglement between church and state.

"living" Constitution The notion that the Constitution was intended to endure for the ages and thus can be adapted by judges to changing social needs and perceptions of liberty and justice.

malapportionment As generally used, a reference to governmental election districts that vary significantly in population, thereby denying urban voters the equal protection of the law.

media search privilege The claim, rejected by the Supreme Court, that media offices should normally be protected from police searches and that evidence should instead be secured by a subpoena, since such searches might inhibit confidential media sources and thus interfere with the First Amendment's commitment to the free flow of information.

***Miranda* warnings** The notice police must give suspects prior to in-custody questioning, informing them they have a right to remain silent, a right to an attorney during any interrogation they choose to permit, the right to court-appointed counsel if indigent, and that anything they do say will be recorded and may be used against them in court; substantially limited in use by the Burger and Rehnquist Courts.

mootness doctrine The doctrine holding that courts cannot decide cases that have already been resolved by circumstances (such as the approaching graduation of a student initially denied admission to law school who then challenged the school's affirmative action admission policies in a lawsuit).

"negative commerce clause" The concept under which the Constitution's grant to Congress of authority over national trade has been held to prevent unduly burdensome or discriminatory state regulations of interstate commerce.

obscenity test The test established in the *Miller* case under which material can be penalized as obscene if its dominant theme appeals to the prurient interest in sex, it depicts or describes specific sexual conduct in a patently offensive manner, and it lacks serious literary, artistic, political, or scientific value.

opinion announcing the court's judgment A signed opinion announcing the Supreme Court's decision in a case in which a majority of the justices were unable to join an opinion explaining the rationale for the ruling.

opinion, concurring A separate opinion expressing the views of a member of the majority in a case.

opinion, dissenting An opinion filed by a justice voting with the minority in a case.

opinion of the court A signed opinion announcing the Supreme Court's decision and rationale in a case; must be joined by a majority of the justices.

opinion, per curiam An unsigned opinion of the Court, usually issued when the justices summarily decide a case without full review and oral argument.

oral argument The series of statements presented by counsel before a court in a case, usually limited to a half hour for each side in the Supreme Court.

overbreadth test The requirement that laws affecting First Amendment rights be narrowly written so that they cannot be used to penalize protected expression as well as conduct subject to government control.

penumbra doctrine The doctrine holding that rights enumerated in the Constitution imply or suggest other rights that lie in the shadow (or penumbra) of the stated rights and are also entitled to constitutional protection.

plain view doctrine The doctrine holding that police lawfully in an area may seize without a warrant evidence they observe in plain sight there, if they have reasonable grounds to believe it is evidence of a crime.

political question doctrine The doctrine holding that federal courts are authorized to decide only justiciable questions, not political questions—those, for example, the Constitution appears to address to one of the political branches of government or for which there are no judicially manageable standards of resolution or that judicial resolution of which would risk substantial embarrassment to the nation abroad.

precedent The concept that courts should decide cases largely according to the legal principle established in earlier similar cases.

preliminary hearing The proceeding in which a judge determines whether there is probable cause for further proceedings against a suspect in a criminal case.

preventive detention Denial of bail to a suspect in a criminal case based on the judge's belief the suspect is probably guilty and likely to commit other violent crimes if released on bail before trial.

prior restraint The name for court orders and laws prohibiting particular publications or broadcasts; long disfavored by the Supreme Court, prior restraints bear a heavy burden of justification.

public forum The name for areas, such as streets, sidewalks, and parks, traditionally considered appropriate places for the exercise of freedom of expression, with government largely limited to regulating the time, place, and manner of expression in such locales.

quasi-suspect classifications Laws that discriminate on the basis of a group's gender, status of birth, or related characteristics, thus calling for heightened (or relatively strict) judicial scrutiny.

rational basis test The judicial test under which economic regulations and other laws that do not discriminate on the basis of a suspect classification or interfere with a fundamental right will be upheld if they are rationally related to some legitimate government purpose.

recess appointments The controversial practice under which the president, when Congress is in recess, can appoint federal judges and other officials without Senate approval; those appointed remain in their positions unless they fail to win confirmation during the next congressional session.

recusal The largely voluntary decision of judges to disqualify themselves from hearing a case in which their participation might constitute a conflict of interest.

Rehnquist Court The Supreme Court during the chief justiceship of William H. Rehnquist, who was appointed chief justice in 1986.

Roosevelt Court The Supreme Court during the chief justiceship of Harlan Fiske Stone (1941–1946), so called since President Franklin D. Roosevelt named all the justices but Stone to the Court and elevated Stone to the Court's center seat.

same evidence rule The rule under which the constitutional guarantee against double jeopardy is violated if a defendant is prosecuted in several trials for separate offenses growing out of the same criminal transaction (such as the robbery of several players in a poker game) and the same evidence (proof of what one person robbed all the poker players) is necessary to convict the accused in each trial.

separate sovereignties doctrine The doctrine that permits both the national government and a state, despite the double jeopardy guarantee, to try a defendant once for a crime that is an offense under both federal and state law but does not extend to state and local prosecutions of the same crime, since local governments are merely creatures of their state governments rather than sovereign bodies.

separation of powers The doctrine under which the powers of government are divided among the legislative, executive, and judicial branches, with each branch maintained by separate officials with separate, albeit at times overlapping, functions and powers.

sodomy The name attached to a variety of so-called unnatural sex acts, especially oral or anal intercourse, traditionally forbidden by state law.

speech and debate clause The provision of Article I, Section 6, of the Constitution protecting members of Congress from civil suit for all expression connected with their legislative duties.

speech-plus Communicative activity consisting of verbal or printed expression as well as other conduct, such as picketing and parading.

standing doctrine The rule requiring litigants seeking to challenge a law or other governmental action to allege direct and substantial personal injury to a legal right or interest for which the court can provide meaningful relief.

Stone Court The Supreme Court during the chief justiceship of Harlan F. Stone (1941–1946); also known as the Roosevelt Court.

subsequent punishment Regulations imposed on expression after it has occurred, for example, through criminal prosecution of a speaker; more likely to withstand First Amendment challenge than a prior restraint on expression.

"Super-Legislature" The pejorative term applied to courts (such as the pre-1937 laissez-faire Supreme Court) that use substantive due process or other general constitutional guarantees as a basis for reviewing the reasonableness or utility of a challenged law, much as legislative bodies take such considerations into account in deciding whether to adopt a statute.

suspect classifications Laws that discriminate on the basis of a group's race, color, national origin, or related characteristics considered inherently questionable by courts and thus subject to strict judicial scrutiny.

symbolic speech Nonverbal conduct, such as flag burning, intended to communicate ideas or emotions; subject to regulations narrowly tailored to further a legitimate and substantial governmental interest unrelated to the suppression of expression.

takings clause The Fifth Amendment provision forbidding government to take private property for a public purpose (through exercise of its eminent domain power) without just compensation.

testimonial evidence The name for statements, letters, and related evidence protected from compulsion by government under the Fifth Amendment guarantee against compulsory self-incrimination; distinguished from blood and hair samples and other physical evidence declared by the Supreme Court to enjoy no protection under the self-incrimination guarantee.

testimonial privilege The claim, rejected by the Supreme Court, that members of the media should ordinarily be exempt from appearing and testifying before grand juries and judicial proceedings, since such testimony might inhibit their confidential sources and interfere with the First Amendment's commitment to the free flow of information.

vagueness test The doctrine that laws violate due process if they are so vague in their meaning that persons of average intelligence cannot know what they require and that, under the First Amendment, laws affecting expression must be very clearly drafted to avoid their use as a weapon against protected speech.

Vinson Court The Supreme Court during the chief justiceship of Fred M. Vinson (1946–1953).

Warren Court The Supreme Court during the chief justiceship of Earl Warren (1953–1969).

Annotated Bibliography

Books

Abraham, Henry J. *Justices and Presidents: A Political History of Appointments to the Supreme Court.* 4th ed. Lanham, Md.: Rowman and Littlefield, 1999.

> A highly readable account of the politics of presidential appointments to the Supreme Court, with excellent summaries of the backgrounds and judicial records of each justice, including members of the Burger Court.

Blasi, Vincent, ed. *The Burger Court: The Counter-Revolution That Wasn't.* New Haven: Yale University Press, 1983.

> A profile of Burger Court decisions that emphasizes its continuity with Warren Court precedents.

Caplan, Lincoln. *The Tenth Justice: The Solicitor General and the Rule of Law.* New York: Alfred A. Knopf, 1987.

> An interesting summary of the office of solicitor general and probing account of the Reagan administration's attempt to use that office in the aggressive pursuit of its conservative constitutional agenda.

Current Biography. New York: H. W. Wilson, various years.

> A collection of helpful biographical profiles of figures in public life, including those connected with the federal judiciary.

Davis, Sue. *Justice Rehnquist and the Constitution.* Princeton, N.J.: Princeton University Press, 1989.

> A thoughtful study of William Rehnquist's record as an associate justice that focuses on positivist elements in the justice's jurisprudence, especially his efforts to find a fixed meaning for constitutional provisions through examination of the Constitution's text and the circumstances surrounding its adoption.

Eisler, K. I. *A Justice for All: William J. Brennan, Jr.* New York: Simon & Schuster, 1994.

> An admiring portrait of one of the most liberal-activist justices in the Supreme Court's history.

Friedman, Leon, and Fred L. Israel, eds. *The Justices of the United States Supreme Court, 1789–1978.* New York: Chelsea House, 1978.

A multivolume collection of profiles of Supreme Court justices, including members of the Burger Court.

Funston, Richard Y. *Constitutional Counterrevolution? The Warren Court and the Burger Court: Judicial Policy Making in Modern America.* New York: John Wiley & Sons, 1977.

A study of the change from the Warren to the Burger Court that emphasizes the Burger Court's continuity with its predecessor's record in a variety of fields.

Goldman, Sheldon. *Constitutional Law: Cases and Essays.* 2d ed. New York: Harper & Row, 1991.

A constitutional law casebook that also includes excellent statistical summaries of the decisional patterns of the Supreme Court and individual justices, including the Burger Court and its members.

Hall, Kermit, ed. *The Oxford Companion to the Supreme Court.* New York: Oxford University Press, 1992.

A fine one-volume collection of profiles relating to the Supreme Court, including its justices and major rulings.

Hutchinson, Dennis J. *The Man Who Once Was Whizzer White: A Portrait of Justice Byron R. White.* New York: Free Press, 1998.

An excellent biography of Justice White by one of his former clerks that focuses more on the justice's pre-Court career than his Supreme Court activities and record.

Jeffries, John C., Jr. *Justice Lewis F. Powell, Jr.* New York: Scribner's, 1994.

Written by one of Justice Powell's former clerks, a detailed examination of the justice's life, as well as his role in abortion litigation and a number of other selected issues.

Lamb, Charles M., and Stephen C. Halpern, eds. *The Burger Court: Political and Judicial Profiles.* Chicago: University of Illinois Press, 1991.

A collection profiling the backgrounds, appointments, and judicial records of Burger Court justices.

"Law Clerks: The Transformation of the Judiciary." *The Long Term View: A Journal of Informed Opinion* 3 (1995): 1–110.

A collection of essays on the roles of Supreme Court clerks.

Levy, Leonard W., ed. *Encyclopedia of the American Constitution.* New York: Macmillan, 1986.

A multivolume collection of essays on topics relating to the U.S. Constitution, including profiles of Supreme Court justices.

———. *Against the Law: The Nixon Court and Criminal Justice.* New York: Harper & Row, 1974.

An analysis of changes in the scope of defendants' rights from the Warren to the Burger Court that is highly critical of what the author considers the illusion of "strict construction" that President Nixon professed to insist upon in his judicial nominees.

Marsell, R. S. "The Constitutional Jurisprudence of Justice Potter Stewart." *Tennessee Law Review* 55 (1987): 1.

A general survey of Justice Stewart's flexible constitutional philosophy.

Maverty, Nancy. *Justice Sandra Day O'Connor: Strategist on the Supreme Court*. Lanham, Md.: Rowman & Littlefield, 1996.

An analysis of Justice O'Connor's influential role as a pivotal vote on the Supreme Court in close decisions.

Newman, Roger K. *Hugo Black: A Biography*. New York: Pantheon, 1994.

A thorough and balanced biography of the influential Alabamian whose Supreme Court career extended from the New Deal to the early years of Chief Justice Burger's tenure.

O'Brien, David M. *Storm Center: The Supreme Court in American Politics*. 4th ed. New York: Norton, 1996.

A leading textbook on the Supreme Court's inner workings during the Burger era as well as other periods in the Court's history.

Schwartz, Bernard, ed. *The Burger Court: Counter-Revolution or Confirmation?* New York: Oxford University Press, 1998.

Intriguing essays that focus not only on the Burger Court's record in a variety of constitutional fields but also assess the Court and its chief justice from a variety of perspectives.

———. *The Unpublished Opinions of the Burger Court*. New York: Oxford University Press, 1988.

A collection of draft opinions of Burger Court justices that ultimately went unfiled.

Schwartz, Herman, ed. *The Burger Years: Rights and Wrongs in the Supreme Court, 1969–1986*. New York: Viking Penguin, 1987.

Fifteen essays, published the year after Chief Justice Burger's retirement, that examine and assess the Court's record in such fields as access to the courts, religious liberty, freedom of expression, and criminal justice.

Sickles, R. J. *John Paul Stevens and the Constitution*. College Station, Pa.: Pennsylvania State University Press, 1988.

An analysis of Justice Stevens's highly independent approach to a variety of constitutional issues.

Simon, James F. *Independent Journey: The Life of William O. Douglas*. New York: Harper & Row, 1980.

An absorbing account of the life and judicial record of perhaps the most liberal-activist jurist in the Supreme Court's history.

————. *In His Own Image: The Supreme Court in Richard Nixon's America*. New York: David McKay, 1973.

> A very readable account by a lawyer-journalist of President Nixon's attempt to alter the course of Supreme Court decision making and the Burger Court's early record in the *Pentagon Papers Cases* and other controversial litigation.

Tushnet, Mark V. *Making Constitutional Law: Thurgood Marshall and the Supreme Court, 1961–1991.* New York: Oxford University Press, 1997.

> The second in a two-volume study of Justice Marshall's career, with this volume concentrating on his work as a court of appeals judge, the first African American solicitor general, and justice.

U.S. Congress. Senate. Committee on the Judiciary. *Hearing, Nomination of Judge Sandra Day O'Connor of Arizona to Serve as an Associate Justice of the Supreme Court of the United States.* 97th Cong., 1st sess., 1981.

> A transcript of the Judiciary Committee hearings on Justice O'Connor's confirmation, including the testimony of the nominee and other witnesses.

————. *Hearing, Nomination of John Paul Stevens, of Illinois, to Be an Associate Justice of the Supreme Court of the United States.* 94th Cong., 1st sess., 1975.

> A transcript of the Judiciary Committee hearings on Justice Stevens's confirmation, including the testimony of the nominee and other witnesses.

————. *Hearing, Nominations of William H. Rehnquist, of Arizona, and Lewis F. Powell, Jr., of Virginia, to Be Associate Justices of the Supreme Court of the United States.* 92d Cong., 1st sess., 1971.

> A transcript of the Judiciary Committee hearings on the confirmation of Justices Powell and Rehnquist, including the testimony of the nominees and other witnesses.

————. *Hearing, Nomination of Harry A. Blackmun, of Minnesota, to Be Associate Justice of the Supreme Court of the United States.* 91st Cong., 2d sess., 1970.

> A transcript of the Judiciary Committee hearings on Justice Blackmun's confirmation, including the testimony of the nominee and other witnesses.

————. *Hearing, Nomination of Warren E. Burger, of Virginia, to Be Chief Justice of the United States*. 91st Cong., 1st sess., 1969.

> A transcript of the Judiciary Committee hearings on Chief Justice Burger's confirmation, including the testimony of the nominee and other witnesses.

Wasby, Stephen L. *Continuity and Change: From the Warren Court to the Burger Court.* Pacific Palisades, Calif.: Goodyear, 1976.

> Another study of the transition from the Warren to the Burger Court, focusing on elements of continuity and change.

Wilkinson, J. Harvie. *From Brown to Bakke: The Supreme Court and School Integration, 1954–1978.* New York: Oxford University Press, 1979.

> A history of school desegregation, including major Burger Court developments during the chief justice's first decade on the bench.

Woodward, Bob, and Scott Armstrong. *The Brethren: Inside the Supreme Court.* New York: Simon & Schuster, 1979.

> A highly readable and provocative journalistic account of the inner workings of the Burger Court, frequently criticized for the authors' reliance on unattributed sources but a stimulating introduction nonetheless to the Court's behind-the-scenes activities.

Yarbrough, Tinsley E. *John Marshall Harlan: Great Dissenter of the Warren Court.* New York: Oxford University Press, 1992.

> The first biography of the Warren and early Burger Court justice who advocated a jurisprudence of judicial self-restraint but embraced an approach to constitutional construction that provided the principal philosophical basis for *Roe v. Wade* (1973) and other Burger Court rulings recognizing unenumerated constitutional rights.

———. *The Rehnquist Court and the Constitution.* New York: Oxford University Press, 2000.

> An analysis of the Rehnquist Court and its justices, focusing on major constitutional trends on the Court during Chief Justice Rehnquist's tenure.

Internet Sources

New Internet sites are introduced frequently. Readers who use the sites listed below are encouraged to explore the countless number of links to other sites that are provided in virtually every site you visit.

There are a number of excellent sites with information about the U.S. Supreme Court, some of which are listed below. The full text of court decisions is available from some of these sites, but generally limited to cases decided since approximately 1900.

Emory University School of Law
http://www.law.emory.edu/LAW/refdesk/toc.html

> The electronic reference desk initial menu offers several useful categories of information including federal and state laws in the United States and selected representation of laws from more than seventy other countries. This site contains a reference option as well as sections on law by subject, law schools, legal periodicals, legal career information, and selected law firms.

http://www.law.emory.edu/FEDCTS

> This U.S. Federal Courts Finder site links the user to all federal appellate courts. Supreme Court link connects the user to the Legal Information Institute site. Excellent source for U.S. Court of Appeals decisions. Click any of the circuits on the U.S. maps to access rulings covering the last several years.

Federal Judicial Center

http://www.fjc.gov/

> Home page for the Federal Judicial Center, the research and education agency of the federal judicial system. Contains links to other courts including the new Supreme Court site and the newly added link to the History of the Federal Judiciary site, which contains a biographical database of all federal judges since 1789, histories of the federal courts, and other historical materials related to the federal judicial branch.

Federal Judiciary Homepage

http://www.uscourts.gov/

> This page is maintained by the administrative office of the U.S. courts and is a good source of information on the federal courts. The site contains a number of links to other valuable court/law-related sites. There is also a link that features recent developments regarding the federal courts including the latest information on the status of federal judicial vacancies.

Federal Legal Information Through Electronics (FLITE)

http://www.fedworld.gov/supcourt/index.htm

> Contains the full text of about 7,500 U.S. Supreme Court decisions from 1937 to 1975. Cases can be retrieved by case name or keyword. Links are provided to other sites such as the Cornell University site.

Findlaw

http://www.findlaw.com/

> Extraordinarily valuable and comprehensive site. Among other things, the site has federal and state cases and codes; U.S. and state resources; news and reference; a legal subject index; and links to bar associations, lawyers, and law firms. Decisions of the U.S. Supreme Court back to 1893 can be accessed as well as federal courts or appeals rulings.

Jurist: The Legal Education Network

http://www.jurist.law.pitt.edu/supremecourt.htm

> Pittsburgh University Law School guide to the U.S. Supreme Court as an online

introduction to the "jurisprudence, structure, history and Justices of America's highest court." Links the user to sites that contain Supreme Court decisions (e.g., Cornell, Findlaw), news about the Court, biographies of the justices, the Court's procedures, and the latest media coverage of the Court.

Legal Information Institute (LII)

http://www.law.cornell.edu/index.html

Cornell Law School site containing Supreme Court decisions since 1990, U.S. and state constitutions and codes, law by source or jurisdiction including international law, and "law about" pages providing summaries of various law topics. The site has a "current awareness" page that contains news about the Court. LII provides a free email service that distributes syllabi of Supreme Court decisions within hours of their release.

Lexis-Nexis Academic Universe

http://www.web.lexis-nexis.com/universe/

Lexis-Nexis is a subscription database that covers a wide range of news, business, and reference information. Free access can be obtained to Lexis-Nexis through Academic Universe, which is available through most educational institutions.

National Center for State Courts

http://www.ncsc.dni.us

A comprehensive site with extensive information on state courts, state judges, and state court caseloads. Links are provided for information about federal courts and international courts.

Oyez Project

http://www.oyez.nwu.edu/

Northwestern University multimedia database that allows users to obtain oral arguments from selected cases, summaries of more than 1,000 Court opinions, biographical information on all the justices who have served on the Court, and a virtual-reality tour of the Supreme Court building.

Supreme Court

http://www.supremecourtus.gov/

A newly accessible site that overviews the Supreme Court as an institution, its functions, traditions, procedures, court rules, docket, and calendar. There is also information available on the justices and the Supreme Court building. "Plug in" capability is required to access information from this site.

Westlaw

http://www.westlaw.com/

> Westlaw is one of the largest and most comprehensive legal and business databases available on the Internet. Subscription is required for access, but prospective subscribers are able to fully explore the site on a "trial" basis.

Yahoo Law

http://www.dir.yahoo.com/Government/Law/

> Yahoo is a search engine with a separate and extensive listing of law-related sites. An easy-to-use and comprehensive searching device.

A number of newspapers provide good coverage of the U.S. Supreme Court. Among the best are the *New York Times* (http://www/nytimes.com) and the *Washington Post* (http://www.washpostco.com).

Index

About the Author

Tinsley E. Yarbrough is Arts and Sciences Distinguished Professor at East Carolina University and a widely published legal scholar who has written books on the Rehnquist Court, Justice John Marshall Harlan, and Justice Hugo Black, among others.